MICROSOFT®

WORD 2000

FOR LAW FIRMS

Send Us Your Comments

To comment on this book or any other PRIMA TECH title, visit our reader response page on the Web at **www.prima-tech.com/comments**.

How to Order

For information on quantity discounts, contact the publisher: Prima Publishing, P.O. Box 1260BK, Rocklin, CA 95677-1260; (916) 632-4400. On your letterhead, include information concerning the intended use of the books and the number of books you wish to purchase. For individual orders, visit PRIMA TECH's Web site at **www.prima-tech.com**.

MICROSOFT®
WORD 2000
FOR LAW FIRMS

Payne Consulting Group, Inc.

A Division of Prima Publishing

A Division of Prima Publishing

Prima Publishing and colophon are registered trademarks and PRIMA TECH is a trademark of Prima Communications, Inc., Rocklin, California 95677.

Publisher: Stacy L. Hiquet
Associate Publisher: Nancy Stevenson
Marketing Manager: Judi Taylor
Managing Editor: Dan J. Foster
Senior Acquisitions Editor: Deborah F. Abshier
Senior Editor: Kelli R. Crump
Project Editor: Estelle Manticas
Copy Editor: Hilary Powers
Technical Editor: Barbara Denz
Interior Layout: Bill Hartman
Cover Design: Prima Design Team
Indexer: Sharon Hilgenberg

Microsoft and Windows are registered trademarks of Microsoft Corporation.

Important: If you have problems installing or running Microsoft Word, go to Microsoft's Web site at **www.microsoft.com**. Prima Publishing cannot provide software support.

Prima Publishing and the authors have attempted throughout this book to distinguish proprietary trademarks from descriptive terms by following the capitalization style used by the manufacturer.

Information contained in this book has been obtained by Prima Publishing from sources believed to be reliable. However, because of the possibility of human or mechanical error by our sources, Prima Publishing, or others, the Publisher does not guarantee the accuracy, adequacy, or completeness of any information and is not responsible for any errors or omissions or the results obtained from the use of such information. Readers should be particularly aware of the fact that the Internet is an ever-changing entity. Some facts may have changed since this book went to press.

ISBN: 0-7615-1803-7

Library of Congress Catalog Card Number: 98-68141

Printed in the United States of America

99 00 01 02 03 DD 10 9 8 7 6 5 4 3 2 1

ACKNOWLEDGMENTS

Payne Consulting Group's previous book with PRIMA TECH, *Word 97 for Law Firms,* currently remains near the top of computer book bestseller lists, and has done so for more than a year. To everyone who has purchased the book, to schools using the book in the classroom, and to the reviewers who have recommended the book to their readers, we can only say thank you. Thank you to our clients, who have taught us what we need to put in the book to meet the needs of the legal profession. We can't mention everyone's name in this brief space, but we appreciate your support nonetheless.

Some of the people that we would like to individually recognize for their help and encouragement are Robert Craig, Carol Creagan, Carrie Davey, Stanley Deutsch, P. Cameron DeVore, Farhad Farhad, Chris French, Michelle Fullbright, Diana Galindo, Bob Gillespie, Shirley Gorman, Jo Haraf, Lisa Michelle Harrell, Joe Hartley, Joy Heath-Porter, Kevin Hendershott, Diane Hintzman, Ron Huffman, Sue Hughes, Andy Jurczyk, Sherry Kappel, Kathleen Kares, Jerome Katchmark, Chris Kitterman, Ross Kodner, Kelli Kohout, Leslie Koons, *Law Office Computing, Law Technology News,* Woody Leonhard, Microsoft Legal Advisory Council, Carol Monteith, Janice Nelson, Rob O'Rielly, Peter Parsons, Alan Pearlman, Alma Perez, Rose and Gary Perkins, Ron Person, Laurie Pinard, Sharyn Powell, Mike Precure, Frank Provenzano, Dee Reichle, Glenn Rogers, John Rogers, Yvonne Shulman, Liz Solomon, Elizabeth South, Madison Spach, Neil Squillante, TechnoLawyer, Daryl Teshima, Rebecca Thompson Nagel, Chip Tilley, Alice Truan, Washington Bar Association, Jolynn Webb, Gloria Webber, Carole West.

At Microsoft, thank you to Tom Bailey, Paul Kim, Eric LeVine, Cory Linton, Kathleen Melle, Michael Strand, and the entire Word development team.

Thank you to Hilary Powers, Barbara Denz, and Estelle Manticas for their great editorial work and for putting all the pieces together. You've made such a difference in this book! At PRIMA TECH, thanks to Kelli Crump, Matt Carleson, Debbie Abshier, Judi Taylor, and the rest of the Prima team, which does much of the hard work behind the scenes that often goes unrecognized.

Finally, thank you for buying this book. We hope you enjoy it.

ABOUT THE AUTHORS

Payne Consulting Group, Inc., is a world leader in software training and development with a specialization in seamlessly migrating law firms to Microsoft products. The company has authored numerous books on Microsoft Office, and has a bevy of legal-specific Word add-ins that make using the software easier. Payne Consulting Group is a Microsoft Certified Solution Provider and has five Microsoft Most Valuable Professionals (MVPs) on staff. For more information, send an e-mail message to info@paynecon-sulting.com or visit them on the Web at **www.payneconsulting.com**.

Donna Payne is president and founder of Payne Consulting Group. She is a Microsoft Certified Trainer (MCT) and a five-time and current recipient of the Microsoft Most Valuable Professional (MVP) award. Donna has authored and co-authored numerous books on Microsoft Office, the most recent being PRIMA TECH's *Word 97 for Law Firms, Outlook 98 Fast & Easy*, and *The Essential Excel 97 Book*. She has worked on development projects at Microsoft and is a technical beta tester for Microsoft Office releases. Donna has written articles for computer and law magazines and has been the subject of syndicated articles on leading women in technology. She is on the Microsoft Legal Advisory Council and gives lectures on software needs in corporate and legal environments.

Tara Byers is a senior trainer and project manager with Payne Consulting Group. She is a Microsoft Certified Expert in Microsoft Word, Excel, and PowerPoint. Tara has traveled internationally to assist in all aspects of law firm migration to Microsoft products, including project management, development of courseware, template design, end-user and technical training, and after-training floor and telephone support. She is a regular speaker with Law Seminars International, presenting ways to master Word's features for law offices.

David Webb is trainer and developer with Payne Consulting Group. He is a Microsoft Certified Trainer (MCT) for Visual Basic. He is a contributing author *of Word 97 for Law Firms* and *Outlook 98 Fast & Easy*. David is co-creator of the Payne Word VBA Workshop class, and has traveled extensively to train and support law firm migrations. David has been in the legal industry for over nine years, starting as a legal secretary for a small firm before doing paralegal work for the American Civil Liberties Union.

Other Contributors from Payne Consulting Group: Robert Affleck, Michelle Bovey, Rob Bovey, Colette Crawford, Kim Serchen, Joy Suttles, Karen Walker, and a special thank you to Andrea Terray and Jan Lightner for all of their hard work in this effort.

CONTENTS AT A GLANCE

Introduction. xxv

Chapter 1 Getting Started 1

Chapter 2 Working with Text. 37

Chapter 3 Formatting Text. 75

Chapter 4 Bullets and Numbering. 105

Chapter 5 Page Setup and Layout 139

Chapter 6 Styles. 177

Chapter 7 Using Tables in Legal Documents. 201

Chapter 8 Spelling and Grammar 237

Chapter 9 Mail Merge. 259

Chapter 10 Creating Legal Templates 295

Chapter 11 Creating Legal Forms. 333

Chapter 12 Working with Long Documents 371

Chapter 13 Sharing Legal Documents 415

Chapter 14 Document Conversion 451

Chapter 15 Publishing Documents to Your Intranet. 487

Chapter 16 Integrating Word with Other Office Applications. 507

Chapter 17 Introduction to VBA. 531

Index 559

TABLE OF CONTENTS

Introduction xv

CHAPTER 1
GETTING STARTED 1

Starting Word 2
Understanding the Word Window 3
    The Title Bar 4
    Single Document Interface 4
    The Menu Bar 4
    Personalized Menus and Toolbars. 5
Understanding Toolbars. 6
    ScreenTips. 7
    Default Toolbars 8
    Other Toolbars 9
    Moving Toolbars 10
Customizing Toolbars. 11
    Adding Toolbar Buttons. 11
    Removing Toolbar Buttons 13
    Creating a Legal Toolbar 14
    Resetting Toolbars. 15
Keyboard Shortcuts 16
Rulers: Not Just for Measuring Anymore! 17
The Status Bar 17
Scroll Bars 18
The Browse Object 18
A Window with a View. 19
    Normal View. 19
    Web Layout View 19
    Print Layout View 20
Working with Documents 21
    Creating a New Document 21
    Locating and Opening Existing Documents 22
    Toolbar Buttons in the Open Dialog Box 24

Places Bar 26
Saving Documents 27
Closing Documents. 28
Working with Multiple Documents Open Simultaneously 28
Getting Help 31
Office Assistant. 32
Customizing the Assistant 33
Standard Help 33
Office on the Web 34
Using the WordPerfect Help Feature 34
Detect and Repair 35
About Microsoft Word 35
Closing Word. 35

CHAPTER 2
WORKING WITH TEXT 37

Entering Text. 38
Moving Around in a Document 39
Using the Mouse to Position the Insertion Point 39
Using Scroll Bars to Move through a Document 39
Using the Keyboard to Position the Insertion Point 40
Inserting and Deleting Text 41
Click and Type 43
Selecting Text 45
Selecting Text Using the Mouse 45
Using the Mouse to Select Large Amounts of Text. 46
Using the Selection Bar 47
Selecting Text Using the Keyboard 47
Finding and Replacing Text 50
Moving and Copying Text 54
The Clipboard. 55
Using Drag and Drop to Move and Copy Text. 57
The Undo Command. 58
Working with Different Views 60
The Document Map 64
The Zoom Feature 65
The Full Screen Command 68
AutoText. 69
Inserting AutoText Entries into a Document. 69

Creating Your Own AutoText Entries 71
Redefining AutoText Entries 72
Deleting AutoText Entries 73
Answering Common Questions 73

CHAPTER 3
FORMATTING TEXT 75
Viewing Paragraph Marks. 76
Using the Formatting Toolbar in Legal Documents. 78
Using the Font Dialog Box 80
Making the Printed Document Match the Screen 81
Inserting Legal Symbols 82
Assigning Shortcut Keys for Legal Symbols 84
Inserting a Nonbreaking Space or Hyphen 85
Setting Paragraph Alignment. 87
Setting Paragraph and Line Spacing 90
Setting Indents 93
Setting Tabs. 96
Creating Borders. 99
Paragraph Borders 100
Page Borders. 101
Formatting Text Automatically as You Type 102
Using the Format Painter. 103

CHAPTER 4
BULLETS AND NUMBERING. 105
Working with Bullets. 106
Applying Bullets. 107
Changing Bullet Styles 110
Removing Bullets. 111
Customizing Bullets 111
Modifying a Bullet Style 114
Working with Numbers. 116
Applying Numbers 116
Editing a Numbered List 119
Interrupting a Numbered List 120
Restarting or Continuing Numbers. 121
Changing or Removing Number Styles 122
Customizing a Numbered List 122

Converting Bullets to Numbers 124
Using Outline Numbering 125
   Applying Outline Numbering 126
   Editing an Outline Numbered List 127
   Customizing an Outline Numbered List 127
Using Outline Numbers Linked to Styles 130
   Numbering Items in a Paragraph 132
Answering Common Bullets and Numbering Questions 133

CHAPTER 5
PAGE SETUP AND LAYOUT. 139

Setting Up a Page 140
   Word 2000 Default Settings 140
   Working with Margins 141
   Setting Margins 142
   Working with Options on the Margins Tab 145
   Working with Paper Sizes 149
   Changing the Paper Source 150
   Changing the Layout 151
Inserting Page Breaks 156
Inserting Section Breaks 158
Headers and Footers 159
   Inserting Information into the Header and Footer 159
   Different First Page 161
   Formatting Page Numbers 162
   Same as Previous 163
Using Print Preview 166
Printing Legal Documents 168
   Using the Print What Feature 171
   Working with Print Options 171
Answering Common Page Setup and Printing Questions 174

CHAPTER 6
STYLES 177

Understanding Styles 178
Using Styles in Legal Documents 179
Applying Styles 180
Displaying Styles in a Document 182
Creating Styles for Legal Documents 184

Modifying Styles 189
Deleting Unwanted Styles 192
Copying Styles 193
Renaming and Replacing Styles 195
Resetting Styles 198
Using Built-In Style Shortcuts 199

CHAPTER 7
USING TABLES IN LEGAL DOCUMENTS. . . . 201

Five Ways to Create a Table 202
    Method 1: Insert from a Menu Command 203
    Method 2: Use the Insert Table Button 204
    Method 3: Copy the Table from Another Application 205
    Method 4: Convert Text to a Table 205
    Method 5: Draw Table 208
The Tables and Borders Toolbar 209
    Text Entry and Table Navigation 215
Modifying Table Structure 216
    Working with Cells 216
    Working with Rows 217
    Working with Columns 220
    Working with the Entire Table 223
    Table Properties 225
    Nested Tables 226
Formatting Tables 227
    AutoFormat 227
    Headings 227
Perform Calculations in Tables 229
    Bookmark Calculations 231
    Aligning Decimals in a Table 232
Answering Common Table Questions 234

CHAPTER 8
SPELLING AND GRAMMAR 237

Automatic Spelling and Grammar Checking 238
    Controlling Automatic Spelling and Grammar Checking 239
    Correct Flagged Spelling and Grammar Errors 240
    Checking Spelling and Grammar Together 241

Spelling and Grammar Options 242

    Spelling Options 243

    Grammar Options 244

Using AutoCorrect with Spelling 245

    Add Misspelled Words to AutoCorrect 246

    Using AutoCorrect to Quickly Insert Text 248

    Adding or Deleting AutoCorrect Entries 248

    AutoCorrect Exceptions 250

Working with a Custom Dictionary 251

    Editing the Custom Dictionary 251

    Create an Exclude Dictionary 252

    Rechecking the Document 253

    Checking Spelling and Grammar in Another Language 254

Using Thesaurus and Hyphenation 255

Hyphenation 256

Word Count 257

Changing Case 258

CHAPTER 9
MAIL MERGE 259

Defining Mail Merge 260

Step 1: Create the Main Document 260

    Creating a Mail Merge Letter 262

Step 2: Specify the Data Source 263

    Create a Data Source Document 263

    Using the Data Form 266

Step 3: Inserting Merge Fields 268

Step 4: Merge the Data with the Document 270

Data Source Options 271

    Editing the Data Source 271

    Attaching a New Data Source 273

    Creating a Data Source from Delimited Text 274

Creating Mailing Labels and Envelopes 275

    Creating File Folder Labels from a Pleading Index 278

    Printing a Single Label or Envelope 280

Query Options 284

    Sorting the Data Source 284

    Filtering Your Data 285

Printing Specific Pages of a Mail Merge 287

Using WordPerfect Merges in Word 288
Customizing the Main Document 289
    Using If . . . Then Fields 289
Creating Catalog Lists with Mail Merge 290
Answering Common Questions 292

CHAPTER 10
CREATING LEGAL TEMPLATES 295

Introducing Templates 296
Template Types 298
    The Normal Template 298
    Attached Templates 299
    Global Templates 303
    What Are Wizards? 304
    Add-In Programs 306
Creating Legal Templates 307
    Creating a FAX Template 308
    Modifying the Fax Template 309
    Using the Fax Template 311
    Creating a Legal Pleading Template 311
Automating a Template 315
Using the Organizer to Copy Custom Settings between Templates . . . 317
Exploring the Legal Toolbar and Macros 319
Customizing Toolbars for Legal Templates 321
Using Workgroup Templates 324
Creating Global Templates 324
Template Hierarchy 329
Automated AutoText Entries 330
Answering Common Template Questions 331

CHAPTER 11
CREATING LEGAL FORMS 333

Introducing Forms 334
Creating Forms 335
    Using the Forms Toolbar 335
    Creating a Form Template 336
    Inserting Text Form Fields into a Form Template 337
    Setting Options for Text Form Fields 339
    Inserting Check Box Form Fields into a Form Template 340
    Setting Options for Check Box Form Fields 341

Inserting Drop-Down Form Fields into a Form Template 342
Setting Options for Drop-Down Form Fields 343
Using Forms 344
Protecting and Unprotecting Forms 345
Completing a Form 348
Moving through a Form with the Keyboard or Mouse 348
Modifying Form Fields 349
Formatting Form Fields 350
Naming Form Fields 350
Disabling Form Fields 351
Deleting Form Fields 352
Clearing Form Fields 352
Calculating Fields 353
Creating Professional-Looking Forms 356
Using Fill-In Fields 357
Adding Help Text to Form Fields 362
Adding Macros to a Form 364
Other Useful Fields 365
Three Kinds of Fields 365
Inserting Fields 366
Preventing a Field From Being Updated 368
Answering Common Forms and Fields Questions 368

CHAPTER 12
WORKING WITH LONG DOCUMENTS 371

Table of Contents 372
Generate a Table of Contents Using Word's Built-In Styles 373
Building a Table of Contents Using Customized Styles 375
Updating a Table of Contents 377
Deleting or Replacing a Table of Contents 378
Modifying Table of Contents Styles 378
Create a Table of Contents by Marking the Entries 380
Table of Authorities 382
Marking Citations 383
Generating a Table of Authorities 385
Updating a Table of Authorities 386
Indices 387
Marking Index Entries 387
Using a Concordance File 390
Updating the Index 390

Footnotes and Endnotes 390
    Viewing and Editing Footnotes and Endnotes 394
    Browsing by Footnotes. 395
    Deleting Footnotes or Endnotes 396
    Converting Footnotes and Endnotes 396
Bookmarks. 397
    Inserting a Bookmark 397
    Using a Bookmark. 398
    Advanced Bookmark Functions. 399
Cross-References 400
    Viewing and Updating Cross-References. 403
    Counting Words. 403
Captions. 404
    Updating Captions 405
Table of Figures 406
Hyperlinks 408
    Viewing Hyperlinks 409
Common Questions on Long Documents 410

CHAPTER 13
SHARING LEGAL DOCUMENTS 415

Sharing Documents. 416
    Copying a File to Disk. 416
    E-Mail a Document from Word 417
Using the Reviewing Toolbar 421
Using Comments 422
    Insert a Comment 423
    Reviewer ScreenTips. 424
    View a Comment 425
    Browsing by Comment. 426
    Editing and Deleting Comments 426
    Deleting All Comments at Once. 427
    Printing Comments. 428
Using the Track Changes Feature. 429
    Track Changes Options 430
    Turning on Track Changes 431
    Viewing Tracked Changes 432
    Reviewing Marked Changes 433
    Printing Tracked Changes 434
    Strange Table and Track Changes Behavior 434

Comparing Documents 435

Merging Documents 437

Versioning 439

Problems with Versioning 442

Protecting Documents 442

Using Master and Subdocuments 444

Expand and Collapse Subdocuments 446

Add Subdocuments to a Master Document 447

Deleting a Subdocument 448

Other Buttons on the Outlining Toolbar 448

Locking Subdocuments 449

Using Master and Subdocuments on a Network 449

CHAPTER 14
DOCUMENT CONVERSION 451

Conversion: The Real Story 452

Round-Tripping 453

File Types That Word Can Convert 453

Converting from WordPerfect 457

Converting from WordPerfect 458

PRIVATE Fields 458

Compatibility Options 459

Section Breaks 460

Quotations and Apostrophes 462

Field Codes 462

Converting Numbered Paragraphs 462

Header and Footer Margins 462

Widow and Orphan Control 463

Unusual Tab Settings 463

Parallel Columns, Tables, and Borders 463

Cleaning Up Converted Documents 463

Why Clean Up? 464

Quick and Dirty (Less Than an Hour) 465

Spic and Span 466

Spring Cleaning (Precedent Documents) 473

Converting Outgoing Files 476

Converting to Previous Versions of Word 476

Automatic Numbering and Other Features 478

Saving a Document to a Different File Format 480

Converting from Word to WordPerfect 481

Converting Several Documents Simultaneously. 483

Troubleshooting Common Conversion Issues 485

CHAPTER 15
PUBLISHING DOCUMENTS TO
YOUR INTRANET 487

Don't You Mean Internet? 488

The Need for an Intranet 489

Create a Web Page 489

Basing a Web Page on a Web Template 490

Using the Web Page Wizard 491

Adding Text to the Web Page 496

Inserting Hyperlinks. 496

Using the Web Toolbar 500

Saving a Document in HTML Format. 501

Web Page Goodies 502

Changing Bullet Styles 502

Changing the Background or Theme of the Page. 503

Inserting Scrolling Text 504

Adding Frames. 505

Viewing HTML Source 505

CHAPTER 16
INTEGRATING WORD WITH OTHER
OFFICE APPLICATIONS 507

Integrating Outlook and Word 508

Exporting an Outlook Contact List for a Mail Merge. 510

Letter to Contact 511

Integrating Excel and Word 512

Using the Insert Microsoft Excel Worksheet Button 513

Using a Menu Command to Insert a Worksheet 514

Using Copy and Paste with Excel Data. 515

Using Copy and Paste Special. 515

Word Hyperlink 516

Maintaining a Link between Excel and Word 517

Basic Excel Functions for Legal Purposes 518

Excel Charts in Word 519

Integrating PowerPoint and Word 521

Exporting PowerPoint Files to Word. 522

Exporting Meeting Minder Notes to Word 523

Exporting Word Documents to PowerPoint 524

Integrating Access and Word. 526

Inserting Objects into Word. 527

Insert Clip Art into Word 527

Change the Layout of the Object 528

Insert Pictures into Table Cells. 529

Insert Organizational Charts 530

CHAPTER 17
INTRODUCTION TO VBA 531

Visual Basic for Applications 532

Does My Firm Need VBA? 533

So How Do I Know If I'm Reinventing the Wheel? 533

OK, I Need a Macro. Do I Try It Myself or Get a Pro? 533

Jumpstart to Creating Macros in VBA 534

Where Macros Live 536

Storing Macros in a Legal Document 536

Storing Macros in a Legal Document Template 536

Storing Macros in the Normal Template 537

Storing Macros in a Legal Global Template. 537

How Word 2000 Works with Macros 538

Recording Legal Macros 540

Assigning Legal Macros to Toolbar Buttons, Keyboard Shortcuts, and
MacroButton Fields. 545

Assigning a Macro to a Keyboard Shortcut 547

Assigning a Macro to a MacroButton Field 548

Editing Macros 549

Navigating within Visual Basic Editor 551

Deleting Macros 552

Run-Time and Macro Errors 553

Macro Security in Word 2000 554

Using Word 97 Macros in Word 2000—and Vice Versa 555

INDEX 559

INTRODUCTION

Most law firms use Microsoft Word as their word-processing software of choice. This is driven by the need to share documents with clients, who are predominantly using Word. *Word 2000 for Law Firms* will make using Word in a law office easier. It provides legal examples and hands-on exercises geared toward producing legal documents. Specific topics covered in this book include tables of authorities, legal numbering styles, conversion issues, pleadings, macros, and more.

Word 2000 for Law Firms continues where *Word 97 for Law Firms* leaves off. It is not simply a rehash of information. It includes comprehensive coverage of the new features in Word 2000, with additional chapters and new legal-specific exercises. Since our last book, we've also received hundreds of questions that we've answered in the book. Most chapters will contain a new section where we answer common questions on the chapter's topic. This book is packed with tips, tricks, and information to get you up to speed on Word 2000 in the least amount of time.

For updated information and additional material that you may find useful, please see our Web site at **www.payneconsulting.com**.

WHO SHOULD USE THIS BOOK

Word 2000 for Law Firms covers the typical areas in which legal users have problems. We give you practical solutions to increase your productivity and decrease the amount of time that you'll need to get up and running as you make the transition to Word 2000. If you are not new to Word, you will still find much of this book helpful because of the in-depth coverage it provides for many of Word's best features. You'll find that this book is packed with ideas and effective approaches for using Word 2000 in your firm.

HOW TO USE THIS BOOK

Every chapter provides an abundance of practical, hands-on exercises. These exercises have been designed in a clear and direct fashion to walk you through the steps to accomplish the tasks you need to get done. In fact, you may find it tempting to skip the chapter text and go straight to the exercises—especially if you have documents to finish that were due yesterday. We recommend that you read through the text as much as possible, however. We've supplemented it with many notes and tips explaining aspects of Word's features that simply following the steps may not make entirely clear.

You don't have to use the book in any particular order; you'll find it useful again and again as a reference source as issues come up. But if you're new to Word, you should spend some time with the first several chapters before you go on to other areas.

CONVENTIONS USED IN THIS BOOK

Wait! Don't turn the page yet! Before you skip over this section, you should know that the conventions used in this book are important to understand. There are more conventions than just those that apply to Windows applications. For example, this book has conventions of its own to make it easier to use.

KEYBOARD SHORTCUTS

Keyboard shortcuts are a combination of keys that you must press to access commands within Word 2000. You will see keyboard shortcuts listed in two ways:

+ **Underlined Letters.** Underlined letters are used to denote hot keys—that is, the keys that allow you to access menus, items on menus, and items in dialog boxes. To access a menu, hold down the Alt key, and then press the underlined letter. Once a menu has been displayed, you no longer need to depress the Alt key. For example, to access the New dialog box in Word, you would press Alt+F (to open the File menu), and then press N for the New command. To access commands in a dialog box, you always hold down the Alt key and press the underlined letter.

+ **Keyboard Combinations.** Keyboard combinations are keys you must hold down simultaneously for them to work. For example, pressing Ctrl+N is the shortcut to create a new blank document in Word. Some key combinations will require three keys to be depressed. For example, Ctrl+Shift+K is the shortcut for turning on and off SMALL CAPITAL LETTERS. When you see a keyboard combination, you must hold down all of the keys at the same time for it to work. If you are new to Windows, the easiest way to do this is to first press and hold down the Ctrl, Alt, and/or Shift key, and then press the specified letter key. Pressing them all simultaneously is difficult.

OTHER CONVENTIONS

◆ **Bold Text.** Bold text has been used to indicate text you must type to complete an exercise. For example, if we ask you to name a document **mybrief.doc**, it means to type **mybrief.doc** into the file name box.

◆ **Extra Capital Letters.** The names of items that appear on menus, dialog boxes, and buttons have initial capital letters on all words, even though the screen elements themselves often have only one initial capital—or none at all. This makes it easier to sort out the narrative text from the screen labels.

◆ **Button Names.** When you see a direction like "Click OK," it means that there is a button on the screen with **"OK"** printed on it. When you see a direction like "Click the Show/Hide button," it means that the button will not actually have "Show/Hide" printed on it. This book contains many pictures to show you what buttons look like. The directions for using screen elements such as buttons always indicate that they should be clicked or chosen, never pressed.

◆ **Primary-Click and Alternate-Click.** These commands relate to the left and right mouse buttons. If you have set up your mouse for right-handed use (according to the Mouse settings in the Windows Control Panel), the primary button is the left button, and the alternate button is the right button. If you have set up your mouse for left-handed use, the primary mouse button is the right button, and the alternate button is the left button. The alternate-click button is very handy and has many uses in Word 2000.

◆ **Toolbar Conventions.** Word 2000 has many toolbars that make your life easier as you work, but generally only two are present when you first open Word. At first glance they may appear as one because the default in Word 2000 is for them to share one row. The first of these default toolbars contains buttons for basic tasks such as opening and printing a file; it is called the Standard toolbar. The second is the Formatting toolbar, which contains buttons for style and font setting and other tools used in formatting a document. Other toolbars can be turned on, usually by choosing Toolbars from the View menu; you can turn off the option for toolbars to share one row by choosing Customize from the Tools menu and deselecting Standard and Formatting Toolbars Share One Row.

• **Key Conventions.** When referring to keys on the keyboard, not in Word, those keys are given the names printed on them whenever possible. The most common are Shift, Ctrl, Alt, Enter, and Spacebar. They all have initial capital letters, and the directions indicate that they should be pressed, not clicked.

SPECIAL ELEMENTS

You will see the following items used throughout this book:

Tips are used to show you shortcuts and alternate methods for accomplishing tasks.

Notes are used when we need to give you more information about a task or feature. We might also use Notes to help you troubleshoot mishaps.

Cautions are used when we need to alert you to a potential problem or misunderstanding.

THIS IS A SIDEBAR

A sidebar is an area of text that provides a discussion on how to best use a particular feature in Word 2000.

That's it. Now you can get started!

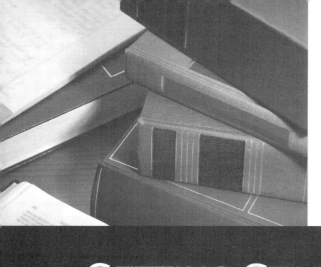

CHAPTER 1

GETTING STARTED

IN THIS CHAPTER

- ◆ Getting Started with Word 2000
- ◆ Exploring elements and tools in the Word window
- ◆ Understanding toolbars
- ◆ Personalized menus and toolbars
- ◆ Customizing the keyboard
- ◆ Understanding page views
- ◆ Working with documents: creating, finding, opening, saving, closing
- ◆ Working with multiple documents simultaneously
- ◆ Getting help fast!

Welcome to Word 2000! If this is your first time viewing Microsoft's word processing program, thanks for allowing us to be your guide. For those readers who are experienced Word users, prepare to be pleasantly surprised by many of the new features in Word 2000. Are you ready to explore the new environment of Word 2000? It's got a whole new look and feel, so sit back, relax, and plan to have a good time!

You're probably excited about using Word to create legal documents, but before you dive into the waters of pleadings, contracts, and letters, you'll want to take a few moments and learn the basics of how Word 2000 works. If you've used Word before and want to skip to the next chapter, that's OK with us; just remember that this chapter is always here as a reference if you need it.

STARTING WORD

In Windows 95, Windows 98, and Windows NT, you can start all applications the same way: by clicking the Start button on the taskbar (the gray bar that spans the bottom of your screen) and then choosing Programs. Most of the programs installed on your computer are listed here. When you find what you're looking for, just point and click.

START WORD

1. Click Start.
2. Select Programs.
3. Click Microsoft Word once.

Other ways to start Word:

- Double-click any file name that ends with a .doc extension. Files that end in .doc are Word documents.

- Create a shortcut on the desktop for Word. Once you've done that, double-click the shortcut icon to start the program with a new blank file open. To create a shortcut, alternate-click the desktop and choose New, and then choose Shortcut. Click Browse and locate Microsoft Word on your computer. Click Next, and then click Finish.

When you start Word, you see the window that you'll learn about next: the Word window.

NOTE If you already know how to use Windows 95, Windows 98, or Windows NT, you have a leg up on learning any Windows application because they use common elements: a title bar, menu and toolbars, scroll bars, the taskbar at the bottom of the screen, and the control buttons: Minimize, Restore, and Close.

UNDERSTANDING THE WORD WINDOW

Microsoft designed the Word window to make using Word easier. In fact, everything in this window either gives you information or provides a tool to assist you in creating and editing documents. Figure 1.1 shows the elements of the Word window. Don't worry about memorizing all the names of the elements right now; you'll see them again as the chapter proceeds.

Before discussing the elements of the Word window, it's important to know that Word 2000 has a new look and feel. What you see on your screen may not match what you see on another person's computer, or some of the pictures in this book. That's because the menus and toolbars are personalized in Word 2000. Instead of having toolbars and menus with extra commands taking up screen space, only the commands you use most often appear.

FIGURE 1.1

The elements that make up the Word window.

THE TITLE BAR

At the top of the window is the title bar. The title bar provides information about which program you're using and what document is open. It also holds a place for the application control buttons, which are Minimize, Restore, and Close.

TIP

If your computer is beeping at you and you are unable to type text, you may have shifted the focus from the document to a dialog box or to another window. If you use the Windows standard color palette, when the title bar is blue, the window is active. When the title bar is gray, or dimmed, the window has become inactive and unavailable. If a dialog box is active, press the Esc key to return to the active document. Otherwise, just click the button in your taskbar that corresponds to the document you'd like to activate.

The first time you start Word, the title bar reads, "Document 1 – Microsoft Word." If you create another new document, a new window opens with "Document 2 – Microsoft Word" on the title bar. Word increments the document number to show how many new documents you've started in the current session. If you save the document, the name on the title bar changes to reflect the new name of the document. Having each open document appear on the taskbar is called the Single Document Interface (SDI).

SINGLE DOCUMENT INTERFACE

Previous to Word 2000, Word had a multi-document interface. The multi-document interface would allow you to have an unlimited number of documents open at once, however only one instance of Word would appear on the taskbar.

Word 2000 has a single document interface. Each open Word document appears as a separate button on the Windows taskbar. To move from one document or program to another, click on the taskbar, or press Ctrl+Tab. With single document interface, you must close all open Word documents before you are able to completely exit Word. For more information on moving between and working in open documents, see "Working with Multiple Documents Open Simultaneously" later in this chapter.

THE MENU BAR

Just below the title bar is the menu bar. The menu bar organizes most Word commands under nine menu headings: File, Edit, View,

Insert, Format, Tools, Table, Window, and Help. Each menu heading logically groups the commands that belong in a particular category. For example, if you want to do something that affects the entire document, such as Print, Save, or Close, you point to the word File and click. To change the formatting of something, choose the Format menu. To view the document in a different way, choose the View menu.

The underscored character in the menu heading provides a way for non–mouse users to access the commands on the menu. To access the File menu, hold down the Alt key and press the letter F. After the menu has expanded, you either press the underscored command (this time without holding down Alt) or use the directional arrows on the keyboard (up or down). Figure 1.2 shows the contents of the File menu.

PERSONALIZED MENUS AND TOOLBARS

When you click a command on the menu bar, a drop-down list of commands appears. Because of the new, personalized menus in Word 2000, the commands you see on your computer may not match exactly the commands displayed in Figure 1.2. Personalized menus remember which commands you have used and adds them to the menu. Only the most frequently used commands appear on

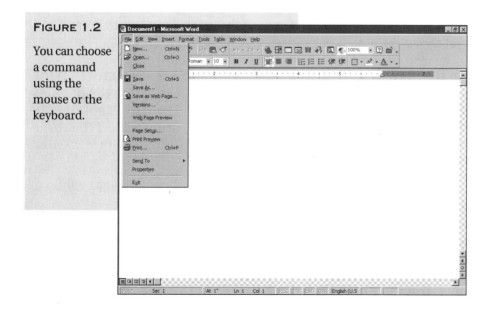

FIGURE 1.2

You can choose a command using the mouse or the keyboard.

the File menu when you first open it; then, after a brief delay, the full list appears. You can click the chevrons at the bottom of any drop-down menu or double-click a menu command to see the full list of commands.

EXPLORE PERSONALIZED MENUS

1. Click File to display the contents of the menu.

2. Rest the mouse pointer over the File command until the menu changes and the full list of commands appears.

NOTE

If the full menu doesn't appear when you pause on the File command, you may have this feature turned off. From the Tools menu, choose Customize. Select the Options tab, and turn on Show Full Menus After A Short Delay.

3. Press Esc to close the File menu.

4. Click the File menu.

5. Click the chevron at the bottom of the drop-down list to display the complete list of menu commands.

TIP

The expanded menu shows two things that can help you use and learn Word: a keyboard shortcut combination on the right side and, in many cases, a picture icon on the left side of the command that shows the equivalent toolbar button, if one is available.

For the purposes of consistency in this book, we have turned off the personalized menus. If you want your screen to match the pictures in this book, you should also turn them off. From the Tools menu, choose Customize. Select the Options tab, and turn off the three options in the Personalized Menus And Toolbars section. Click Reset My Usage Data, and then click Close.

Now that you know some of the basic elements of the Word window, it's time to focus on the toolbars and their buttons.

UNDERSTANDING TOOLBARS

Toolbars and toolbar buttons can save a great deal of time because they provide a one-click shortcut for performing tasks that you repeat over and over. For example, as you use Word, you'll want to save your documents every few minutes so that if you lose power or there is a problem with your computer, you don't lose what you've been working on. You can save a document by choosing <u>S</u>ave from the <u>F</u>ile menu, but this method requires two steps. To save your document using one step, click the Save button on the Standard toolbar.

NOTE

Word 2000 has over 700 toolbar buttons, not counting the ones for each of the fonts installed on your computer.

SCREENTIPS

If you're looking at those tiny pictures on the toolbar and wondering what each one does, don't worry. Word provides a tool called ScreenTips that helps you identify them. Rest the mouse pointer (without clicking) over a button on the toolbar to make a ScreenTip containing the name of the button pop up (see Figure 1.3).

USE SCREENTIPS

1. Rest the mouse pointer over the button that looks like a diskette (some people think it looks like a television set!). This is the Save button.

2. Move the mouse pointer to the button showing a clipboard and piece of paper. This is the Paste button.

3. Rest the mouse pointer over a button showing the numbers 1, 2, and 3. This is the Numbering button.

4. Move your mouse pointer over the button to the right of the numbering button. This is the Bullets button.

TIP

If you don't get a ScreenTip when you rest your mouse pointer over a toolbar button, your ScreenTips may be deactivated. From the <u>T</u>ools menu, choose <u>C</u>ustomize, and then select the <u>O</u>ptions tab. Select Show Screen<u>T</u>ips On Toolbars to turn the ScreenTips on.

FIGURE 1.3

ScreenTips help you learn which buttons to select.

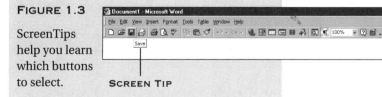

SCREEN TIP

Keyboard users can also display shortcut keys in the ScreenTips. From the Tools menu, choose Customize, and then select the Options tab. Select Show Shortcut Keys In ScreenTips to turn the shortcut keys on.

DEFAULT TOOLBARS

Word 2000 includes 16 toolbars. The Standard and Formatting toolbars initially share the same row, directly under the menu bar (see Figures 1.4 and 1.5). The buttons on these two toolbars provide the most commonly used commands, such as Save, Close, Copy, Paste, Bold, Italic, and Underline.

To place the Standard and Formatting toolbars on separate rows, from the Tools menu, choose Customize, and then select the Options tab. Turn off Standard And Formatting Toolbars Share One Row, and then click Close.

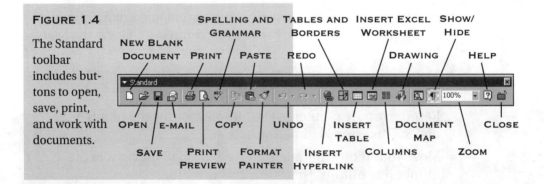

FIGURE 1.4

The Standard toolbar includes buttons to open, save, print, and work with documents.

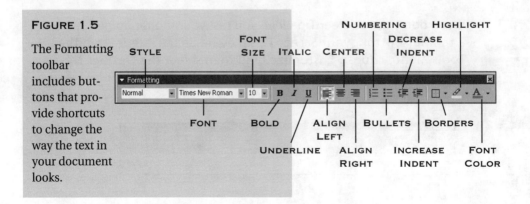

FIGURE 1.5

The Formatting toolbar includes buttons that provide shortcuts to change the way the text in your document looks.

OTHER TOOLBARS

Word's other toolbars can be uncovered by choosing Toolbars from the View menu. Toolbars that are currently displayed will have a check mark next to them. If you click a name with a check mark next to it, the toolbar toggles off. Figure 1.6 shows the list of available toolbars.

TIP

Alternate-click any toolbar to quickly display the toolbar list.

Not all of the available toolbars are listed in the shortcut menu of toolbars. In fact, while there are only 16 toolbars listed in the shortcut menu, there are 23 toolbars in the list of toolbars in the Customize dialog box. The Function Key Display toolbar, which is new to Word 2000, is shown in Figure 1.7.

FIGURE 1.6

A check mark next to a toolbar's name indicates that the toolbar is currently active.

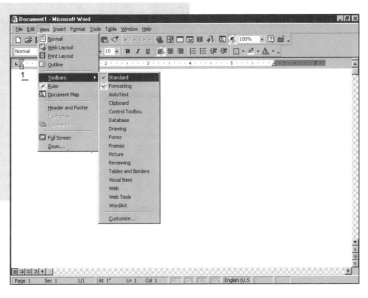

FIGURE 1.7

The Function Key Display toolbar has some handy shortcuts.

MOVING TOOLBARS

The first time you use Word, the toolbars are located at the edge of the document window. These toolbars are called *docked toolbars*. They don't have to be docked at the top edge of the window; they can also be located on the left, right, or bottom edge of the window.

When the toolbar is not attached to the edge of the window, it is referred to as a *floating toolbar*. Floating toolbars place the commands that you need right where you need them. For example, when you view the header or footer in a document by choosing <u>H</u>eader And Footer from the <u>V</u>iew menu, a floating Header and Footer toolbar appears right next to the header or footer.

You can move toolbars by clicking and dragging the move handle. The handle is the single gray vertical line on the left edge of each toolbar. When you place the mouse pointer over the move handle, the pointer changes to a four-sided arrow, indicating that you can drag the toolbar to a new location. The next exercise shows you how to make a toolbar float over text and how to dock it back in the default toolbar location. Figure 1.8 shows a floating toolbar.

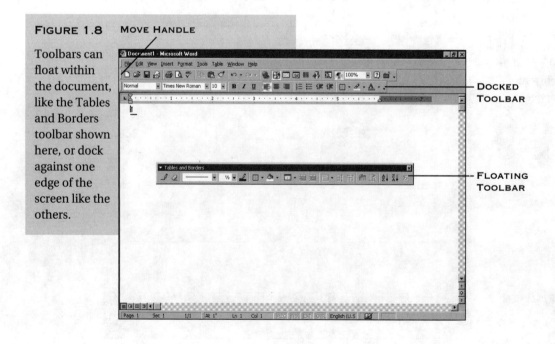

FIGURE 1.8   MOVE HANDLE

Toolbars can float within the document, like the Tables and Borders toolbar shown here, or dock against one edge of the screen like the others.

DOCKED TOOLBAR

FLOATING TOOLBAR

MOVE A TOOLBAR

1. Click the move handle on the left edge of the Standard toolbar.
2. Drag the toolbar to the middle of the document window. Release the mouse button.
3. The toolbar is now a floating toolbar.

Double-click the title bar of the toolbar to dock it back in its previous location.

When a toolbar is floating, you can resize it by placing the mouse pointer over any edge of the toolbar. When the pointer changes to a double-headed arrow, begin clicking and dragging to resize the toolbar.

If you accidentally grab and undock the menu bar, just double-click its title bar—the line that says "Menu Bar." Doing so docks the menu bar where it was before the unintentional move.

CUSTOMIZING TOOLBARS

Let's face it, everyone works differently. The toolbar button that I find most useful, you may never use. That's why Microsoft created personalized menus and toolbars. Word 2000 lets you completely customize each toolbar, or create your own.

ADDING TOOLBAR BUTTONS

You can add buttons to any toolbar, or you can create your own toolbar. One toolbar button that most people like to add to the Standard toolbar is Close All. This command closes all open documents with one click.

TIP

Holding down the Shift key before you click the File menu also displays the Close All command.

Some toolbar buttons you might want to add to your toolbars may be closer than you think. In Word 2000, an Add Or Remove Buttons command has been added to every toolbar. This command gives you quick access for customizing toolbars.

FIGURE 1.9

Click Add Or Remove Buttons to quickly customize a toolbar.

You can access the Add Or Remove Buttons command by clicking the More Buttons command at the right end of the toolbar, then selecting Add Or Remove Buttons, as shown in Figure 1.9.

If a toolbar is floating, you can access the Add Or Remove Buttons command by clicking the small triangle to the left of the toolbar name on the title bar of the toolbar.

Once you have activated the Add Or Remove Buttons command, a list of buttons is revealed with check marks to the left of each of the buttons. Add buttons from the list to your toolbar by clicking them.

CUSTOMIZE TOOLBARS

1. Click the More Buttons command at the end of the Formatting toolbar.

2. Click Add Or Remove Buttons.

3. Click the Superscript command.

4. Click the Subscript command.

5. Click in the document to close the list of commands.

FIGURE 1.10

You can cus-
tomize any of
Word's tool-
bars.

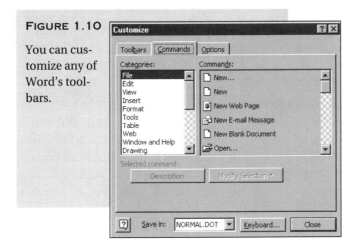

What if you don't see the button you want in the list of buttons to
add or remove? Just click the Customize command at the bottom of
the list to open the Customize dialog box. Then select the
Commands tab, as shown in Figure 1.10.

ADD TOOLBAR BUTTONS

1. From the Tools menu, choose Customize.
2. Select the Commands tab (refer to Figure 1.10).
3. Select File in the Categories window.
4. In the Commands window, click Close All.
5. Holding down the mouse button, drag the Close All button to
   the Standard toolbar. As you drag the button, note the letter X
   that is attached to the mouse pointer. When the pointer is in a
   position where the button can be dropped, the X will change to
   a plus sign (+).
6. Release the mouse button when the Close All button is next to
   the Save button, represented by an image of a floppy disk.

REMOVING TOOLBAR BUTTONS

A toolbar has only so much room for buttons, so you may have to
decide which buttons you won't need as often as others. For exam-

ple, how often are you going to need the Insert Hyperlink button, or the Highlight, Columns, or Drawing buttons? If your answer is "not very often," you can remove these four buttons and replace them with something more useful to you.

To quickly delete a button from a toolbar, press the Alt key on the keyboard and drag the button downward off the toolbar and into the document window. Or click the More Buttons command on the toolbar, and then choose Add Or Remove Buttons. Click any command with a check mark next to it to remove the command from the toolbar.

CREATING A LEGAL TOOLBAR

We recommend adding a few toolbar buttons that can help you with legal documents. You can either add these buttons to an existing toolbar, or create a new toolbar with these buttons added. Table 1.1 shows the categories and command options in the Customize dialog box for each button. The next exercise walks you through all the steps necessary for creating a new toolbar.

TABLE 1.1   A LEGAL TOOLBAR

CATEGORIES	COMMAND	DESCRIPTION
Insert	Footnote	Inserts a footnote or endnote into your document.
Insert	AutoText	Displays the words *All Entries* with an arrow. When you click the button, all of the categories of AutoText are displayed.
Insert	Symbol	Opens the Symbol dialog box.
Insert	Mark Citation	Marks the citation that you want to be included in the selected Table of Authorities.
Insert	Cross Reference	Inserts a cross-reference to an item in the document.
Format	Single Spacing	Changes the line spacing to single space.
Format	Double Spacing	Changes the line spacing to double space.
Format	Hanging Indent	Applies a hanging indent to the selected paragraphs or increases the indents of an indented paragraph to the next indent level.
Format	Un Hang	Decreases the Hanging Indent.
Format	Para Keep with Next	Prevents a page break between the selected paragraph and the next paragraph.
Format	Change Case	Changes the capitalization of selected text.

FIGURE 1.11

Create tool-
bars that give
you quick
access to fre-
quently used
buttons.

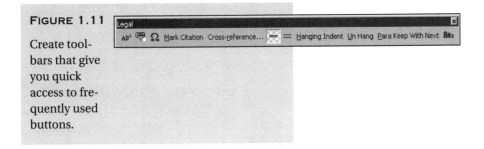

CREATE A NEW LEGAL TOOLBAR

1. Alternate-click any toolbar button.
2. From the shortcut menu, choose Customize.
3. In the Customize dialog box, select the Toolbars tab.
4. Click New. The New Toolbar dialog box appears.
5. In the Toolbar name box, type **Legal**. The Normal.dot template should appear in the Make Toolbar Available To box to make this toolbar available for every new document that you create in Word.
6. Click OK. A new toolbar named Legal is now floating in your document window.
7. Select the Commands tab.
8. Drag the buttons listed in Table 1.1 to the new legal toolbar. Click OK to close the dialog box. You can place the tools in any order that is convenient. Figure 1.11 shows the new Legal toolbar.

RESETTING TOOLBARS

If you want to return any toolbar to its original state, you can reset it. Click the More Buttons command at the end of the toolbar, and then select Add Or Remove Buttons. Click Reset Toolbar to reset the toolbar. Click Yes when you are asked if you want to reset the toolbar. If you want to reset toolbars from one dialog box, from the Tools menu, choose Customize, and then select the Toolbars tab. Select the toolbar that you want to reset from the list of toolbars, and then click Reset.

TIP

You can also delete a custom toolbar from the Toolbars tab by selecting it and clicking <u>D</u>elete.

After you reset the toolbars, make sure to exit Word to cement the changes. Word may prompt you to save changes to the blank document template, Normal.dot. If so, click <u>Y</u>es and start Word again.

NOTE

A quick way to access the Customize dialog box is to alternate-click any existing toolbar. You can then select <u>C</u>ustomize from the shortcut menu that appears.

KEYBOARD SHORTCUTS

Although keyboard shortcuts don't appear on the screen, they certainly can affect everything you do in Word! Many users like to rely on the keyboard instead of the mouse. Word has numerous keyboard shortcuts, and you can add even more.

CUSTOMIZE THE KEYBOARD

1. From the <u>T</u>ools menu, choose <u>C</u>ustomize.
2. Click <u>K</u>eyboard. The Customize Keyboard dialog box appears, as shown in Figure 1.12.
3. Select a category in the Categories window.
4. Select a command in the C<u>o</u>mmands window.
5. Click in the Press <u>N</u>ew Shortcut Key box.

TIP

If the shortcut key combination you press is already assigned, it appears below the Press New Shortcut Key box. You can overwrite the assigned shortcut if you want, or press Backspace to delete the shortcut key you press. Keep trying shortcut key assignments until you find one that is unassigned.

6. Press the new shortcut key combination. It must contain a combination of Ctrl, Alt, Shift, or one of the function keys.
7. Click <u>A</u>ssign to assign the shortcut key combination.
8. Click Close.

FIGURE 1.12

You can create a keyboard shortcut for any Word command.

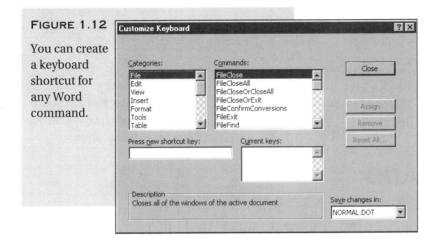

For a list of all shortcut keys, you can run a built-in Word macro called ListCommands. For more information, see Chapter 17, "Introduction to VBA."

RULERS: NOT JUST FOR MEASURING ANYMORE!

In Word, you use the horizontal ruler located below the toolbars (refer to Figure 1.1) for more than just keeping track of where you are on the page. This ruler is used for setting margins, indents, and tabs, and even for changing the width of newspaper and tabular columns. If you don't see this ruler, from the View menu, choose the Ruler command.

The ruler has so much information on it that using your ScreenTips to see each element of the ruler is a good idea.

THE STATUS BAR

The horizontal bar that appears at the bottom of the Word document is called the Status bar. The Status bar is very important and useful because it gives you information about where you are in the document, displays contextual messages, and lets you turn on options such as Record Macro, Track Changes, Extend Selection, Overtype, WordPerfect Help, and Spelling.

If you don't see the Status bar, on the Tools menu, choose Options. Click the View tab, and then in the Show section, select the Status bar check box.

Occasionally, you can see other icons on the Status bar depending on the background actions. While Word is performing a Background Save, a pulsating disk appears in the Status bar. When Background printing is taking place, a printer icon appears in the Status bar.

SCROLL BARS

Word has two scroll bars: vertical and horizontal. The horizontal scroll bar has a left and a right arrow that move you through the width of a document. If no movement occurs when you click either of these arrows, it means that you are already looking at the entire width of the document and it doesn't need to be adjusted.

The vertical scroll bar also contains arrows for navigation. The up and down arrows scroll you through the document one line at a time. The double up arrows move you to the previous page, the double down arrows to the next page. Between the double up and down arrows is a dot, also known as the Browse Object.

THE BROWSE OBJECT

The Browse Object is a shortcut to finding and moving to items within a document. When you click the Browse Object, it expands to show 12 additional icons. By clicking one of the exposed icons, you can quickly move to fields, footnotes, endnotes, comments, sections, pages, edits, headings, graphics, and tables within the document. Figure 1.13 shows the Browse Object and the Next and Previous buttons.

When you click one of the browse icons, you set the Browse Object to search for that type of item within the document. To move to the next or previous item of this type, click the Next or Previous arrows located above and below the Browse Object on the scroll bar. To cancel the search, click the Browse Object and at the bottom of the palette.

All the options available to you in Browse Object become available when you press F5. The difference is that the Browse Object displays pictures, whereas the Go To dialog box displays the listings as text. Many people find it easier to use the F5 method to navigate to different locations in Word. You can also use the keyboard with the Browse Object; just click Alt+Ctrl+Home to activate it.

FIGURE 1.13

Use the
Browse Object
to move
quickly though
the document.

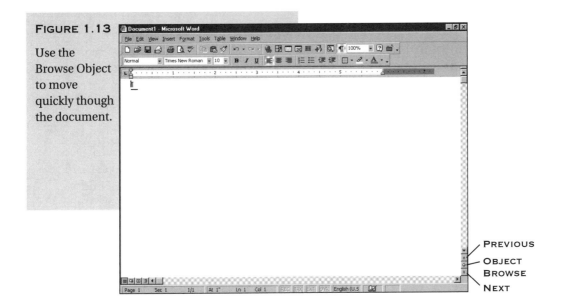

PREVIOUS

OBJECT
BROWSE

NEXT

A WINDOW WITH A VIEW

Word provides more than just one view; it has four primary ways
you can view a document: Normal, Web Layout, Print Layout, and
Outline. The easiest way to change views is by clicking the view buttons in the lower-left corner of the window.

NORMAL VIEW

Many fast typists prefer Word's Normal view because it allows them to
type as fast as they can without the machine slowing down to repagi-
nate. One thing to remember about documents in Normal view is that
this view is not a true WYSIWYG (What You See Is What You Get) view,
meaning that the document will not print exactly as it appears on
screen in the Normal view window. You will not see headers, footers,
footnotes, or endnotes while you are in Normal view.

To put your document into Normal view, click the leftmost button
in the row of view buttons, or from the View menu, choose Normal.

WEB LAYOUT VIEW

The Web Layout view is new to Word 2000, and replaces Word 97's
Online Layout View. This view makes your text appear as it would be
viewed through a Web browser or on an Intranet. It allows you to
view backgrounds and pictures as if they were on a Web page, and

offers a Web page's overall look and feel. Web Layout view is very different from Print Layout, however; it doesn't show your headers or footers, and it makes your text wrap to the window rather than to the page. If you plan to share your documents over an Intranet or the Internet, consider designing them in Web Layout view.

You might notice that the Status bar becomes dim and doesn't report page numbers when you switch to Web Layout view. That's because with Web Layout view, what you see is *not necessarily* what you get. Because the text on the page wraps to the window instead of the page, Word can't calculate the pages to report them to you in the Status bar. When you return to Normal or Print Layout view, the accurate number of pages appears.

The Web Layout view can be advantageous when you work remotely via a laptop. Laptops with small screens normally require scrolling left and right to view the entire width of your document. The wrapping feature within the Web Layout view eliminates the need to scroll horizontally.

PRINT LAYOUT VIEW

Print Layout view is convenient to work in because it shows you exactly what the document will look like when it's printed. Print Layout view allows you to see pictures and clip art, columns, headers and footers, footnotes and endnotes, text boxes, and frames. In Print Layout view, you can adjust not only the left and right but also the top and bottom margins.

Print Layout view may take longer to arrange all the items on your screen, but for most documents, virtually no time difference between the views exists.

Here are three keyboard shortcuts for switching views:

Normal	Alt+Ctrl+N
Print Layout	Alt+Ctrl+P
Outline View	Alt+Ctrl+O

Another tool in Word 2000 that you can use to navigate documents more effectively is the Document Map. The Document Map pulls out any headings or significant items from the document and lists them in the navigation pane on the left side of the screen. By clicking any of the headings that appear there, you can quickly move to that part of the document. If nothing appears in your Document Map or you don't find it useful, you can switch it off by clicking the Document Map button on the Standard Toolbar, or by going to the View menu and choosing Document Map.

WORKING WITH DOCUMENTS

Now that you know all you've ever wanted to know about the Word window (and then some), you can take a look at how to create a new document.

CREATING A NEW DOCUMENT

Word provides three methods for creating a new document: a toolbar button, a menu command, or a keyboard shortcut. You might be surprised at the different results you can achieve with each method.

If you press the New button on the Standard toolbar, you get a blank new document based on Word's default document template, Normal.dot (you'll learn more about templates later in this book). This is a generic blank document. If you press Ctrl+N, you get the same result. If, however, you go to the File menu and choose New, you get to choose what type of document you want to create from all of Word's built-in templates and any that have been created for your firm. Figure 1.14 shows the New dialog box.

FIGURE 1.14

All templates, whether you create them or they come with Word, appear in this dialog box.

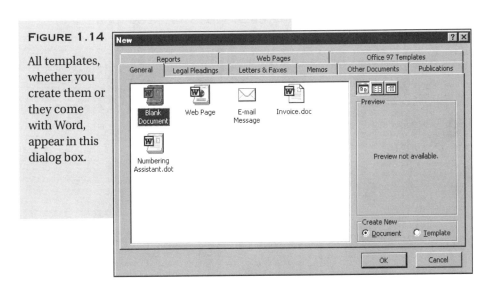

CREATE NEW DOCUMENTS

1. On the Standard toolbar, click the New button.

2. Press Ctrl+N.

3. Select File, and then choose New. In the New dialog box, select the Memos tab.

4. Click Elegant Memo.dot once to see a preview on the right side of the dialog box.

5. Click OK to create a new document based on the Elegant Memo template.

LOCATING AND OPENING EXISTING DOCUMENTS

You've probably guessed that Word provides more than one way to open documents. This book concentrates on one way, but keep in mind that you can choose a keyboard shortcut or a menu command if you don't like the suggested method.

To open existing documents, click the Open button on the Standard toolbar. The Open dialog box, shown in Figure 1.15, is a powerful component of Word because it enables you not only to open a document but also to sort, search, copy, and paste documents. The Places bar on the left side of the Open dialog box gives you quick access to the documents you recently worked on, your favorites, the desktop, and more.

FIGURE 1.15

You can do more than just open documents with the Open dialog box.

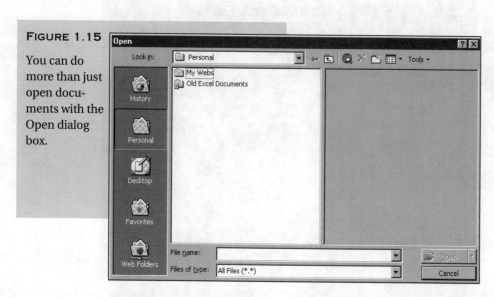

Of course, the main function of this dialog box is to help you find and open documents. The Open dialog box has a number of major components, described in the following sections.

LOOK IN

The Look In box shows you which drive or folder you're currently searching through. By clicking the drop-down arrow on the right side of the Look In box, you can get a map of all of the local and network drives to which your computer currently has access. After you select the appropriate drive, you can open folders on the drive by double-clicking the folder icon in the document window of the Open dialog box. If you go too far into the depths of your computer, don't panic; there is a button to take you back up one level.

DOCUMENT WINDOW

This is a list of files or folders and other resources within the selected Look In location.

FILE NAME

The File Name box allows you to enter the name of the file that you want to find. Sometimes, if you know the path of your document, typing the full path or document name in the File Name box is better than using the Look In drop-down box. That's because in some larger law firms, client directories can be huge and therefore take a lot of time to appear in the document list.

TIP

A quick way to look at files in a different location is by typing the location in the File Name box. For example, to look at what's on your floppy disk, you could type A:\ and press Enter. To look at files on your computer, you could type C:\ and press Enter. To look in My Documents on the C drive, type C:\My Documents and press Enter.

So what happens if you don't know the exact name of the document? If you know only a part of the file name, try typing as much as you remember. If your entry matches any part of a file name in the current folder, Word automatically selects that file for you.

If that doesn't work, click the Tools button. Doing so allows you to enter search terms in a specialized search dialog box. You may not find the file that you're after right away, but you will at least narrow down your search from hundreds of files to just a few.

FILES OF TYPE

If you don't see the file that you're looking for, you may have the wrong file type showing in the Files Of Type box. This box narrows down your search to a specific type of document. For example, to open a WordPerfect 6.1 file in Word 2000, select the WordPerfect 6.x file type. Depending on how Word was installed, you may have up to 26 file types from which to choose.

The last file type that you've selected is the default the next time you open a document. If you select and stay with the All Files option, you can avoid many problems locating files.

TOOLBAR BUTTONS IN THE OPEN DIALOG BOX

The Open dialog box has toolbar buttons that help you locate, view, and manage files. These buttons are described in the following sections.

BACK

The first button next to the Look In folder is the Back button. This button jumps you from the current location that you're browsing in to the location you were in previously. The Back button is disabled when you first enter the Open dialog box.

UP ONE LEVEL

Next to the Back button is the Up One Level button. This button is useful if you need to go up one level in your folder and file structure. Say that you're looking in a folder named Client A inside the My Documents folder. If you click the Up One Level button, you will change the view from the contents of Client A to the contents of the My Documents Folder.

SEARCH THE WEB

The button with a globe on it opens up your Internet browser, allowing you to search the World Wide Web, if you have access.

DELETE

This button deletes the selected file or folder. Deleted files or folders move to the Recycle Bin. To permanently delete a file or folder and bypass the Recycle Bin, hold down the Shift key while clicking Delete.

CREATE NEW FOLDER

Click the Create New Folder button to create a new folder in the current directory. In prior versions of Word, this command was found only in the Save As dialog box. Now, you can create folders in either the Open or Save As dialog boxes.

VIEW

The View button controls how the documents and folders presented in the box appear. Clicking the button cycles you through the view options. You can click the small drop-down arrow next to the View button for a list of available views. Here is an explanation of the choices on the list:

- **List**. Shows the names of the files. If the file is a Word file, you'll see an icon that shows a page with a *W* over it. If it is another kind of file, you'll see a different icon. These icons give you some idea of what the document is.

- **Details**. Shows the name of the file along with the size, file type, and date it was last saved. This view is useful when you're looking for a specific file and you know some attributes of the document but not the file name itself. You can sort files in the document window by Name, Size, Type or Date Modified by clicking the column headers.

- **Properties.** Lists more attributes of each document than you probably knew existed! Use this view to determine the author's name, how many pages, words, and characters are in the document, when the document was created and last modified, and so on. For some people, all this information is very handy; for others, it's just too much.

- **Preview.** This view displays a small portion of the selected document in the preview box. Many people find the preview setting handy when they are trying to locate a file that they would recognize by appearance but can't identify any other way. One reminder, though: preview view can take a little longer than other views to give you the information you need. If you're just browsing, you might consider one of the other three views.

- **Arrange Icons.** Just as in Windows 95, Windows 98, or Windows NT, you can arrange the icons in the Open dialog box by name, type, size, or date.

TOOLS

The Tools button allows you to search for files, delete or rename files, add a file to your list of favorites, map a network drive, or view a file or folder's properties.

TIP

One of the easiest ways to open a document that you've been working on is to access your most recently used file list. This is a list of Word documents that you've been working on from your computer. The list can include up to nine document names and appears on the File menu.

You can customize this number from the Tools menu by choosing Options, and then selecting the General tab.

Word 2000 also records a history of documents you've worked with recently; this feature is discussed in the next section.

PLACES BAR

The Places bar gives you quick access to several locations where you commonly search for documents. The Places bar appears on the left side of the Open dialog box, and contains shortcuts to several places where you store documents. If you have used Microsoft Outlook, you'll find the Places bar very similar to the Outlook Bar.

To use the Places bar, click any one of the five shortcuts to navigate to the folder. That folder's contents then appear in the document window. An explanation of the Places bar's components is given below.

HISTORY

If you've used a Web browser in the past few years, you've probably noticed a feature most of them have called History. Its equivalent in Word 2000 shows you the 20 to 50 files and folders you've accessed recently. If you can't find a file that you've worked with before, and it's not on the list of recently used files in your File menu, consider using this feature.

MY DOCUMENTS

This button gives you quick and easy access to the My Documents folder. It's also the default location for saving files when you first begin Word.

In the Open dialog box, the Places bar will say "Personal" rather than "My Documents" if you're using Windows NT. It works with your Personal folder rather than your My Documents folder.

DESKTOP

Believe it or not, your desktop is actually a folder! You can access your desktop in a snap with this tool.

FAVORITES

If you access a certain folder frequently, you might consider placing it in your Favorites. Favorites is a place for you to keep shortcuts to your most frequently used files so that you can get in and out of them quickly. Click the Favorites button to access your Favorites; click the Tools button in the Open dialog to add a selected item to your Favorites.

WEB FOLDERS

If you have access to certain folders via the World Wide Web, using the Web Folders tool will allow you to log on (if necessary) and access those folders over the Internet.

SAVING DOCUMENTS

You can spare yourself a lot of trouble by saving your document and saving it often. In a Word for Law Firms Master Series class, we had the class go through a long document-building exercise. Just as the class members were about to save, the power went off in the building! This is very frustrating and we don't want it to happen to you. Form the habit of saving your document when you get to the bottom of each new page, or every few minutes if you're working with a small document. Remember: save early, and save often!

The keyboard shortcut for saving a document is Ctrl+S.

Word has a feature called Allow Fast Saves that is, in theory, a good idea. The goal is to speed up processing by reducing the amount of hard disk activity. A fast save appends the editing changes to the end of a document, which increases the size of the document. By contrast, when you turn off the Allow Fast Saves option and save the document, Word performs a full save, which incorporates all the revisions (instead of appending them). In plain terms, Allow Fast Saves can make files much larger than they need to be. Even though performing a full save after a file was fast saved reduces the size of the file, *turn Fast Save off!* Disable it by going to the Tools menu, choosing Options, selecting the Save tab, and clearing the option to Allow Fast Saves.

CLOSING DOCUMENTS

Closing documents is even easier than opening them. From the File menu, choosing Close starts the ball rolling. If you've saved your work, Word will close the current document and display either another open document or a blank screen, depending on whether you have any other documents open. If you haven't saved changes made to your document, a dialog box opens, asking, "Do you want to save the changes made to '*document name*'?" You may then select Yes, No, or Cancel to return to the document.

Another way to close documents is with the application control button in the upper-right corner of the screen. The Close button is the one with an "X" on it. If you have several documents open, there is only one Close button available. Click it to close documents, one at a time. When there is only one document remaining open, two close buttons appear. The upper Close button closes Word. The lower Close button closes the last open document, but leaves Word open.

TIP

To reopen a document that you recently closed, choose File and look down at the bottom of the expanded menu to view the most recently used file list. If you see what you're looking for, point and click. The selected document will open automatically.

WORKING WITH MULTIPLE DOCUMENTS OPEN SIMULTANEOUSLY

In Word, you can have as many documents open as you want, provided that you have enough memory in your computer. This is useful when you need to refer back to another document for information that you're putting into a document, or even to copy and paste information between the two documents.

If you have used previous versions of Word, you'll remember that the extra documents you opened all stayed in a single iteration of Word. If you worked in many documents, the workspace got very messy, finding the document you wanted wasn't easy, and working between two or more documents was a nightmare. Things have changed in Word 2000. Each new document you open begins a new Word document window. You can move the windows around separately. If you minimize them, they will each have a separate Word icon in the taskbar at the bottom of your screen.

Word provides you not only with the ability to open multiple documents but also gives you tools to make working with multiple documents easy. These tools, which you will find on the Window menu, are described in the following sections.

NEW WINDOW

Say that you want to view different parts of one of the documents at the same time. One way to do this is to create a new window for the document and then arrange the windows so that you can see both at the same time. You can arrange them on your desktop side by side or on top of each other or above and below each other. This is very handy if you are cutting text from one part of a document and moving (pasting) it in another and want to see the results in both places.

CREATE A NEW WINDOW

1. Create a new document and save it with the name **Test**.

2. From the Windows menu, choose New Window.

3. Looking at the title bar, notice that the name is now Test.doc:2. This means that you're looking at a second window of the same document. Any changes you make in either window will be updated and stored in the original Test file.

ARRANGE ALL

You can arrange all open documents so that you can see them simultaneously.

ARRANGE WINDOWS

1. From the <u>W</u>indow menu, choose <u>A</u>rrange All to tile the two documents (or any number of open documents) on your desktop. Previous versions of Word only arranged within a single version of Word. Now you have your entire desktop to work on. This feature allows Word to duplicate a WordPerfect feature, Tile Vertical, allowing side-by side document comparison. Figure 1.16 shows an example of tiling documents.

2. Locate Test.doc:1 and click the title bar to activate the document. Click the Maximize button to make Test.doc:1 fill the screen. The other document is still open; it's just waiting on your desktop behind this document.

3. Choose Test.doc:2 from the <u>W</u>indow menu to make this document the current document.

4. Close Test.doc:2 and the original file name, Test.doc, appears in the title bar.

TIP

This exercise showed you how to use features under the <u>W</u>indow menu. You can also use the <u>W</u>indow menu to switch between open documents. Keyboard users can press Ctrl+F6 to switch between open documents.

FIGURE 1.16

All open documents are arranged in the window.

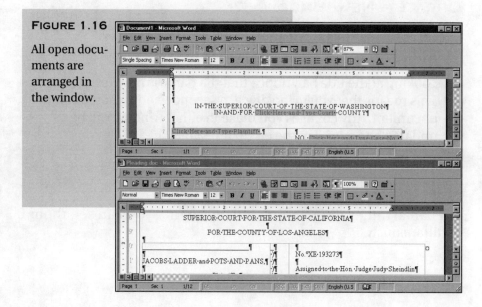

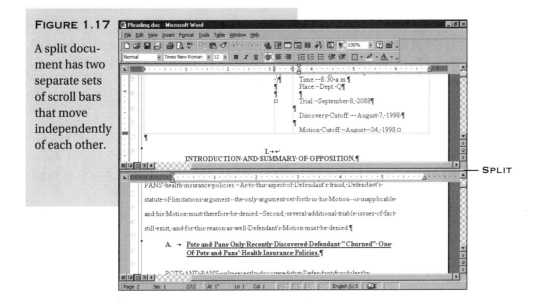

FIGURE 1.17

A split document has two separate sets of scroll bars that move independently of each other.

SPLIT

SPLIT

The <u>W</u>indow, <u>S</u>plit command enables you to work at two different points in the same document. Applying a split divides your document into two independent halves. You can scroll the top half of the screen to one location and the bottom half to another. This allows you to cut and paste information between two parts of your document with ease. Figure 1.17 shows a document that has been split.

You can put the split where you want it on the screen by moving the line with the mouse and then clicking it when you want it to stay in that spot. To remove a split, either double-click the line or choose Remove <u>S</u>plit from the <u>W</u>indow menu.

GETTING HELP

You probably won't remember everything covered in this chapter, and the same holds true throughout this book. You can thumb back through the text or consult the index for help on specific topics, or you can access Word's help feature, the Office Assistant.

The fastest way to access the Office Assistant is by pressing the F1 key on your keyboard. If you don't have an extended keyboard, you can click the Office Assistant button on the Standard toolbar, or from the <u>H</u>elp menu, you can choose Microsoft Word <u>H</u>elp.

If you have used the Office Assistant in previous versions of Word, you'll notice something different in Word 2000. Now the Assistant is "thinking outside of the box," or floating and available to assist you anywhere in the document.

OFFICE ASSISTANT

The Office Assistant feature offers the following characters (or actors, as they're sometimes called): Clippit, the Dot, F1 the Robot, the Genius (shown in Figure 1.18), Office Logo, Mother Nature, Links the Cat, and Rocky the Dog.

NOTE

Not all of the actors may be installed on your computer because they have to be installed from the ValuPack that comes with Microsoft Office 2000. If you can't live without seeing these other characters, contact your firm's systems help desk or the person who installed Word on your computer.

To select an actor, alternate-click the Office Assistant and select Choose Assistant from the shortcut menu. You can hide it by alternate-clicking the Office Assistant and choosing Hide.

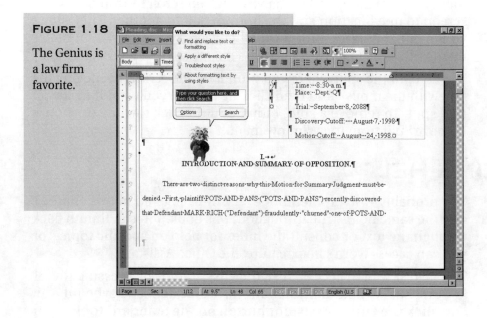

FIGURE 1.18

The Genius is a law firm favorite.

The Office Assistant begins by asking what you want help with. Just type your question in the box provided and click Search or press Enter on the keyboard. Amazingly, this feature can "understand" sentences or segments of your question and return information on any topics that seem to be most related to the words in your question.

CUSTOMIZING THE ASSISTANT

Do you find the Office Assistant providing more help than you need? Luckily, you can tailor the Office Assistant to act and react any way you want. Choose Options from the Assistant's pop-up dialog box to view all the available features. You can set the Assistant to move when it's in the way, be quiet, offer only high-priority tips (as opposed to always popping up with ideas), or show you the shortcut keys to help you work more quickly.

NOTE

If you hide the Office Assistant frequently, you may ask yourself whether you ought to hide it permanently. The answer you give to that question will depend on your attitude toward the Office Assistant (which varies widely—folks either love it or hate it!).

STANDARD HELP

If you prefer a different type of help, other options are available. If, after choosing a topic proposed by the Office Assistant, you decide to venture into other help topics, you can use the Help pane to browse the Contents, Index, or Answer Wizard.

If you don't see the Contents, Index, or Answer Wizard tabs, click the Show button on the Help pane. Contents and Index are like an electronic software manual. You can search for help from a table of contents of topics, or by clicking the Index tab.

Once a Help topic is selected, a pane appears with instructions or further topics to explore (see Figure 1.19). Many of the topics are hyperlinks, which means you can click them to jump to another Help topic.

TIP

If the Help topic instructions involve multiple steps, click the printer icon in the Help pane and print the topic.

FIGURE 1.19

Help displays help for the selected topic and hyperlinks that allow you to jump to additional topics.

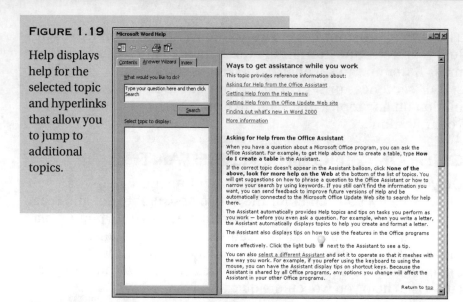

OFFICE ON THE WEB

Microsoft has included a way for you to get the latest and greatest information about Word: a shortcut called Office On The Web under the Help menu. Choosing Office On The Web reveals a list of free stuff, product news, frequently asked questions, and other online support. If you don't find what you're looking for here, try visiting Payne Consulting Group's home page at http://www.paynecon-sulting.com/. We constantly update our Web page to provide tips and tricks for working with Word and other Office applications.

Another great resource for getting your questions answered is on the product newsgroups hosted by Microsoft on the Web. Here you can post your question and have it answered "for free" by your peers—who may have the answer—or by people designated by Microsoft as Microsoft Most Valuable Professionals. Payne Consulting Group currently has five MVPs who answer questions on the newsgroups. To access the newsgroups, go to http://support.microsoft.com/ and select the option to go to the newsgroups.

USING THE WORDPERFECT HELP FEATURE

What if you are converting from WordPerfect for DOS and you need help finding Word's way of doing things? Word has a special type of built-in help called WordPerfect help. It will help you learn the Word equivalents for WordPerfect for DOS commands and keystrokes. Just click the command that you used in WordPerfect, and Help will tell you how to do the same function in Word.

GETTING WORDPERFECT HELP

1. From the Help menu, choose WordPerfect Help.

2. Scroll down the Command Keys list to Reveal codes. Click it once.

3. The right side of the screen shows you how to get the equivalent to "Reveal Codes" in Word.

DETECT AND REPAIR

Each time you start Word, it performs a routine under-the-hood maintenance check to make sure that everything is running smoothly. If you experience problems with Word, you can run a diagnostic check to see what the problem is by choosing Help, Detect and Repair. You may need to close other programs and provide installation source information when running Detect and Repair.

ABOUT MICROSOFT WORD

When you choose About Microsoft Word from the Help menu, a dialog box opens with information about what version of the product you're using, copyright, license, system information, and instructions on how to access technical support. Once you finish with the About Microsoft Word dialog box, click OK.

CLOSING WORD

When you're ready to close Word, you can use a menu command, the mouse, or a keyboard shortcut.

Here are the various ways to close Word:

◆ From the File menu, choose Exit.

◆ Use the keyboard shortcut of pressing ALT+F4.

◆ Click the upper-right button on the title bar in the Word window, the one that has an "X" on it.

Do not go to the File menu and choose Close—that closes only the active document and leaves Word open.

If you've made any changes to the document since the last time it was saved, Word prompts you to choose whether to save changes before it closes the document.

If you clicked the Close button in error, just press the ESC key or click the Cancel button and you return to the document window.

If you've used prior versions of Word, you may have noticed that the application control buttons in the upper right corner of the screen have changed. Word used to have two sets of Maximize, Restore, and Close buttons. The upper set controlled the application, and the lower set controlled the document. Word 2000 displays only one set of application control buttons when there are multiple documents open. Clicking the Close button closes the current document, not the application.

When only one document remains open, Word 2000 displays two Close buttons. The upper Close button closes the program. The lower Close button closes the document, and leaves Word open.

Remember, you can hold down the SHIFT key and click the File menu to display a Close All command.

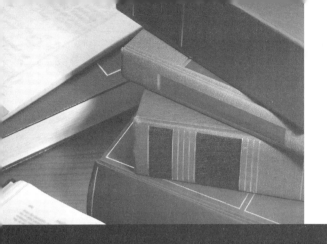

CHAPTER 2

WORKING WITH TEXT

IN THIS CHAPTER

- ◆ Inserting text into a document
- ◆ Using Click and Type
- ◆ Selecting text
- ◆ Moving and copying text
- ◆ Working in different views
- ◆ Using the Document Map
- ◆ Creating and using AutoText entries

Word processing programs have revolutionized the way documents are produced in law firms. Even relatively new computer users have the ability to quickly insert, move, and delete text, and to use more sophisticated functions such as formatting and styles to create documents with a professional flair.

New features in Word 2000 like Click and Type and the expanded Office Clipboard for copying and moving information make it more powerful than earlier versions. Word makes creating complex documents easy, making it an amazingly useful tool in the legal office.

ENTERING TEXT

When you first start Word, you see an empty document resembling a blank sheet of paper. A blinking cursor appears at the top left of the screen, ready for you to begin entering text. As you begin typing, the text appears on the screen. The *word-wrap* feature automatically wraps (moves down) the text to the next line when it reaches the end of a line. You do not need to use the Return (Enter) key to force the text to wrap as you do on a typewriter; the word processor does it for you. Don't worry about pressing the Enter key until you are ready for a new paragraph or would like to insert a blank line.

The blinking cursor is referred to as the *insertion point* since its location determines where text is inserted as you type.

ENTER TEXT INTO A DOCUMENT

1. Type the following paragraph into the document. If you have different text that you would like to use, that's OK; you can enter your own text instead.

   Pursuant to Federal Rule of Civil Procedure 36, you are requested to respond to the following requests. Please answer each request within the blank space provided, inserting additional pages where necessary; verify your answers on the form provided after the last request; and serve a completed set of requests and the answers on this defendant within thirty (30) days after receipt of these requests. Service should be made to the office of plaintiff's attorneys, Jones and Associates, 123 Main Street, Anywhere, Washington 98003.

2. When you have finished typing the paragraph, press the Enter key to start a new paragraph.

Don't worry if you make a mistake. Mistakes are easy to correct in a word processing program! Correcting mistakes is covered later in this chapter.

MOVING AROUND IN A DOCUMENT

Before you can begin correcting mistakes and formatting text, you must know how to move around in a document. For example, if you leave out a word while typing, you will want to move back to that location to insert the missing word. You can move around a document using either the mouse or the keyboard.

USING THE MOUSE TO POSITION THE INSERTION POINT

To use the mouse, position the mouse pointer over the text where you want to begin typing. The mouse pointer appears in the shape of a capital I when it's in the text area. It indicates where the insertion point will be placed when you click the primary mouse button. Click one time with the primary mouse button to move the insertion point to the location of the mouse pointer. When you begin typing, Word puts what you type at the location of the insertion point. The insertion point moves to the right of the inserted text as you type.

NOTE If text is overwritten as you type, then you have accidentally turned on the *Overtype* feature in Word. To turn off this feature, locate the OVR characters on the Status bar at the bottom of the screen and double-click it.

USING SCROLL BARS TO MOVE THROUGH A DOCUMENT

Sometimes the text that you want to edit is not visible on the screen. Mouse users can move through a document by using the vertical and horizontal scroll bars. To use the scroll bars, click the single-headed arrows at the ends of the scroll bars to scroll the screen in the desired direction—up, down, right, or left (see Figure 2.1).

To scroll through the document one entire screen at a time, click above or below the scroll box on the vertical scroll bar.

To move through a document page by page, drag the scroll box along the vertical scroll bar. Word presents you with a ScreenTip that contains information about the current page.

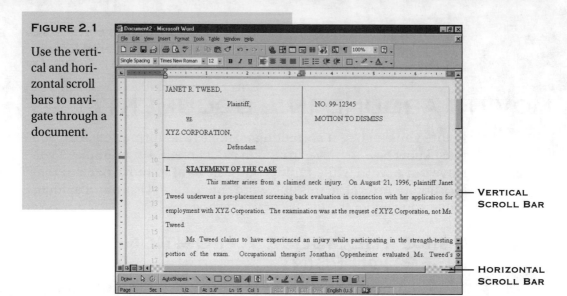

FIGURE 2.1

Use the vertical and horizontal scroll bars to navigate through a document.

VERTICAL SCROLL BAR

HORIZONTAL SCROLL BAR

NOTE

When you find the text you want to edit, you must click in the document with the primary mouse button to move the insertion point to the desired location.

USING THE KEYBOARD TO POSITION THE INSERTION POINT

The arrow keys and the Home and End keys allow you to use the keyboard to move the insertion point within a document. Several useful keys and key combinations for movement are available on the keyboard, as described in Table 2.1.

TABLE 2.1   KEYBOARD MOVEMENT KEYS

TO MOVE . . .	DO THIS . . .
Left or right one or more characters	Press the Left Arrow or Right Arrow key
Up or down one or more lines	Press the Up Arrow or Down Arrow key
Left or right one word at a time	Hold down the Ctrl key and press the Left Arrow or Right Arrow key
Up or down one paragraph at a time	Hold down the Ctrl key and press the Up Arrow or Down Arrow key
To the beginning of a line	Press the Home key
To the end of a line	Press the End key

TO MOVE . . .	DO THIS . . .
Up or down one full screen of text at a time	Press the Page Up or Page Down key
To the start of a document	Hold down the Ctrl key and press the Home key
To the end of a document	Hold down the Ctrl key and press the End key
To the previous insertion point	Press Shift+F5
To the next screen	Press PageDown
To the previous screen	Press PageUp
To the next open document in Word	Ctrl+F6
To the previous open document in Word	Ctrl+Shift+F6

USE THE MOUSE AND KEYBOARD TO MOVE THROUGH A DOCUMENT

1. Move the mouse pointer over the middle of any paragraph of text.
2. Click the primary mouse button one time. The insertion point moves to the location where you clicked.
3. Experiment with the scroll bars by clicking the arrows and dragging the scroll box.

NOTE When you drag the scroll box, Word presents a ScreenTip showing the current page number only if the document is longer than one page.

4. Experiment by pressing the different keyboard movement combinations, as described back in Table 2.1.

INSERTING AND DELETING TEXT

If you create a document and realize you inadvertently left out an important topic or comment, just place the insertion point where you want to add text and start typing. The text is automatically placed at the location of the insertion point, and nothing is over-written or deleted. Imagine the power of such a tool for the legal office, where documents can have hundreds of revisions!

Deleting text is also simple. To delete text, position the insertion point at the beginning of the text you want to delete, and then press the Delete key to remove the text from the document (see Figure 2.2).

NOTE

You can also use the Backspace key to delete text. However, unlike the Delete key, you must position the insertion point at the *end* of the text to be deleted, and then press the Backspace key.

In Figure 2.2, if you wanted to delete the word *plaintiff's,* you would press the Backspace key. To delete the word *attorneys,* you would press the Delete key.

TIP

Pressing the Delete or Backspace key will delete one character at a time. To delete entire words with one keystroke, hold down the Ctrl key and then press either the Delete or Backspace key.

DELETE TEXT FROM A DOCUMENT

1. Use the mouse or keyboard to position the insertion point at the beginning of the text that you want to delete.
2. Press the Delete key several times until the text is deleted.

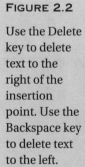

FIGURE 2.2

Use the Delete key to delete text to the right of the insertion point. Use the Backspace key to delete text to the left.

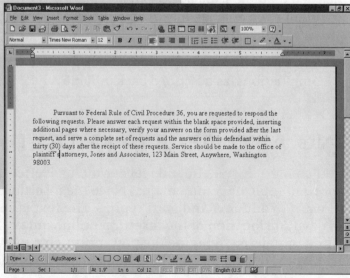

To delete large amounts of text, you *select* the text first. Selecting text is covered in the next section.

If you delete text accidentally, you can restore the text using the Undo command, which is covered later in this chapter, under "Undo Command."

CLICK AND TYPE

What would you do if you needed to move to the bottom of a blank page and type something? Normally, you press the Enter key numerous times until the insertion point reaches the bottom. Word 2000's new Click and Type feature changes all that. Now, you can scroll to any blank area of the document and quickly insert text, graphics, tables or other items, just by clicking the mouse.

To use Click and Type, double-click your mouse at the location where you want to insert an item. For example, to type a centered heading in the middle of the page, all you need to do is double-click in the middle of the page and start typing. Word automatically applies the correct formatting and inserts tabs and paragraph marks if necessary.

Click and Type only works when you are in Print Layout or Web Layout view and does not work if you are in Normal or Outline view. Views are covered later in this chapter, in the section titled "Working with Different Views."

You can see what type of formatting Click and Type automatically applies by watching your mouse pointer as you move it across the page. The Click and Type marker displays the alignment—that is, center, left, or right aligned—applied when you double-click.

If you want to see the tab characters and paragraph marks inserted by Click and Type, turn on the Show/Hide button on your Standard toolbar—or press Ctrl+Shift+*. Table 2.2 shows the different types of Click and Type markers.

One of the great things about the Click and Type feature is that it can duplicate the Flush Right feature of WordPerfect. This is handy in signature blocks, or any time you need text flush left and flush right on the same line. The document shown in Figure 2.3 was created using the Click and Type feature.

TABLE 2.2 CLICK AND TYPE MARKERS

MARKER IMAGE	MARKER DESCRIPTION	RESULT
I⁼	Left-aligned marker	Creates a left-aligned paragraph
I≣	Centered marker	Creates a centered paragraph
⁼I	Right-aligned marker	Creates a right-aligned paragraph
I≟	Indent marker	Creates a paragraph with a first-line indent where you double-clicked

FIGURE 2.3

Word 2000 automatically formats the document with Click and Type.

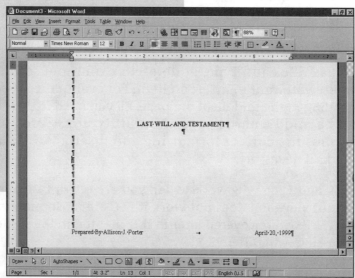

USE CLICK AND TYPE

1. Place your mouse pointer in the middle of the page in a new blank document.
2. Double-click the primary mouse button.

NOTE

If Click and Type doesn't work, it may not be enabled. From the Tools menu, choose Options, and then select the Edit tab. Select Enable Click And Type and click OK.

3. Type **LAST WILL AND TESTAMENT** and press Enter.

4. Double-click at the beginning of a line at the bottom of the page and type your firm name.

5. Double-click at the end of the same line and type today's date.

SELECTING TEXT

Often, you want to change the text after you've typed it—this is one of the main reasons for using a word processor. Changes you want to make may include altering the appearance of text (bold, italic, underline), moving or copying text to a new location, or simply deleting or replacing text. Word operates on the "Select, Then Do" principle. In other words, before you can manipulate existing text, you must first select it.

Selecting text means that you will block, or highlight, the area you want to change. If you try to make a change without selecting text first, you most likely will not get the changes you desire. Selecting indicates to Word that this is the text to be manipulated. Word offers many different methods for selecting text, and, like all features in Word, you can use the mouse or the keyboard to accomplish this task.

NOTE

In WordPerfect for DOS, this technique is called *blocking* text. WordPerfect for Windows and Word refer to it to as *selecting* text.

SELECTING TEXT USING THE MOUSE

Table 2.3 illustrates methods for selecting text using the mouse.

TABLE 2.3 SELECTING TEXT WITH THE MOUSE

TO SELECT . . .	DO THIS . . .
One or more characters	Drag the mouse pointer across the characters that you want to select.
	Dragging is a term used to describe sliding the mouse pointer across the screen while holding down the primary mouse button
One word	Double-click the word.
Multiple words	To select multiple words, click the first word, continue to hold down the mouse button and drag the mouse pointer over the words that you want to select. Word will automatically select the entire first word where you clicked, even if the pointer wasn't at the beginning of the word.

TABLE 2.3   SELECTING TEXT WITH THE MOUSE (CONTINUED)

TO SELECT . . .	DO THIS . . .
One sentence	Hold down the Ctrl key and click anywhere inside the sentence that you want to select.
Multiple sentences	To select multiple sentences, continue to hold down the mouse button and drag the mouse pointer over the sentences that you want to select.
One paragraph	Triple-click any word in the paragraph.
Multiple paragraphs	To select multiple paragraphs, triple-click the first paragraph, but continue to hold down the mouse button on the third click. Then drag the mouse over the paragraphs that you want to select.

It's easy to move text accidentally when you are learning to select text. If this happens, choose the <u>U</u>ndo command from the <u>E</u>dit menu. The Undo command is covered in more detail later in this chapter.

USING THE MOUSE TO SELECT LARGE AMOUNTS OF TEXT

If you select large blocks of text with the mouse, the selection can be difficult to control. When you select a block of text larger than one screen, you often end up with more text selected than you intended.

One way to use the mouse and still control the scroll rate is to use the Shift+Click method. Click where you want to start the selection, and then scroll down using the scroll bar, *not* the keyboard (if you use the keyboard, the insertion point will move). Locate the end of the text that you want to select. Hold down the Shift key and click one time after the last character of the text that you want to select. All text between the insertion point and the Shift+Click is selected.

If you still aren't comfortable with the mouse, you can place the insertion point where you want to begin selecting text, and then double-click the Extend Selection button (EXT) on the Status bar. This activates the Extend Selection feature in Word. Click where you want the selected text to end. To turn Extend Selection off, double-click the EXT button again or use the Escape key. Extend Selection will automatically turn off when a Word command that affects the selection, such as Delete, is executed.

USING THE SELECTION BAR

Mouse users also have the option of using the Selection bar. This area is located along the left margin of the document. It's not marked on the screen, but if you move the mouse pointer inside the Selection bar area, it will change to an arrow that points in toward the text. When you are in the Selection bar area, point at the line you want to select and click one time. Word selects the entire line of text. If you double-click in the Selection bar, Word selects the entire paragraph. A triple-click in the Selection bar selects the entire document. You can also drag the mouse up and down in the Selection bar area to select multiple lines and paragraphs.

CAUTION

To deselect text with the mouse, click the mouse anywhere inside the document. If you press a key other than an arrow, Home, or End, the selected text is deleted. If this happens, choose <u>U</u>ndo from the <u>E</u>dit menu. The deleted text will reappear. When the text reappears, it will still be selected; click in the document to deselect it.

SELECT TEXT USING THE MOUSE

1. Move the mouse pointer into the Selection bar area.
2. Drag the mouse pointer up and down to select multiple lines of text.
3. Click anywhere in the document to deselect the text.
4. Double-click one word to select it.
5. Press the Delete key. The selected word is deleted.
6. Triple-click one paragraph to select it.
7. Click anywhere in the document to deselect it.

SELECTING TEXT USING THE KEYBOARD

Power typists (such as secretaries and others who do a lot of word processing) may prefer to use the keyboard to select text. Several keyboard combinations allow you to select text without taking your fingers off the keyboard. In the earlier sections, you learned how to use the keyboard to move the insertion point around in a document. By using the same keys and key combinations in conjunction with the Shift key, you can select text. Table 2.4 illustrates methods for selecting text with the keyboard.

TABLE 2.4   SELECTING TEXT WITH THE KEYBOARD

TO SELECT . . .	DO THIS . . .
One or more characters	Hold down the Shift key and press the Left Arrow or Right Arrow key.
One or more lines	Hold down the Shift key and press the Up Arrow or Down Arrow key.
Current word	Press F8, F8.
One or more words	Hold down Ctrl+Shift and press the Left Arrow or Right Arrow key.
Current sentence	Press F8, F8, F8.
Insertion point to beginning of line	Press Shift+Home.
Insertion point to end of line	Press Shift+End.
One or more paragraphs	Hold down Ctrl+Shift and press the Up Arrow or Down Arrow key.
To the beginning of a document	Press Ctrl+Shift+Home.
To the end of a document	Press Ctrl+Shift+End.
To the previous screen	Press Shift+PageUp.
To the next screen	Press Shift+PageDown.
The entire document	Ctrl+A (hold down the Ctrl key and press A on the keyboard). It's easy to remember "A" because it refers to *all*.

To deselect text with the keyboard, press any movement key without holding down the Shift key. If you press a key other than an arrow, Home, or End, the selected text is deleted. If this happens, choose Undo from the Edit menu. The deleted text will reappear. When the text reappears, it will still be selected; press any movement key to deselect it.

Another keyboard selection technique is Extend Selection. If you want to select text up to a certain character, that is, select everything from the insertion point to the next colon, you can use the Extend Selection feature. Activate the Extend Selection by pressing F8; you'll see the EXT light up in the Status bar, and now simply type the character you want selected through. Your text is now selected. Table 2.5 summarizes the various uses of Extend Selection.

TABLE 2.5 SELECTING TEXT USING EXTENDED SELECTION

To Select . . .	Do This . . .
One or more characters	F8, then press Left Arrow or Right Arrows.
One or more words	F8 twice to select a word, three times to select a sentence
One or more paragraphs	F8 four times to select a paragraph, five times to select the document
To a specific character	F8, then type the character
Reduce the size of selection	Shift+F8
Turn off Extend Selection	Press Esc

CAUTION   Once you have turned on the Extend Selection feature by pressing the F8 key, it will stay turned on until you press Esc or perform some other formatting task (for example, applying bold, italic, or underline; copying or moving text, and so on). If text is being selected every time you press a key or click your mouse, check to see if EXT appears in your Status bar.

SELECT TEXT USING THE KEYBOARD

1. Hold down the Shift key and press the Left Arrow or Right Arrow key. The text is selected as the arrow keys are pressed.
2. Press the Left Arrow or Right Arrow key without holding down the Shift key to deselect the text.
3. Position the insertion point at the beginning of a word.
4. Hold down Ctrl+Shift and then press the Right Arrow key to select the word.
5. Press the Delete key to delete the selected word.
6. Press Ctrl+A to select the entire document.
7. Press Ctrl+Home to move the insertion point to the start of the document and deselect the text simultaneously.
8. Press F8 and type a comma to select text from the insertion point to the first comma. Type another comma.
9. Press Shift+F8 to shrink the selected area.
10. Press Esc to turn off Extend Selection mode.

FINDING AND REPLACING TEXT

Legal users need the ability to search for a string of text within a long document. As documents are edited in law firms, pages automatically renumber because large amounts of text are removed and added. Eventually, the printed draft of a document no longer matches the on-screen version. A secretary wanting to edit a portion of text appearing on page 50 of a printed document may find that the text has moved to a new page during editing. Fortunately, Word's Find feature is the perfect tool to help you locate text anywhere in a document.

Legal users also need to be able to replace one string of text in a document with another. For example, it may be necessary to change the name of a company throughout an entire document. Word's Replace feature allows users to search for one string of text and replace it with another. Users can search for and replace text throughout an entire document, or they can select a portion of a document and replace only those instances of the text that fall within the selection.

Sometimes, you might need to find or replace specific instances of text. For example, you might want to search a document for all instances of a client's name in bold type and have the bold formatting automatically removed. Replace can search for and replace or remove formatting from text within a document. For information about replacing styles within a document, see Chapter 6, "Styles."

NOTE

This chapter covers an introduction to Word's Find and Replace feature. However, this feature is quite comprehensive and powerful. You will find details on advanced Find and Replace options such as using wildcards, special characters, and formatted text in Word's Help files. Legal users are encouraged to take a moment to review Help after familiarizing themselves with the less advanced functions of Find and Replace that are covered in this chapter.

Word offers a Typing Replaces Selection feature. This feature allows users to select text and replace it by typing new text. For example, to quickly change one instance of a date within your document, select the old date and then type the new one. Word will replace the selected text with the new text you typed. The old string of text and the new one do not need to be the same number of characters.

This feature is useful because it turns a three-step process (selecting, deleting, and typing new text) into a two-step process (selecting and typing new text).

NOTE

You can turn off the Typing Replaces Selection feature in the Options dialog box. To turn this feature off or on, from the Tools menu, choose Options and then click the Edit tab. Clear or select the option for Typing Replaces Selection and click OK.

FIND TEXT IN A DOCUMENT

1. From the Edit menu, choose Find. Keyboard users can press Ctrl+F. The Find and Replace dialog box appears.

NOTE

If you want to search for text only in a specific section of a document, select that portion of the document first.

2. Click the Find tab.

3. Click More to show additional options for finding text. If the dialog box is already extended, More will change to Less.

4. In the Find What box, type the text that you want to find in the document.

5. Select a search option, if desired. The options shown in Table 2.6 are available.

6. After selecting the desired options, click the Find Next button to find the next occurrence of the text within the document.

TABLE 2.6 FIND AND REPLACE OPTIONS

OPTION	FUNCTION
Search:	Set the search direction:
	Select All to search through the entire document or selection, regardless of where the insertion point is when you begin.
	Select Down to search forward from the insertion point through the document or selection. When the end of the document or selection is reached, Word asks whether you want to continue the search at the beginning of the document or selection back to the location where the search began.

TABLE 2.6 FIND AND REPLACE OPTIONS (CONTINUED)

OPTION	FUNCTION
	Select Up to search backward from the insertion point toward the beginning of the document or selection. When the top of the document or selection is reached, Word asks whether you want to continue searching from the bottom back to where the search began.
Match Case:	Select this option to designate a case-sensitive search.
	If you select this box, Word will find only text that matches the capitalization of the text that you type in the Find What box. For example, if this feature is selected and you search for "Law Firm," Word will find only instances where the phrase appears with a capital "L" and "F." It will not find "law firm" or "LAW FIRM".
Find Whole Words Only:	Select this option to find only whole-word instances of the text in the Find what box.
	Word will not find words that are part of a larger word. For example, if you type "legal" in the Find what box and select this option, Word will not find "legally," "paralegal," or "illegal." It will find "legal" anywhere, however, even if it's followed by a punctuation mark such as a period or comma ("legal." Or "legal,"). Note that Word would find "legal" in a combination such as "legal-minded" but not in "legalminded."
Use Wildcards:	Select this option to use a wildcard in a search.
	You might use a wildcard when you are unsure of the spelling, or if you want to search for a special character. To find a single character, use "?". For example, "t?e" finds "the" and "tie". To find a string of characters, use "*". For example, t*m finds "them", "team" and "theorem". The wildcard to locate one of the specified characters is []. For example, "s[ou]n" finds "son" and "sun". To find any character except the one specified, use the "[!]" wildcard. For example, use "m[!a]n" to find "men" and "mon" but not "man". For a complete list of available wildcards in Word, from the Help menu, choose Microsoft Word Help. Type "Find and Replace" and click Search. Click Find and Replace Text or Formatting and then click Fine-tune a search by using wildcard characters.
Sounds Like:	Select this option when you want to search for words that sound the same but are spelled differently.
	For example, you might want to find all occurrences of "color" and "colour" in a document, but are unsure of how the document originator spelled the word. Searching for "color" and selecting Sounds Like finds both spellings in the document.

OPTION	FUNCTION
Find All Word Forms:	Use this feature to find all instances of a word regardless of the form.
	This tool is especially useful when replacing text. Word finds and replaces all forms of a word. For example, if you need to replace all forms of a verb such as "drink" with "eat" and its forms, Word will also find and replace "drank" with "ate" and "drunk" with "eaten." You do not need to perform additional searches to replace these other forms.

If Word does not find the text that you are searching for, and if you are certain that it exists, it could be that an unwanted formatting or search option is active in Find and Replace. Word defaults Find and Replace options to the same settings used in the previous Find or Replace. To reset these options, clear each option in the dialog box and click No Formatting. If No Formatting is inactive, then no special formatting options have been set.

At any time during a Find or Replace, you can move out of the Find and Replace dialog box and edit text directly in the document. To do this, click with the mouse inside the document. The insertion point will appear there, but the dialog box will remain on the screen. Make any desired edits and then click back inside the Find and Replace dialog box to continue searching for or replacing text. When the dialog box is open, keyboard users can press Alt+Shift+F6 to move into and out of the Find and Replace dialog box.

SEARCH FOR AND REPLACE TEXT IN A DOCUMENT

1. From the Edit menu, choose Replace. Keyboard users can press Ctrl+H. The Find and Replace dialog box opens.

If you want to search for and replace text only in a specific section of a document, select that portion of the document first.

2. Select the Replace tab.
3. Click More to view additional options for replacing text. If the additional options are already visible, More changes to Less.
4. Type the text that you want to replace in the Find What box.

5. Type the new text that you want to insert in the Replace With box.

6. Select any desired options. Refer back to Table 2.6 for a list of available options. See Word's help for a list of Format and Special options.

7. To find the next occurrence of the text you typed in the Find What box, click Find Next.

8. To replace a single selected occurrence of the text that you typed in the Find What box with the text that you typed in the Replace With box, click Replace.

9. To replace all occurrences of the text that you typed in the Find What box with the text that you typed in the Replace With box, click Replace All.

NOTE

If you select text in the document before performing a Replace, then clicking Replace All will replace text only within the selection.

Finding and replacing text can also be activated from the Browse Object—the round button at the bottom of the vertical scroll bar. Click the Browse Object and then click the Find icon, represented by a picture of binoculars. This will open the Find and Replace dialog box.

After you have finished finding or replacing text, notice that the double-headed arrows above and below the Browse Object have changed color. The arrows are blue to indicate that the Browse Object is set to search for something other than the next or previous page. Place your mouse pointer over the double-headed arrows to see a ScreenTip showing you what the current Browse Object setting is.

TIP

To reset the Browse Object to search for the next or previous page, click the Browse Object and select Browse By Page, represented by the icon of a single sheet of paper.

MOVING AND COPYING TEXT

Typically, as you work through an agreement or pleading, things start out one way but end up different by the time the document is completed. For example, attorneys might start with a dictated outline of thoughts, whereas secretaries and word processing staff put the text plus formatting details into a document. The ability to move and copy text from one location to another is necessary for arranging thoughts and completing complex legal documents. Word's Cut, Copy, and Paste commands allow you to quickly move text from one location to another.

These special editing commands are on the Standard toolbar as well as in the Edit menu. Keyboard users can press Ctrl+X to Cut, Ctrl+C to copy, and Ctrl+V to paste.

THE CLIPBOARD

When you cut or copy text, Word places it on the Office Clipboard. The Office Clipboard is separate from the Windows Clipboard and is a new feature in Microsoft Office 2000. Text is held on the Clipboard as separate items that you can paste into your document at a new location. Each time you select text and copy or cut it, a new Clipboard item is created and becomes visible on the Clipboard toolbar. You can paste items into your current document or into a different document.

If you forget what you have placed in the different Clipboard items, you can see the first 50 characters of your text by resting the mouse pointer on the item's icon on the Clipboard toolbar. You can paste individual items by clicking the appropriate item's icon on the Clipboard toolbar, or paste all the items *in the order you copied or cut them* by clicking the Paste All button on the Clipboard. Figure 2.4 shows the Office Clipboard.

You can paste the text repeatedly because it is not removed from the Clipboard until you clear the Clipboard or turn off your computer. You can also paste text into another Word document or other Windows file, such as an e-mail message or an Excel spreadsheet.

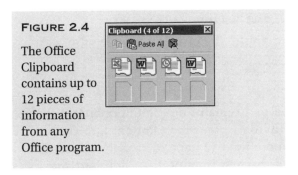

FIGURE 2.4

The Office Clipboard contains up to 12 pieces of information from any Office program.

CUT AND COPY TEXT

1. Select some text that you want to copy.

2. Click the Copy button on the Standard toolbar. Keyboard users can press Ctrl+C to copy text.

The Clipboard toolbar appears showing an icon for each item of text that has been collected. A total of 12 items may be placed on the Clipboard at any one time. If the Clipboard toolbar did not appear, alternate-click on any toolbar button and click once on Clipboard.

3. Move the mouse pointer to the location where you want to insert the copied text and click once to bring the insertion point there.

4. Click the icon of the item you want to paste. Keyboard users can press Ctrl+V to paste the last item copied. Word inserts the text.

5. Select a piece of text that you want to move.

6. Click the Cut button on the Standard toolbar. Keyboard users can press Ctrl+X to cut text. A new Clipboard icon is added every time you cut. You can have a combination of copied and cut text in the Clipboard at any time—up to 12 items.

If you have multiple items of the same type on the Clipboard, it's often confusing what information is stored in each item. You can hover your mouse pointer over an item to have a ScreenTip appear with text from the beginning of each icon.

7. Move the insertion point to the location where you want to insert the cut text.

8. Click the icon of the item you want to paste. Keyboard users can press Ctrl+V to paste the last item cut.

9. Move to another location in the document and paste the text again.

Remember that cut or copied text remains on the Clipboard until you cut or copy more than 12 items, clear the Clipboard, or close Windows. If you cut or copy more than 12 items, a message appears asking if you want to discard the first item on the Clipboard and add the new item to the end of the Clipboard. If you click OK, the next time you cut or copy an item, the Clipboard automatically discards the first item and adds the new item at the end of the Clipboard.

USING DRAG AND DROP TO MOVE AND COPY TEXT

Using the Cut and Copy commands with the Clipboard toolbar is easy to do, but sometimes the drag-and-drop feature may be easier or faster. For example, if all you need to do is transpose two words or move one paragraph before another, the drag-and-drop feature may provide a quicker solution than using Cut or Copy.

Another good time to use the drag-and-drop feature is when your Clipboard is full of things you want to keep. You can move or copy text without erasing any Clipboard items by using drag-and-drop. This bypasses the Clipboard so no existing Clipboard item is overwritten.

USE DRAG-AND-DROP EDITING TO MOVE TEXT

1. Select some text that you want to move.

2. After you select the text, hover the mouse pointer over the selected text. Notice that the mouse pointer changes to an arrow.

NOTE

If you do not see an arrow when you reposition the mouse pointer over the selected text, it is for one of the following reasons:

If you did not move the mouse after selecting the text, the arrow will not appear. Be sure to move the mouse pointer across the selected text after you have selected it.

If you have moved the mouse pointer over the selected text and still do not see an arrow, the drag-and-drop editing feature has been turned off. To turn on drag-and-drop editing, from the Tools menu, choose Options. Click the Edit tab and select Drag-And-Drop Text Editing and click OK.

3. Drag the selected text to the new location. When you release the mouse button at the new location, the text will move.

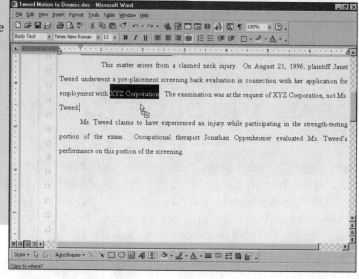

If you like the drag-and-drop method of editing and want to use it to copy as well, follow the same instructions but hold down the Ctrl key and then drag the text. A plus sign appears beside the mouse pointer to indicate you are copying text rather than moving it. Figure 2.5 shows how the mouse pointer looks when using drag-and-drop to copy text.

TIP

If you select text and drag it with the alternate mouse button clicked, when you release the mouse, you can choose whether to move, copy, link or create a hyperlink to the text from the shortcut menu.

THE UNDO COMMAND

"Oops! I didn't want that to happen!" Do those words have a familiar ring? When people work with computers, mistakes happen. Fortunately, Word's extensive Undo command allows you to reverse actions. The Undo command is one of the most important and helpful features in Word. Imagine inadvertently deleting a large portion of text from an unsaved pleading or brief. Being able to restore the deleted material saves hours of time you might otherwise spend reconstructing the document.

Word allows you to undo all of the actions performed from the time you opened the document. Every action (typing, deleting, formatting, copying, moving, or whatever) you perform is stored in the *undo stack* in case you need to undo an action—but not indefinitely. Word clears portions of the undo stack when memory is low. Therefore, it is a good idea to undo an action as soon as you realize a mistake has been made.

Mouse users can access Undo on the Standard toolbar. Keyboard users can access the command from the Edit menu, or by pressing Ctrl+Z.

When actions are undone they move to the *redo stack*. This means that they can be redone if needed. You can only redo actions that have been undone. The Redo command is available by clicking the Redo button on the Standard toolbar. Keyboard users can press Ctrl+Y.

USE THE UNDO AND REDO COMMANDS

1. Select and delete a portion of text in a document.
2. Click the Undo button on the Standard toolbar. Keyboard users can press Ctrl+Z.
3. Click the Redo button on the Standard toolbar to redo the deletion. Keyboard users can press Ctrl+Y.

Word undoes actions in the order in which they were executed. If you need to undo an action performed earlier, continue clicking Undo until the desired action is undone. For example, if you delete some text, copy some text, and then insert more text, to undo the Delete command, you must first undo the Insert action as well as the Copy action.

If you need to undo several actions, click the drop-down arrow attached to the Undo button on the Standard toolbar. A drop-down list of all available actions to be undone appears. Move the mouse to the action you want to undo and click it. Remember that Word can only undo commands contiguously—even with the list, you can't skip back and undo only the third-from-last change you made. Figure 2.6 shows the Standard toolbar with the Undo list displayed.

If you just got the paragraph fixed the way you want it and then discover you need to undo a deletion you did a few minutes ago, you might want to copy the revised text to the Clipboard, undo what you

FIGURE 2.6

You can undo more than one action from the undo stack.

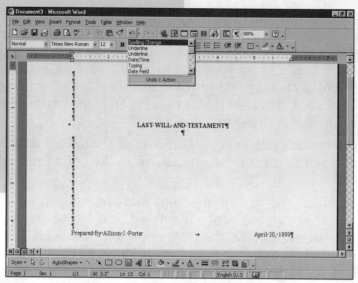

need to using the Undo drop-down list box, and then paste the perfect paragraph back where it should go.

The Delete command will show as "Clear" in the Undo list.

WORKING WITH DIFFERENT VIEWS

In Word, you can choose how you see your document on the screen by selecting different views. Each view has its own function or use. You might find you switch between several views depending on the task you are performing. For example, a power typist may prefer working in Normal view most of the time, but choose Print Layout view to see how headers, footers, and footnotes look. Likewise, an attorney might prefer working in Print Layout view to see exactly how the printed document will appear, but switch to Outline view when drafting a new pleading or contract.

In the bottom-left corner of the Word window, you will see four buttons allowing mouse users to switch between views. Refer to Figure 2.7 for an example of the view buttons. Keyboard users can use the View menu or shortcut keys to switch among views.

FIGURE 2.7

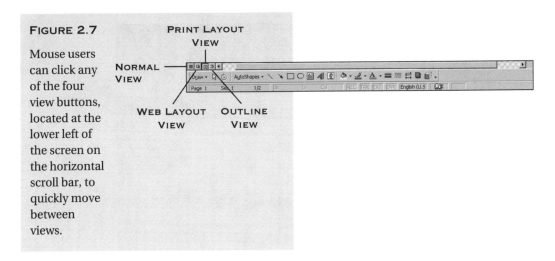

Mouse users can click any of the four view buttons, located at the lower left of the screen on the horizontal scroll bar, to quickly move between views.

Several shortcut keys are available to switch views. They are listed in Table 2.7.

TABLE 2.7 KEYBOARD SHORTCUTS FOR SWITCHING VIEWS

TO SWITCH TO . . .	PRESS . . .
Normal view	Alt+Ctrl+N
Print Layout view	Alt+Ctrl+P
Outline view	Alt+Ctrl+O

The two most commonly used views are Normal and Print Layout:

◆ **Normal view** is often used when entering, editing, and formatting text.

Page boundaries, headers, footers, footnotes, columns, backgrounds, and pictures don't appear in Normal view. Normal view shows text formatting but simplifies the layout of the page so you can type and edit quickly.

Page breaks are displayed as dotted lines across the screen in Normal view. Figure 2.8 shows a document in Normal view.

TIP

To make Word even faster, you can turn pagination off. To do this, from the Tools menu, choose Options. Then select the General tab and clear the option for Background Repagination. This option is available only when you are in Normal view.

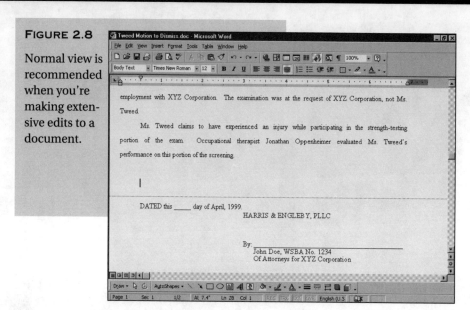

- ◆ **Print Layout view** shows text on the screen exactly as it will print. You will usually use Print Layout view when working with columns and other special formats. For example, Normal view shows all the text in a columnar document in one long column along the left side of the page; Print Layout view shows multiple columns across a page. (WordPerfect users should not confuse Word's column feature with WordPerfect's parallel column feature. For more information about columns and tables, see Chapter 7, "Using Tables in Legal Documents.")

  Print Layout shows margins and displays headers, footers, footnotes, and endnotes as unavailable (dimmed) text.

  In Print Layout view, a blank area appears between pages when you scroll from one page to another. Figure 2.9 shows a document in Print Layout view.

- ◆ **Outline view** is for organizing the structure of a document. You can format a document quickly by assigning heading styles to different paragraphs. After you have heading styles established, manipulating and moving large blocks of text in Outline view is easy. If you drag a heading paragraph in this view, all the body text associated with the heading moves as well. For more information about using styles, see Chapter 6, "Styles." Figure 2.10 shows a document in Outline view.

FIGURE 2.9

Use Print Layout view when you need to see headers, footers, margins, and an accurate representation of how a document will look when it prints.

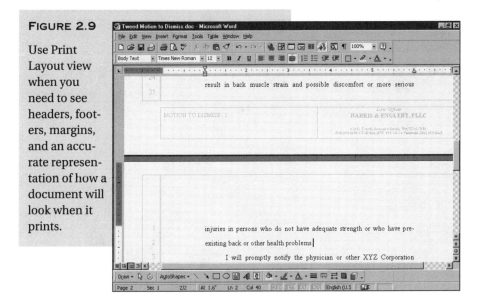

FIGURE 2.10

Use Outline view with heading styles to quickly organize text and ideas in a document.

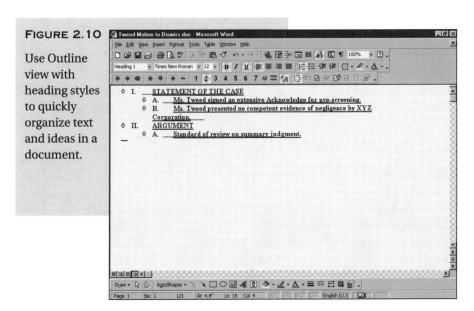

♦ **Web Layout view** shows how the document will look in a Web browser, showing background colors and patterns along with the text. Word saves a copy of your document and then opens it in your default browser. Text appears larger and wraps to the width of the window, making it easier to read (see Figure 2.11).

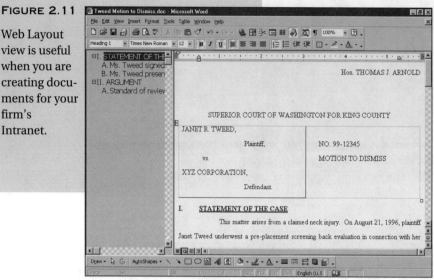

For more information about creating Web documents, see Chapter 15, "Publishing Word Documents on Your Firm's Intranet."

If you are working on a laptop and have limited screen space, the ability to see all the text simultaneously is invaluable.

THE DOCUMENT MAP

The Document Map is a feature that makes navigating through a large document easy. You can use the Document Map in any view; however, if you have the Document Map visible—as in figure 2.11— and then switch to Outline view, the Document Map closes. You activate this feature by clicking the Document Map button on the Standard toolbar. Keyboard users can access the Document Map from the View menu. When activated, a pane appears on the left side of the document window showing all the headings and titles within the document. You can adjust the width of the Document Map by placing the mouse pointer over the right edge of the pane and dragging to resize it.

To navigate through a document using the Document Map, click any heading or title that appears in the Document Map window. For example, if you want to move quickly to Article XII in a large document, click the appropriate heading in the Document Map; the insertion point will jump to that location.

Word pulls text into the Document Map if it is formatted with outline levels. If Word can't find any text formatted this way, it looks through the document for paragraphs that look like headings and titles. For example, a short paragraph that is centered, bold, or in a larger font than other text will be displayed in the Document Map window. If Word can't find any headings or titles in a document, the Document Map window is empty.

To place paragraphs in the Document Map without changing the formatting of the paragraph, set an Outline level. First, select the paragraph you want in the Document Map. Then from the Format menu. choose Paragraph, and select the Indents and spacing tab. Change the Outline level from Body text to any of the levels, 1 through 9.

ACTIVATE AND USE THE DOCUMENT MAP

1. Open a document containing headings or titles.
2. On the Standard toolbar, click the Document Map button, or choose Document Map from the View menu.
3. Click any heading or title in the Document Map to jump to that location in the document.
4. Close the Document Map by clicking the Document Map button on the Standard toolbar. Keyboard users can choose Document Map from the View menu.

THE ZOOM FEATURE

Sometimes the font in a document may look very small on the screen, or you may not be able to see from one margin to the other without using the horizontal scroll bar. Changing the magnification of the document will allow you to get the best view of your document.

The magnification of a document can be controlled through the Zoom dialog box, or by changing the percentage in the Zoom box on the Standard toolbar. Figure 2.12 shows the Zoom box on the Standard toolbar.

Changing the zoom percentage for a document does not physically change the size of the font. It merely changes the magnification of the text on the screen (making it larger or smaller). When the document prints, the text will print according to the size set in the Font

FIGURE 2.12

Use the Zoom box on the Standard tool-bar to change the screen magnification of a document.

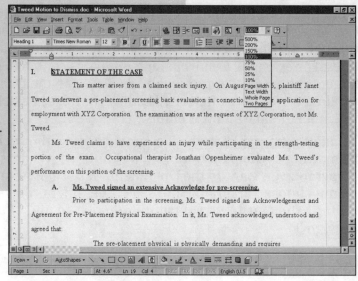

Size box on the Formatting toolbar. For more information about set-ting the font size and using the Formatting toolbar, see Chapter 3.

CHANGE THE MAGNIFICATION OF A DOCUMENT

1. Click the drop-down arrow to the right of the Zoom list box on the Standard toolbar. The zoom choices are displayed (see Figure 2.12).

2. Choose "200%." You should now have a close-up view of your document. A close-up view is helpful when you're trying to align text and graphics.

3. Click the arrow again and choose "50%." Notice how the docu-ment magnification changes. Text will still print in the original size. It appears smaller only on the screen.

4. Click the Zoom box again and choose Page Width. Word will shrink or enlarge the magnification so that the page width fits within the Word window. This is helpful when you're working with wide documents that cause the window to jump back and forth while you type.

The options described in Table 2.8 are available in the Zoom box.

TABLE 2.8 ZOOM OPTIONS

SELECT . . .	TO . . .
Page Width	Reduce the view enough to see the entire width of the page.
Text Width	Reduces or enlarges the view of the text from margin to margin.
Whole Page	Reduce the page dramatically so that one complete page fits onscreen.
	You cannot read the text in this view, but you can see the overall layout of the page.
	This option is available only in Print Layout view.
Many Pages (Zoom dialog box)	When you select Many Pages in the Zoom dialog box, you must click the button to the right of the option to select the number of pages that you want to see.
Two Pages (Zoom box on Standard toolbar)	View two pages simultaneously. Use the scroll bars to move to the previous or next pages.
	These options are useful if you want to compare the layout of two or more pages. They are available only in Print Layout view.

You will notice when you choose one of the preceding options that the percentage showing in the Zoom box may not match one of the options listed in that box when you click the drop-down arrow. You can type a percentage into the Zoom box even if it does not appear on the list. To do this, click the number inside of the Zoom box, and then type the percentage that you would like (you don't have to type the percent symbol). Make certain to press the Enter key after you type the number.

Changing the view does not change the look of the printed document. If the document is too large or too small when it prints, change the font size, *not* the magnification. For more information about formatting text, see Chapter 3.

Zoom settings belong to a document, not to a computer. WordPerfect users accustomed to setting their environment and never having it change are in for a surprise. Word remembers the zoom percentage of a document based on the last time it was saved. If someone in your firm saves and closes a document in 200% view, when you open the document, it will also be in 200% view.

THE FULL SCREEN COMMAND

The Full Screen command, found on the View menu, allows you to see a document by hiding all toolbars, scroll bars, and the Status bar. You can still type and format text while in this view.

When Full Screen mode is activated, you can still use the mouse and keyboard to access Word's menus. To use the mouse, position the pointer along the top edge of the screen; the menu bar will appear. Keyboard users need only press the Alt key to make the menu visible.

When Full Screen mode is activated, the Full Screen toolbar appears on the screen. Click Close Full Screen (or press Alt+C) to close Full Screen view and return to one of Word's regular views. You can also press Esc to exit Full Screen view. Figure 2.13 shows a document in Full Screen mode with the Full Screen toolbar floating near the bottom edge of the screen.

NOTE

The location of the Full Screen toolbar will vary. It may float above the text or it may be located along the top edge of the screen. You can move the toolbar by dragging it. The toolbar will always appear in the last position in which it was located in this view.

FIGURE 2.13

Use Full Screen mode when you need to see as much of a document as possible on the screen.

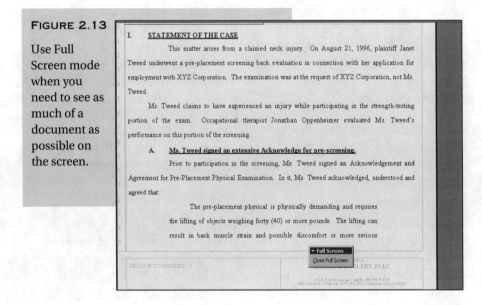

AUTOTEXT

The AutoText feature allows you to store and easily retrieve commonly used text or graphics. For example, you can save your firm's address as an AutoText entry and then quickly insert it when needed.

NOTE

If you are converting from WordPerfect for DOS, you can replicate many of your WordPerfect macros for inserting text with the AutoText feature. If you are converting from a more recent version of WordPerfect, you will find Word's AutoText very similar to WordPerfect's Abbreviations feature.

AutoText entries can contain a few words or large blocks (even pages) of text. Entries can include complex formatting, graphics, tables, and field codes. This feature is used to store items that you use often in one or more documents. Word also has predefined AutoText entries, such as sample headers and footers, common closings, salutations, mailing instructions, and more.

AutoText entries can be stored only in templates. If you store them in a document template, they are available only in documents created with that specific template. For example, you might create an AutoText entry to insert an attorney's name and direct-dial number into the header of a letter. Because you would not need this entry available in all documents, you would store it in the letter template. By limiting AutoText entries to specific documents, you will keep the AutoText entry dialog box from becoming cluttered. This will make finding the entries that you need easier. To make AutoText entries available in all documents, store them in the Normal template or a global template (see Chapter 10 for more information about storing AutoText entries in templates).

Word comes with several predefined AutoText entries. To see Word's default AutoText entries, select AutoText from the Insert menu. A drop-down menu will appear. Select AutoText again. You can insert any of the entries listed into a document.

INSERTING AUTOTEXT ENTRIES INTO A DOCUMENT

Word provides several ways to insert an AutoText entry into a document. You can use the AutoText menu, the AutoText dialog box, a keyboard shortcut, or you can accept an AutoComplete Tip. Figure 2.14 shows the AutoText dialog box.

FIGURE 2.14

Use the AutoText dialog box to insert AutoText entries into documents.

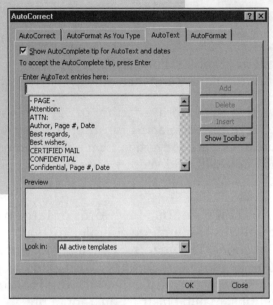

INSERT AN AUTOTEXT ENTRY USING AUTOCOMPLETE

1. Begin typing today's date into a document. Make certain that you spell out the name of the month. For example, type **September**.

2. Notice that a yellow AutoComplete Tip appears on the screen as you type the fourth character of the month.

NOTE

If you do not see an AutoComplete Tip, this feature may be turned off. You can activate the AutoComplete Tip feature from the Insert menu by choosing AutoText. Then select AutoText from the drop-down menu. The AutoText dialog box will appear (refer back to Figure 2.14). Select the option to Show AutoComplete Tip For AutoText And Dates.

3. To insert the suggested text, press the Enter key while the AutoComplete Tip is showing onscreen. The month is automatically inserted.

CREATING YOUR OWN AUTOTEXT ENTRIES

You may want to create your own AutoText entries. For example, you might create an entry that inserts your firm's name and address so that you don't have to type it each time you want to insert it into a document. Creating an AutoText entry is as easy as typing the text one time and then selecting it.

CREATE A GLOBAL AUTOTEXT ENTRY

1. Type your firm's name and address into a document. Make certain to format it the way you want it to appear most often. If you will need other formats, you can create additional entries for them later. (For information about formatting text, see Chapter 3.)

2. Select the entire name and address. Make certain to include in the selection the final paragraph mark at the end of the address.

3. From the Insert menu, choose AutoText.

4. Choose New. The Create AutoText dialog box appears (see Figure 2.15).

5. Click OK to accept the default name.

NOTE

AutoText entries are, by default, stored in the Normal template, meaning that they are available in all documents. If you want to create an AutoText entry for a specific template, you must create the entry in the AutoText dialog box (refer back to Figure 2.14) and change the Look In box to specify the template. For more information about templates, see Chapter 10.

FIGURE 2.15

The Create AutoText dialog box allows you to create an AutoText entry.

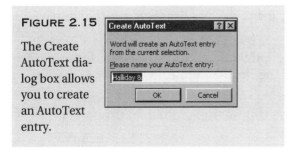

If you open the AutoText dialog box, the new entry should be listed. To insert it into your document, select it and then click Insert.

To insert the entry using an AutoComplete Tip, simply begin typing the firm name into the document. The AutoComplete Tip will appear. Press the Enter key to insert the complete name and address in the format in which you saved it.

NOTE

Sometimes an AutoComplete Tip will not appear. If this happens, press the F3 key to force the entry to be inserted. You won't get an AutoComplete Tip when multiple entries have similar names in the AutoText dialog box, or when the AutoText name is less than four characters.

If you do not like the AutoComplete Tip feature, you can turn it off. To do this, from the Insert menu, choose AutoText. Choose AutoText again to display the AutoText dialog box. Clear the Show AutoComplete Tip For AutoText And Dates option and click OK.

TIP

If you use AutoText often, you may want to display the AutoText toolbar. The toolbar has three buttons: AutoText, All Entries, and Create AutoText (labeled New). The AutoText button when clicked displays the AutoCorrect dialog box with the AutoText tab selected. The All Entries button displays a drop-down list of categorized AutoText entries. The Create AutoText button is enabled when text is selected and is a shortcut to creating new AutoText entries.

REDEFINING AUTOTEXT ENTRIES

You can add as many AutoText entries as you want. You can also delete or change existing entries when necessary. When you modify an existing entry, you "redefine" it.

REDEFINE AN AUTOTEXT ENTRY

1. Insert the entry for your firm address, or insert another entry you want to redefine.

2. Modify the text as desired. If you are modifying your firm address, you might add the firm's telephone number at the bottom of the entry.

3. Select the *entire* entry, including the original text and the new text that you have added.

4. From the Insert menu, choose AutoText.

5. Choose New. Make certain to name the entry the same as before.

6. If you have named the entry correctly, Word asks whether you want to redefine the existing entry. Choose Yes to redefine it, or No to leave the original entry as it is. The next time that you insert the entry, the newly modified entry is inserted.

DELETING AUTOTEXT ENTRIES

Sometimes you may want to delete an AutoText entry that you no longer need.

DELETE AN AUTOTEXT ENTRY

1. From the Insert menu, choose AutoText. Choose AutoText again to access the AutoText dialog box. (Refer back to Figure 2.14 to see the AutoText dialog box.)

2. Locate and select the entry that you want to delete.

3. Click Delete.

4. Click Close to close the dialog box.

Word does not ask you to confirm an AutoText entry deletion. It deletes the entry immediately.

ANSWERING COMMON QUESTIONS

Why do I keep losing the two spaces between sentences when I copy and paste text?

Many law firms still follow the practice of having two spaces after every sentence. Word has a feature called Smart Cut And Paste that automatically deletes extra spaces between sentences when you cut or drag them, leaving only one space between sentences when they are moved. To turn this feature off, from the Tools menu, choose Options and then select the Edit tab. Clear the Use Smart Cut And Paste option and click OK.

When I try to select text, sometimes I accidentally move it instead. What can I do?

Sometimes, you drag text without meaning to do so. When this happens, you can move the text back to its original location by choosing the Undo command from the Edit menu, pressing Ctrl+Z on the keyboard, or clicking the Undo icon on the Standard toolbar. If this happens to you often, you can disable the Drag and Drop feature. From the Tools menu, choose Options and then select the Edit tab. Clear the check box next to Drag And Drop Text Editing.

Sometimes when I try to select a few characters, I end up selecting the entire word or several words.

Word has a feature that automatically selects an entire word when you are selecting text with the mouse. This feature can be a great time saver because you don't have to worry about placing the mouse pointer directly in front of the word that you want to select. However, the feature may become frustrating if you want to select one or two characters in a word and you select the entire word instead. Don't worry, you can turn this feature off by choosing Options from the Tools menu and then clicking the Edit tab. Clear the When Selecting, Automatically Select Entire Word option and click OK.

Why doesn't my Office Clipboard appear automatically when I copy text?

The Clipboard toolbar will not appear automatically if you have closed it consecutively three times without pasting. If the Clipboard toolbar isn't showing automatically when you copy an item, you can redisplay it by choosing Toolbars from the View menu and then clicking Clipboard.

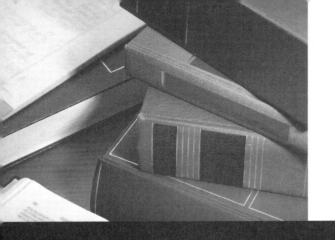

CHAPTER 3

FORMATTING TEXT

IN THIS CHAPTER

- Using the Formatting toolbar and dialog boxes
- Inserting legal symbols
- Setting alignment, spacing, tabs, and indents
- Creating borders
- Formatting text automatically as you type
- Using the Format Painter

The biggest reason for using a word processor is to apply formatting to a document. After all, if you didn't need formatting, you could just use a typewriter! While most legal documents are fairly plain-looking, there is actually a great deal of formatting that takes place behind the scenes to give the document its professional appearance. For example, when you prepare a court document and use a required font size, you are formatting. When you insert a legal description in a document and indent the text one inch on both sides, again, you are formatting. You can use formatting to meet court requirements or to emphasize various points in your documents.

After you have typed text in your document, almost all your work from that point forward involves formatting. Word provides several ways for you to easily apply formatting. Menu commands, toolbar buttons, and shortcut keys are available for the most commonly used formatting. You can apply formatting as you type, or type your text first and then go back and format it later.

This chapter addresses two types of formatting—character and paragraph formatting—plus a few formatting options, such as borders, that can apply either to individual characters or to entire paragraphs.

Character formatting includes features that affect the font characteristics, such as bold, underline, font size, and font type. You can apply character formatting to one or several characters within a document.

Paragraph formatting includes centering, indenting, and tabs as well as other features. You cannot apply paragraph formatting to single characters; you must apply it to entire paragraphs within a document.

VIEWING PARAGRAPH MARKS

The first time you open a Word document with paragraph marks showing, you may be inclined to hide them to make your screen less cluttered. Wait! Before you do that, you need to understand why paragraph marks are so important in Word.

Corel WordPerfect has a feature called Reveal Codes that allows you to see the commands hidden in text. These commands indicate where formatting has been turned on and where it has been turned off. By reading the codes, you can determine why your text looks the way it does when you print it.

Word doesn't need a Reveal Codes type of feature because you can see the formatting right on your screen. This is called WYSIWYG (What You See Is What You Get). For example, if bold formatting has been applied to text, that text will appear bold right on your screen. Likewise, if a paragraph is centered, it will appear centered on your screen.

The paragraph marks in a document store the codes that align text and set spacing. If you delete a paragraph mark at the end of a paragraph, you remove whatever paragraph formatting codes it contained, which can dramatically change the appearance of the text. For these reasons, leaving paragraph marks showing while you are editing is best; you should turn them off only when you are reading your document on the screen.

To display paragraph marks, click the paragraph symbol (¶) on the Standard toolbar, or press Ctrl+Shift+*. This toggles the Show/Hide button, which displays other nonprinting symbols in your document as well. Nonprinting symbols include paragraph marks, spaces between words, tab characters, optional hyphens, and hidden text.

TIP

If you want to display paragraph marks but not tabs and spaces on the screen, choose Options from the Tools menu. Select the View tab. Select the option for Paragraph Marks, and then clear any other items that you do not wish to see on the screen.

If you want to find out which codes are stored in the paragraph marks, you can use a Word feature called What's This? This feature allows you to view formatting stored within paragraph marks and text. Click What's This? from the Help menu, and the mouse pointer turns into a question mark. When you click any text or paragraph symbols, a balloon appears that lists the formatting codes. Keyboard users can press Shift+F1 to activate this feature.

To turn off this feature, press the Esc key. For more information on this Help feature and other ways to get help, see Chapter 1, "Getting Started." Figure 3.1 shows an example of the What's This? balloon.

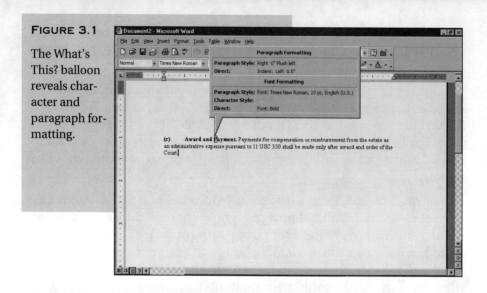

FIGURE 3.1

The What's This? balloon reveals character and paragraph formatting.

USING THE FORMATTING TOOLBAR IN LEGAL DOCUMENTS

Most of the commands that you use to format legal documents are located on the Formatting toolbar. By clicking a button, you can make text bold, italic, or underlined, or you can change the style or size of the font. Keyboard users can use shortcuts to perform the formatting commands. Figure 3.2 shows the Formatting toolbar (see Chapter 1 for the button names on this toolbar).

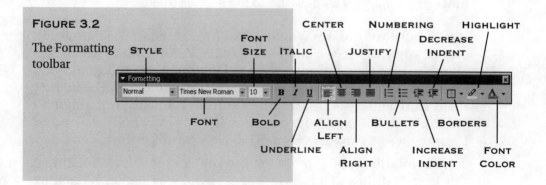

FIGURE 3.2

The Formatting toolbar

TIP

You can use Word's Help feature to print a list of keyboard short-cuts for formatting text. Choose Microsoft Word <u>H</u>elp from the Help menu. In the Office Assistant text box, type **keyboard short-cuts**, and then select the keyboard shortcuts topic in the Topics Found dialog box. When the Help pane appears, select Format Characters and Paragraphs. Click the printer icon on the Help pane to print the topic.

Commands that change the appearance of text are referred to as character formatting commands. To apply character formatting, you select the text that you want formatted, and then click the corresponding button on the toolbar.

Have you ever applied a font change in your document and then regretted it because the font was not what you expected? Word 2000 offers a new WYSIWYG (What You See Is What You Get) font list on the Formatting toolbar. So before you select a font, you get a preview of what your text will look like if you apply the font. Figure 3.3 shows the WYSIWYG font list.

FORMAT TEXT

1. Create a new blank document by clicking the New icon on the Standard toolbar. Keyboard users can press Ctrl+N.

2. Type **Seller sells the products being sold hereunder to Buyer as is where is**.

3. Select the text "as is where is."

4. Click the Bold button on the Formatting toolbar, or press Ctrl+B.

FIGURE 3.3

The WYSIWYG font command on the Formatting toolbar

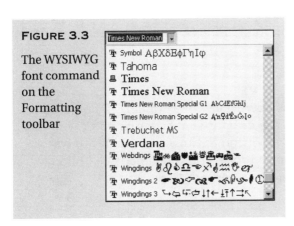

To remove bold formatting from the selected text, click the Bold button again. It works as a toggle. If you have applied several formats to the selected text and wish to remove all of them, select the text and press Ctrl+Spacebar. This command removes all manually applied formatting.

Are you a keyboard user who doesn't want to lift a hand off the keyboard? You can turn formatting off and on as you type without ever touching the mouse. For example, let's say you need to type an underlined title. As mentioned earlier, one way to format the title is to type the text, select the text, and then click the Underline button on the Formatting toolbar. To stay on the keyboard, press Ctrl+U to turn on underlining, type the underlined text, and then press Ctrl+U to turn underlining off. Your hands never have to leave the keyboard.

USING THE FONT DIALOG BOX

What if you need a command that is not available on the Formatting toolbar? Perhaps you need to make a word appear with a double underline, or you need superscript formatting. All of Word's character formatting commands are available in the Font dialog box. These include multiple forms of underlining (single, double, words only, different colored underlines, and so on), shadowed text, outlined text, and many other formatting options for legal documents.

USE THE FONT MENU

1. Select the text that you typed in the previous exercise.
2. Choose Font from the Format menu.
3. Click the All Caps option in the Effects section.
4. Click the OK button.

Word's 2000's default font is now Times New Roman, 12 point. In previous versions of Word, the default font size was 10 pt. One caveat however; If you open a document in Word 2000 that was created in a previous version of Word, your document will retain the default font size of the previous version (10 points).

If you find that you are always changing the font to a different size and type, you can change it permanently in the Normal template. The following exercise shows you how to change your default font. Note that this change only affects *new* documents based on the Normal template, that is, new blank documents. For more information on working with templates, see Chapter 10, "Creating Legal Templates." For more information on modifying existing styles, see Chapter 6, "Styles."

SET THE DEFAULT FONT

1. Choose Font from the Format menu. Keyboard users can press Ctrl+D.

2. Select Courier New in the Font box, and 12 points in the Size box.

3. Click the Default button in the lower-left corner of the dialog box.

4. You will receive the following message: "Do you want to change your default font to Courier New? This change will affect all new documents based on the Normal template."

5. Click the Yes button if you wish to make this change; otherwise, click No.

MAKING THE PRINTED DOCUMENT MATCH THE SCREEN

In legal documents, it's important that the characters that appear on the screen match the printed document. If the screen display does not match what is printed, change the font to a TrueType font. TrueType fonts are marked with a TT in the Font box on the Formatting toolbar. TrueType fonts are installed with Windows and have been designed to appear on the screen and on paper in an identical format. Non-TrueType fonts appear with a printer icon next to their name in the Font box.

If the text layout changes each time you open a document, make certain that you are using the same printer settings each time. Word automatically adjusts the text on the screen to match output from the currently selected printer. You can change the selected printer by choosing Print from the File menu. Next, select a different printer in the Name box. Another option is to turn on printer metrics. This feature is found under Tools, Options, on the Compatibility tab. Select the Use Printer Metrics To Lay Out Document box to have the document preserve exact formatting.

INSERTING LEGAL SYMBOLS

Inserting copyright, trademark, paragraph, section, and other legal symbols into a document is easy. The Symbol menu contains all the symbols that you need to create legal documents. Keyboard shortcuts are also available to quickly insert legal symbols into a document. Figure 3.4 shows the Special Characters tab of the Symbols menu.

INSERT LEGAL SYMBOLS

1. Type **Microsoft**.

2. Choose Symbol from the Insert menu and then select the Special Characters tab.

3. Click the Registered symbol (®) entry once and then click the Insert button.

4. Click the Close button.

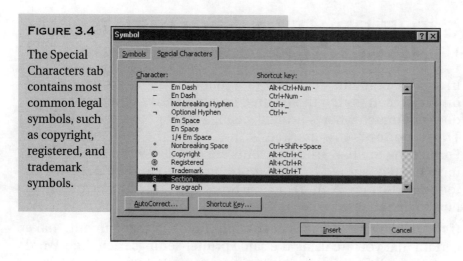

FIGURE 3.4

The Special Characters tab contains most common legal symbols, such as copyright, registered, and trademark symbols.

FIGURE 3.5

You can find symbols and international characters in the Symbol dialog box. Changing the font selection will display different character sets.

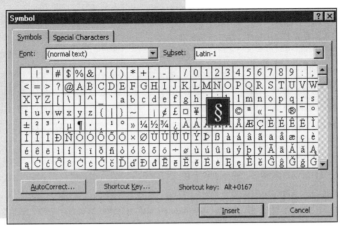

Only the most commonly used symbols appear on the Special Characters tab. Others are available on the Symbols tab. You will find international characters, typographical symbols, and many other symbols available there. Figure 3.5 gives an example of the symbols available in the normal text font, Latin-1 subset.

INSERT INTERNATIONAL CHARACTERS FOR THE WORD RÉSUMÉ

1. Type **r**.
2. Choose Symbol from the Insert menu. Select the Symbols tab.
3. Select (normal text) in the Font box, and Latin-1 in the Subset box.
4. Select the é symbol and click the Insert button.
5. Click the Close button.
6. Type **sum**.
7. Press [Ctrl]+['],[e] to insert another é.

TIP

If you are having difficulty viewing the symbols in the Symbol box, click one time on a symbol to magnify it.

ASSIGNING SHORTCUT KEYS FOR LEGAL SYMBOLS

If you don't want to use the Symbol menu, you can insert legal symbols into documents using shortcut keys. Shortcut keys work by combining the Ctrl, Alt, and Shift keys with other characters. If Word does not have a shortcut key assigned to a particular symbol, you can assign one.

TIP

To determine if a symbol has a keyboard shortcut assigned, click a symbol in the Symbols tab once. If a keyboard shortcut is assigned, it appears in the dialog box, directly above the Insert button.

For example, the Section (§) and Paragraph (¶) symbols do not have shortcut keys assigned by default, so you may want to assign shortcut key combinations for them. Shortcut keys can be assigned from the Symbol dialog box by clicking the Shortcut Key button. This opens the Customize Keyboard dialog box (see Figure 3.6).

ASSIGN A SHORTCUT KEY TO A SYMBOL

1. Choose Symbol from the Insert menu.
2. Select the Special Characters tab.
3. Select the Paragraph symbol in the list of characters.
4. Click the Shortcut Key button.

FIGURE 3.6

You can customize the keyboard by assigning shortcut keys to any Word command.

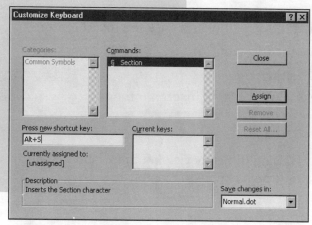

5. Press the shortcut key combination that you would like to assign, such as Alt+P.

6. Click the <u>A</u>ssign button and then click Close.

If you select the Customize Keyboard dialog box and then press the new shortcut key combination, Word tells you whether the shortcut is currently assigned to another command. For example, if you press Ctrl+P, Word tells you that Ctrl+P is currently assigned to FilePrint. You could reassign Ctrl+P to the Paragraph symbol, but others who use your machine would not be aware of the different shortcut keys. It's best not to override Word's built-in shortcut keys; instead, try to find a combination that is unassigned. For the Paragraph symbol, you may find Alt+P a good alternative.

NOTE You can use the numeric keypad on the keyboard to insert symbols by typing their ANSI equivalent. For example, Alt+0182 inserts a paragraph symbol, and Alt+0167 inserts a section symbol. Just remember to turn the numeric keypad on before pressing the Alt key.

INSERTING A NONBREAKING SPACE OR HYPHEN

Nonbreaking spaces prevent text from being separated when it falls at the end of a line. For example, if you were entering a date such as January 15, 2000, you would not want "January" at the end of one line and "15" at the beginning of the next. You can use a nonbreaking space to prevent this separation from occurring.

This feature is also helpful with names. If your law firm is named Smith Jones & Reed, LLPC, you might want to guarantee that the names "Smith" and "Jones" will always stay together. You can do this by inserting a nonbreaking space between them.

Nonbreaking hyphens keep hyphenated text together across a line. A good time to use a nonbreaking hyphen is when typing a telephone number.

INSERT A NONBREAKING SPACE AND HYPHEN

1. Type **Pursuant to Federal Rules of Civil Procedure**.

2. Rather than press the spacebar after "Procedure," insert a nonbreaking space by choosing <u>S</u>ymbol from the <u>I</u>nsert menu.

3. Select the Special Characters tab.

4. Click Nonbreaking Space in the list of characters.

5. Click the Insert button and then click Close.

6. Type **26** after the Nonbreaking space.

Keyboard users can press Ctrl+Shift+Spacebar to insert a nonbreaking space. Mouse users will probably find this shortcut easier as well.

On the screen, a nonbreaking space looks like a degree symbol. It is a nonprinting character, however, meaning that it will show on the screen but not appear in the printed document. Inserting a nonbreaking space between "Procedure" and "26" keeps them together, never to be placed on separate lines.

The flow of text will change as you edit a document (because you are adding and removing text), so habitually inserting nonbreaking spaces between words that should remain together is a good idea. This way, as the document layout changes, you do not need to worry about dates and other phrases becoming separated.

Word also provides AutoCorrect entries for common legal symbols. AutoCorrect entries allow you to type a few characters and automatically produce a symbol onscreen. For example, you can type **(c)** and it will automatically turn into a copyright symbol. (Don't worry, you can press Ctrl+Z to undo the change if you're typing a list, and you can remove any or all AutoCorrect entries if you find them annoying) Table 3.1 shows some common shortcut keys and AutoCorrect entries for legal symbols. You can assign your own AutoCorrect entries as well as delete any that are currently in the system. Figure 3.7 shows the shortcut keys and AutoCorrect entries for common legal symbols.

TABLE 3.1 AUTOCORRECT ENTRIES FOR LEGAL SYMBOLS

SYMBOL	RESULT	SHORTCUT KEY	AUTOCORRECT ENTRY
Copyright	©	Ctrl+Alt+C	(c)
Registered	®	Ctrl+Alt+R	(r)
Trademark	™	Ctrl+Alt+T	(t)

FIGURE 3.7

You can assign AutoCorrect entries for any symbol or international character.

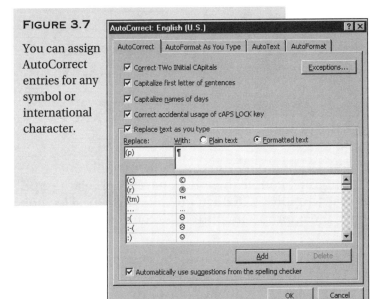

ASSIGN AUTOCORRECT ENTRIES

1. Choose Symbol from the Insert menu.
2. Select the Special Characters tab.
3. Select the Paragraph symbol in the list of characters.
4. Click the AutoCorrect button.
5. Type **(p)** in the Replace box.
6. Click the Add button.
7. Click OK.

AutoCorrect is covered in more detail in Chapter 8, "Spelling and Grammar."

SETTING PARAGRAPH ALIGNMENT

So far, you've seen various forms of character formatting, such as making text bold, italic, or underlined. The next level of formatting is paragraph formatting.

Although you can apply character formatting to one or more characters within a paragraph, you must apply paragraph formatting to

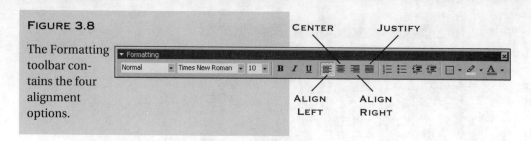

FIGURE 3.8

The Formatting toolbar contains the four alignment options.

an entire paragraph. For example, you cannot center only one word of a paragraph. You must center the entire paragraph. Paragraph formatting is as easy to apply as character formatting: you select the text and then click the appropriate button on the Formatting toolbar.

Paragraph alignment allows you to control the alignment of a paragraph on a page. For example, when you create a pleading, you usually center the court's name. You might right-align the date in a letter, or justify the text in a brief. Four types of paragraph alignment are available in Word: left-aligned, centered, right-aligned, and justified. The Formatting toolbar, shown in Figure 3.8, has buttons available for all four types of alignment.

Many paragraph formatting options are available on the Formatting toolbar. These include paragraph alignment, bullets and numbering, and commands to increase or decrease a paragraph indent. As with the character formatting options, there are more paragraph formatting options besides the ones available on the Formatting toolbar. You can find additional options such as line spacing, paragraph spacing, and special indents in the Paragraph dialog box.

One of the great features of paragraph formatting is that formatting applied in one paragraph automatically copies down to the next. For example, assume that you have set a first line indent in a paragraph. Every time you press Enter, the new paragraph has the same first line indent. No more need to press the Tab key at the beginning of every paragraph!

For new users, this feature may seem tricky at first. For example, if you type a centered paragraph and then press Enter to begin the next line, the new paragraph will also be centered, which may not be what you want. Remember that you do not "turn off" paragraph alignment; you change it by selecting a different option. To change the alignment, choose a new type of alignment *after* you press the

Enter key to begin the new paragraph. You can do this by clicking the appropriate alignment button on the toolbar. If you click a toolbar button *before* you press the Enter key, you change the alignment of the current paragraph.

ALIGN A PARAGRAPH

1. Type **Employment Agreement** and press Enter.
2. Select the paragraph that you just typed and then click the Center button on the Formatting toolbar (or press Ctrl+E).
3. Click the other alignment buttons on the toolbar so that you can see the various types of paragraph alignment.

Table 3.2 lists keyboard shortcuts for aligning text.

You can apply only one type of paragraph alignment to a paragraph. If you try to replicate the Flush Right command that is available in WordPerfect by right-aligning selected text in a paragraph, the entire paragraph will become right-aligned. You can replicate the Flush Right feature of WordPerfect using right tabs, and in Word 2000, it's easier than ever to do this. See "Setting Tabs" later in this chapter for more information.

TIP

If you use justified text, you may have experienced problems when pressing Shift+Enter to insert a manual line break. Word 2000 has a new feature that prevents the text in a justified paragraph from expanding. To turn this feature on, choose Options from the Tools menu and select the Compatibility tab. Select Don't Expand Character Spaces on the line ending Shift-Return and click OK.

TABLE 3.2 PARAGRAPH ALIGNMENT SHORTCUT KEYS

KEYBOARD SHORTCUT	PARAGRAPH ALIGNMENT
Ctrl+L	Left-aligned
Ctrl+E	Centered
Ctrl+R	Right-aligned
Ctrl+J	Justified

TIP

You can reset some paragraph formats by pressing Ctrl+Q. Ctrl+Q will return the paragraph to its original formatting and remove any manual, or direct, formatting.

SETTING PARAGRAPH AND LINE SPACING

Word has two types of spacing: line spacing and paragraph spacing. Paragraph spacing determines how much space is inserted between paragraphs, whereas line spacing determines how much space exists between lines within a paragraph.

For example, you might set paragraph spacing to 12 points and line spacing to Single. This setting would cause Word to single-space the text as it wraps within the paragraph. A double space would occur when you press the Enter key, making the current paragraph end and a new one ready to begin.

As you can imagine, this feature is extremely powerful. It allows you maximum flexibility with a reduced number of keystrokes. Figure 3.9 shows the Indents and Spacing tab in the Paragraph dialog box, which contains the options for line and paragraph spacing.

FIGURE 3.9

The Paragraph dialog box contains all the spacing options for paragraphs and lines.

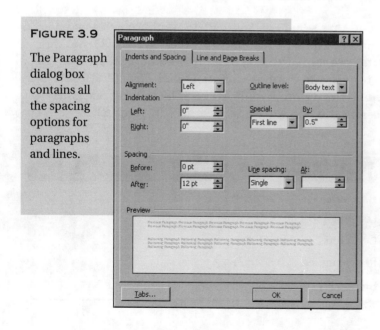

Two types of paragraph spacing are available: spacing before and spacing after the paragraph. In Word, a blank line is equal to 12 points. Therefore, if you want a blank line between paragraphs, you set the spacing before *or* after to 12 points. When you set paragraph spacing, you must consider whether to use spacing before or after the paragraph, or a combination of both.

If space within a document is limited, you can set the space before or after to 6 points, or half a line. This still provides a double-spacing effect, but will increase the amount of text that can fit on a single page. This feature offers quite a bit more flexibility when it comes to spacing than using the Enter key.

Remember that setting spacing before *and* after the paragraph will result in a cumulative effect. For example, setting 12 points of space before and after the paragraph will result in 24 points of space between paragraphs. This would be the same as having two blank lines between every pair of paragraphs.

SET PARAGRAPH SPACING

1. Type two paragraphs.
2. Select the two paragraphs.
3. Choose Paragraph from the Format menu.
4. Select the Indents And Spacing tab.
5. Change the amount of space in the After box to 12. This adds a blank line between the first and second paragraphs.
6. Click OK.

TIP

Keyboard users can press Ctrl+0 (zero) to add 12 points of space before a paragraph. Pressing Ctrl+0 again removes the 12 points of space.

You can also use "auto" spacing, which sets an automatic amount of space, before or after the paragraph,. To select auto, in the Paragraph dialog box, find the Before And After sections. Click the down arrow on the spin box. A *spin box* is a control on a dialog box that presents two arrows, one pointing up and the other pointing down. By clicking these arrows, you move ("spin") through a fixed set of values, such as dates, by increasing or decreasing the number. A Word 2000 document with auto spacing is converted to 5 points of space before and after the paragraph if the document is later opened in Word 97.

Line spacing determines the amount of vertical space between the lines of a paragraph. The most common types of line spacing are single, double, or 1.5 line spacing. Single line spacing adjusts automatically to the largest font in the line. Double spacing doubles the amount of the largest font in the line.

When you use single and double spacing, the space between lines may widen when you apply formatting such as bold, superscript, and other formatting that enlarges the text. If you don't want Word to adjust the spacing automatically, you can set spacing to an exact amount by selecting Exactly in the Line Spacing box. This is especially helpful when you're creating pleadings, briefs, and other documents in which text must line up with the line numbers along the left margin. By using exact spacing, you guarantee that the text will line up correctly. Using a 12-point font and setting line spacing to exactly 12 points or exactly 24 points produces paragraphs that look as if they are single or double spaced.

NOTE

If you use a 12-point font and exactly 12 points of line spacing, some of your text or underlining may not show up in the printed document—12 point spacing is designed to work with a 10 point font by providing 20 percent more space than the text. This extra space allows underlines and letters with "descenders" (j, g, p, and so on) to print completely. To remedy this problem, switch to At Least spacing, or set the Exact line spacing 20 percent higher than the font size.

Table 3.3 provides a list of keyboard shortcuts for applying the most common paragraph and line spacing commands.

TABLE 3.3   SPACING OPTIONS

TYPE OF SPACING	SPACING	KEYBOARD SHORTCUT
Line	Single	Ctrl+1
Line	One and one-half (1.5)	Ctrl+5
Line	Double	Ctrl+2
Paragraph	12 points of space before	Ctrl+0 (zero) (toggle)

SETTING INDENTS

Word provides four types of indents: a first-line indent, a hanging indent, a left indent, and a right indent.

A *first-line* indent affects only the first line of text in a paragraph. Setting a first-line indent in a paragraph can save time and keystrokes because you are not required to press the Tab key at the beginning of each paragraph. Editing is also simplified because you do not have to insert and remove extra tabs when you're cutting and pasting text.

A *hanging indent* is an indent that affects every line except the first line of text. Using a hanging indent makes the first line of text more prominent than the rest of the paragraph. Hanging indents are often used in bulleted and numbered lists.

Left indents set a temporary left margin; *right* indents set a temporary right margin. Left and right indents affect all lines of the paragraph. For example, you might set a left and right indent when you insert a quote into a document. You can also use negative left and right indents to move beyond the margins when you need additional room in a paragraph.

The document shown in Figure 3.10 has paragraphs formatted with the different types of indents.

FIGURE 3.10

An example of the different types of indents available in Word.

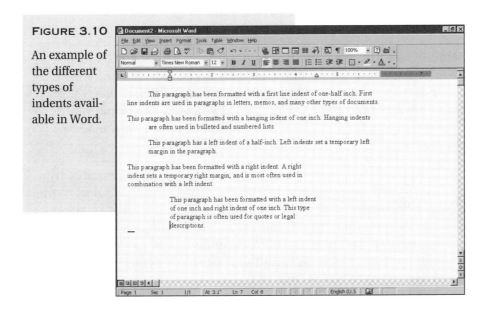

FIGURE 3.11   FIRST
              LINE
The horizontal INDENT
ruler has four
indent
markers.

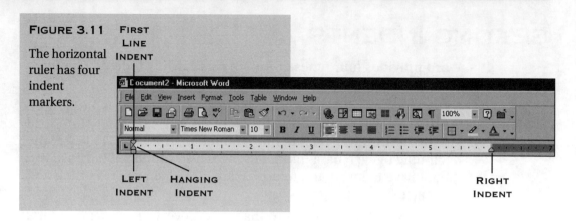

LEFT   HANGING   RIGHT
INDENT INDENT   INDENT

One way to set indents is by using the horizontal ruler. The ruler is located under the Formatting toolbar. If you don't see the ruler on the screen, click the View menu and then select Ruler. If the ruler is activated, a check mark appears next to Ruler on the View menu.

You should notice small gray triangles and a box on the ruler. Each triangle represents a different type of indent. Figure 3.11 shows a picture of a ruler and the indent markers.

CHANGE INDENTS WITH THE RULER

1. Type a paragraph of text.
2. Click the mouse anywhere within the paragraph.

NOTE

Because indents are a type of paragraph formatting, Word applies them to the entire paragraph. This means you can click the insertion point anywhere within a paragraph rather than select the entire paragraph. Keep in mind that if you wish to format more than one paragraph, you must select the paragraphs before applying the format.

3. Drag the first-line indent marker on the ruler (represented by a downward-pointing triangle on the left edge of the ruler) to the one-half-inch mark. This may also be accomplished by selecting the First Line Indent marker in the tab alignment box at the left edge of the ruler and clicking once on the ruler at the one-half inch mark. See "Setting Tabs" later in this chapter for more information. The first line of the paragraph is then indented one-half inch.

4. Type a new paragraph.

5. Click the mouse anywhere within the paragraph.

6. Drag the Hanging Indent marker on the ruler (represented by an upward-pointing triangle on the left edge of the ruler) to the one-inch mark. You may also select the Hanging Indent marker in the tab alignment box and click once on the one-inch mark.

NOTE

The Hanging Indent marker does not move independently of the Left Indent marker.

A *dual indent* is a paragraph that has both left and right indents. Law firms use dual indents for several types of text, most often with quotes or legal descriptions.

Although using the ruler is fast, it can be difficult to guarantee that the indent markers are placed exactly where you need them. The following exercise demonstrates an alternative to using the ruler to set indents.

USE THE PARAGRAPH DIALOG BOX TO SET A DUAL INDENT FOR A QUOTE

1. Type several lines of text to represent a quote in your document.

2. Click the mouse anywhere within the paragraph.

3. Choose Paragraph from the Format menu.

4. Select the Indents And Spacing tab.

5. Set the Left Indentation to one inch by clicking the up arrow on the spin box or by typing the number **1** in the box.

TIP

Make sure that the indent is set to one inch (1"), not one-tenth of an inch (0.1").

6. Set the Right Indentation to one inch by clicking the up arrow on the spin box or by typing the number **1** within the box.

7. Click OK.

Later in the book, you will learn how to create *styles* for quotes, as well as how to assign keyboard shortcuts for your styles. Setting dual indents by creating a style and assigning a keyboard shortcut is easy. For more information on styles, see Chapter 6.

Notice the change in the indent markers on the ruler after you make changes in the Paragraph dialog box. Another way to adjust the indents is by dragging them along the ruler.

SETTING TABS

Tab settings allow you to quickly indent one line of text by pressing the Tab key at the beginning of each line. Tabs are also useful for aligning text at specific locations. Word has default tabs set every one-half inch.

You might use a tab setting when you type a signature line in a letter, because signatures are usually located on the right side of the page at 3.5 inches. Rather than pressing the Tab key repeatedly to move the insertion point to the 3.5 point, consider setting a tab stop instead. The text in Figure 3.12 shows the different tab settings available in Word 2000.

FIGURE 3.12

The selection in the tab alignment box determines what type of tab is set—left, right, center, bar, or decimal.

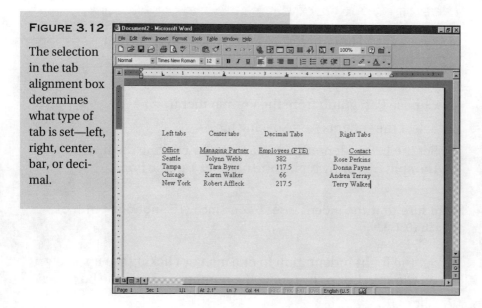

Five types of tabs are available in Word: left, right, bar, center, and decimal tabs. You can set a tab by using the Tab Alignment box on the ruler, located on the left edge of the horizontal ruler. Click the Tab Alignment box until you have the type of tab you want, and then click the location on the ruler where you want to put the tab.

SET TABS FOR A SIGNATURE BLOCK

1. On a blank line in the document, click the Tab Alignment box until you have a Left Tab selected.

2. Click the ruler at 3.5 inches to set a left tab at that location.

3. Press the Tab key and type your preferred closing (for example, **Very Truly Yours,**). Then, press Enter several times.

4. Press the Tab key again and type your name.

After you have set a tab in a paragraph, the tab settings are copied down to the next paragraph when you press Enter. In the previous exercise, this feature allowed you to set the tabs in one paragraph, type your preferred closing, press the Enter key, and automatically duplicate the tab settings for the next paragraph.

If you need to clear tabs from a paragraph, click each tab on the ruler and drag it down off of the ruler (into the document area). When you release the mouse button, the tab is deleted.

If a paragraph has many tabs, using the Tabs dialog box (see Figure 3.13) to clear all of the tabs may be easier.

FIGURE 3.13

In the Tabs dialog box, you can set new tabs, change the type of tab being used, choose a tab leader, or clear tab settings.

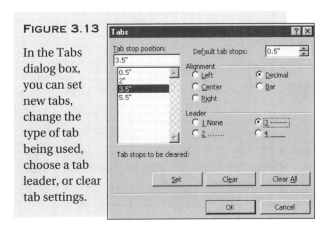

USE THE TAB DIALOG BOX TO CLEAR ALL TABS

1. Select the signature block that you typed in the previous exercise.

NOTE

Because paragraph codes are stored in the paragraph symbols, and because you are formatting more than one paragraph, you must first select each of the paragraphs that you wish to format.

2. Choose Tabs from the Format menu.

3. Click the Clear All button to clear all the tab settings in the selected paragraphs.

You can also set tab leaders from the Tabs dialog box. Tab leaders are dotted, dashed, or solid lines that fill the space of a tab. Leader characters are often used in tables of contents, for example:

   I. DEFINITIONS. 2

SET A TAB LEADER IN A TELEPHONE LIST

1. Choose Tabs from the Format menu.

2. Type **6.5** in the Tab position box.

3. Select Right in the Alignment area.

4. Select a dotted Leader (select 2) in the Leader area.

5. Click the Set button. When you have successfully set a tab, it appears in the area below the Tab Stop Position box.

6. Click OK.

7. Type **Name** and press the Tab key.

8. Type **Extension** and press Enter.

9. Type your name and press the Tab key, and then type your extension.

If you are trying to replicate the Flush Right feature of WordPerfect, you can use right tabs to achieve the same effect. In Word 2000, it is easier than ever to set a right tab. You can use the new Click and Type feature to set tabs for a signature line, as shown in Figure 3.14.

FIGURE 3.14

Using right tabs allows text to be flush left and flush right on the same line.

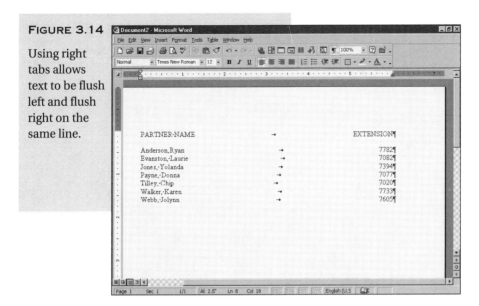

SET A RIGHT TAB FOR A SIGNATURE LINE

1. Choose <u>P</u>rint Layout from the <u>V</u>iew menu.

2. On a blank line, type **Name**.

3. Move the insertion point to the end of the line, near the right margin, until the Click-and-Type pointer changes to a right-aligned paragraph.

4. Double-click to set a right tab at the right margin.

NOTE

You must be in Print Layout or Web Layout view for the Click and Type feature to work. If it isn't working, choose <u>T</u>ools, <u>O</u>ptions, and select the Edit tab. Make sure the option Enable <u>C</u>lick And Type is selected, and then close the dialog box by clicking OK.

5. Type **Signature**.

CREATING BORDERS

Word allows you to add a border to selected text, a paragraph, or an entire page. Borders can be single black lines, colored double lines, or even artwork.

FIGURE 3.15

The Borders and Shading dialog box allows you to choose different line styles, widths, and colors for borders.

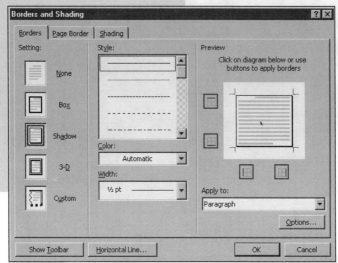

You might want to put a border such as a box around the first page of an agreement or will to give the document a more professional appearance. In pleadings, borders can be used in captions and to separate line numbers from text. You might also use a border to place a box around an exhibit or graphic to make the document easier to read. The Borders and Shading dialog box, shown in Figure 3.15, contains settings for line styles, line widths, and available colors. The Borders and Shading dialog box can be accessed from the Format menu.

PARAGRAPH BORDERS

You can apply borders as easily as you apply other paragraph formatting. You first select the text or the paragraph that you would like to enclose with a border, and then use the Borders and Shading dialog box to apply the border.

USE BORDERS IN A MEMO

1. Type **TO: John Morris** and press Enter.
2. Type **FROM: Janet L. Smith** and press Enter.
3. Type **RE: Partner Retreat** and press Enter.

4. Select the paragraph "RE: Partner Retreat" (including the paragraph mark at the end). Selecting the paragraph mark is important; if you don't, Word places a border around the selected text only.

If you place the insertion point within the paragraph and do not select any portion of the text, Word will apply a paragraph format rather than a border around specific text.

5. Choose Borders And Shading from the Format menu.

6. Select the Borders tab.

7. Select the Custom option under the Setting section and click the double underline option under Style.

8. To have only a bottom border, click the bottom border in the Preview box to insert a border.

PAGE BORDERS

A page border wraps around the entire page, creating the look of a preprinted frame. Page borders can be simple black boxes or elaborate artwork. Regardless of which type of border you use, the procedures for creating one are the same. Figure 3.16 shows a page border around a document.

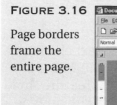

FIGURE 3.16

Page borders frame the entire page.

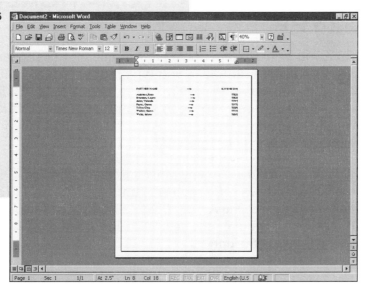

ADD A PAGE BORDER

1. Open a multiple-page document with a title page.
2. Click anywhere on the title page to place the insertion point.
3. Choose <u>B</u>orders And Shading from the F<u>o</u>rmat menu.
4. Select the <u>P</u>age Border tab.
5. Click the Bo<u>x</u>, Sh<u>a</u>dow, or 3-<u>D</u> setting.
6. Select a St<u>y</u>le for the lines of the border.
7. Select a <u>C</u>olor for the lines of the border.
8. Select a <u>W</u>idth for the lines of the border.
9. If desired, select an A<u>r</u>t frame.
10. Select This Section – First Page Only in the App<u>l</u>y To list box.

If you select Whole Document in the Apply To section, then all the document's pages will have borders. Choosing This Section – First Page Only affects only the first page of the section you are in. For more information about sections, see Chapter 5, "Page Setup and Layout."

11. Click OK.

FORMATTING TEXT AUTOMATICALLY AS YOU TYPE

When you begin to type in Word, you may notice the text changing as you type. For example, if you type **January 15th, 2000**, Word formats it as **January 15th, 2000**. This is an example of a feature that adds superscript formatting to any ordinal numbers that you type. Word also formats fractions. For example, if you type a fraction character such as 1/4, Word changes it to 1/4 .

If you do not like these or any other automatic formatting changes, you can turn them off. To do so, choose <u>A</u>utoCorrect from the <u>T</u>ools menu. Select the AutoFormat As You Type tab and turn off any option that you do not need. To turn off an option, clear the check box beside the option.

Here's a partial list of automatic formatting features in Word:

- **Borders.** If you type three or more characters and press Enter, the automatic border is generated. The characters that you can type and their results are as follows: a thin line for hyphens (-); a single bold line for underscores (_); a double line for equal signs (=); a single wavy line for tildes (~); a dotted line for asterisks (*); and a fancy triple line for number signs (#).

- **Automatic Bulleted Lists.** If you want a bulleted list, type an asterisk followed by a space or a tab, and then type some text and press Enter. Word automatically converts the typing to a bulleted list. For more information on creating and customizing bulleted and numbered lists, see Chapter 4.

- **Automatic Numbered Lists.** If you want a numbered list, type a number or letter followed by a period (**1.**, **A.**, **a.**, **I.**, or **i.**), a space, or a tab, and then some text. When you press Enter, Word automatically converts the typing to a numbered list and starts the next paragraph with the next number or letter in the series you specified.

- **Ordinals (1st) with Superscript.** If you want ordinals, such as 1st, 2nd, or 3rd, to appear in superscript, type the number and its ordinal letters (1st) and have Word automatically convert the typing to superscript (1st, 2nd, or 3rd).

- **Fractions (1/2) with Fraction Character (½).** Word automatically converts 1/2, 1/4, and 3/4 to fraction characters.

One of the unpredictable AutoFormat features is the one that automatically defines styles as you type. With this feature active, Word takes a look at the manual formatting used in the document and applies and redefines styles on the fly. This is a potentially dangerous feature, and it should always be disabled. To turn off Automatically Define Styles As You Type, choose Tools, AutoCorrect, and select the AutoFormat As You Type tab. Then uncheck Define Styles Based On Your Formatting.

USING THE FORMAT PAINTER

To copy the format of existing text, you can use the Format Painter button on the Standard toolbar. This feature copies all character formatting including bold, italic, underline, effects, character spacing and animation–the formatting available when you choose <u>F</u>ont from the F<u>o</u>rmat menu. If you want to copy the paragraph format, all you have to do is select the entire paragraph including the paragraph mark at the ned and the Format Painter copies all the paragraph formatting and styles along with the character formatting.

To use the Format Painter, select the text from which you want to copy the format. Click the Format Painter once to use the tool one time or double-click to use it multiple times. Select the text to be reformatted and release the mouse. If you double-clicked the Format Painter, press Esc to cancel.

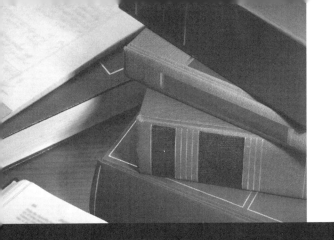

CHAPTER 4

BULLETS AND NUMBERING

IN THIS CHAPTER

- ◆ Using, customizing, and removing automatic bullets
- ◆ Using and customizing automatic numbers
- ◆ Using and customizing outline numbering
- ◆ Converting bullets to numbers
- ◆ Linking outline numbers to styles
- ◆ Answering common bullet and numbering questions

To say that numbering is important to law firms is an understatement! In fact, automatic numbering is so important that many of our clients consider it a major factor in deciding which word processing software package to buy.

The good news is that Word can handle almost every type of numbering style used in law firms. Word comes with multiple numbered styles, including many of the most common numbering styles law firms use in documents. You can customize Word's built-in numbering extensively to exactly match the style that your firm uses. If you used previous versions of Word, you may notice some improvements.

Any bad news? Word's outline numbering sometimes changes in midstream when you customize the outline numbering scheme. Understanding how Word handles bullets and numbering is the first step toward customizing Word for your firm so that bulleted and numbered lists meet your needs.

WORKING WITH BULLETS

You generally see bullets alongside a list of items, most often appearing as small black dots. Bullets can also appear as triangles, diamonds, hyphens, or squares, however. See Figure 4.1 for an example of a document with bullets.

FIGURE 4.1

Bullets appear in the space along the left side of a list.

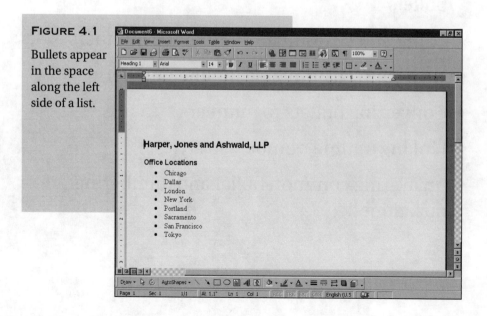

In Word 2000, you can use any character that appears in the Symbol dialog box as a bullet. Depending on the fonts you have installed, more than 200 options for bullets can exist! You can even use your firm logo, a picture, or a bit of clip art as a bullet. Although you will probably use only two or three types of bullets regularly in legal documents, it's nice to know that Word has so many options available.

APPLYING BULLETS

Word provides several ways to apply bullets. You can use a feature to make them appear automatically as you type, or you can insert them using a toolbar button or a menu command. You can apply them before you start typing a list or after you have completed it. When bullets are in place in a document, they can be easily converted to another type of bullet style or to a numbered list. You can also remove bullets from a list with a single mouse click.

APPLYING BULLETS AS YOU TYPE

Ready to get started? The following exercise shows you how to make bullets appear automatically just by typing a few characters. Word can interpret an asterisk (*), a greater-than sign (>), one or two hyphens (-), or an arrow made up of a hyphen followed by a greater-than sign or an equal sign followed by a greater-than sign (->; =>); you just have to follow one of these characters by a space (press the Spacebar) or a tab (press Tab). Type some text, and when you press Enter, Word converts your typing to a bulleted list.

APPLY BULLETS AS YOU TYPE

1. Create a new blank document.
2. Type an * (asterisk) on the first line. Press the Spacebar or the Tab key.
3. Type some text and press Enter.
4. Word converts the text to a bulleted list by inserting a bullet before the new paragraph.

If the list was not converted to bullets, check to make sure that you typed a space after the asterisk, and then typed some text before pressing Enter.

Your typing will not be converted to bullets if the AutoFormatting option is turned off. From the <u>T</u>ools menu, choose <u>A</u>utoCorrect, and then select the AutoFormat As You Type tab. In the Apply As You Type section, select A̲utomatic Bulleted Lists.

5. Press Enter once more to finish the bulleted list.

Pressing Enter twice is a quick way to turn off bullet formatting.

6. On a new blank line, type a greater-than sign (>) followed by a space or a tab, and then type some text. Press Enter. Word converts the typing to a bulleted list.

7. Continue typing items for the list.

8. To finish, press Enter twice to turn the bullet formatting off.

9. Close the document without saving it.

Pressing Ctrl+Z after Word has converted a paragraph into a bulleted list will undo the action. You must press Ctrl+Z immediately after pressing Enter for the bullets to be removed.

To permanently disable automatic bulleting as you type, from the T̲ools menu, choose A̲utoCorrect and then select the AutoFormat As You Type tab. Clear the A̲utomatic Numbered Lists option and click OK.

From the I̲nsert menu, you can apply bullets automatically by selecting S̲ymbol. Type two spaces or press Tab after the symbol, and then type some text. When you press Enter, Word converts the symbol into a bullet. Continue typing, or press Enter twice to finish the list.

New Word users often confuse bullets and paragraph position marks. Word places a paragraph position mark next to paragraphs that have Keep With Next or Keep Lines Together formatting applied to them. The paragraph position mark is a small black box that looks like a bullet and is only visible if you show nonprinting characters. Although this symbol appears on the screen, it does not print. There are two ways to determine whether a paragraph has a bullet rather than a paragraph position mark:

On the Standard toolbar, look for the Show/Hide button (¶). Click it once. If the black box goes away, it's a paragraph positioning mark.

Highlight the "bulleted" paragraph. On the Formatting toolbar, check to see whether the Bullets button is enabled. If it is, the paragraph is really bulleted.

APPLYING BULLETS THROUGH THE BULLETS AND NUMBERING MENU

Another way to apply bullets is through the Bullets And Numbering command on the Format menu. Applying bullets as you type is quick, but you are limited in the selection of bullets. Using the Bullets And Numbering command gives you a choice of seven different types of bullets, and the ability to create hundreds more.

APPLY BULLETS WITH THE BULLETS MENU

1. Create a new blank document.
2. From the Format menu, choose Bullets And Numbering.
3. Select the Bulleted tab (see Figure 4.2).
4. Select one of the seven types of bullets and click OK.
5. Type some text and press Enter.
6. Type several more lines of text to create a bulleted list.
7. Press Enter twice after the last item to turn off bullets.
8. Save and close the document so that you can use it for the next exercise.

FIGURE 4.2

The Bulleted tab contains seven default gallery positions for bullets, each of which can be customized.

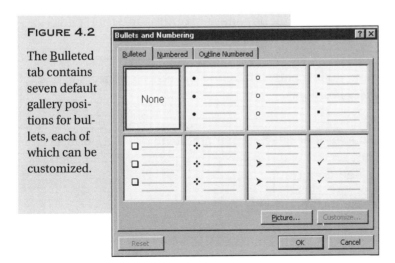

APPLYING BULLETS THROUGH THE BULLETS BUTTON

If you select any of the bulleted paragraphs, notice that the Bullets button on the Formatting toolbar is enabled.

Using the Bullets button is another way to apply bullets in the document. Click the Bullets button to add a bullet to the selected paragraph, or to remove bullets if they are already applied.

When you click the Bullets button on the Formatting toolbar, Word uses the bullet format last selected in the Bullets And Numbering dialog box. To change to a different bullet , choose Bullets And Numberingfrom the Format menu and then select a different bullet.

CHANGING BULLET STYLES

If you receive a document that has a bulleted list, converting the bullet style is easy.

CHANGE A BULLETED LIST

1. Open the document created in the previous exercise.
2. Select all of the bulleted paragraphs.

Don't try to select the actual bullet character to the left of the paragraph. Word won't allow you to select automatic bullets.

3. From the Format menu, choose Bullets And Numbering.
4. Select the Bulleted tab.
5. The bullet currently in use is selected. To use a different type of bullet, click another item, or gallery position, and then click OK.

Each picture in the Bullets and Numbering dialog box appears in a slot called a *gallery position.*

If you have any paragraphs selected that are blank (no text), notice that Word did not apply bullets to those paragraphs. Word applies bullets only to paragraphs containing text.

6. Save and close the document.

Word's default bullets come with preset formatting characteristics, such as a hanging indent and tab settings. After you apply bulleting to a paragraph, you can select the paragraph and apply any of the formatting commands discussed in Chapter 3, "Formatting Text."

If you need to modify a paragraph's tab or indent settings, apply the bullets first and then change any indent or tab settings. You must do this because each bullet comes with its own tab and indent setting. Applying a bullet to a previously indented or tabbed paragraph changes any tab and indent settings to match those associated with the bullet.

REMOVING BULLETS

You've already discovered two easy ways to turn bullets off: by clicking the Bullets button on the Formatting toolbar or by pressing Enter twice at the end of a paragraph. You can also choose Bullets and Numbering from the Format menu, select the Bulleted tab, and then double-click None.

CUSTOMIZING BULLETS

You can customize the available bullets by changing the font color or size, adjusting the text position or bullet position, or even by selecting a different bullet character altogether.

If you find yourself repeatedly modifying a certain type of bulleted list by selecting the paragraphs and applying formatting, it's best to customize the bulleted list instead. Customizing a bulleted list makes the list format available at all times and in any document. You can customize bulleted lists by using the Bullets and Numbering command on the Format menu.

CUSTOMIZE A BULLET

1. Create a new document.
2. From the Format menu, choose Bullets And Numbering.
3. Select the Bulleted tab.
4. Select a bullet to be customized.
5. Click Customize. The Customize Bulleted List dialog box appears, as shown in Figure 4.3.

FIGURE 4.3

You can make changes to the font, select a different bullet character, or adjust the position of the bullet or text in the Customize Bulleted List dialog box.

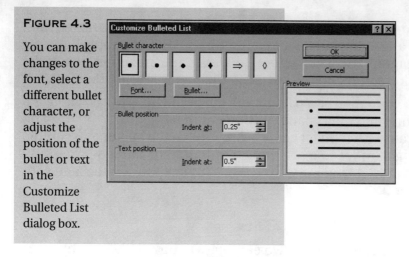

6. Click <u>F</u>ont to change any of the font attributes. For example, you may want to make the bullet larger or smaller by changing the font size.

7. Click <u>B</u>ullet to select a new character for bullets. The Symbols dialog box appears. Double-click any symbol to choose a new bullet character.

8. Adjust the bullet position by changing the measurement in the Indent <u>A</u>t box. This change affects the first-line and left indent.

9. Adjust the text position by changing the measurement in the <u>I</u>ndent At box. This change affects the hanging indent.

NOTE

If you want a bullet that is flush left with a half-inch tab, select 0" in the Bullet Position Indent <u>A</u>t box, and .5" in the Text Position Indent At box.

10. Click OK.

11. Close the document without saving it.

You need to customize a bullet only once to make it available in all Word documents. Once you have customized a bullet, you can choose it from the Bullets and <u>N</u>umbering dialog box.

TIP

You can share customizations by sending a document that includes the customized bullet or number to another person. They will need to select the Format menu, choose Bullets And Numbering, and select the appropriate tab. The trick to saving the customized bullet or number is to click Cus<u>t</u>omize and then click OK. The bullet or number will be available to all Word documents and it will appear in a gallery position.

To reset customized bullets and return to Word's default bullet styles, from the Format menu choose the Bullets And Numbering command. Select the Bulleted tab. Select one of the modified bullets and click Reset in the lower-left corner of the Bulleted tab. Word displays a message asking whether the bullet should be reset to the default setting. Click Yes to reset the bullet, or No to retain the customized bullet and then click OK.

Word 2000 allows you to use a picture or clip art for a bullet, so you can create lists with graphical bullets. If you don't already have a copy of your firm logo in graphic format, first scan the image so you have a graphic file available to use for the bullet. For smaller files, you can save images to .jpg or .gif formats. These are readable in Word and are much smaller than standard graphic formats.

NOTE

Word 2000 turns the graphics into bullets with automatic formatting. To activate this feature, choose AutoCorrect from the Tools menu. Select the AutoFormat As You Type tab and turn on Automatic Bulleted Lists. In a graphical bulleted list, you can select and resize the bullet character, directly in the document.

USE A PICTURE FOR A BULLET

1. Create a new document.
2. From the Format menu, choose Bullets and Numbering.
3. Select the Bulleted tab.
4. Select a bullet to be customized.
5. Click Picture.
6. Click once on a picture of the bullet you want. A drop-down list of options appears, as shown in Figure 4.4.
7. Click the Insert Clip button.
8. Click OK.

TIP

To use your firm's logo as a bullet, click Import Clips and navigate to where the logo is stored. Select the logo, click Import, and then click OK.

FIGURE 4.4

Use any of the clip art images as a bullet.

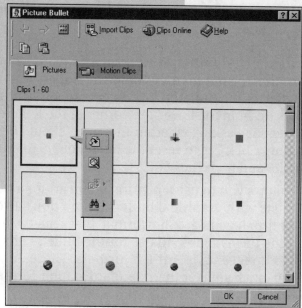

9. Type some text after the graphic, and press Enter. Notice the graphic is copied down to the next paragraph automatically.

MODIFYING A BULLET STYLE

A style is a collection of formats applied to a paragraph. Word comes with more than 90 built-in styles that can be applied to paragraphs and customized extensively. Chapter 6, "Styles," fully explores the topic of styles, so this chapter won't spend a lot of space on the topic. However, you can modify a bullet style to get exactly the result that you need for legal documents.

Why would you need to modify a bullet style rather than customize a bullet? As you may have noticed, some paragraph characteristics, such as spacing and alignment, were not available on the Customize Bulleted List dialog box. Modifying a bullet style allows you to modify paragraph characteristics such as paragraph and line spacing or paragraph alignment.

TIP

If you've ever tried to get a blank line between bulleted paragraphs, you'll love knowing how to modify bulleted styles. Some people press Enter twice to get an extra blank line between paragraphs. But remember, pressing Enter twice turns bullets off! Learning how to modify the bulleted style will save you much time and allow you to put that extra blank line between bulleted paragraphs.

Word comes with five bulleted styles, called List Bullet 1 through List Bullet 5. Your firm might customize these styles, apply bullets to other built-in styles, or create new styles that have bullets. Modifying Word's bulleted styles will guarantee consistency in documents and save time.

MODIFY THE LIST BULLET STYLE

1. To apply the List Bullet style to a paragraph, place the insertion point in the paragraph to be formatted and press Ctrl+Shift+L.

TIP

Word provides many ways for you to apply styles to paragraphs. See "Using Styles" in Chapter 6 for more information.

2. Make sure that the insertion point is still in the bulleted paragraph.
3. From the Format menu, choose Paragraph.

NOTE

Because the List Bullet style is set to automatically update, you do not need to modify the style to change it in the document. Modifying the format of one paragraph will update all paragraphs formatted with this style. If you want to permanently change the style in the template, you need to modify the style and select the option to Add To Template in the Modify Style dialog box. See Chapter 6 for information about modifying styles.

4. Select the Indents and Spacing tab.
5. Under Spacing, change the After setting to 12pt.
6. Click OK.

Figure 4.5 shows a document with a modified List Bullet style applied. Each paragraph is single spaced and there are 12 points of space after each paragraph.

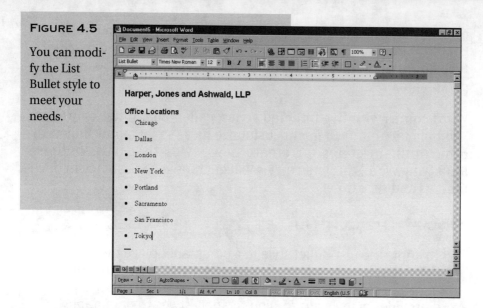

WORKING WITH NUMBERS

Law firms use numbered lists daily in contracts, pleadings, letters, and memos. Most firms have developed a specific numbering style for general use, as well as additional styles for each practice group. Word makes activating and customizing automatic numbering fairly straightforward. Word has ordinary numbered lists, such as 1, 2, 3 and A, B, C. You can customize these lists extensively to duplicate the numbering styles used in your law firm. Multilevel lists such as I, A, 1 are handled through Word's Outline Numbering feature, which is explained later in this chapter. Many firms rely on outline numbered lists to draw up contracts and pleadings. Like numbered lists, outline numbered lists can be customized.

APPLYING NUMBERS

You can apply everything that you learned in the section about working with bullets to working with numbers. As with bullets, you can have Word apply numbers automatically as you type, or you can apply them using a toolbar button or a menu command. You can turn number formatting on before you begin a list, or you can select paragraphs and apply formatting to them.

APPLYING NUMBERS AS YOU TYPE

Perhaps the easiest way to begin applying numbers is by starting to type a numbered list. Word recognizes that you are creating a list and responds accordingly by converting text that you type into numbered items.

APPLY NUMBERS AS YOU TYPE

1. Create a new blank document.

2. Type the number **1** (one) on the first line, followed by a period, and then press the Spacebar or the Tab key.

3. Type some text and then press Enter.

4. Word automatically converts the typing to a numbered list and inserts the next sequential number before the following paragraph.

TIP

If Word did not convert the list, check to make sure that you typed a period after the number, pressed the Spacebar or the Tab key, and then typed some text before you pressed Enter.

NOTE

Word does not convert typing to an automatic numbered list if the AutoFormatting option is not activated. From the Tools menu, choose AutoCorrect and then select the AutoFormat As You Type tab. Under Apply As You Type, select Automatic Numbered Lists.

5. Unlike previous versions of Word, you can press Tab to promote the list level. Press Shift+Tab to demote the list level, or click the Increase Indent or Decrease Indent buttons on the Formatting toolbar.

CAUTION

When you press Tab to indent the list level, Word uses AutoFormatting to apply outline numbering. To avoid confusion, start an outline numbered list by choosing a numbering scheme from the Outline Numbered tab in the Bullets and Numbering dialog box.

6. To discontinue numbering, press Enter twice.

7. Close the document without saving it.

You activate Automatic Numbered Lists whenever you type a number-type character followed by a period, hyphen, or parenthesis, and then a space or a tab. For example, you can type **1.**, **A-**, **I)**, **i.**, or **a.** followed by a space or a tab and then some text. When you press Enter, Word converts the paragraph into a numbered list item using the same format you've specified.

TIP

Pressing Ctrl+Z after Word has converted typing to a numbered list will undo the action. You must press Ctrl+Z immediately after pressing the Enter key for this to work.

To permanently disable automatic numbering as you type, from the Tools menu choose AutoCorrect and then select the AutoFormat As You Type tab. Clear the Automatic Numbered Lists option.

APPLYING NUMBERING USING THE MENU COMMAND

Another way to add numbers to lists is to use the Bullets And Numbering command from the Format menu. Using Automatic Numbered Lists as you type is quick and easy, but using the menu provides more numbering options. Numbers have seven default gallery positions, and you can fully customize each.

APPLY NUMBERS USING THE MENU COMMAND

1. Type a list with six items.
2. Select the list.
3. From the Format menu, choose Bullets And Numbering.
4. Select the Numbered tab (Figure 4.6 shows the Numbered dialog box).
5. Select one of the seven types of numbers. Click OK.
6. Save the document and leave it open for the next exercise.

APPLYING NUMBERING USING A TOOLBAR BUTTON

From the Formatting toolbar, the Numbering button gives you an easy way to apply numbers in a document. Looking at the Numbering button is also a good way to determine whether a paragraph has automatic numbering or a number that was typed manually.

FIGURE 4.6

The Numbered tab contains seven default gallery positions for numbers, each of which can be customized.

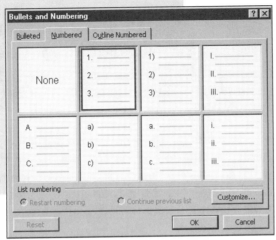

TIP Some converted documents may not contain automatic numbering. To troubleshoot numbering in converted documents, click in the paragraph to see whether the Numbering button on the Formatting toolbar is enabled.

When you click the Numbering button on the Formatting toolbar, Word uses the number format that was last chosen in the Bullets and Numbering dialog box. To choose a different numbering scheme, from the Format menu, choose Bullets And Numbering and then select a different numbered scheme.

EDITING A NUMBERED LIST

You already know how to move text by using the Cut and Paste commands or the drag-and-drop feature. You can use these techniques when you move items in a numbered list. To review these techniques, see Chapter 2, "Working with Text."

Although the techniques for moving text are the same, you should keep certain points in mind when you move items in a numbered list. Because you cannot select the number itself, selecting the paragraph mark at the end of the paragraph is important. The paragraph mark stores the code that tells Word that the paragraph is numbered. If you select the text but not the paragraph mark, Word moves the text, but not the number.

CUT AND PASTE NUMBERED ITEMS

1. Open the document that you created in the previous exercise.
2. If paragraph marks are not visible, click the Show/Hide button on the Standard toolbar. Keyboard users can press Ctrl+Shift+* to display nonprinting characters.

TIP

If you click the Show/Hide button and the paragraph marks and nonprinting characters still do not appear, the option to display them might have been cleared. You can select the option to display any nonprinting character. From the Tools menu, choose Options and then select the View tab in the Options dialog box.

3. Select the fourth paragraph, including the paragraph mark.
4. Press Ctrl+X or click the Cut button on the Standard toolbar.
5. Click the insertion point in the space after the tab character in the first paragraph.
6. Press Ctrl+V or click the Paste button on the Standard toolbar.
7. The fourth paragraph is now the first paragraph. Word automatically renumbers the list.
8. Close the document without saving it.

INTERRUPTING A NUMBERED LIST

Many times, you will want to interrupt numbering in the middle of a list. One way to accomplish this is by clicking the Numbering button on the Formatting toolbar to remove numbering in a specific paragraph. Another technique is to <u>enter a manual line break by</u> <u>pressing Shift+Enter</u>. A manual line break moves the insertion point to the next line without beginning a new paragraph. A manual line break is a nonprinting character that appears on the screen as an arrow that points down first and then left if nonprinting characters are displayed. Figure 4.7 shows a document with a list interrupted by a manual line break.

INTERRUPT A LIST

1. On the Formatting toolbar, click the Numbering button to activate numbering.

FIGURE 4.7

A list can be
interrupted
with a line
break
(Shift+Enter)
to include
nonnumbered
information
between para-
graphs that are
numbered.

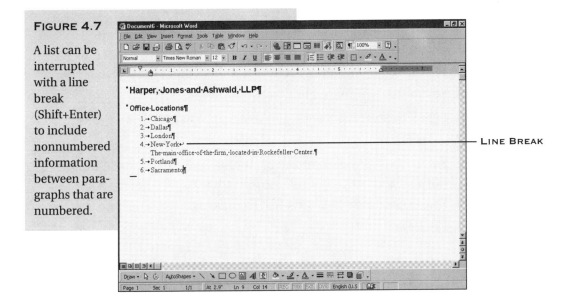

FIGURE 4.7

A list can be
interrupted
with a line
break
(Shift+Enter)
to include
nonnumbered
information
between para-
graphs that are
numbered.

2. Type a three-item list. Do not press Enter when you are finished typing the third item.

3. Press Shift+Enter to insert a manual line break. Mouse users
   can choose <u>B</u>reak from the <u>I</u>nsert menu, and then select a Text
   <u>W</u>rapping Break.

4. Type some text and press Enter.

5. Continue typing the list and then press Enter twice to complete
   the list.

6. Close the document without saving it.

RESTARTING OR CONTINUING NUMBERS

Word has a way of determining when a numbered list should be
restarted or when it should be continued from a previous list.
Sometimes you will not agree with Word's logic, but that's OK. You
can easily tell Word whether to restart the numbering or to continue
a numbered list from a previous list.

RESTART OR CONTINUE A NUMBERED LIST

1. On the Formatting toolbar, turn on numbering by clicking the
   Numbering button.

2. Create a list with five numbered paragraphs.

3. Select the third item in the list.

4. From the Format menu, choose Bullets and Numbering.

5. Select the Numbered tab.

6. Select Restart Numbering to restart the list.

7. Click OK.

8. Select the third item in the list again, and then choose Bullets and Numbering from the Format menu.

9. Select Continue Previous List to make the list continue.

10. Click OK.

CHANGING OR REMOVING NUMBER STYLES

To switch from one number style to another, or to remove numbers from a list, you can follow the same procedures discussed earlier in this chapter, in the "Changing Bullet Styles" and "Removing Bullets" sections. These actions are as easy as selecting the list and then choosing a different number style from the Numbered tab, or clicking the Numbering button on the Formatting toolbar to remove the numbering.

CUSTOMIZING A NUMBERED LIST

Word has seven default numbered lists, such as 1, 2, 3 and A, B, C. You can customize many aspects of the default numbers. Word allows you to change the font, the number positions, or the position of the text that follows the numbers. You can change the style of the number so that your list uses First, Second, Third or One, Two, Three. You can even type customized text before or after the number.

NOTE

For interrogatories, requests for production, and requests for admissions, we recommend using field codes instead of automatic numbering. See "Answering Common Bullets and Numbering Questions" at the end of this chapter.

CUSTOMIZE A NUMBERED LIST

1. From the Format menu, choose Bullets And Numbering.

2. Select the Numbered tab.

3. Select one of the seven default number styles and then click Customize. The Customize Numbered List dialog box appears (see Figure 4.8).

4. Type any text before or after the number in the Number Format box. You can also change or delete the character (period or parenthesis) that follows the number, or add a new character in front of the number.

If you accidentally delete the number that appears in the Number Format box, do not type a number in the box. Instead, select an option in the Number Style box. The number that appears in the Number Format box is a field. The field increments with each new line. If you manually type a number in this box, you get that number on each new line.

5. Click Font to choose bold, underline, or any other font formatting. Changing the font of the number results in numbers that Word formats differently from the text.

6. Select an option in the Number Style box.

7. Change the number in the Start At box if you want the list to start at a different number.

FIGURE 4.8

Word provides numerous formatting options for numbered lists.

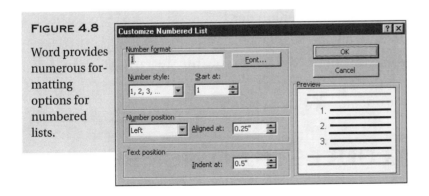

FIGURE 4.9

Numbers can be left-aligned, centered, or right-aligned.

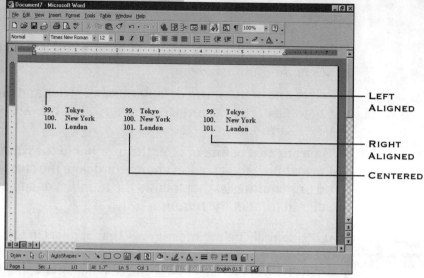

You do not need to customize a numbered list to get two lists in separate parts of the document to have continuous numbering. See the earlier section called "Restarting or Continuing Numbers."

8. Change the position of the number by choosing Left, Center, or Right in the Number Position box and adjusting the Aligned At measurement. This action adjusts the first-line and left indent. Figure 4.9 shows the differences among left-aligned, centered, and right-aligned numbers.

9. Change the position of the text by adjusting the Indent At measurement in the Text Position box.

10. Click OK until all open dialog boxes are closed.

11. Start typing the numbered list. Press Enter twice to finish the list.

12. Close the document without saving it.

CONVERTING BULLETS TO NUMBERS

What if a list has been formatted with bullets and you decide to use numbering instead? Just select the list and then choose Bullets And Numbering from the Format menu. If the list is bulleted, the

Bulleted tab is displayed. Change to a numbered list by selecting the Numbered tab and double-clicking any of the gallery positions.

NOTE You can use a combination of bullets and numbers within the same list. Just remember to select the paragraphs first, and then apply bullets or numbers.

USING OUTLINE NUMBERING

Understanding outline numbering and how it interacts with styles is crucial to your success in using Word with your legal documents. Styles are covered in detail in Chapter 6.

Basic outline numbering can be handled much the same way as bullets and numbering. Seven default outline numbered lists come with Word. Three of the lists format the paragraphs with outline numbers. The remaining four format the paragraphs with outline numbers and apply heading styles to the paragraphs. To select outline numbering without changing the formatting of the paragraph, make sure that you select an outline numbered list that is *not* linked to the Heading Styles feature. Figure 4.10 shows the available outline numbering styles.

Each Outline Numbered paragraph is assigned a level. Word provides nine levels for each outline numbering scheme. Figure 4.11 shows a document displaying outline numbering, with each level identified.

FIGURE 4.10

Word has seven default outline numbering styles.

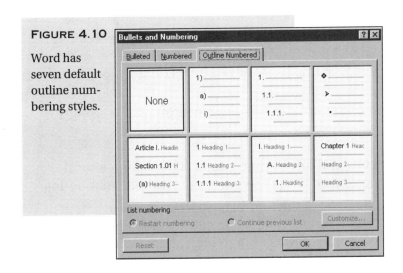

FIGURE 4.11

Word's default outline numbering scheme has nine levels.

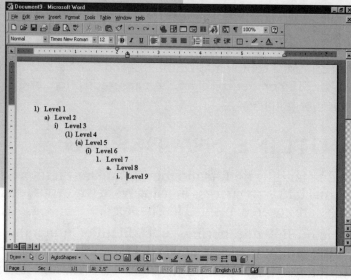

APPLYING OUTLINE NUMBERING

You apply outline numbering from the F̲ormat menu. Select Bullets And N̲umbering and then select the O̲utline Numbered tab from the Bullets and N̲umbering dialog box to view the various outline numbering options.

CREATE AN OUTLINE NUMBERED LIST

1. From the F̲ormat menu, choose Bullets And N̲umbering.
2. Select the O̲utline Numbered tab.
3. Select one of the numbering options that does not contain the text "Heading 1." Selecting one of these options starts an outline numbered list that is *not* linked to heading styles.

Outline numbers that are not linked to heading styles usually appear on the top row of the Outline Numbered tab.

4. Type some text and press Enter. The next paragraph is automatically numbered with the same level of outline numbering.
5. To change the level of the number, click the Increase Indent or Decrease Indent button on the Formatting toolbar. Keyboard users can press Tab or Shift+Tab to increase or decrease the indent.

TIP

If Tabs And Backspace Set Left Indent is turned off, Tab and Shift+Tab will not change the indent of the paragraph. From the Tools menu, choose Options and select the Edit tab; then, select Tabs And Backspace Set Left Indent to control this setting.

Some users prefer to keep this feature turned off. If you've taken this approach, you can press the Alt+Shift+Right Arrow or Alt+Shift+Left Arrow to change the level of the outline number.

6. Continue typing the list until you have at least three numbered paragraphs. Press Enter twice to finish the list.

7. Save the document and leave it open for the next exercise.

EDITING AN OUTLINE NUMBERED LIST

To modify an outline numbered list, you can use the same techniques that you use to modify a bulleted or numbered list. When Outline Numbering is activated, Word automatically renumbers the document for you when you move and delete paragraphs. You can place nonnumbered paragraphs, tables, or pictures between the numbered paragraphs, and you can choose to restart the numbering or continue a list anywhere in the document.

CUSTOMIZING AN OUTLINE NUMBERED LIST

Word's default Outline Numbered List feature has predefined tab settings and indents. If you need to temporarily change an outline numbered list, you can easily select the paragraph and apply formatting. If, however, you continually make the same changes to an outline numbered list, customizing the list is a far better solution.

Because Word provides so many options for customizing an outline numbered list, we highly recommend that you have several documents on hand with the number scheme that you are trying to replicate. You can customize up to nine levels of the outline numbering scheme, and to avoid mistakes, you should follow the same steps when customizing each level.

CUSTOMIZE AN OUTLINE NUMBERED LIST

1. Open the document from the preceding exercise.

2. From the Format menu, choose Bullets And Numbering.

3. Select the Outline Numbered tab.

4. Select an outline numbering scheme that is not linked to heading styles.

5. Click Customize. The Customize Outline Numbered List dialog box, as shown in Figure 4.12, appears.

6. Click More to open the expanded dialog box.

NOTE

If the dialog box is already expanded, the button will read Less rather than More.

7. Select 1 in the Level box to customize the Level 1 numbering scheme.

8. Add, edit, or delete text in the Number Format box.

9. Select a number style in the Number Style box.

10. Select a starting number for the Level in the Start At box.

11. To include the number of the previous level as part of the current level, select the level in the Previous Level Number box. For example, you can use this for numbers such as Section 1.1.

FIGURE 4.12

Use Customize Outline Numbered List to change number style or formatting, indents, tabs, and numbering styles.

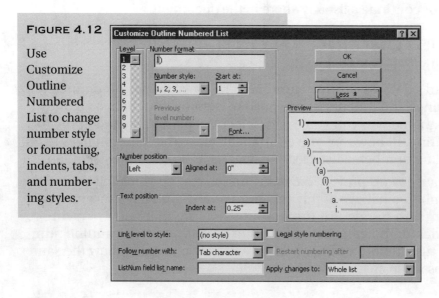

The Previous Level Number box is unavailable while the Level box is set to Level 1. When the Level box option is set to anything other than 1, you can make changes in the Previous Level Number box.

12. Click Font to make changes to the font formatting of the number.

13. Change the number position by selecting Left, Center, or Right in the Number Position box. Adjust the Aligned At measurement to change the first-line and the left indent.

14. Change Text Position by changing the measurement in the Indent At box. This change affects the hanging indent.

15. Select (no style) in the Link Level To Style box.

16. Select a Tab character, a space, or nothing in the Follow Number With box. This selection determines the character that will follow the number.

If you select a Tab character Word places a .25" tab after the number. If you need a .5" tab, you'll need to further customize the outline numbering scheme through the Tab dialog box.

17. Leave the ListNum Field List Name blank. You will learn more about the ListNum field later in the chapter.

18. Select Legal Style Numbering to convert numerals to their Arabic values. For example, Section II will be converted to Section 2.

19. Select Restart Numbering After to restart the level whenever it follows a higher list level. This option is selected by default on Levels 2 through 9. This option is unavailable if Level 1 is selected in the Level box.

20. Select Whole List, This Point Forward, Selected Text, or Current Paragraph in the Apply To box. The default, Whole List, applies the customizations of the level to the entire list throughout the document.

21. Select a new level in the Level box and repeat Step 8 through Step 22.

22. Click OK to return to the document.

Whew! As you can see, Word provides numerous options for formatting an outline numbered list. You can create whatever numbering scheme your firm uses by customizing a numbered list.

USING OUTLINE NUMBERS LINKED TO STYLES

The ability to link outline numbers to styles is an even more powerful feature of outline numbered lists. Using styles in documents guarantees consistency and reduces the need for additional training. Assigning keyboard shortcuts to styles that are linked to outline numbering gives users an incredibly easy and fast way to generate complex outline numbered lists.

Another reason to use outline numbers linked to styles is for the ease of generating a table of contents. Instead of manually marking text to be included in a table of contents, you can tell Word to use the outline numbered styles in the document for the table.

The most powerful way to customize outline numbers is by linking them to the styles available in templates. You can link outline numbers to Word's built-in styles, such as Heading 1, 2, and 3, or to any user-defined styles that you have created.

APPLY AN OUTLINE NUMBERED STYLE USING BUILT-IN HEADINGS

1. Open a document that contains paragraphs formatted with Word's built-in heading styles (Heading 1, Heading 2, and so on).

TIP

If you do not have a document formatted with heading styles, apply these styles quickly with keyboard shortcuts. Click anywhere in the paragraph to be formatted and press Alt+Ctrl+1 for Heading 1, Alt+Ctrl+2 for Heading 2, and Alt+Ctrl+3 for Heading 3.

If you have customized Word's built-in heading styles to match your firm's formatting, make sure that you open a document or template that contains the customized styles.

2. From the Format menu, choose Bullets And Numbering.

3. Select the Outline Numbered tab.

4. Select an Outline Numbering scheme that includes the text "Heading 1."

5. Click OK.

Notice that every paragraph in the document formatted with a heading style is now automatically numbered with the appropriate outline level. This is an extremely powerful tool that allows you to quickly number a document.

When you press Enter after an outline numbered paragraph formatted with a style, you won't get a new numbered paragraph. Instead, you begin a paragraph formatted with Normal style. If you don't like this, don't worry—you can specify what follows an outline numbered paragraph, whether it's another numbered paragraph or a nonnumbered paragraph.

Problems with numbering occur when an outline numbered style linked to headings is applied in a document formatted with heading styles. When a paragraph is selected and outline numbering is applied, *all* of the paragraphs in the document formatted with heading styles will be numbered, even if they were not part of the selected text. This is *not* a bug. Using outline numbered styles linked to headings adds an great amount of flexibility and power to Word. Only when a user is unaware of the connection between numbers and headings do problems arise.

Working with outline numbers linked to styles makes numbering much easier. When you have turned outline numbering on, you can change the outline level of a paragraph simply by switching the style. Figure 4.13 shows the Style list box.

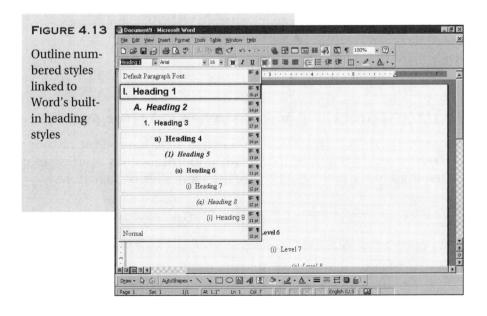

FIGURE 4.13

Outline numbered styles linked to Word's built-in heading styles

In some cases, you may want to link outline numbering to custom styles in the document rather than use Word's built-in heading styles. You can link any style to an outline numbering scheme.

LINK OUTLINE NUMBERS TO CUSTOM HEADINGS

1. Open a document formatted with custom styles.

If you want to read more about creating custom styles, skip ahead to Chapter 6.

2. From the Format menu, choose Bullets And Numbering.
3. Select the Outline Numbered tab.
4. Select any outline numbering scheme.
5. Click Customize.
6. Click More.
7. Select the appropriate level for the style in the Level box. For example, if you want to automatically number a top-level heading style that you have named "Outline level 1," select 1 in the Level box.
8. Select the style to link to the level in the Link Level To Style box. The style should correspond to the level that you selected in Step 7 of this exercise.
9. Repeat Steps 7 and 8 for each custom style that should be linked to an outline level.
10. Click OK.

NUMBERING ITEMS IN A PARAGRAPH

As you've probably noticed, numbering is a paragraph formatting characteristic. If you need to apply numbering within a paragraph rather than to the entire paragraph, use Word's ListNum feature.

INSERT LISTNUM FIELDS IN A PARAGRAPH

1. Create a new blank document.
2. Type **Please include the following information with your application** and press the Spacebar.

3. Press Alt+Ctrl+L to insert the ListNum field.

You can also insert fields by choosing Field from the Insert menu. For more information about fields, see Chapter 11, "Creating Legal Forms."

4. To change the level of the ListNum field, select the number and press the Tab key. Continue to press Tab or Shift+Tab to increase or decrease the level of the field.

If Tabs And Backspace Set Left Indent is turned off, press Alt+Shift+Right Arrow or Alt+Shift+Left Arrow to change the level of the ListNum field.

5. Press the Spacebar after the number and type **driver's license**. Press the Spacebar.

6. Press Alt+Ctrl+L to insert another ListNum field.

7. Press the Spacebar after the number, type **birth certificate**, and press the Spacebar.

8. Press Alt+Ctrl+L to insert another ListNum field.

9. Press the Spacebar after the number and type **law degree**.

You may wonder whether typing 1, 2, and 3 would be easier than using the ListNum field. Although doing so may be easier initially, the value of using the ListNum field becomes apparent when you cut and paste. When a paragraph contains multiple numbered items that you move or delete, Word automatically updates the ListNum fields. Using ListNum fields assures you of accurate numbering within a paragraph throughout the document.

Another advantage of ListNum fields is the ability to easily cross-reference them. ListNum fields show up on the list of numbered items available for cross-referencing.

ANSWERING COMMON BULLETS AND NUMBERING QUESTIONS

There are a few questions that we hear repeatedly from our clients concerning bullets and numbering. Some are easy to answer; others have prompted us to develop a solution through Word 2000's macro language, Visual Basic for Applications (VBA). Here are some frequently asked numbering questions.

Why do I keep losing my tabs settings when I customize Word's outline numbered styles?

This is one of the biggest complaints we hear from users. Unfortunately, Word 2000 hasn't solved the problem that plagued our clients in Word 97. The fact is, it's really hard to get rid of Word's default quarter-inch tabs. Even if you've cleared all the tab settings in an outline numbered scheme, going back in to customize one more thing can cause all the default tabs to reappear.

We were frustrated, too. And that's why we created our add-in, The Numbering Assistant©. The Numbering Assistant provides your firm with numerous intuitive, easy-to-apply outline numbered schemes. Best of all, the Numbering Assistant uses native Word functionality, which means you can easily share documents with your clients. Figure 4.14 shows the Numbering Assistant.

Each outline numbered scheme in the Assistant is completely customized for your firm. We include a description of each scheme and a preview picture of a document formatted with the scheme. All you have to do is select the numbering scheme that you want and then use the keyboard shortcuts or the style list to apply automatic numbering. E-mail Payne Consulting Group at legaldev@payneconsulting.com for more information or visit our Web page at `http://www.payneconsulting.com/`.

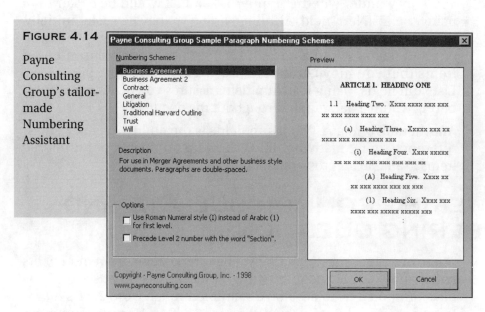

FIGURE 4.14

Payne Consulting Group's tailor-made Numbering Assistant

How do I format text on the left of the line and bullets or numbers on the right, like in a pleading index?

A two-column table solves this problem. Insert a table into the document by choosing Insert from the Table menu, and then selecting Table. Select two columns and one row and then click OK. Type the text needed in the first column and press the Tab key to move to the next column. Click either the Bullets or Numbering button on the Formatting toolbar to activate one or the other. Type text and press Enter when you need a new bulleted or numbered paragraph. Press the Tab key in the last cell of the table to create a new row.

When you finish typing, remove the border from the table by choosing Borders And Shading from the Format menu. Select the Borders tab and select None under Setting. Keyboard users can press Ctrl+Alt+U to remove table borders. For more information about tables, see Chapter 7, "Using Tables in Legal Documents."

How do I type plain text on the same line after the heading, but have only the heading appear in the table of contents?

As you will learn in Chapter 12, "Working with Long Documents," Word uses styles to create tables of contents. A common practice in law firms is to generate outline numbered styles that have bold or underlined heading text immediately followed by paragraph text on the same line. Because the paragraph is formatted with a style, Word tries to place the entire paragraph in the table of contents.

One solution is to format the heading with the style and follow it with a hidden paragraph mark. You can create a hidden paragraph mark by selecting the paragraph mark at the end of the numbered paragraph, and then pressing Ctrl+Shift+H. You should format the text in the next paragraph with a style that is not included in the table of contents. A hidden paragraph mark keeps the text together on one line when it is printed, even though it is actually two separate paragraphs. To see the hidden paragraph marks on the screen, click the Show/Hide button, or press Ctrl+Shift+*. The Table Of Contents command picks up only those paragraphs with heading styles and places them into the table of contents.

Payne Consulting Group has a macro called the *Table of Contents Builder* that lets you easily mark text for a Table of Contents. Please note, however, that the macro works in Word 2000 or Word 97 Service Release 1 (SR-1) only. It does not work in Service Release 2 of Word 97.

How do I create an outline numbered list that uses both Roman and Arabic numerals? Our firm uses "Article I." as the first level, and "Section 1.1." as the second level. Right now it appears as "Section I.1."

You can customize the Outline Numbered list and turn on Legal Style Numbering in Level 2 to fix this problem. Open a document formatted with the Outline Numbered List feature. From the Format menu, choose Bullets And Numbering. Select the Outline Numbered tab and then select the scheme that you want to customize. Click Customize to display the Customize Outline Numbered List dialog box. Select 2 in the Level box and then select Legal Style Numbering. You may have to click More if you do not see the option for Legal Style Numbering. Click OK.

How do I keep several separate numbered lists in a document, such as interrogatories, requests for production, and requests for admission?

You can do this by using Sequence fields saved as AutoText entries. Sequence fields keep track of several numbered lists within a document. The following exercise shows you how to create the entries.

INSERT SEQUENCE FIELDS

1. Type **INTERROGATORY** and press the Spacebar.
2. Press Ctrl+F9 to insert a field.
3. Type **SEQ**, a space, and then **Rog**. When you are finished, the field should look like this { SEQ Rog }.
4. Press F9 to update the field. The number 1 appears.
5. Select the text and the number.
6. Press Alt+F3 to create the AutoText entry. Type **Rog** for the AutoText entry name.
7. To insert the entry, type **Rog** and press F3.
8. To create entries for Requests for Production and Admission, follow the same steps. In Step 3, use different identifiers after the sequence fields; for example, **SEQ rfp** and **SEQ rfa**. In Step 6, use different AutoText entry names, such as **rfp** and **rfa**.

Each time you insert the AutoText entry, the number will increase by one. If you cut and paste SEQ fields, they will not automatically update. To renumber the document, select the numbers and then press F9 to update the fields. To update all fields within a document, press Ctrl+A to select the entire document, and then press F9 to update fields.

How do I underline heading text but not the number. For example:
2.2   Definitions?

Since numbering is a paragraph format, by default, formatting applied to the text is also applied to the paragraph number.

REMOVE UNDERLINE FORMAT FROM NUMBER

1. Select the paragraph with outline numbering applied.
2. Click the Underline toolbar button. Underline formatting will be applied to both the text and number.
3. From the Format menu, choose Bullets And Numbering.
4. Select the Outline Numbered tab.
5. Click Customize.
6. Select the level that is to be modified. In most cases, it will be Level 2, 3, or higher.
7. Click Font.
8. Select None from the Underline drop-down list. Do not choose Blank as this option follows the formatting of the text. None specifies that the number will not be underlined, regardless of text formatting.
9. Click OK.

Can I center Article I and have the actual heading appear centered beneath it?

Many law firms center their heading information and then want the text associated with this heading to appear centered on the next line. If you attempt to center the information, the text often appears off-center. To correct this problem, try the following exercise.

CENTER TEXT BENEATH A NUMBER

1. Create a new blank document.
2. From the Format menu, choose Bullets And Numbering.
3. Select the Outline Numbered tab and then double-click on gallery position that includes the word Article.

4. Type the **Agreement**.

5. From the Format menu, choose Bullets And Numbering, and select the Outline Numbered tab.

6. Click Customize.

7. Set the Numbered Position to be Left. Do not choose Center as this centers only the number and not the text.

8. The Number Position Aligned At position should be 0. Set the Indent At Text Position to 0 as well.

9. Click More to expand the dialog box if necessary.

10. Select None in the Follow Number With drop-down list and click OK.

11. Click the Center button on the Formatting toolbar.

12. Click in front of the word "Agreement" and press Shift +Enter.

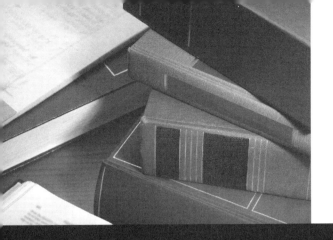

CHAPTER 5

PAGE SETUP AND LAYOUT

IN THIS CHAPTER

- ◆ Setting margins
- ◆ Laying out a page
- ◆ Inserting page breaks
- ◆ Inserting section breaks
- ◆ Creating headers and footers
- ◆ Print and preview a document

To make legal documents look exactly the way you want them, you need to know how to set up and lay out a document. Word makes layout easy by providing you with the means to do everything visually. Word has no tricky keyboard combinations to remember, and you can use everything you've read up to this point to lay out your legal documents quickly.

Although most concepts in Word are fairly simple, a few, such as section breaks, may take some time to understand. You'll find other concepts to be the same in Word as they were in your old word processing software.

This chapter shows you how to set page margins, change the way the document is laid out, insert page breaks, create and modify headers and footers, and insert section breaks. The best way to learn these features is to follow the exercises.

SETTING UP A PAGE

Creating a document is as easy as starting Word and typing text. If you choose, you can work with Word's default settings. However, many legal documents use a different standard layout. It's important to know how to change the settings so that you can change the way the text looks on the page.

Setting up legal documents entails working with four main components: margins, paper size, paper source, and layout. You will find each component in the Page Setup dialog box that appears when you choose Page Setup from the File menu. This section describes each of these components.

WORD 2000 DEFAULT SETTINGS

If you haven't changed the settings in your Normal template, you'll find the defaults (in the U.S. version of Word 2000) to include top and bottom margins set to 1 inch, left and right margins at 1.25 inches, header and footer margins at .5 inches, gutter position left, paper size is 8.5x11 inches, portrait page orientation, section starts on a new page, and vertical alignment set to top.

Page Setup options apply to the entire document in Word unless you have divided the document into sections. See "Using Section Breaks" in the next section for more information.

NOTE

WORKING WITH MARGINS

Knowing how to set margins is necessary for submitting all types of legal documents to the courts. Margins are the boundaries to the left, right, top, and bottom of the document. They determine the space between the text in the document and the edge of the page.

It's important not to confuse margins with paragraph indenting. Margins affect the overall appearance of the document, whereas indents apply to specific paragraphs.

When you switch to Print Layout view, you see darker areas on the left and right side of the horizontal ruler that indicate the margin area. If you don't see the horizontal ruler, choose Ruler from the View menu. Top and bottom margin indicators on the vertical ruler appear as well.

TIP

If the vertical ruler does not appear, make sure that you are in Print Layout view, and choose Options from the Tools menu. Select the View tab and then click the Vertical Ruler (Print View Only).

LOCATE THE PAGE MARGINS

1. Create a new Word document.

2. If you are not already in Print Layout view, switch to it by choosing Print Layout from the View menu. Keyboard users can press Alt+Ctrl+P.

NOTE

If you are new to Word 2000 and are not certain whether you are in Print Layout view, click the View menu. The current view appears selected (the icon beside the view is depressed) on the menu. To change views, from the View menu, click the icon next to the view you want to display. To learn more about the different views, see Chapter 2, "Working with Text."

3. Hold the mouse over the right margin boundary on the horizontal ruler where the margin is located. The mouse pointer changes to a double-sided arrow when you hold it over the margin, and a ScreenTip appears that says "Right Margin" (see Figure 5.1).

FIGURE 5.1

Holding the
mouse over
the margin
boundary
makes a
ScreenTip
appear.

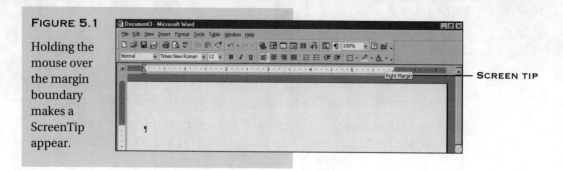

SCREEN TIP

SETTING MARGINS

Word gives you two ways to set margins. You can click and drag
margins in the ruler or open the Page Setup dialog box and type
the desired margins. There are specific reasons for using each
method; the method you choose depends on the complexity of
your document.

SETTING MARGINS WITH THE MOUSE

When you're working on letters and other short documents where
the precise size of the margin is not important, you can control the
size of a margin the easy way, by dragging the mouse to move the
margin. This allows you to change the margin of a document and
immediately see the result.

SET MARGINS WITH THE MOUSE

1. Place the mouse over the right margin boundary on the ruler
   until the double-sided arrow and ScreenTip appear.

It's important that you see a pointer and that the ScreenTip reads,
"Right Margin" and not "Right Indent." Otherwise, you are changing
the indent for the selected paragraph rather than the margin for
the entire document.

2. Drag the mouse to the left, moving the margin to the "5" for the
   five-inch mark on the ruler. The margin for the right side of the
   document is increased to approximately two inches.

3. Click the Undo button on the Standard toolbar to undo the
   margin change. Keyboard users can press Ctrl+Z to undo an
   action.

To see the margin's measurement as you drag with the mouse, hold down the Alt key as you drag. If you don't want to use the keyboard, you can hold down the primary and alternate mouse buttons simultaneously as you drag the margin.

SETTING MARGINS IN THE PAGE SETUP DIALOG BOX

Dragging margins on the ruler is a quick way to change margins for a document. Unfortunately, you may find that you do not have a lot of control with this technique because it can be difficult to determine the exact measurement on the ruler. When you must have a specific margin, the Page Setup dialog box lets you plug in the precise numbers you need.

For example, if you know that you want a 1.17-inch margin, you might find typing that number into a dialog box easier than trying to drag the margin. You can also control other margin settings, such as mirror margins, in the Page Setup dialog box.

Sometimes, though, you will want to change the margins for only one part of a document rather than for the entire text. For example, you may want to change the margins just for an exhibit appearing at the end of a document. Word 2000 refers to *parts* of documents as *sections*.

To change margins for sections, the Page Setup dialog box contains an option that allows you to specify changes for the particular sections of a document. For more information on dividing your document into sections, see "Inserting Section Breaks" later in this chapter.

USE THE PAGE SETUP DIALOG BOX TO SET MARGINS

1. Choose Page Setup from the File menu.

A shortcut for displaying the Page Setup dialog box is to double-click anywhere along either the horizontal or the vertical ruler. Make certain to double-click the dark gray margin area only, however. If you double-click in the white area of the ruler or in some of the light gray areas, you may accidentally set a tab. If you do accidentally set a tab, you can remove it by dragging it off the ruler and into the text area of the document.

2. Select the Margins tab. Figure 5.2 shows the Page Setup dialog box with the Margins tab selected.

FIGURE 5.2

Margin
options in
Page Setup
dialog box. Set
exact margins
by typing
numbers in
each box.

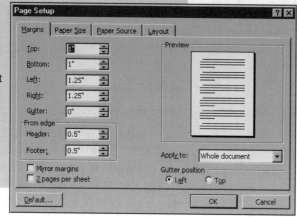

3. Change settings for the Top, Bottom, Left, or Right margins. (All the options available in this dialog box are explained immediately following this exercise.)

NOTE

By default, Word 2000 fixes the top and bottom margins at 1 inch, and the left and right margins at 1.25 inches. Enter the number for exactly how far you want the text from the edge of the page, or click one of the spin box buttons (the up and down arrows beside the numbers) to change the distance.

TIP

Many law firms use one-inch margins at the top, bottom, left, and right. To change Word's default margins, choose Page Setup from the File menu. Enter the number **1** in the Top, Bottom, Left, and Right boxes. Click the Default button in the lower-left corner of the dialog box. Word displays a message informing you that the default page margins will be changed, affecting all new documents based on the Normal template. Click Yes to continue or No to cancel.

4. Click the OK button to apply the new margin settings to the document or click Cancel to cancel the changes.

TIP

You can set negative top and bottom margins in the document to create a "fixed" margin. This prevents the header and footer area from pushing text in the document up or down. For example, the court requires certain documents to begin one inch from the top of the page. To guarantee that the one inch is always there, type -1" in the Top Margin and Bottom Margin settings. Now, no matter how much text is in the Header or Footer, the text in the document will start one inch from the top of the page and end one inch from the bottom of the page. Be careful when using this setting; if the text in the header or footer is more than one inch long, it can overlap the document text.

WORKING WITH OPTIONS ON THE MARGINS TAB

Several options are available on the Margins tab in the Page Setup dialog box. These options give you total control over the setup and layout of your documents. For example, a document that will be bound and duplexed requires very different settings than the ones you need for a pleading or letter. The sections that follow describe the options available on the Margins tab.

GUTTER CONTROL

Below the Right Margin box is the Gutter box. This option is a great feature to use if your document will be printed on both sides (duplexed) and bound. By defining a gutter distance, you define how much extra space the document needs along the bound edge of each page. Creating a gutter ensures that the binding will not overlap the text along the inside margin. If you are duplexing a bound document, then you need to *mirror* the margins as well. Mirroring margins is explained next.

In Word 2000, you also have the option to choose whether the gutter position is set at the top or left of each page, which allows for different printing needs.

MIRROR MARGINS

When you choose the Mirror Margins option, you create equal space for the inside and outside margins of each page, just as you see in the layout of this book. This is such an important feature that it's worth taking a moment to make sure you understand its use.

This setting is used for documents that will be duplexed and bound, so that the inside and outside margins appear correctly in the final, bound document. For example, imagine creating a document that has a left margin of two inches, a right margin of one inch, and a gutter of one-half inch (.5"). If you print the document without using mirror margins, the left side of each page will have a two-and-a-half-inch (2.5") margin (the left margin *plus* the gutter setting) and the right side of each page will have a one-inch margin. Now, imagine duplexing and binding the same document. The layout of the document will look very strange because the even-numbered pages will have a smaller margin along the edge of the book when it is bound. This can be a real problem, and can even cause the text on the even-numbered pages to be covered up by the binding.

You can solve this problem by setting the Mirror Margins option in the Page Setup dialog box. When you set this option, Word changes the left and right margins to be *inside* and *outside* margins, respectively. The inside margins are the ones that appear along the bound edge of the document, and the outside margins appear along the outside edge of the pages (the nonbound side).

NOTE If you select the Mirror Margins option, the Left and Right options in the Page Setup dialog box change to read Inside and Outside, respectively.

TWO (2) PAGES PER SHEET

Have you ever wished you could fold a piece of paper in half to create a booklet? A new feature in Word 2000 allows you to do this. When you select 2 Pages Per Sheet on the Margins tab of the Page Setup dialog box, the second page of the document prints on the same page as the first.

With this option, you can fold the paper in half either vertically or horizontally, depending on the orientation of the paper. Figure 5.3 shows a document in Landscape orientation with two pages per sheet.

The exercise below shows you how to set up a document with two pages per sheet.

This is not to be used to print a multi-page booklet, since that requires printing pages one and four on the first sheet and pages two and three on the second. This works well for a single sheet to be folded and placed in a cover.

PRINT TWO PAGES PER SHEET

1. Open a document with several pages of text.
2. Choose Page Setup from the File menu.
3. Select the Margins tab.
4. Check the box for 2 Pages Per Sheet.

FIGURE 5.3

Document with two pages of text printed on one page.

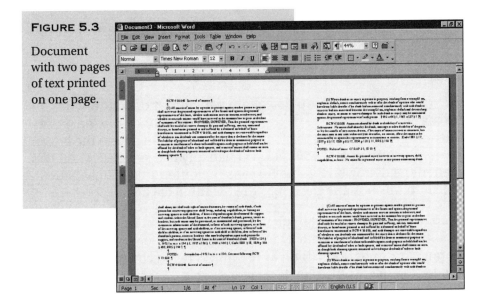

5. Select the Paper Size tab.

6. Choose Landscape for the Orientation and click OK.

PREVIEW

As you make changes to the settings in the Page Setup dialog box, the Preview picture updates to reflect how the document would look. The preview won't change much if you're making small adjustments, but the effects of an accidental keystroke are easy to see. This feature is extremely helpful when you set a gutter and use mirror margins. Go ahead and enter an amount for a gutter and select the Mirror Margins option. The preview changes to reflect the gutter running along the inside of each page. The preview makes understanding the impact of these options easier as you learn to use them.

HEADER AND FOOTER DISTANCE

Below the margin controls are two options that allow you to change how far the header and footer in a document begin from the edge of a page. The default is half an inch. Often printers have default settings that restrict how close to the edge of a page a margin can be set. If you decrease the distance to less than three-tenths of an inch, your printer is likely to be unable to handle the new settings—and your header or footer won't print! The setting of 0.3" or higher works best when you change header or footer distance.

APPLY TO

The Apply To box lets you designate which part of your document the margin changes affect: the whole document or just part of it. The options available in this box change depending upon the layout of your document and whether you had any text selected when you opened the dialog box. Table 5.1 lists the different options that can appear in this box and describes the meaning of each.

CAUTION If you drag a margin in the ruler in a document that contains sections, the margins change only for the selected sections. As you can imagine, it can get confusing as to what is being changed when you use the ruler to change document margins. For example, suppose you're responsible for maintenance on a document someone else created. If you drag the ruler to change the margins without realizing that the document contains sections, the results may be an unpleasant surprise. The safest way to change margins is to use the Page Setup dialog box and select the appropriate setting in the Apply To box.

TABLE 5.1 "APPLY TO" SETTINGS ON THE MARGINS TAB

OPTION	DESCRIPTION
Whole Document	Changes that you make in the Page Setup dialog box apply to the entire document.
This Point Forward	Word inserts a section break into the document and applies the changes that you make only from this point forward in the document. Text before the insertion point retains its original formatting.
Selected Text	Changes apply only to the text that was selected when you displayed the Page Setup dialog box. Word inserts Next Page section breaks before and after the selected text. Text outside of the new section (before and after the selected text) retains its original formatting.
This Section	Your document contains section breaks, and the changes that you make apply to the selected section only. The selected section is the one in which the insertion point resides when the dialog box is opened. Text in all other sections retains its original formatting.
Selected Sections	Your document contains section breaks, and text has been selected in one or more of the sections. The changes apply to the entire sections that are selected. Text outside of these sections retains its original formatting.

WORKING WITH PAPER SIZES

The United States uses the 8.5"×11" (Letter) paper size for most standard documents. Legal documents often require 8.5"×14" legal-sized paper; however, many other countries use a paper standard called A4. If you receive a document from someone who uses A4 paper, you don't need to switch the paper size and readjust all the margins to conform to the 8.5"×11" size. Word can automatically reformat A4 size documents to retain their original layout when printed on 8.5"×11" paper.

NOTE

When you change the paper size of a document, all of the document indents change accordingly. For example, if a paragraph contains a right indent of one inch, the indent remains at one inch if you change the document margins or page size. Although this feature can be helpful, you may need to adjust items such as tab settings and tables. For example, if you have set a right-align tab at the right margin for specific paragraphs, the tab will not move when the margins change for the document. Therefore, converting a U.S. letter-sized document to A4 will make the tab setting fall outside the document margin. The same is true of centered tabs; they will no longer be centered in the document margins. This is a real problem if you've used the centered tab setting in the document's header or footer. Likewise, a table that runs the width of a page will also fall outside the new document margin. Word 2000 offers an option in the Print dialog box that allows you to scale the document to different page sizes. This is a time-saving option if all you need to do is print it on specific paper.

Choose the paper size that you want to use for the document by using the Paper Size tab. Word has options for Letter, Legal, A4, and other paper sizes. Figure 5.4 shows the Paper Size tab in the Page Setup dialog box.

CHANGE PAPER SIZE OPTIONS

1. Choose Page Setup from the File menu.

2. Select the Paper Size tab.

3. Click the arrow to display the options in the Paper Size box. For U.S. setups, the default paper size is Letter (8.5"×11").

FIGURE 5.4

Paper size and orientation are set on the Paper Size tab.

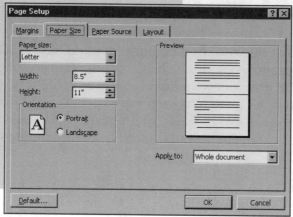

If you have chosen Letter in the Paper Size box, the Width and Height controls will reflect the dimensions of the pages in the document. If you choose Custom Size in the Paper Size box, you will need to specify the specially sized paper format using these controls.

If you want your changes to become the default settings that Word uses each time you create a new document, click the Default button in the lower-left corner of the Page Setup dialog box.

ORIENTATION

The Orientation section allows you to choose whether you want the page to be portrait or landscape. When the paper is oriented as portrait, it stands taller than it is wide; when oriented as landscape, it is wider than it is tall.

There is no need to manually adjust width and height of your paper when you want to change to a different orientation. As soon as you choose landscape, Word automatically adjusts the width and height settings for your page.

CHANGING THE PAPER SOURCE

Many printers on the market have multiple paper trays that allow you to print on more than one kind of paper during a single print job. Hewlett-Packard printers are especially well known for this feature. Multiple paper trays are popular because most law firms and businesses print the first page of a letter on letterhead, and subse-

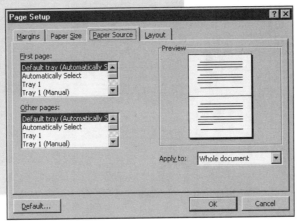

quent pages on regular (or at least letterhead-free) paper. Figure 5.5 shows the Paper Source tab.

The Paper Source tab contains the controls to print from one tray (the one with your letterhead pages) for the first page and another tray (the one with the regular paper) for the remaining pages.

To print from different trays, select the tray that you want to use for the first page of the document in the First Page box. Next, select the tray to use for subsequent pages in the Other Pages box. Depending on the selection in the Apply To box, the First Page setting can refer to the first page of the document or the first page of a section. Click the OK button to confirm the changes.

CHANGING THE LAYOUT

The Layout tab allows you to apply sophisticated document formatting techniques for special documents. You can change the vertical alignment of your text, or insert line numbers for documents such as pleadings, briefs, agreements, and patent applications. Figure 5.6 shows the Layout tab.

SECTION START

If your document has sections, you can change the selected section's break type in this box. For example, you might insert a continuous section break and realize later that you want a new page section break. Rather than remove and reinsert the break, which can wreak havoc on formatting in the surrounding sections, you can simply change the section type on the Layout tab.

FIGURE 5.6

Set advanced document layout options by clicking the Layout tab.

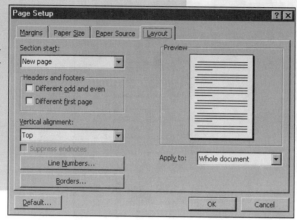

Word has an annoying habit of changing section types in complex documents as you modify text and sections in the document. Luckily, this occurs only rarely, but when it does, you can use the Layout tab to reset the section break type. You might see this occur in documents converted from WordPerfect or in documents that have been damaged in the course of processing.

HEADERS AND FOOTERS

Select the Different Odd And Even option for headers and footers if you are creating a document for publication and want to create different headers and footers for odd and even pages.

Select the Different First Page option to print different headers and footers on the first page of the document or section. See the "Headers and Footers" section later in this chapter for a detailed explanation of this feature.

VERTICAL ALIGNMENT

If you want to center your document content vertically on the page, change the vertical alignment setting to Center. This option centers the text on the page relative to the margins; therefore, if you want to center the text but make it appear a little bit higher than the center of the page, make the bottom margin larger than the top margin. This option is often used to create the title page for a document.

Choose Justified to justify the vertical alignment of a full page of text. This option forces the final line of text for a page to print so that it is even with the bottom margin.

SUPPRESS ENDNOTES

This prevents the endnotes from printing at the end of the selected section. If this option is chosen, the endnotes print in the next section directly before the endnotes for that section.

LINE NUMBERS

This feature is especially important because it allows you to create documents that have numbers down the left side. Click the Line Numbers button to activate this feature. The Line Numbers dialog box appears, as shown in Figure 5.7.

When the Line Numbers dialog box appears, select the Add Line Numbering option. To indicate the beginning number for the line numbering, change the value in the Start At box. To control the distance between the line numbers and text, change the value in the From Text box. Select Auto, if you want the numbers to print in the default position of 0.25" from the left edge of the text.

Change the value in the Count By box to tell Word how many lines to skip (if any) when it positions line numbers on the left side of the page. For example, some patent applications require you to number every fifth line rather than every line. By adjusting this control, you can conform to any necessary filing requirements. Figure 5.8 shows the Line Numbers dialog box and a document that contains line numbers.

Finally, you must choose a Numbering option. You can choose to have the numbers restart with each new page or section, or have the document numbered continuously from beginning to end. If you want the numbering to start at 1 for each paragraph, you would first need to separate each paragraph with a continuous section break and then tell Word to restart numbering at each section.

FIGURE 5.7

You can apply line numbers to the entire document or to selected paragraphs.

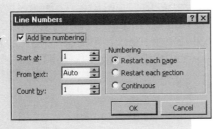

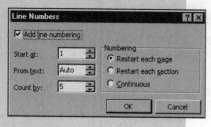

FIGURE 5.8

The count for line numbers is set to 5 as required for certain patent applications.

Line number spacing is based on the line spacing of the paragraph. For example, if a paragraph is double-spaced, the line numbers next to it will be double-spaced. If a paragraph is single-spaced, the line numbers will also be single-spaced. To change the line numbering to double-space, select the entire document (Ctrl+A) and then press Ctrl+2. The result will be double spacing for both the document and the line numbers.

If you are using line numbers for your patent applications, and need a number to occur every five lines, you need to be aware of a problem with line numbers and tables. When line numbers are turned on, and a table is inserted, the line numbers are discontinued until the text resumes. If your patent application needs the line numbering, use a text box with the line numbers inserted. A text box can be inserted by displaying the Drawing toolbar, clicking the Text Box button and drawing the size of the text box within the document. To remove the border of the text box, select the text box and choose Text Box from the Format menu. Select the Colors And Lines tab and set Line Color to No Line.

For pleadings, many law firms use a text box filled with numbers rather than Word's line numbering feature. This method gives users more control over line numbering and allows them to place a vertical line between the line numbers and the text. Read about the Pleading wizard in Chapter 10, "Creating Legal Templates," for more information.

PAGE BORDERS

When you need a border around the entire page, such as in an agreement or a will, you can use Word's page borders. Even if you don't have a legal document that needs a page border, you'll be the star of the office when you create eye-catching newsletters, notices, or bulletins using this feature.

You can have the traditional black border around the page, but Word lets you do much more. By giving you options to apply color, art, and different line styles, Word lets your borders be as simple or complex as you need.

ADD A PAGE BORDER

1. Create a new document.
2. Choose Page Setup from the File menu and select the Layout tab.
3. Click the Borders button. The Borders tab of the Borders and Shading dialog box is shown in Figure 5.9.
4. Select the Page Borders tab.
5. Click the Box button in the Setting section of the dialog box.
6. Select a desired line style in the Style section.
7. Click the Art drop-down and select a graphic page border.
8. Continue to select desired options for the border to see the many options this feature provides.

FIGURE 5.9

Use borders to make a document stand out.

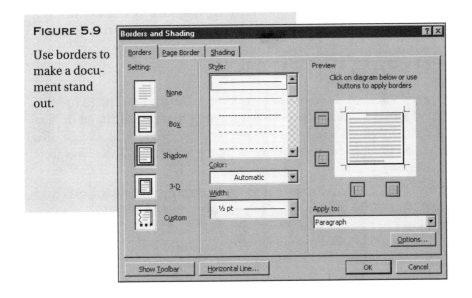

The default for the page border is to apply it to the whole document. Before you click OK, make sure you have changed the Apply To setting to place the border in the correct location.

9. Click OK.

If you need to change the distance between the border and the edge of the page, or specify whether the border surrounds the footer, click the Options button on the Page Border tab.

 When you click the Show Toolbar button from the Page Border dialog box, the Tables and Borders toolbar appears and the dialog box disappears. You can get the dialog box back without losing the toolbar by going to the Format menu and choosing Borders And Shading.

The Horizontal Line button opens a separate window of fancy lines for Web page design. The Show Toolbar button turns on the Tables and Borders toolbar, which applies paragraph and table borders and shading. See Chapter 7, "Using Tables in Legal Documents," for more information on this toolbar.

The Page Setup dialog box contains a rich set of options that give you control over how a document prints. Word has other features, however, that are equally important for formatting the layout of a page. Those features are the subject of the remainder of this chapter.

INSERTING PAGE BREAKS

Three types of Page Breaks are available in Word: hard page breaks, soft page breaks, and section breaks. Word inserts soft page breaks automatically when you have entered enough text to fill a page. You insert hard page breaks manually when you want to force the start of a new page.

Section breaks allow you to divide a document into sections and apply different formatting to each section. Section breaks are discussed later in this chapter.

INSERT A PAGE BREAK

1. Create a new document.

2. Choose Normal from the View menu. (You can see the page breaks better in Normal view.)

3. Type **Page One** and press Enter.

4. Choose Break from the Insert menu and then select Page Break and click OK. Word inserts a page break into the document, as shown in Figure 5.10. Keyboard users can press Ctrl+Enter to insert a page break.

5. Type **Page Two**.

In Normal view, a hard page break appears on your screen as a dotted line with the words *Page Break* in the center. Soft page breaks appear on the screen as just a dotted line. You can delete a hard page break by clicking the mouse anywhere on the page break and pressing the Delete key. You cannot delete a soft page break, but you can control where it appears by applying formatting to the text in a document. For information about formatting paragraphs to control page breaks, see Chapter 3, "Formatting Text."

FIGURE 5.10

The dotted line with the words *Page Break* indicates that a page break was manually inserted.

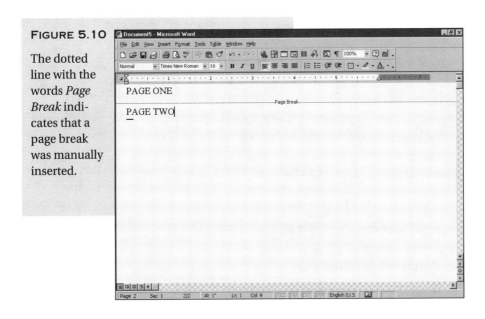

INSERTING SECTION BREAKS

In a complex legal document, there will be times that you need to have formatting changes apply to only certain parts of the document. By default, Word documents are set up as one section. Therefore, any changes made to the page format of a document apply to the entire document.

Section breaks allow you to break up the document and apply different page formatting to the individual parts. Think of a *section break* as a mark that tells Word to end one type of document formatting and begin another.

You must insert a section break to do the following:

- Create multiple columns of text in the middle of a page.
- Use different margin settings for different pages within the same document.
- Format page numbers differently on different pages within the same document. For example, you may want different styles of numbering for a table of contents and an appendix than for the rest of the document.
- Switch from portrait to landscape orientation in the middle of a document.
- Store a letter and an envelope in the same document.
- Control the layout of a document to make new chapters always begin on an odd page.
- Use different headers and footers within the same document.

A section break appears on the screen in Normal view as a double dotted line with the words *Section Break*.

INSERT SECTION BREAKS

1. Create a new Word document.
2. Switch to Normal view by choosing Normal from the View menu.
3. Type **Table of Contents** and press Enter.
4. Insert a Next Page section break by choosing Break from the Insert menu. Select the option for a Next Page section break and then click the OK button. Word inserts a section break that is also the beginning of a new page.

If you insert the wrong type of section break, you can change the type by clicking the Layout tab in the Page Setup dialog box.

5. Type **Contract** and press Enter.

6. Insert another Next Page Section break by following the instructions in Step 4.

7. Type **Appendix** and press Enter.

8. Save this document and name it **my contract.doc**.

You now have a document with three different sections. Because each section has its own footer, you can use different page number formats for each section. To determine which section you are in, click anywhere in the document and then look at the Status bar. The letters *Sec* followed by a number tell you what section is active.

HEADERS AND FOOTERS

The header and footer areas in the document allow you to store information that should appear on each page. For example, you can put page numbers, document name, date, company confidentiality information, and much more in a header or footer.

To insert multiple headers and footers in your document, you need a complete understanding of these topics:

◆ Inserting section breaks

◆ Using the Different First Page feature

◆ Linking headers or footers together with the previous using the Same As Previous feature

The preceding section of this chapter covered section breaks. In this section we will explore how section breaks apply in headers and footers as well as how they relate to the Different First Page and Same As Previous features.

INSERTING INFORMATION INTO THE HEADER AND FOOTER

You can plug commonly used information into the header and footer by using the buttons on the Header and Footer toolbar, or you can add text by typing it manually. Figure 5.11 shows the Header and Footer toolbar.

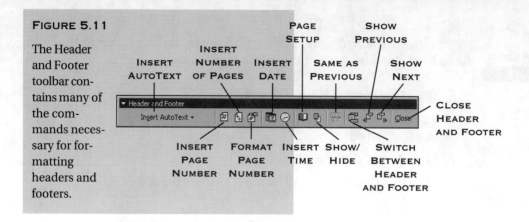

FIGURE 5.11

The Header and Footer toolbar contains many of the commands necessary for formatting headers and footers.

INSERT A FOOTER

1. Open the document created in the previous exercise (mycontract.doc).

2. Choose Header And Footer from the View menu.

3. Switch to the Footer by clicking the Switch Between Header And Footer button on the Header and Footer toolbar.

TIP

Keyboard users can press the Down Arrow key to move the insertion point into the footer, and the Up Arrow key to move the insertion point back into the header.

4. Click the Insert AutoText button and choose Filename And Path.

5. Press the Tab key to move to the center of the footer.

TIP

Headers and footers have different tab settings from the rest of the document. Word sets a center tab at three inches and a right tab at six inches in headers and footers. These tab settings are stored in styles. See Chapter 6, "Styles," for further explanation.

6. Click the Page Number button on the Header and Footer toolbar to insert the page number. Keyboard users can press Alt+Shift+P to insert a page number.

7. Press Tab to move to the right side of the footer.

8. Click the Insert Date button on the Header and Footer toolbar to insert the date.

9. Close the footer by clicking the Close button on the Header and Footer toolbar.

10. Save this document. You will use it the "Formatting Page Numbers" exercise later in this chapter.

DIFFERENT FIRST PAGE

Select the Different First Page option to print different headers and footers on the first page of the document or section. On a letter, for example, you might want to have no header or footer on the first page, but have the client name and page number in the headers and footers on the remaining pages. To do this, you would select this option and then remove any text appearing in the header and footer for the first page of the document. If this option is selected, the header and footer on the first page will always be distinct from the headers and footers on the remaining pages.

Keep in mind that header and footer options are set distinctly for each section of a document. You can therefore create different headers and footers for sections such as exhibits. For example, you might use a different first-page header and footer in the first section of a brief, but clear this option for the exhibit pages. You could then give the exhibit pages a different header and footer, with no distinct first page header and footer for that section. The result would be a brief with one first-page header and footer, remaining pages with a different header and footer, and an exhibit section whose pages show yet another header and footer.

When you have this feature turned on, the first-page header and footer will read "First Page Header" and "First Page Footer" when you choose Header And Footer from the View menu. This helps you identify which header or footer you're currently editing.

In this exercise, you will create a document with a title page and use the Different First Page command to turn off the page number in the footer on the title page but leave it on for the rest of the document.

CREATING A DIFFERENT FIRST PAGE FOOTER

1. Create a new blank document.

2. Type **Title Page**, and then press Ctrl+Enter to insert a page break.

3. Type **This is the first page**, and then insert another page break by pressing Ctrl+Enter.

4. Type **This is the second page**, and then press Ctrl+Home to move to the top of the document.

5. Choose Header And Footer from the View menu.

6. Switch to the Footer by clicking the Switch Between Header And Footer button on the Header and Footer toolbar.

7. Select the –PAGE- AutoText entry from the Insert AutoText command to insert the page number.

8. Click the Page Setup button on the Header and Footer toolbar and select Different First Page on the Layout tab.

9. Click OK. You have just created a first page footer, which by default is empty.

10. Click the Show Next button on the Header and Footer toolbar to move to the next footer. This footer reads "Footer" and has page number (2) showing.

FORMATTING PAGE NUMBERS

You can easily format page numbers for a document. You can place page numbers anywhere in the header or footer, and there are numerous formats available, such as Arabic or Roman numerals. You can also choose to start page numbering at a specific page number.

The following exercise walks you through the process of formatting the page numbers inserted in the preceding exercise. Each section's page number will be formatted differently. The table of contents will be formatted with lowercase Roman numerals, the contract will have Arabic numbers, and the appendix will have uppercase Roman numerals.

FORMATTING PAGE NUMBERS

1. Open the **my contract.doc** document created in the Section Break exercise.

2. Press Ctrl+Home to move to the top of the document. Check the section number displayed on the Status bar to verify that the insertion point is in Section 1.

3. Choose Header And Footer from the View menu.

FIGURE 5.12

Format page numbers in the Page Number format dialog box.

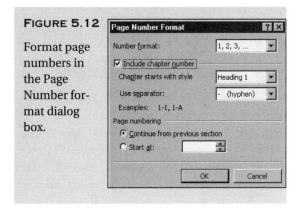

4. Switch to the Footer by clicking the Switch Between Header And Footer button on the Header and Footer toolbar.

5. Click the Format Page Number button on the Header and Footer toolbar. The Page Number Format dialog box appears, as shown in Figure 5.12.

6. Select the lowercase Roman numerals (i,ii,iii) in the Number Format box and click the OK button.

In the next section you will format the rest of the page numbers.

Formatting a page number and inserting a page number are two separate steps. If you had formatted the page number before inserting it, you would still need to insert the page number in the footer.

SAME AS PREVIOUS

Earlier, you saw that in order to have different formatting in the headers or footers, you must insert section breaks. There is still one more step that is crucial to making the header and footer formatting work correctly in each section.

This is where the Same As Previous command comes in. Even when a document is divided into sections, Word connects all the sections with the Same As Previous option. Therefore, if you make a change in one footer, all the rest of the footers change unless this option is turned off. Figure 5.13 shows a document with Same As Previous turned on.

FIGURE 5.13

Same as
Previous
showing in
footer

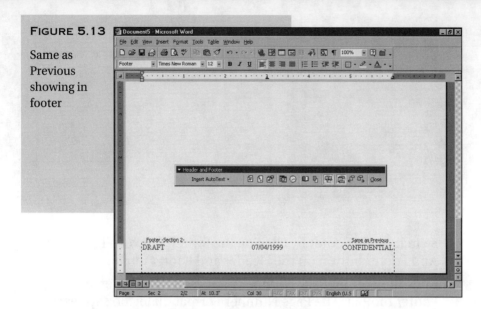

Imagine moving through your footers, making changes as you go: adding a date in one section, formatting the page number correctly and even adjusting the alignment in the appendix area. Now you print the document and all of the footers look like the last footer you modified! To prevent this from happening, Same As Previous must be turned off in each section. In this exercise, you will go to the remaining sections and turn off this command.

SAME AS PREVIOUS

1. Make sure the document created in the previous exercise is still open, with your insertion point in the footer of Section 1.

2. Click the Show Next button on the Header and Footer toolbar to move to the footer for Section 2. The page number already appears in the footer, so you need change only the formatting.

3. Turn off Same As Previous by clicking the Same As Previous button on the Header and Footer toolbar.

4. Click the Format Page number button.

5. Select the regular Arabic numbers (1,2,3) in the Number Format box.

6. Choose Start At 1 in the Page Numbering section, and then click OK.

7. Click the Show Next button to move to the footer for Section 3. The page number already appears in the footer; you need change only the formatting.

8. Turn off Same As Previous by clicking the Same As Previous button.

9. Click the Format Page number button.

10. Choose the uppercase Roman numerals (I,II,III) in the Number Format box.

11. Choose Start At I in the Page Numbering section, and then click OK.

12. Close the header and footer by clicking the Close button on the Header and Footer toolbar.

You now have three different types of page numbering in your document. The table of contents has lowercase Roman numerals, the contract has Arabic numbers, and the appendix has uppercase Roman numerals.

If you commonly create documents with different page numbering styles, you will save time by creating all the sections in a template that you can then use to create new documents. See Chapter 10, "Creating Legal Templates," for information about this technique.

Sections are also used to change the layout within the middle of a document. For example, you might want to use multiple columns in the middle of a document, or change to landscape orientation.

CREATE NEWSPAPER-STYLE COLUMNS

1. Create a new blank document.

2. Type a title for the document and press Enter.

3. Choose Break from the Insert menu.

4. Select the option for a Continuous Section Break. This will insert a section break without creating a new page.

5. Choose Columns from the Format menu to open the Columns dialog box.

6. Select the option for Two Columns and click the OK button.

7. Enter the text for your article. The text that you type will fill up the first column until it is forced into the next column. To manually move to the next column, press Ctrl+Shift+Enter to insert a column break, or select Break from the Insert menu, and then select Column Break.

8. When you finish the article, press Enter.

9. Insert another continuous section break.

10. Display the Columns dialog box and select the option for One Column.

11. Click the OK button.

12. Enter summary or other text for your document.

If your document already contains the text that you want formatted in columns, you do not need to insert the continuous section breaks. Select the text and choose how many columns you would like in the Columns dialog box. Word inserts the continuous section breaks for you.

If you are working in Print Layout view, you will see the columns on the page as soon as you insert the section break following the columns. If you are in Normal view, you will not see the columns (they appear as one column on the left of the screen), but they will print correctly. If you prefer to work in Normal view, you can check the layout of the columns by switching to Print Preview. Print Preview is covered next.

USING PRINT PREVIEW

Before you print legal documents, you can use the Print Preview feature in Word to see what the documents will look like on the page. This allows you to see whether the document is truly ready to be printed or still needs changes to the layout. Catching and correcting mistakes before printing saves both time and paper–not to mention trees.

You can access Print Preview in three ways: by clicking the Print Preview button on the Standard toolbar, choosing Print Preview from the File menu, or pressing Ctrl+F2.

FIGURE 5.14

You can adjust
margins, edit
text, or shrink
a document
while you're in
Print Preview.

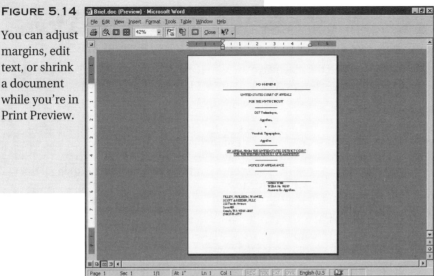

PREVIEW A DOCUMENT IN PRINT PREVIEW

1. Open an existing Word document.
2. Click the Print Preview button on the Standard toolbar. The document appears in Print Preview, as shown in Figure 5.14.

When you're in Print Preview mode, you will notice that the only toolbar visible is the Print Preview toolbar. Table 5.2 provides a description of each button and its function.

TABLE 5.2 PRINT PREVIEW TOOLBAR

BUTTON	FUNCTION
Print	Prints the active document without opening the Print dialog box.
Magnifier	Zooms in and out of the document.
One Page	Shows a single page of the document. Use the scroll bar or Page Up and Page Down keys to move to the previous and next pages.
Multiple Pages	Shows up to 24 pages simultaneously and reduces the view depending on the number of pages displayed. To view multiple pages at once, click and hold your mouse and drag out to the number of pages you wish to view.

TABLE 5.2   PRINT PREVIEW TOOLBAR (CONTINUED)

BUTTON	FUNCTION
Zoom	Lets you adjust the magnification from 10 percent to 500 percent. To select a number not listed, type directly into the magnification box and press Enter.
View Ruler	Displays or hides the horizontal and vertical ruler.
Shrink to Fit	Reduces the number of pages in a document by one by reducing the font size, so if a small amount of text is spilling over onto the last page, you can force it all onto one page. (*Note:* Use this feature only with documents such as letters and memorandums. Do not use it on legal documents that must adhere to court rules. Otherwise, you might change the formatting of the document so that it no longer qualifies for filing.)
Full Screen	Hides most of the screen elements so that you can see more of your document. To restore the view, click the Close Full Screen button, or press the Esc key on your keyboard.
Close	Exits Print Preview and returns to your document view.
Context Sensitive	Displays context-sensitive help. Click this button and then click Help on any button or screen element to display help for that feature.

PRINTING LEGAL DOCUMENTS

Printing legal documents is a snap; you just point and click. If you want to print one copy of the entire active document, the easiest way is to click the Print button on the Standard toolbar. If you want to print multiple copies, define exactly what to print, or select a particular printer, you need to use the Print dialog box. To open the Print dialog box, press Ctrl+P or choose Print from the File menu. Figure 5.15 shows the Print dialog box.

In the Print dialog box, you can select a specific printer for the print job and set attributes for the selected printer. You can also specify what page range of the document to print, how many copies, and whether to collate them. The following exercise will show you how to use the Print dialog box.

USE THE PRINT DIALOG BOX TO PRINT A LEGAL DOCUMENT

1. Choose Print from the File menu. Keyboard users can press Ctrl+P to open the Print dialog box.
2. Click the arrow next to the Name box to view all available printers. Select the printer that you want to use.

FIGURE 5.15

You can define what to print and where to print it from the Print dialog box.

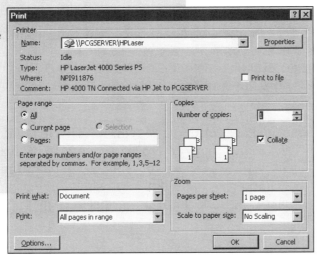

NOTE

Only printers that have been installed and properly set up will appear in the Name box. However, you can install and set up a printer your firm doesn't actually own, if you need to format documents that will be printed elsewhere, as long as the printer drivers are available to you.

3. Click the Properties button to view options for paper size, draft print, graphics, fonts, and device options.

NOTE

Printer options will vary depending upon the printer that you selected in Step 2.

4. Click the Cancel button to close the Printer Properties dialog box without saving changes. To save the selections that you made, click the OK button.

TIP

If you alter the printer's settings accidentally, you can restore the original settings by clicking the Restore Defaults button in the Properties dialog box.

5. In the Page Range section, select a desired option.

NOTE

The options available in the Page Range section will vary, depending upon whether or not text was selected when the Print dialog box was opened.

TIP

If you select Current Page, it is not necessarily the page that you see behind the Print dialog box. The current page is the page that contains the insertion point. If you used the scroll bars to move to another part of the document but didn't click to change the insertion point, the Current Page selection may return unexpected results.

6. Choose the Pages option and type **1,3**. This tells Word to print only Page 1 and Page 3 and to skip Page 2. To print a range of consecutive pages, use a hyphen between page numbers. For example, typing **1-3** would print the first three pages. Table 5.3 shows all the options for printing specific pages and sections.

CAUTION

If you type a starting page number in the Pages box that is greater than the ending page number, Word will print the document backwards. For example, typing **10-5** will cause Word to print pages 10 through 5 in reverse order. Although this can be helpful if you have a printer that prints pages face up, it can result in a crisis if a large document is printed this way on a face-down printer.

TABLE 5.3 OPTIONS FOR PRINTING SPECIFIC PAGES AND SECTIONS

TO PRINT . . .	TYPE THIS IN THE PAGES BOX . . .
Noncontiguous pages	Page numbers with commas between them. For example, **2,4,6**.
A range of pages	Page numbers with a hyphen between them. For example, **1-5**.
A range of pages within a section	"p#" for page number and "s#" for section number. For example, typing **p2s1-p5s3** prints Page 2, Section 1 through Page 5, Section 3.
An entire section	"s#" to specify a section. For example, typing **s2** prints Section 2.
Noncontiguous sections	Sections with commas between them. For example, **s1,s3,s5** prints sections 1, 3, and 5.
A range of pages across sections	A range of page numbers and sections with a hyphen between the start and end numbers in the range. For example, typing **p1s1-p3s4** prints Page 1, Section 1, through Page 3, Section 3.
From a specified page to the end	A page number followed by a hyphen. For example, typing **47-** prints Page 47 through the end of the document.

USING THE PRINT WHAT FEATURE

This is a great but often underused feature. You can use this option to print a document, document properties, comments, styles, AutoText entries, or assigned keyboard shortcuts. To change what is printed, click the drop-down arrow and select a different option from the list. If your firm has created firmwide AutoText entries to allow you to quickly insert commonly used phrases and clauses, you can get a list of the AutoText entries by choosing to print AutoText.

TIP

Choosing assigned keyboard shortcuts will not show you all of Word's shortcuts. It lists only the shortcuts that you have customized in the document or template. To get a printout of all keyboard shortcuts, look up "Keys" in Word Help and select "Shortcut Keys." Then print the associated topic.

WORKING WITH PRINT OPTIONS

You can choose to print odd- or even-numbered pages if you're using a printer that does not print double-sided, and you have to turn the document over and refeed it through the printer. The default is to print the entire document in straight numerical order.

PRINT TO FILE

You choose Print To File when you need to distribute a file for printing on a machine that does not have Word installed. Also, use this option to control elements, such as resolution, for files that you plan to send to a print shop. For example, it's possible to format files with a special type of printer format—even if you don't have that kind of printer—and then place them on a floppy disk so that print shops can manipulate them for special types of printing.

COPIES

To print multiple copies of the document, you can either click the spin box controls or type a number directly into the box next to Number of Copies. If you want the copies collated, check the Collate option.

ZOOM

The following two features, which come under zoom in the print setup dialog box, help you preview the layout of your document and allow you to print it on different sizes of paper.

- ◆ **Pages Per Sheet.** Use this option to print multiple pages on one sheet of paper. This is a great way to preview the layout of your document without wasting paper.

- ◆ **Scale to Paper Size.** If you like the feature on copy machines that allows you to reduce or enlarge your document, you'll love the Scale to Paper Size feature, which allows you to take a document formatted for one size of paper and scale it for a different size of paper by manipulating the size of fonts and graphics. The scaling change is for the current printing session only.

OPTIONS

When you click the <u>O</u>ptions button, a new Print dialog box appears that lets you set all sorts of options for printing a document. Figure 5.16 shows the Print Options dialog box, and Table 5.4 goes into the details.

Be very careful when you set printing options. After they are set, they remain in place until you change them. For example, if you select the option to print hidden text, that option will remain selected when you print other documents.

FIGURE 5.16

Select Print Options to further customize your print jobs.

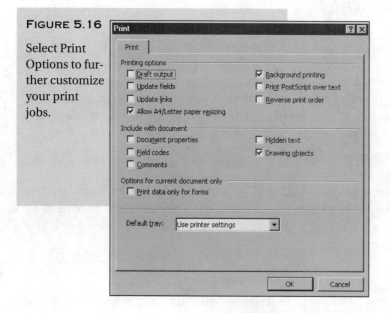

TABLE 5.4 AVAILABLE PRINT OPTIONS

OPTION	DESCRIPTION
Print Options	
Draft Output	Prints in Draft Output mode to speed up a print job in a document. Most of the formatting will not be printed.
Update Fields	All fields, such as tables of contents, indexes, and tables of authorities, will be updated when printing.
Update Links	Word locates any linked files and updates any changes in the document.
Allow A4/Letter Paper Resizing	Word automatically adjusts a document formatted for A4 paper to print on 8.5"×11" paper.
Background Printing	Turns off background printing to speed up print jobs. You will not be able to work in Word until the print job is finished if this option is turned off.
Print PostScript Over Text	Used when printing documents from a Macintosh.
Reverse Print Order	If you have a printer that prints face up, choose this option to have pages print in the correct order.
Include with Document	
Document Properties	Prints document statistics, such as number of pages and words, with the document.
Field Codes	Prints field codes rather than field results. Useful for troubleshooting problems with field codes.
Comments	Prints a separate sheet containing all of the comments.
Hidden Text	Prints any hidden text in documents.
Drawing Objects	Prints Drawing Objects.
Options for Current Document Only	
Print Data Only for Forms	Prints the data entered into an online form without printing the form. Use when you are feeding preprinted forms through the printer.
Default Tray	These options will vary depending upon the printer that has been selected.

ANSWERING COMMON PAGE SETUP AND PRINTING QUESTIONS

Is it possible to lock a document so that users cannot edit a header or footer?

Press Ctrl+Home to move to the beginning of the document. From the Insert menu, choose Break. In the Section Break Types section, choose Continuous, and then click OK. Now you'll need to protect the section in the document. From the Tools menu, choose Protect Document. In the Protect Document dialog box, click the Forms option button, and click Sections. In the Protect Sections list box, be sure Section 1 is selected and click OK. You can assign a password if you like, and then click OK again. Now when you go to the View menu, the Headers and Footers feature is disabled.

How can I insert the word "draft" on every page and have it appear behind the text?

There are a few different ways to do this. One way is to go into the header and footer by choosing Header and Footer from the View menu. Display the Drawing toolbar and click the Insert WordArt button. Select the first row, second column WordArt style (or any other that you prefer) and click OK. Type **DRAFT** and click the OK button. With the WordArt selected, click the Format WordArt button on the WordArt toolbar. Select the Layout tab and set the Wrapping Style to Behind Text. On the Colors and Lines tab, click the Color drop-down arrow and select the lightest gray available and select the Semitransparent option. Set the Line Color to No Line, and then click OK.

How do I copy formatting from one section to another?

You can copy section formatting such as newspaper columns or margins by switching to Normal view and selecting the section break at the end of the section. Click the Copy button on the Standard toolbar. Place the insertion point to the new location and click the Paste button. The text above the new section break takes on its formatting

Is there an easy way to find and replace section breaks?

You can use the Find and Replace dialog box to search for and replace section breaks. From the Edit menu, choose Replace. Keyboard user can press Ctrl+H. Click the More button to expand the dialog box. Click the Special button and choose Section Break.

To delete the section break, leave the Replace With box empty and click Replace or Replace All.

How can I speed up printing?

The default is for Word to use background printing, which allows you to work while a document is printing. While this is a great feature, occasionally with long or complex documents, printing can take a long time, or worse, Word may experience a General Protection Fault (GPF) because background printing uses additional system memory. If you experience slow printing or the a GPF error, turn background printing off by choosing Options from the Tools menu, and then select the Print tab. Under Printing Options, clear the Background Printing option. While you're on the Print tab, you can speed printing by selecting Draft Output, which prints the document with a minimal amount of formatting.

Why do the line numbers of my pleading show on screen but not print?

When you use the Pleading wizard to initially setup a pleading, the line numbers are placed in a text box in the header and footer layer. Because a text box is a drawing object, it will not print if you've selected the option not to print drawing objects. To control this option, from the Tools menu, choose Options and select the Print tab. Check or uncheck the Drawing Objects option and click OK.

Is there a way to maintain document settings when our attorneys send a document to a client to be signed?

Word repaginates the document depending on which type of printer it is printing on. Therefore, a document that you send to a client might look one way when printed, but when you print it, it looks very different. You can change this by opening the document, and choosing Options from the Tools menu, and selecting the Compatibility tab. Select the Use Printer Metrics To Lay Out Document option and then save the document.

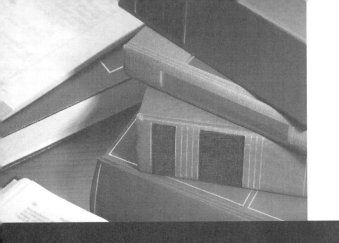

CHAPTER 6

STYLES

IN THIS CHAPTER

- ◆ Understanding styles
- ◆ Using styles in legal documents
- ◆ Applying and displaying styles
- ◆ Creating and modifying styles
- ◆ Copying and deleting styles
- ◆ Renaming, replacing, and resetting styles

UNDERSTANDING STYLES

Styles are stored sets of formatting commands that you can call upon while you create and edit documents. For example, suppose that each heading in a document must be centered, bold, uppercase 14-point text, and automatically numbered. As you can imagine, you would have to use quite a few keystrokes to accomplish this task each time you insert a heading. However, if you store the formatting commands in a style, you can retrieve the heading formatting with a single keystroke each time you need it (for more information about formatting text, see Chapter 3, "Formatting Text").

You can apply styles to entire paragraphs (paragraph styles) or to sections of text (character styles).

Paragraph styles allow you to apply font *and* paragraph formatting to entire paragraphs of text. Character styles allow you to apply font formatting to one or more selected characters.

Word comes with a complete set of built-in styles. These built-in styles are in use all the time, even if you are not aware of them. For example, when you insert a footnote, Word uses the Footnote Text style to format the footnote text, and the Footnote Reference style to format the footnote number. When you generate a table of contents, Word uses TOC styles. Built-in styles are available to you in all templates when you install Word. Depending on the template used, the list of styles varies—some templates have more styles than others, some styles with the same name may produce a different look on the page, and some styles may have unique names.

Some styles are used for more than just formatting text. For example, when you insert heading styles into a document, you can automatically generate a table of contents based on these headings. Likewise, you can use various other styles to control the automatic numbering of items such as paragraphs, figures, and captions. For more information about generating a table of contents, see Chapter 12, "Working with Long Documents."

The really good news is that Word doesn't limit you to using its built-in styles. You can create your own styles and store them in documents and templates. Styles created by users are called *user-defined* styles. Storing a style in a document makes the style available within the current document. Storing a style in a template makes the style available in all documents based on that template. Once you understand how styles work, you become more productive while working in documents because you have a clearer knowledge of what Word can do for you.

You can also create your own styles for including text in a table of contents or to automatically number paragraphs within a document. For example, you may want to create a heading style for exhibits that is different from the other headings in your document. You can create a different style for Exhibit headings, and then include that style in the table of contents so that the exhibits are listed there.

USING STYLES IN LEGAL DOCUMENTS

Styles are one of the most powerful and exciting features in Word. In the legal environment, they can make users more efficient and productive as well as make Word easier to use. The following list provides some examples of why styles are so powerful:

- **Consistent Formatting**: Using styles ensures that all of your documents are formatted consistently. In a legal environment, many different people work on the same document. Styles keep the formatting consistent and allow you to put all your focus on the content of the document.

  Clients who receive documents from multiple authors find these documents easier to understand because the style of formatting is familiar (no need to relearn how to read your firm's documents each time something arrives). Clients also immediately recognize documents from your firm because the formatting looks the same.

- **Legal Practice and Court Rules**: Documents such as pleadings can be set up to adhere automatically to court rules.

  Using styles in pleading templates ensures that text is formatted correctly for any court. It also allows staff to provide support across practice groups. For example, a secretary working in Corporate Finance can create a document for Litigation by using the styles associated with the litigation templates.

  For more information about this feature, see Chapter 10, "Creating Legal Templates."

- **Create Tables of Contents without Codes**: By using headings and other styles, you can automatically create tables of contents and other tables for documents.

Unlike other word processing programs, Word does not require you to code headings for inclusion in the table of contents. Word generates the table of contents based on heading styles.

If someone modifies the headings, you can update the text automatically in the table of contents. No codes need to be edited for the document to be updated correctly. For information about generating a table of contents, see Chapter 12, "Working with Long Documents."

♦ **Reduce Editing Time**: Secretaries and word processors can make major formatting changes with only a few keystrokes.

Text formatted with styles is formatted the same throughout the document. If you modify and update the style, all text formatted with the same style is reformatted automatically throughout the document.

♦ **Reduce Training Time**: Each template can contain identical style names.

Styles that have the same name can look different in each template. For example, Body Text style in a letter might be single-spaced with a first-line indent of half an inch. In a pleading, Body Text style might be double-spaced and flush left.

Using the same style names reduces the amount of training necessary for new and temporary employees. Simply provide a list of style names and examples of different document types, and users who already know Word can step right in where needed.

Overall, styles make Word easier to learn and use. They also make users at your law firm more productive. Keep in mind that you are *always* using styles while working in Word, so why not take advantage of their features and flexibility?

APPLYING STYLES

You can apply styles from the Style box on the Formatting toolbar, or by choosing Style from the Format menu. Figure 6.1 shows the Style box. For more information about the Formatting toolbar, see the section called "Using the Formatting Toolbar in Legal Documents" in Chapter 3. As with most features in Word, you can use the mouse or keyboard to apply styles.

FIGURE 6.1

You can apply styles quickly using the Style box on the Formatting toolbar.

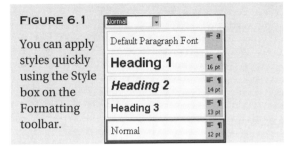

When applying paragraph styles, make sure the entire paragraph is selected, or that the insertion point is clicked within the paragraph. If one or several characters are selected when applying a paragraph style, only the font characteristics of the style are applied to the selected text.

APPLY STYLES THREE DIFFERENT WAYS

1. Type your firm name and press Enter. Type your name and press Enter. Type your job title and press Enter.

2. Select the paragraph with your firm's name.

3. On the Formatting toolbar, click the down arrow on the right side of the Style box (refer to Figure 6.1).

When you click Style on the Formatting toolbar, you won't see all of the built-in Word styles. Word displays only the styles in use along with the most commonly used built-in styles. In most cases and for less advanced users, this list is sufficient. To see a complete list of available styles, hold down the Shift key as you click the Style box.

In Word 97, styles listed in the drop-down list did not appear in alphabetical order. In Word 2000, they are listed in alphabetical order.

4. To the right of each style name is information about the point size and paragraph alignment of each style. A symbol indicates whether the style is a paragraph (¶) or character (a) style. Figure 6.2 shows style indicators.

5. Select Heading 1. The paragraph is formatted as Heading 1.

FIGURE 6.2

The style list in the Style box indicates whether a style is a paragraph (¶) or character (a) style.

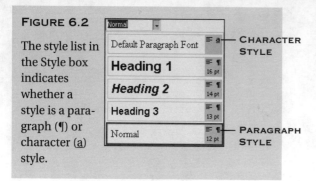

If you do not see the style listed, click the up or down arrows on the scroll bar to the right of the style list to find the style. If you find scrolling too tedious, you can type the name into the Style box and then press the Enter key to apply it. You can also type in the first few letters of the style name and click the down arrow on your keyboard to locate the style. If Word finds the style that you're looking for, press Enter to apply the style to the current area within the document.

NOTE

6. Select the paragraph with your name.

7. Press Ctrl+Shift+S, and type **Heading 2** in the Style box.

TIP

To apply the same style to additional paragraphs, select the paragraphs and then press Ctrl+Y or F4 (the Repeat command). Mouse users can choose Repeat Style from the Edit menu.

8. Select the paragraph with your job title.

9. Press Ctrl+Alt+3 to apply Heading 3.

DISPLAYING STYLES IN A DOCUMENT

You can activate the Style Area onscreen to see the styles currently assigned to each paragraph. Figure 6.3 shows a document with the Style Area activated.

The Style Area is helpful when you're trying to familiarize yourself with a document that you did not create. It also allows you to quickly see how a document has been formatted.

FIGURE 6.3

Activate the
Style Area of a
document to
see which
styles are in
use.

STYLE AREA ———

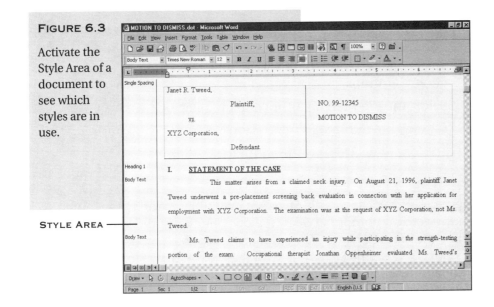

You cannot view the names of character styles in the Style Area.
Only paragraph style names appear there.

You can only activate the Style Area while you work in Normal or
Outline views. You can change the current view to Normal by going
to the View menu and selecting Normal. For more information, see
"Working with Different Views" in Chapter 2.

ACTIVATE THE STYLE AREA

1. From the Tools menu, choose Options.

2. Select the View tab if it is not already selected.

3. In the Style Area Width box, type the size of the area that you
   want to display. For example, type **1.5** to display a Style Area of
   one and one-half inches.

4. Click OK.

When Style Area is activated, mouse users have new shortcuts available to them. To select a paragraph, single-click the style name to
the left of the paragraph in the Style Area. To quickly access the
Style dialog box, double-click the style name (the Style dialog box is
discussed later in this chapter).

CHANGE THE STYLE AREA WIDTH

1. To change the width of the Style Area, from the Tools menu, choose Options.

2. Select the View tab if it is not already selected.

3. Change the number in the Style Area Width box as desired.

4. To close Style Area, set the width to 0 (zero).

NOTE

Mouse users can change the Style Area width by placing the mouse on the vertical border between the document and the Style Area. When the mouse pointer changes shape, drag the border to the left or right. To close the Style Area with the mouse, drag the border all the way to the left edge of the screen and then release the mouse.

CREATING STYLES FOR LEGAL DOCUMENTS

User-defined firmwide styles keep documents consistent and guarantee adherence to court rules. You can create paragraph styles on the fly by selecting an example of text that already has the formatting you want, or you can set them up using the Style dialog box.

You can override any style by applying your own formatting to any text or paragraph. If you use the style again later, however, it won't contain the manual formatting that you applied previously. This is OK because sometimes you want to apply manual formatting in a few specific instances. For example, you might want to apply the Body Text style to many paragraphs in your document but for one of those paragraphs, you may also want to indent it on the right and left side.

NOTE

Character styles must be created using the Style dialog box. You cannot create them by selecting an example of formatted text.

CREATE A PARAGRAPH STYLE BY EXAMPLE

1. Format some text in your document with a one-inch left and right indent. For information about formatting text, see Chapter 3.

2. Select the formatted paragraph. For information about selecting text, see "Selecting Text" in Chapter 2.

3. Press Ctrl+Shift+S to access the Style box on the Formatting toolbar (or click inside the Style box with the mouse).

4. Delete the existing style name and then type a name for the style that you want to create, such as **Quote.**

NOTE Style names can be more than one word and can contain spaces, numbers, and any special characters except for the semicolon (;), curly braces ({}), and back slash (\). Do not use a comma in a style name. The comma denotes an alias. Alias names are covered later in this chapter.

5. Press Enter. You have created a new style.

6. To use the style, move to a new location in the document and apply the style from the Style box on the Formatting toolbar.

CREATE A PARAGRAPH STYLE USING THE STYLE DIALOG BOX

1. From the Format menu, choose Style. The Style dialog box appears (see Figure 6.4).

2. Click New. The New Style dialog box appears (see Figure 6.5).

FIGURE 6.4

Use the Style dialog box to access a full range of style options.

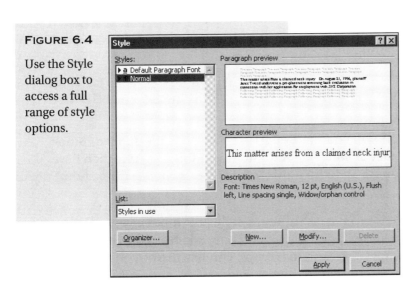

FIGURE 6.5

Use the New
Style dialog
box to create
legal styles.

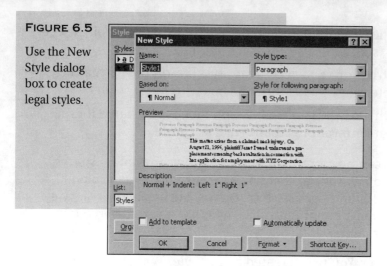

FIGURE 6.5

Use the New
Style dialog
box to create
legal styles.

3. In the Name box, enter the name of the new style.

4. From the Style Type list, select Paragraph.

5. From the Based On list, select an existing style on which to base the new style. Select a style that most closely matches the new style. For example, if you are creating a block quote style, you might select the style used for your body text.

CAUTION

Keep in mind that if you change the formatting of the Based On style, the new style may change as well. For example, say that you base a new block quote style on an existing body text style. If you later make the body text style double-spaced, or change the size of the font, the block quote style also changes unless those attributes have been specifically set for this style.

The way that Word interprets a style might look as follows: Block Quote Style = Body Text + 1-inch left indent + 1-inch right indent.

Therefore, if you change Body Text to be double-spaced, Block Quote changes as well. If you do not want this to occur, then base the block quote style on a different style or choose "(no style)" from the Based On list.

6. If you wish to have a different style automatically applied when you press the Enter key, select that style from the Style For Following Paragraph list. When you use the new style in the document and press the Enter key at the end of the paragraph,

the new paragraph automatically defaults to the style selected in the Style For Following Paragraph list.

7. Click Format to format the font, paragraph, and other settings for the new style. For information about formatting text, see Chapter 3.

8. If you want the style to be available in all documents based on the existing template, select the Add To Template option. If you do not select this option, the style is available in the current document only (and in any copies of this document).

TIP

If you need to create a large number of styles for a template, you might find opening the template first easier, because the styles that you create are then added directly to the template.

9. To create a shortcut key for applying the style, click Shortcut Key.

10. Select Automatically Update if you want Word to update the style automatically as you make formatting changes in the document.

CAUTION

You should use the Automatically Update option only for items such as table of contents styles, because you might change the indent or tab settings and want all of the associated table of contents levels to change automatically. This option is dangerous for regular text styles, because any formatting changes you make to one paragraph automatically change all like-style paragraphs throughout the document, even when you only wanted a one-time adjustment in the formatting.

11. Click OK to create the style. The New Style dialog box closes and the Style dialog box appears.

12. Click Close to close the Style dialog box, or click New to create more new styles.

CAUTION

A third way to create new styles is by using an AutoFormat feature called Define Styles Based On Your Formatting. To access this feature, from the Tools menu, choose AutoCorrect and then select the AutoFormat As You Type tab. This creates new paragraph styles in your documents based on the manual formatting that you have applied. For example, if you type a few words and format them with 15-point font, bold, and underline, Word creates a new style named Heading 1 that is 15 points, bold, and underlined.

You can imagine some of the problems that can arise from using this feature. In the preceding example, the Heading 1 style was completely redefined without any warning! It's a good idea to turn this feature off to avoid problems.

CREATE A CHARACTER STYLE USING THE STYLE DIALOG BOX

1. From the Format menu, choose Style. The Style dialog box appears (refer back to Figure 6.4).

2. Click New. The New Style dialog box appears (refer back to Figure 6.5).

3. In the Name box, type the name of the new style.

4. From the Style Type list, select Character.

5. From the Based On list, select an existing style on which to base the new style, if desired.

TIP

If you want the text to remain the same as the selected style and add only the attributes associated with the style that you are creating, choose Default Paragraph Font from the Based On list. Doing so ensures that the font and point size remain the same as the current paragraph (unless they are modified as part of the character style).

6. Click Format to apply character formatting to the style. (For more information about formatting text, see Chapter 3.)

7. If you want the style to be available in all documents based on the existing template, select the Add To Template option. If you do not select this option, the style is available only in the current document (and any copies based on this document).

8. To create a shortcut key for applying the style, click Shortcut Key.

9. Click OK to create the style. The New Style dialog box closes and the Style dialog box appears.

10. Click Close to close the Style dialog box, or click New to create more new styles.

MODIFYING STYLES

One of the most powerful features of styles is the way you can change an entire document by modifying the look of an existing style. If you modify a style, Word applies the modifications throughout the document. Imagine the benefit of such a feature in the legal environment, in which meeting a deadline can make the difference between winning and losing a case!

You can modify both built-in and user-defined styles. You can apply modifications to both character and paragraph styles directly from within the document, or you can do so using the Style dialog box.

Don't confuse *modifying* styles with *resetting* styles. Modifying a style changes the attributes of an existing style. For example, you might change the attributes of a heading style so that it is bold and italic rather than just bold. This action changes the look of all headings based on that style throughout the document. Resetting a style removes manually applied formatting from text and paragraphs. For more information about resetting styles, see "Resetting Styles" later in this chapter.

MODIFY A STYLE WITHIN A DOCUMENT

1. Locate one instance of text formatted with the style that you want to modify. Apply new formatting as desired (for more information about formatting text, see Chapter 3).

2. Select the newly formatted text.

3. Press Ctrl+Shift+S (or click inside the Style box on the Formatting toolbar).

4. Do not change the style name. Instead, press the Enter key.

5. Word prompts you with a dialog box that asks whether you wish to update the existing style or reapply the original style attributes. See Figure 6.6 for an example of this dialog box.

NOTE

The Modify Style dialog box only appears if the text that you have selected has different formatting than the style specifies. For example, if you have not made any formatting changes when you follow the first four steps of the exercise, the Modify Style dialog box does *not* appear.

FIGURE 6.6

When you're updating styles by example, Word prompts you regarding what action to take.

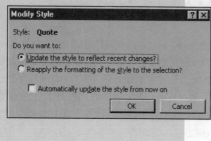

NOTE You may not always want to update a style throughout a document. Refer to Table 6.1 for an explanation of the options presented in the Modify Style dialog box (see Figure 6.6).

6. Select any of the options described in Table 6.1.

7. Click OK.

MODIFY A STYLE USING THE STYLE DIALOG BOX

1. From the Format menu, choose Style. The Style dialog box appears (see Figure 6.4).

2. Select the style that you wish to modify from the Styles list.

TABLE 6.1 MODIFY STYLE OPTIONS

SELECT . . .	TO . . .
Update the Style to Reflect Recent Changes?	Update the look of this style throughout the document. All existing text formatted with this style is modified to look like the current selection.
Reapply the Formatting of the Style to the Selection?	Reset the formatting of the currently selected text. The formatting for the current selection returns to the original format of the style.
Automatically Update the Style from Now On	Set the style so that any future changes you make to text formatted with this style is applied automatically through out the document (Word changes the style throughout the document without prompting you first).

FIGURE 6.7

Use the Modify Style dialog box to modify legal styles.

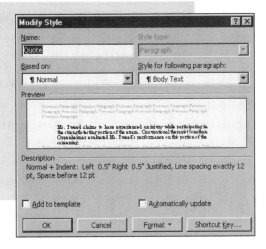

TIP

As a shortcut, place your insertion point in text that is formatted with the style you wish to change. Select Format and then select Style. The style is automatically selected in the Styles list.

NOTE

If the Styles list does not include the style that you wish to modify, the List option might not be set to display all styles. To change this, select All Styles from the List option. Likewise, if so many styles are displayed that you cannot find the one you wish to modify, select User-Defined Styles from List.

3. Click Modify. The Modify Style dialog box appears (see Figure 6.7).

4. Make changes to the style options and formatting as desired (see the exercise called "Create a Paragraph Style Using the Style Dialog Box" earlier in this chapter for information about the various options in this dialog box).

5. If you wish to apply this change to all future documents that are based on this template, select the Add To Template option.

NOTE

If you add these modifications to the template, it will only change the style in future documents that are based on this template. Existing documents will not change when opened. The styles in existing documents must be modified within those documents. To force an existing document to update all styles automatically, from the <u>T</u>ools menu choose Templates And Add-<u>I</u>ns. Select the option Automatically <u>U</u>pdate Document Styles and then click OK.

6. Click OK. The Modify Style dialog box closes and the Style dialog box appears.

7. Click Close to close the Style dialog box, or click <u>M</u>odify to modify another style.

DELETING UNWANTED STYLES

You may want to delete styles that you no longer use. Unwanted styles make Word more difficult to learn for new users because knowing which styles to select can be confusing. Removing unwanted styles reduces training and support time.

At times, court rules change and some styles are no longer necessary. Removing obsolete styles from a document template helps prevent them from being used in error.

Because you can create styles by example, you might create a style accidentally (see "Create a Paragraph Style by Example" earlier in this chapter). Making a typo within the Style dialog box creates a new style with the misspelled name. You may want to delete these styles so that when others edit your document, they don't become confused about which styles to use.

DELETE A STYLE

1. From the F<u>o</u>rmat menu, choose <u>S</u>tyle.

2. Select the style that you want to delete from the <u>S</u>tyles list.

3. Click <u>D</u>elete (refer back to Figure 6.4).

4. Word asks whether you wish to delete the selected style.

5. Choose <u>Y</u>es to delete the style, or <u>N</u>o to leave the style in the document.

NOTE

Deleting a style deletes the style from the current document only. If you wish to remove a style from a template, you must either open the template and delete the style from within the open template, or click Organizer in the Style dialog box (see the next section, "Copying Styles," for information about using the Organizer).

Deleting a style that is in use in a document or template will cause all text formatted with the deleted style to change to Normal style.

6. Click Close to close the Style dialog box.

COPYING STYLES

Sometimes you need to copy styles from one template to another. This is helpful if you have a template containing styles that would be appropriate in other templates that you are creating. You can use the Organizer to copy styles from one template (or document) to another. For more information about creating templates, see Chapter 10.

Copying styles from one template to another is an extremely useful feature for law firms. Imagine the convenience of having templates for several courts in numerous states and districts. Because most of the styles will be the same in each pleading, it's useful to be able to copy styles from one pleading template to another.

You can also copy styles between documents by using Word's Copy and Paste commands.

COPY STYLES FROM ONE TEMPLATE TO ANOTHER

1. From the Format menu, choose Style.

2. Click Organizer (refer back to Figure 6.4). The Organizer dialog box appears, with the Styles tab activated. Figure 6.8 shows the Organizer dialog box.

3. Open the template that you want to copy from and the template that you want to copy to. To do this, click one of the Close File buttons to close the associated template. Then, click Open File to open the desired template.

4. Select the style that you want to copy.

TIP

To select multiple styles, hold down the Ctrl key and click each of the styles that you want to copy.

5. Click Copy to copy the styles to the other template.

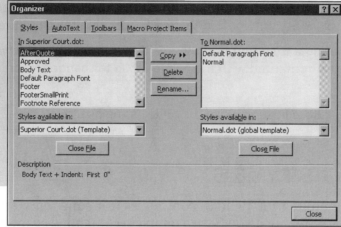

FIGURE 6.8

Use the Organizer dialog box to quickly copy styles between templates and documents.

6. Click Close to close the Organizer dialog box, or open another template and continue to copy styles.

7. You may be prompted to save changes to one or more of the templates. Click Yes to save the changes, or No to reset the template.

COPY STYLES FROM ONE DOCUMENT TO ANOTHER USING COPY AND PASTE

1. Select some text in the document that contains the style you wish to copy. Make certain that the text you select is formatted with the style you wish to copy (for more information about copying text, see Chapter 2).

TIP

When you copy paragraph styles, copying the paragraph symbol along with the text is important. The paragraph symbol holds the formatting codes associated with the current style. If you copy text without including the paragraph symbol, the text is pasted with Normal style.

2. From the Edit menu, choose Copy.

3. Create or open the other document. If the other document is already open, use the Window menu to activate it.

4. From the Edit menu, choose Paste to paste the copied text into the other document. The document now contains the style that was applied to the copied text.

If you copy style-formatted text to a new document and include the paragraph mark, the paragraph style is automatically added to the document.

What happens if you copy text formatted with a specific paragraph style into a document that contains a style with the same name? The pasted text takes on the formatting of the style in the destination document. Think of this rule as "the destination document always wins."

This is a great feature if your templates use the same style names. For example, you may have a paragraph of text in a memo that you would like to paste into a pleading. If both of the paragraphs use a style called Body Text, you don't have to worry about reformatting. When you copy the Body Text paragraph from the memo and paste it into the pleading, the paragraph takes on the formatting of the Body Text style as it is defined in the pleading.

RENAMING AND REPLACING STYLES

Sometimes you may need to rename existing styles to make a document or template compatible with other documents in the firm. For example, you may share documents with another firm that uses different style names. You can rename their styles, or you can create aliases to make their style names match yours.

You can rename only user-defined styles, but you can create an *alias* for a built-in style to make the name compatible with an existing document, or to make the name easier to type. For example, you might create an alias of BT for Body Text style. This makes it a little faster to apply the style using the keyboard. With the alias, you can press Ctrl+Shift+S to place the insertion point in the Style box, and then type BT instead of Body Text to apply the style.

Aliases can also be very handy if you are comfortable with a certain set of style names and open a client's document that uses different names for similar styles. Rather than rename the styles, you can create an alias of their style with your style names. For example, maybe the client uses a Quote style to indent both sides of a paragraph and you call that same format Block Indent. You could create an alias called Block Indent for their Quote style.

Creating aliases makes the system easier to use for keyboard users and reduces the opportunity for users to make typos when they enter style names. Because styles can be created by example, making a typo when you enter a style name will create a new style. For more information about creating styles by example, see the "Create a Paragraph Style by Example" exercise that appeared earlier in this chapter.

You can also use Word's Replace feature to replace one style with another throughout a document.

RENAME A USER-DEFINED STYLE

1. From the Format menu, choose Style.
2. In the list that appears, select the style that you want to rename. If necessary, refer back to Figure 6.4 for an example of the Style dialog box.
3. Click Modify. If necessary, refer to Figure 6.7 for an example of the Modify Style dialog box.
4. In the Name box, type the new name for the style. If you wish to rename the style in the template as well as in the document, select the Add To Template option.
5. Click OK and then click Close to close the Style dialog box. The style is renamed throughout the document.

TIP

Remember that you can rename only user-defined styles. If you want to rename a built-in style, you must create an alias. If you try to rename a built-in style, Word will create an alias for that style rather than change its name (see the following exercise, "Create an Alias for a Built-In or User-Defined Style").

CREATE AN ALIAS FOR A BUILT-IN OR USER-DEFINED STYLE

1. From the Format menu, choose Style.
2. Select the style to which you will assign the alias.
3. Click Modify.
4. In the Name box, type a comma after the style name and then type the new alias for the style (see Figure 6.9).
5. Click OK. The style name appears in the Styles list with the original name followed by a comma and then the new alias.

FIGURE 6.9

Use a comma in the Name box to define an alias for an existing style.

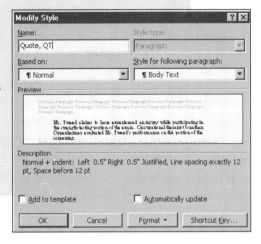

6. To apply the style, press Ctrl+Shift+S and type either the original name or the alias.

REPLACE A STYLE

1. From the Edit menu, choose Replace. The Find and Replace dialog box appears (for information about Find and Replace, see Chapter 2).

2. Click More in the Find and Replace dialog box (if the extended dialog box is not already displayed).

3. Delete any text appearing in the Find What box.

4. Click Format and then choose Style. The Find Style dialog box appears (see Figure 6.10).

FIGURE 6.10

Select a style in the Find Style dialog box when you replace a style using Find and Replace.

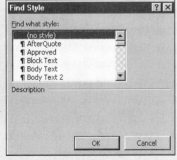

5. Select the style that you want to replace. Click OK.

6. Move to the Replace With box. You can move there by pressing the Tab key, or by clicking inside the box with the mouse. Delete any existing text in this box.

7. Click F**o**rmat and then choose S**t**yle. The Find Style dialog box appears (see Figure 6.10).

8. Select the style that you want to apply. Click OK.

9. Click R**e**place or Replace A**ll** to replace the old style with the new one that you have selected.

NOTE Keep in mind that the next time you perform a Find or Replace, the style format will still be active in the Find and Replace dialog box. To clear this setting, in the Find and Replace dialog box, click F**o**rmat, and then click S**t**yle. Then select "(no style)" from the F**i**nd what Style list in the Find Style dialog box.

To quickly clear all formatting options in the Find and Replace dialog box, click No Formatting. You will need to clear options one time for Fi**n**d What and a second time for Replace W**i**th (the insertion point must be in the box that you wish to clear when you click No Forma**tt**ing).

RESETTING STYLES

Sometimes you need to apply manual formatting to text and it no longer matches the applied style attributes. For example, you might apply italics to a heading style that is normally only bold. You can quickly reset formatting for text and paragraphs using two shortcuts. Table 6.2 lists the shortcuts.

TABLE 6.2 SHORTCUTS FOR RESETTING STYLES

TO RESET . . .	SELECT THE TEXT AND PRESS . . .	ACTION
Paragraphs	Ctrl+Q	This key command removes all manually applied paragraph formatting, such as indents, tabs, and margin settings.
Characters	Ctrl+Spacebar	This key command removes all manually applied character formatting, such as bold, italics, and underline.

USING BUILT-IN STYLE SHORTCUTS

Word comes with several predefined keyboard shortcuts for built-in styles.

You can also assign your own keyboard shortcuts to any of the built-in or user-defined styles that do not already have keyboard shortcuts assigned to them (for information about assigning your own keyboard shortcuts, see the "Creating Styles for Legal Documents" section earlier in this chapter).

Table 6.3 lists the predefined keyboard shortcuts for built-in styles.

Table 6.4 lists the shortcuts you can use to demote and promote heading levels. Continue to press the key combination until you obtain the desired heading level.

TABLE 6.3 STYLE SHORTCUTS

TO APPLY THIS STYLE . . .	PRESS . . .
Normal	Ctrl+Shift+N
Heading 1	Alt+Ctrl+1
Heading 2	Alt+Ctrl+2
Heading 3	Alt+Ctrl+3
List Bullet	Ctrl+Shift+L

TABLE 6.4 PROMOTE AND DEMOTE SHORTCUTS

TO . . .	PRESS . . .
Promote to the next higher heading style level	Alt+Shift+Right Arrow
Demote to the next lower heading style level	Alt+Shift+Left Arrow

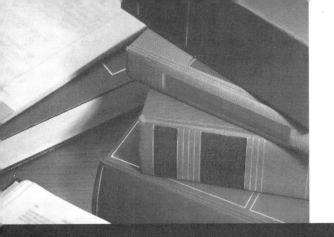

CHAPTER 7

USING TABLES IN LEGAL DOCUMENTS

IN THIS CHAPTER

- ◆ Creating a table
- ◆ Using table tools in Microsoft Word
- ◆ Entering data into a Word table
- ◆ Selecting and manipulating tables
- ◆ Formatting tables
- ◆ Working with table headings
- ◆ Using math in tables

Legal documents use tables in more places than you might imagine. Tables are used in captions for pleadings and briefs, in signature blocks, and in place of parallel columns. Tables can also be used in other legal documents such as damages charts, offering statements and holdings lists, as well as to keep track of documents during discovery. Don't worry: even if you don't use these types of documents, Word's tables feature lets you create documents that keep information organized, correctly aligned, and presentable.

The fax cover sheet appearing in Figure 7.1 shows one example of how you can use tables in documents that don't present arrays of tabular data.

A Word table closely resembles a table in Excel or Lotus 1-2-3, in which columns and rows intersect to create cells. Each cell can contain text, numbers, or even pictures. You can format information in cells just as you can any other text in Microsoft Word.

FIVE WAYS TO CREATE A TABLE

Word provides at least five methods for inserting a table into a document, but the result is the same no matter which method you choose: you get a table. Each method and the reason for using the method are described in this section. As you'll see, Method 5 seems

FIGURE 7.1

Use tables any time you need to line up information.

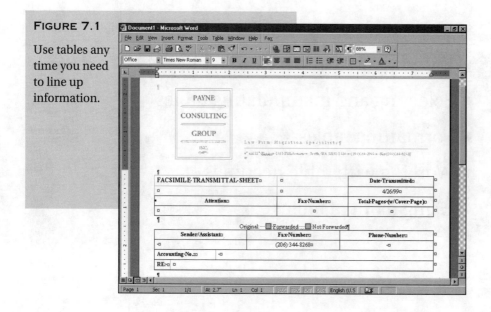

the most fun, but it is also very powerful in the creation of custom tables to fit unique document needs. You can build tables from scratch or you can build on the structure of existing text.

METHOD 1: INSERT FROM A MENU COMMAND

A fail-proof way to insert a table is to place the insertion point where you want the table to appear. From the Table menu, choose Insert, and then choose Table. You will see the Insert Table dialog box, which is shown in Figure 7.2. Word asks you to select how many columns and rows you want in the table, and how you want the table formatted. You are also given the option to save these choices as defaults for any new table you create. This method is great for creating large tables.

CREATE A TABLE USING A MENU COMMAND

1. Create a new document.
2. From the Table menu, choose Insert.
3. Select Table.
4. Specify two rows and two columns, and then click OK. That's how simple creating a table within a Word document is.

NOTE

The maximum number of columns in Microsoft Word 2000 is 63.

FIGURE 7.2

The Insert Table dialog box enables you to define the size of the table.

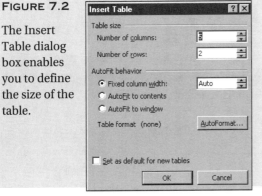

METHOD 2: USE THE INSERT TABLE BUTTON

The Insert Table button on the Standard toolbar is a shortcut for creating a table. When you click this button, you see a grid that represents the number of rows and columns in a table. Drag the mouse pointer across the grid to select the number of columns in the table, and then drag the mouse pointer down to select the number of rows in the table. When you release the mouse—presto! You have the table. Figure 7.3 shows the expanded Insert Table button.

USE THE INSERT TABLE BUTTON

1. Create a new document.
2. Click the Insert Table button on the Standard toolbar.
3. Drag the mouse pointer across three cells and down one cell. This represents a three-column, two-row table.

NOTE

When the Table grid initially appears, it is only five columns wide and four columns deep. For a larger grid, drag the mouse pointer past the borders of the grid.

4. Release the mouse button to insert the table.

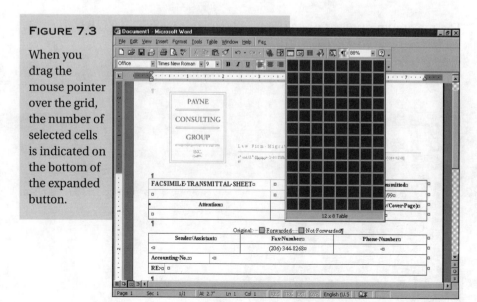

FIGURE 7.3

When you drag the mouse pointer over the grid, the number of selected cells is indicated on the bottom of the expanded button.

METHOD 3: COPY THE TABLE FROM ANOTHER APPLICATION

Why reinvent the wheel if you don't have to? Word integrates well with other applications, even non-Microsoft products. If the table exists in another application, try to copy and paste it into Word.

COPY A TABLE FROM ANOTHER APPLICATION

1. Open Word, and then open the other application and the file that contains the table.
2. Copy the table from the source file.
3. Press Alt+Tab to switch back to Word. You can do this to move through any open applications.
4. From the Edit menu, choose Paste.

TIP

The keyboard shortcut for pasting is Ctrl+V.

METHOD 4: CONVERT TEXT TO A TABLE

You may already have a document filled with information that you would like to put into a table to provide a clean format. Think of those reports downloaded from mainframe-based programs, accounting or financial reports, and lists of addresses that already exist. These files can have information jumbled together or separated by commas, tabs, spaces, paragraph marks, or other characters. These documents are prime candidates for conversion into Word tables because tables can distribute information into separate cells, making them easier to read.

CONVERT TEXT TO TABLE

1. Type the following information, using tabs (indicated by [Tab]) rather than spaces to separate items and pressing Enter at the end of each line.

    Date[Tab]Client/Matter[Tab]Document

    9/12/99[Tab]100/1[Tab]Motion to Appeal

    9/24/99[Tab]100/2[Tab]Certificate of Service

FIGURE 7.4

FIGURE 7.4

Word sepa-
rates informa-
tion into
columns
based on the
characters
used to sepa-
rate the text.

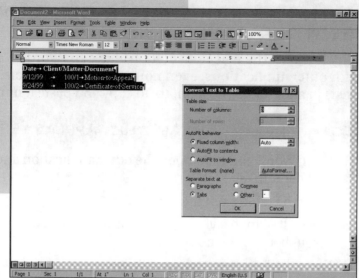

2. Select all the text entered in Step 1.

3. From the Table menu, choose Convert.

4. Select Text To Table. The Convert Text to Table dialog box
   appears. Figure 7.4 shows the selected text and the Convert
   Text to Table dialog box.

5. Word should determine that the table needs to be three
   columns and that the existing text is separated by tabs. If it
   doesn't, in the Separate Text At section, select Tabs. Word will
   know that the text is in three columns after Tabs is selected.

6. Click OK.

7. Click anywhere within the table, and then from the Table
   menu, choose Select Table.

SORTING A CONVERTED TABLE

You can sort lists of text, numbers, or dates in Word. If you receive
information that needs to be sorted but is not formatted in a way
that makes sorting possible, consider turning the information into a
table. For example, say that you need to sort a list of names by last
name, but the text was entered as first name followed by last name.

When you convert the text to a table, you can sort by last name easily. Although you can sort lists that aren't organized in tables, you can do so faster and easier when they are in tables.

SEPARATE FIRST AND LAST NAME

1. On a blank line in a document, type the following pressing Enter after each name:

    John Marshall

    Thurgood Marshall

    William Taft

    Salmon Chase

    Antonin Scalia

    William Rehnquist

2. Select the six names.

3. From the Table menu, choose Convert.

4. Select Text To Table.

5. Word guesses *incorrectly* how many columns to use until you specify how the text is separated. Locate the Separate Text At section of the dialog box and then click in the box to the right of Other.

6. Delete any character that appears in the Other box and then press the Spacebar. This tells Word to separate the text after it detects a space.

7. Click OK to create the table.

8. From the Table menu, choose Sort. Figure 7.5 shows the Sort dialog box.

9. Sort by Column 2 (last name) and click OK.

TIP

If the tables have column headings, when you choose Sort, instead of seeing Column 1 and Column 2, you will see the name of each column. In this example, a good heading for Column 1 is "First Name" and for Column 2, "Last Name." You can create column headings by inserting a row at the top of the table and formatting it as a heading. You will learn how to do both these tasks later in this chapter.

FIGURE 7.5

The Sort dialog box lets you sort by up to three criteria at a time.

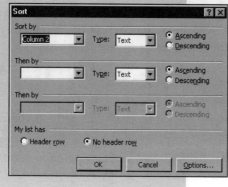

NOTE

If you use column headers, make sure to format them differently from the text so that Word can determine where the header stops and the body of the table begins. If Word doesn't recognize the table headings, you can indicate that a header row exists. In the Sort dialog box, select Header Row in the My List Has section.

METHOD 5: DRAW TABLE

If you look on the Standard toolbar, you'll see a button with a pencil held over a line in a table. Unlike many toolbar buttons, this one gives you an entire toolbar, the Tables and Borders toolbar, in the Word window. The first toolbar button is activated when the toolbar first appears. You can also activate this command from the Table menu by choosing Draw Table, or by alternate-clicking just about anywhere in the document window.

DRAW A WORD TABLE

1. Click the Tables And Borders button on the Standard toolbar.

NOTE

If you are in Normal view, Word switches to Print Layout view when you click the Tables And Borders button.

2. Move the mouse pointer over a blank area in the document. The mouse pointer changes to a pencil.

3. Drag the mouse pointer diagonally to draw a square the size of the table that you want to create, then release the mouse button.

4. Drag the mouse pointer from the top of the box to the bottom of the box to divide the box into two columns.

5. Drag the mouse pointer from the left edge of the box to the right edge of the box to divide the table into two rows.

6. Create more cells by clicking and dragging the mouse pointer within the table.

NOTE

In Word 2000, you can draw diagonal lines in your tables. For more information on this feature, see the "Draw a Table with a Nonstandard Layout" exercise in the next section.

7. When you finish drawing, you can get out of drawing mode by clicking the first button on the Tables and Borders toolbar or double-clicking the mouse anywhere in the document outside of the table, or you can just press Esc on the keyboard.

8. Close any open documents without saving.

The next section teaches you more about how to use some of the buttons on the Tables and Borders toolbar.

TIP

There's a nifty and little known keyboard shortcut that you can use to create a one row table quickly. On a blank line, type +-----+-----+-----+ (this will give you three columns) and press Enter. If the typing does not change into a table, from the Tools menu, choose AutoCorrect, select the AutoFormat As You Type tab and check the Tables check box. Click OK to close the dialog box.

THE TABLES AND BORDERS TOOLBAR

Microsoft created the Tables and Borders toolbar with 18 of the functions that you're likeliest to want to use with a table. To see what each one does, hold the mouse pointer over each button and read the ScreenTip that appears with the button's name. If a ScreenTip does not appear, this feature may not be turned on. From the Tools menu, choose Customize, and then select the Options tab. Select Show ScreenTips on toolbars, and click OK to close the dialog box. Figure 7.6 shows the Tables and Borders toolbar.

Table 7.1 provides a brief overview of the function of each button on the toolbar.

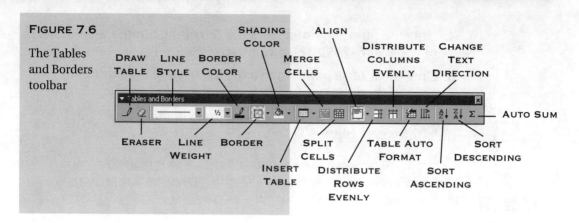

FIGURE 7.6

The Tables
and Borders
toolbar

TABLE 7.1 RESOURCES OF THE TABLES AND BORDERS TOOLBAR

BUTTON NAME	DESCRIPTION
Draw Table	Lets you draw a table in the document.
Eraser	Erases the cell lines and merges adjacent cells that were separated by the lines.
Line Style	Adds a border style to the lines of the table.
Line Weight	Changes the thickness of the line.
Border Color	Adds color for the border of the table.
Border	Gives you several border alternatives for the table on a drop-down list.
Shading Color	Fills active cells with a color that is selected in the list.
Insert Table	Gives you a menu of choices for inserting a table or individual rows, columns, or cells.
Merge Cells	Merges any selected cells into one cell.
Split Cells	Splits a cell into multiple columns or rows.
Align	Lets you choose from nine different alignments for the text within the table both vertically and horizontally.
Distribute Rows Evenly	Changes the selected rows to equivalent row heights.
Distribute Columns Evenly	Changes the selected columns to equivalent column widths.
Table AutoFormat	Opens the AutoFormat dialog box, with options for applying built-in formatting styles to the active table.
Change Text Direction	Changes the direction of the text in the active cells.

BUTTON NAME	DESCRIPTION
Sort Ascending	Sorts the table in ascending order.
Sort Descending	Sorts the table in descending order.
AutoSum	Inserts an =(Formula) field that calculates and displays the sum of the values in the table cells above or to the left of the cell containing the insertion point.

The following exercises show you how to use most of the tools on this toolbar. For more information on the function of these buttons, see Word's help or try them on your own.

DRAW A TABLE WITH A NONSTANDARD LAYOUT

1. Create a new Word document.

2. On the Standard toolbar, click the Tables And Borders button.

3. Draw a table approximately four inches wide by three inches tall. If the rulers are not visible, from the View menu, choose Ruler.

4. Drag the mouse pointer down the center of the box to split the table into two columns.

5. Create two rows in the table by dragging the mouse pointer to draw a horizontal line from one side of the table to the other.

6. Click in the first cell of the table.

7. Drag the mouse pointer from the bottom left corner of this cell to the top right corner to draw a diagonal line.

NOTE The diagonal drawing feature is new in Word 2000. It doesn't truly split your cell into two cells the way drawing a horizontal or vertical line does. You will need to use the Click and Type feature to type text anywhere in the divided cell. For more information see "Using Click and Type" in Chapter 2.

8. Divide the table into more rows and columns.

9. Click in a cell and type information if you want. Figure 7.7 shows a drawn sample table.

FIGURE 7.7

Use the Tables and Borders toolbar to create nonstandard table structures.

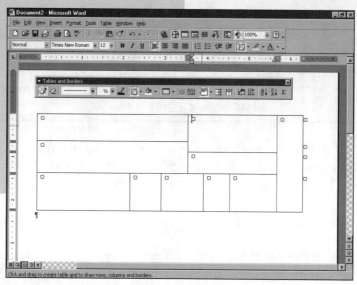

USE THE ERASER TOOL

1. Click the Eraser button on the Tables and Borders toolbar. When you rest the mouse pointer over a line in the table without clicking the mouse, the pointer is the shape of an eraser.

2. Trace any interior line from one side of the table to the other by dragging along the line until the line disappears. That's how simple this tool is to use.

NOTE

When you erase a line that separates two cells, the two cells merge into one cell. If you erase an outside line or a line that does not separate two cells, the border is erased but you will still see the gridline. Gridlines do not print. If you do not want to see the gridlines while you work, from the Table menu, choose Hide Gridlines.

CHANGE THE LINE STYLE AND WEIGHT

1. Click the arrow next to the Line Style button and select a thicker line style.

2. Drag the mouse pointer along the top outside border of the table to change the line style.

3. Change the Line Weight button to a different line width, and then drag the mouse pointer along the bottom outside border of the table to change the line weight.

NOTE

You can also apply the new line style, weight, and color using the Border button. See the upcoming exercises for more information on this technique.

CHANGE THE BORDER COLOR

1. Click the Border Color button to open the color palette, and click the desired border color.

2. Drag along the outside border of the table to change the line color.

CHANGE THE BORDER

1. Select the cells to which you want to apply the border. To select the entire table, from the Table menu, choose Select, and then choose Table.

TIP

Sometimes it is difficult to select a cell if there is no text in the cell. Click at the left edge of the cell to select the entire cell. You will see a thick black arrow when your mouse pointer is in the correct location. To select multiple cells, click and drag across the cells. Or, click in the table and then from the Table menu, choose one of the Select commands.

2. Click the drop-down arrow to the right of the Border button. (The button's name will change depending on which border style was selected last.) A palette of different borders will appear.

TIP

If you want this palette to be a toolbar all to itself, you can click the title bar of the border palette and drag it to a new location.

3. Select the type of border that you want to apply to the selected cells.

SHADE SELECTED CELLS

1. Select one or multiple cells within the table.
2. Click the arrow to the right of the Shading Color button to see colors available for shading the cell.
3. Select a color by clicking it with the mouse.

MERGE TWO CELLS

1. Select two cells in the table.
2. Click the Merge Cells button. The command is also available on the Table menu or by alternate-clicking the selected cells.

SPLIT CELLS

1. Click in one cell within the table.

NOTE

To select a single cell, you do not need to highlight it. If you place the insertion point within a cell and click, that cell is automatically selected.

2. Click the Split Cells button. The command is also available on the Table menu.
3. Specify how many columns and rows you want to create.
4. Click OK.

ENTER AND ROTATE TEXT

1. Type **City** in any cell within the table.
2. Click the Change Text Direction button to rotate the text. In addition to the button on the Tables and Borders toolbar, the Text Direction command can be accessed from the Format menu.
3. Click the same button two more times to have the text change direction again.
4. Close the document without saving it.

The other buttons on the Table and Borders toolbar will be discussed later in this section.

TEXT ENTRY AND TABLE NAVIGATION

To add text to any cell, click in the cell and start typing. When you finish entering text in a cell, move to the next cell by pressing movement keys on the keyboard or by using the mouse. Table 7.2 shows the quickest way to move around in a table by using keyboard shortcuts.

NOTE

To set a tab inside of a table cell, press Ctrl+Tab.

In Word 2000, table columns are set to automatically resize to fit text or graphics. This is a great feature when you add new columns because the table width stays the same and your columns do not fall off the page, as in previous versions of Word. Further, when you

TABLE 7.2   TABLE NAVIGATION SHORTCUTS

KEYS	NAVIGATION
Tab	Move to the next cell
Shift+Tab	Move to the previous cell
Alt+Home	Move to the first cell in a row
Alt+End	Move to the last cell in a row
Alt+Page Up	Move to the first cell in a column
Alt+Page Down	Move to the last cell in a column
Shift+Left Arrow or Right Arrow	Select character by character in the current cell, and then select the entire adjacent cell
Shift+Up Arrow or Down Arrow	Select text row by row in the current cell, and then select the entire adjacent cell
F8+Up Arrow or Down Arrow	Select the current cell and the cell above or below (press the Esc key to end the selection)
F8+ Left Arrow or Right Arrow	Select the characters in the current cell and then all adjacent cells (press the Esc key to end the selection)
Alt+5 (numeric keyboard)	Select the entire table; the Num Lock key must be turned off

type, if your text is longer than the width of a column, the column automatically becomes larger to accommodate the text. If you do not want the column width to change automatically, make sure the insertion point is in the table, and then open the Table menu and choose Table Properties. On the Table tab, click Options and clear the check box next to Automatically Resize To Fit Contents.

MODIFYING TABLE STRUCTURE

It's a snap to change the layout of a table after it has been created. Whether you want to add a row or column, change the size of a cell or entire table, or change the formatting, you can accomplish this in several quick and easy ways.

The new Table Properties dialog box gives you the ability to change properties of individual cells, rows, columns, or the entire table with ease.

WORKING WITH CELLS

Word tables have default text options set to have the text align at the top of the cell and the column width automatically change to fit the amount of text. For complex tables, however, you want more control of the individual cell properties within the table.

Using the drop-down list of choices on the Tables and Borders toolbar, you can align your text both horizontally and vertically in a cell. Table Properties lets you make the text size change to fit the cell rather than the cell change to fit the text.

ALIGN THE TEXT

1. Draw a new table with four columns and four rows.
2. Type text in a cell in the first column.
3. Select the cell that you typed in.
4. On the Tables and Border toolbar, click the drop-down arrow to the right of the Alignment button. (The button's name changes depending on the last alignment option chosen).
5. Select the type of alignment that you want to apply to the selected cell.
6. Leave this table open for the next exercise.

USE FIT TEXT

1. Click in a cell in the last row.
2. From the Table menu, choose Table Properties.
3. Select the Cell tab.
4. Click Options.
5. Check the option for Fit Text.
6. Click OK to accept this change.
7. Click OK to exit the Table Properties dialog box.
8. Type **http://www.payneconsulting.com/**.

The font size does not change when you use the Fit Text feature. Word adjusts the character spacing instead.

When you click inside a cell that has the Fit Text option turned on, you will see a thick turquoise line under the text. This line does not print, rather, it's a visual indication that Fit Text is enabled.

WORKING WITH ROWS

When you are working in a table and you come to the end of the table, you often need to add a new row. To do this, press the Tab key while you are in the last cell, and Word inserts a new row. It's that easy!

Word 2000 provides new options for inserting rows between existing rows of data: whether to insert above or below the existing row. To insert a row, from the Table menu, choose Insert. You can then choose to insert the row above or below the current row. You can also alternate-click or use the Tables and Borders toolbar button method to insert rows.

The following exercises show you how to add and delete rows in a table.

ADD A ROW TO THE END OF A TABLE

1. Create a new Word document and insert a table with two columns and two rows.

2. In the first cell of the first column, type **Office**. Press the Tab key to move to the next cell, and then type **Staff Needed**.

3. Press the Tab key to move to the next cell in the table.

4. Type **San Francisco** and then press the Tab key.

5. Type **14**.

6. Press the Tab key to add a row to the end of the table.

INSERT A ROW BETWEEN EXISTING ROWS

1. Click in the cell where you just typed "14."

2. Alternate-click and choose Insert Rows to insert a row above the active row.

3. With a row selected, from the Table menu, choose Insert, and then Rows Below. Word 2000 allows you to choose where the new row should go.

TIP

If you want to insert multiple rows in a table, first select the number of rows that you want to insert. If you have three rows selected, Word will insert three new rows when you insert rows.

DELETE A ROW

Unfortunately, you cannot simply press Delete on the keyboard to delete table rows. If you've tried it, you know what we mean. Instead, first select the rows you want to delete and then from the Table menu, choose Delete and then choose Rows. You can also alternate-click the selected row and then choose the Delete Rows command from the shortcut menu.

DELETE ROWS IN A TABLE

1. Move the mouse pointer without clicking to the left of the left border of the table until you see an arrow pointing to the table. This area of the document is referred to as the Selection bar.

2. While the mouse pointer is an arrow, drag it to select the adjacent table rows.

3. From the Table menu, choose Delete.

4. Select <u>R</u>ows.

5. Press the Undo toolbar button, or from the <u>E</u>dit menu, choose <u>U</u>ndo Delete, to restore the deleted rows.

6. Select the entire row.

7. Alternate-click the selection and then choose <u>D</u>elete Rows from the shortcut menu.

CHANGING THE HEIGHT OF A ROW

The easiest way to change the height of a row is to place the mouse pointer over one of the rows until you see a double-sided arrow that points both up and down. This is called a *sizing pointer*. Drag the mouse to increase or decrease the size of the row. If you prefer, you can set exactly how high the row should be by first selecting it, and then from the T<u>a</u>ble menu, choosing Table P<u>r</u>operties. The Row Height setting is controlled on the Row tab.

NOTE

The sizing pointer for row height can only be accessed in the Web Layout and Print Layout views.

KEEPING ROWS TOGETHER ACROSS PAGES

If you have a large amount of information in one cell, the cell may split across two pages. The default for Word tables is to allow rows to break across pages, but you can turn this setting off.

KEEP A ROW TOGETHER

1. Insert a table with two columns and 65 rows.

2. Click in the last cell on the first page. Type several sentences of text until the text splits onto the second page. (Switch to Print Layout view to see the pages).

3. From the T<u>a</u>ble menu, choose Table P<u>r</u>operties.

4. Select the <u>R</u>ow tab.

5. Clear the Allow Row To Brea<u>k</u> Across Pages option.

6. Click OK.

To prevent page breaks from being inserted within any of the rows in a table, select the entire table (from the Table menu, choose Select, and then choose Table) and then clear the option to allow rows to break across pages. If you add new rows to the table after clearing this option, the new rows will also have this formatting applied.

The option to allow rows to break across pages is a formatting setting. If you clear this format for the last row of a table and then insert additional rows at the end of the table, the new rows will also have this option cleared.

WORKING WITH COLUMNS

In Word tables, you work with columns the same way that you work with rows. To select a column, hold down the Alt key and click anywhere within the column that you want to select. Mouse users can choose Select Column from the Table menu to select the column in which the insertion point is currently located.

After you have selected one column, you can hold down the Shift key and press Left Arrow or Right Arrow on the keyboard to extend the selection.

ADD A COLUMN

1. Select a column within the table.
2. From the Table menu, choose Insert.
3. Select the Columns To The Right option to add a column to the right of the active column.

If you alternate-click a column to insert another column, Word does not give you the option to insert the column on the left or right of the selected column. It always inserts the column to the left.

DELETE A COLUMN USING ALTERNATE-CLICK

1. Select a column in the table.
2. Alternate-click the selected column and then choose Delete Columns from the shortcut menu.

You cannot use the alternate-click method when the table has only one column.

CHANGING THE WIDTH OF A COLUMN

There are three ways to change the column width of a table:

- ◆ Drag the border of the table.
- ◆ Drag the column marker on the ruler.
- ◆ From the Table menu, choose Table Properties. Select the Column tab.
- ◆ Double-click the column boundary on the right side to expand the column to AutoFit the longest string of text in the cell.

Be aware that you can affect the overall layout of the table by dragging with the mouse.

Hold the Alt key while dragging to get exact measurements of the column widths displayed on the ruler.

An example of a document that might have three different column sizes within a table is a pleading caption.

CREATE A PLEADING CAPTION

1. Create a new Word document and press Enter several times to give yourself some room at the top of the document.
2. Insert a table with three columns and one row.
3. From the Table menu, select the middle column and choose Table Properties.
4. From the Table Properties dialog box, select the Column tab. Set the Preferred Width of Column 2 to 0.09".
5. Click Previous Column to select the first column of the table. Set the Preferred Width of Column 1 to 3.31".
6. Click Next Column twice to select the third column of the table. Set the Preferred Width of Column 3 to 3".
7. Click OK to close the dialog box.
8. Click in Column 2 and press the) key (the close parenthesis) and the Enter key on the keyboard 10 times.

Many firms no longer use parentheses (sometimes called *scallops* in this context) for pleading borders; instead, they create a two-column table for the caption and use table borders to apply straight-line borders to the caption.

9. From the Format menu, remove the borders of the table by choosing Borders and Shading. Select the Borders tab and then in the Settings section, select None. Keyboard shortcut users can press Alt+Ctrl+U.

Even when the borders are removed from the table, gray gridlines will appear on the screen. The gridlines do not print, but they will help orient you when you are working in a table. If you do not see the gridlines, from the Table menu, choose Show Gridlines to display them.

Figure 7.8 shows a generic pleading caption. Columns 1 and 2 contain fields plaintiff and defendant as well as other information specific to the case. A table border separates the two columns in the caption. You'll learn how to use fields in legal documents in Chapter 11, "Creating Legal Forms." Chapter 10, "Creating Legal Templates," shows you how to create a pleading template.

FIGURE 7.8

Pleading captions are just one type of legal document that uses tables.

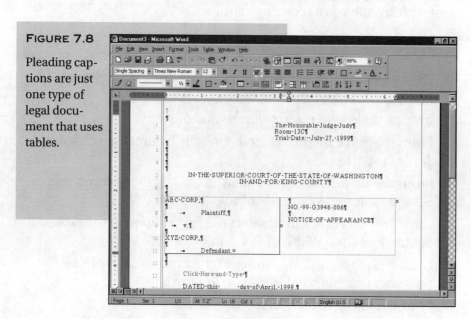

WORKING WITH THE ENTIRE TABLE

When you work in tables in a legal environment, there will undoubtedly be times when you need to change the look of the entire table. Word 2000 has added easy options to resize the table, customize the AutoFit options, or move the table to a new location in your document.

TABLE MOVE HANDLE

The Table Move Handle is a quick and easy method to select a table or move one to a new location.

Rest your mouse pointer over the table without clicking until you see the table move handle on the upper-left corner of the table. The handle looks like a four-way arrow in a square, as shown in Figure 7.9.

MOVE A TABLE

1. Create a new Word document and insert a table with three columns and five rows.

2. Type some text under the table and press Enter several times.

3. Rest your mouse pointer over the table until the move handle appears.

FIGURE 7.9

Table move handle

TABLE MOVE HANDLE

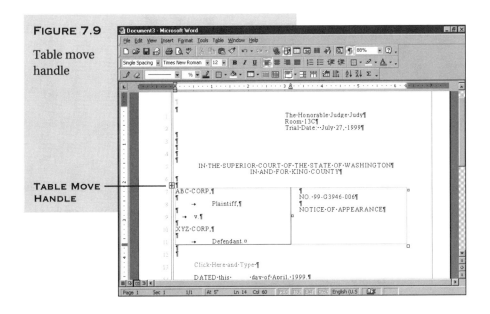

4. Click and hold the move handle.

5. Drag the table under the text.

TABLE RESIZE HANDLE

You can resize an individual column or row as shown earlier in the sections on working with columns and rows. But what if you need to change the size of the entire table? Word 2000 gives you a resize handle in the bottom-right corner of the table that allows you to do just that.

RESIZE A TABLE

1. Create a new Word document and insert a table with four columns and eight rows.

2. Rest your mouse pointer over the table until you see the table resize handle on the lower-right corner of the table, as shown in Figure 7.10.

3. Drag the resize handle until the table is a little larger.

4. Close the document without saving.

FIGURE 7.10

The Table Resize handle lets you change the size of an entire table.

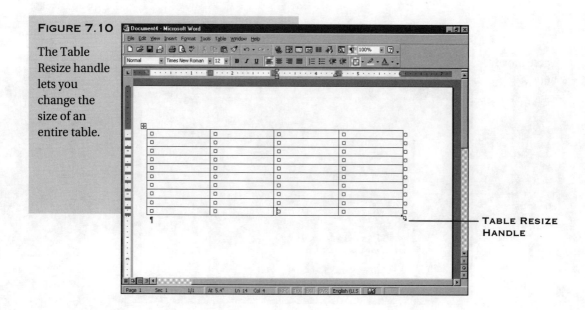

TABLE RESIZE HANDLE

NOTE

The Table Resize and Table Move handles only appear in Print Layout and Web Layout views. For more information on available views in Word, see "Viewing a Document" in Chapter 2.

SPLIT TABLE

If you need to split the table into two separate tables, move the mouse pointer to the cell within the row where the new table should begin. From the Table menu, choose Split Table. The table is divided in two and the insertion pointer is in the row that separates the table. Keyboard users can press Ctrl+Shift+Enter to split a table.

TABLE PROPERTIES

If you've worked with tables in either Word or WordPerfect before, you've probably been impressed with the functionality tables offer, but maybe you've also wished that you could do certain other things like quickly changing a table's width or getting text to wrap around the table as if it were a graphic. With the Table Properties feature, you can do these things and more! The Table Properties dialog box also allows you to adjust the amount of space between your cells and set your cell margins to prevent your text from clinging too close to the top or bottom of the cell.

MANIPULATE TABLE WIDTH

1. Create a new Word document and insert a table with three columns and five rows.
2. From the File menu, choose Page Setup.
3. On the Paper Size tab, choose Landscape. For more information on page setup, see Chapter 5.
4. Click OK. Notice that your table width does not change.
5. Click in the table.
6. From the Table menu, choose Table Properties.
7. Type **10** in the Preferred Width field.
8. Click OK.
9. Close the document without saving.

APPLY TEXT WRAPPING

1. Create a new Word document and draw a small table with two columns and three rows.

2. Ensure that Show/Hide is turned on to see paragraph marks.

3. From the Table menu, choose Table Properties and select the Table tab.

4. Under Text Wrapping choose Around.

5. Click OK. Notice the paragraph mark is now positioned to the right of the table.

6. Click beside the paragraph mark and type in some text. Continue to type text until it wraps under the table.

7. Close the document without saving.

Hold down the Ctrl key when drawing your table to automatically apply text wrapping to your table.

NESTED TABLES

New to Word 2000 is the ability to *nest* tables. *Nesting* is a term used to refer to similar objects that can live inside each other. Basically, you put a table inside another table. Have you ever found yourself wanting to put a great deal of detail in a table, only to give up and make a whole new table? If so, nested tables may be your solution.

Click in the cell where you want to insert your nested table and create a new table. For more information on creating a new table see the section titled "Five Ways to Create a Table" earlier in this chapter.

INSERT A NESTED TABLE

1. Create a new Word document and insert a table with two columns and four rows.

2. In the first row, type **Name** in the first column and **Expense** in the second column.

3. In the second row, type **Daniel Thomas** in column 1 and press Tab to get to Column 2.

4. From the Table menu, choose Insert.

5. Select Table.

6. Choose four columns and two rows. Click OK.

7. In your new table, type **Type, Jan., Feb.,** and **Mar.** in the columns of the first row.

8. In the second row, type **Meals, 125.50, 135.60,** and **127.80** in the columns of the second row.

9. Close the document without saving.

FORMATTING TABLES

The purpose of tables is to organize information and make it easier to read. You can also jazz up your tables by adding some formatting.

AUTOFORMAT

If you want something a bit more impressive than a bold column header or underlined words, you can use Word's Table AutoFormat feature to access built-in formatting that Word can apply instantly.

You can access Table AutoFormat in three ways: from the Table menu, through the Table AutoFormat button on the Tables and Borders toolbar, or by alternate-clicking a table. When you choose Table AutoFormat, the AutoFormat dialog box shown in Figure 7.11 appears. This dialog box lists a group of predefined table formats that you can apply to the selected table (the Preview area shows you what the selected format looks like).

TIP
You can customize the AutoFormats by selecting or clearing the options in the Formats To Apply or the Apply Special Formats To section. For example, if you like the Grid 8 format and need special formatting for the Totals row, select Last Row in the Apply Special Formats To section option.

HEADINGS

When you work with large tables that span several pages, you generally have a heading at the top of the table that you'll want to repeat at the top of every page. This feature in Word is called Heading Rows Repeat and is found on the Table menu.

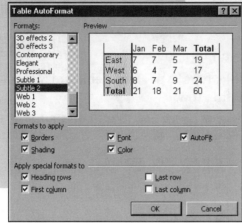

FIGURE 7.11

Word has 42 predefined formats that you can apply to tables.

You can see repeated headings only when you use Print Layout view.

If you insert a manual page break with a table, Word does not repeat the heading.

REPEAT HEADING ROWS IN A LARGE TABLE

1. Create a new Word document.

2. Insert a 2-column, 200-row table.

3. Click in the first cell of the table and type **Client Name**. Press the Tab key to move to the next column.

4. Type **Client/Matter #** and press the Tab key.

5. Select the first row of the table where you entered the information.

6. From the Table menu, choose Heading Rows Repeat.

7. Click the Print Preview button on the Standard toolbar and note how the headings repeat on subsequent pages.

8. Close Print Preview by pressing the Esc key.

9. Close the document without saving.

You can have more than one row selected as a heading; however, you must include the first row of the table in the selection.

PERFORM CALCULATIONS IN TABLES

You can do all sorts of math in Word tables, from simple addition to advanced functions. The fastest way to get a sum is to click in a cell adjacent to the numbers that you want to add and then move the mouse pointer to the Tables and Borders toolbar and click the AutoSum button. More advanced functions such as average, count, and number formatting require you to choose Formula from the Table menu.

ADD NUMBERS TOGETHER USING AUTOSUM

1. Create a new Word document.
2. From the Table menu, choose Insert Table.
3. Make a table that has one column and three rows.
4. In the first cell, type **655**. Press the Tab key to move to the second row.
5. In the second cell, type **815**. Press the Tab key.
6. Click in the third cell and activate the Tables and Borders toolbar.
7. Click the AutoSum button to add the two numbers together.
8. Close the document without saving it.

The AutoSum button is great for quick and simple math. For more complex calculations, you'll need to create formulas. Formulas are covered later in this section.

If you need to do a lot of math, you might consider inserting a Microsoft Excel worksheet into the Word document or using Excel. To insert an Excel worksheet into a Word document, click the Insert Microsoft Excel Worksheet toolbar button on the Standard toolbar. Double-click to activate the Excel worksheet. Now you have the full functionality of Excel without leaving the Word window. See Chapter 16, "Integrating Word with Other Office Applications" for more information on using Word and Excel together.

USE FORMULAS IN A TABLE

1. Create a table with two rows and three columns, and then type the numbers **6** and **15** in the first two cells of the first row and **7** and **12** in the first two cells of the second row.

2. Click in the third column, first row. Make sure that the Tables and Borders toolbar is showing.

3. Click the AutoSum button on the Tables and Borders toolbar. Word calculates the sum of the cells to the left and puts the sum into the table. This number is a calculated field and may appear shaded.

NOTE If you have any blank cells in the rows or columns that you are calculating, Word adds the cells above or to the left of the formula until it reaches a blank cell. This is a great way to use subtotals in a table. If you want to add all of the cells in a row or column, type a zero in each blank cell.

4. Change the number 6 in the first cell to **106**.

NOTE Calculations in Word tables do not update automatically. If you are using tables with many calculations, consider inserting *text form fields* that will calculate on exit. See Chapter 11, "Creating Legal Forms," for more information. See Chapter 16, "Integrating Word with Other Office Applications," for more information on using Excel for calculations.

5. Click in the cell that contains the calculation and click the AutoSum button again to update the formula, or press the F9 key.

6. Click the cell below the calculation.

7. From the Table menu, choose Formula. Notice that Word assumes that you want to sum the numbers above the insertion point. Delete the text that appears in the Formula box.

8. In the Formula box, type **=sum(left)** and then press Enter.

TIP To update a calculation, click the calculated field and press F9. To toggle between the field code and the value data, select the field code and press Shift+F9. If you have trouble remembering these keyboard shortcuts, you can always alternate-click a formula and then choose <u>U</u>pdate Field or choose <u>T</u>oggle Field Codes from the shortcut menu.

9. Add a new row to the bottom of the table by pressing the Tab key in the last cell of the table.

10. Click in the first cell in the last row. From the T<u>a</u>ble menu, choose F<u>o</u>rmula.

11. Word assumes that you want to add the numbers above the current cell. Delete "sum(above)" in the <u>F</u>ormula box, and let the equal sign (=) remain.

12. Click the arrow next to the Paste F<u>u</u>nction box and select PRODUCT.

13. Type **ABOVE** between the parentheses in the <u>F</u>ormula box. The result will be a calculation multiplying the cells above the insertion point.

The formulas in a Word table can be formatted as currency, percentages, decimal points, or other formats. In the Formula dialog box, select a <u>N</u>umber Format from the list of available formats.

Numbers typed as text in the table cannot be formatted with percentages, decimals, or currency through a Word command. Of course, you can type dollar signs, percent signs, or decimal points when you enter the numbers. Consider inserting an Excel worksheet in a document if number formatting is important, or if the table needs to contain a large number of complex calculations.

BOOKMARK CALCULATIONS

If you are calculating cells within a table, inserting formulas is fairly simple. If you want to calculate values from cells in different tables, however, you need to use a bookmark and apply a calculation using the bookmark.

A bookmark is simply a named range that you can use for either navigation or calculations.

USE BOOKMARKS TO CREATE CALCULATIONS

1. Create three tables:
   - One column, three rows, with the numbers **1215** and **310** in the first two cells and the formula **=sum(above)** in the third cell.
   - One column, three rows, with the numbers **90** and **850** in the first two cells and the formula **=sum(above)** in the third cell.
   - One column, one row. Leave this table blank for the present.

2. Select the last cell in the first table, and then from the Insert menu, choose Bookmark.

3. Type **Table1Total** in the Bookmark Name box. Click the Add button.

4. Select the field in the third row of the second table and from the Insert menu, choose Bookmark.

5. Type **Table2Total** in the Bookmark Name box and click the Add button.

6. In the third table, from the Table menu, choose Formula.

7. Select SUM from the Paste Function list.

8. Click the Paste Bookmark arrow and choose "TableTotal1."

9. Type a comma (,), click the Paste Bookmark arrow, and choose "TableTotal2." Your formula should look like this: "=SUM(Table1Total,Table2Total)."

10. Click OK.

ALIGNING DECIMALS IN A TABLE

Any time that you have figures with decimals in a table, you will want to set decimal tabs to align the numbers in the table. Make certain that you choose only to align numbers with decimal tabs, as opposed to text.

ALIGN FIGURES AROUND THE DECIMAL POINT

1. Insert a table with three columns and four rows.

2. In the first cell in the first column, type **Attorney** as that column's header and press the Tab key; type **Billable Hours** as the

second column header and press the Tab key; type **Total Dollars** as the third column header and press the Tab key.

3. Type attorney names in the Attorney column and numbers in the Billable Hours and Total Dollars columns. Use the same format for each number (if you use commas in one cell, use commas in the other cells, too). Include decimal points in the numbers you type.

4. Add a new row to the table by pressing Tab in the last cell of the table.

5. Type **Total** in the first column of the last row and then press Tab.

6. Click the AutoSum button on the Tables and Borders toolbar to total the Billable Hours column, and then press Tab.

7. Click the AutoSum button on the Tables and Borders toolbar to total the Total Dollars column.

8. Select the numbers in the Total Dollars column and set a decimal tab in the column. To set a decimal tab, click the Tab Alignment box until the Decimal Tab marker appears; then, click the ruler to set the tab. For more information about tabs, see Chapter 3.

Do not select columns with text when setting a decimal tab. Because text has no decimals, Word will assume that the decimal is at the end of the text. This will cause the text to be out of alignment with the numbers in the cells. To align text, use paragraph alignment or another type of tab.

Do not set a decimal tab in a column that has been centered or right-aligned. If you do so, the numbers may not align correctly on the decimal. Select the numbers and press Ctrl+L to left-align the cells before setting the decimal tab.

You do not have to press the Tab key to get numbers in cells to line up on the decimal tab. Pressing the Tab key moves the insertion point to an adjacent cell. If you use another type of tab in a table cell, such as a center tab or a right tab, press Ctrl+Tab to move the insertion point to the tab stop within the cell.

ANSWERING COMMON TABLE QUESTIONS

Although using tables in Word is fairly straightforward, there are a few additional tips, tricks, and cautions that you'll want to know.

How do I get text above my table?

If you insert a table at the beginning of a document and later want to insert a line before the table, click in the first cell of the table and press Enter. This adds a line before the table begins.

How do I change the default for tables to insert them without borders?

Word 2000 enables you to set your default table options including number of rows or columns, AutoFit control, and formatting choices.

In the AutoFormat dialog, you can choose not to have borders applied to your new table. The following exercise demonstrates how this works.

CHANGE TABLE DEFAULTS

1. From the Table menu, choose Insert, and then choose Table. The Insert Table dialog box appears.

2. Choose how many rows and columns you would like.

3. Click AutoFormat.

4. Clear Borders in the Formats To Apply section.

5. Click OK.

6. Select Set As Default For New Tables option, as shown in Figure 7.12.

7. Click OK to save these defaults and insert the table.

8. Start a new Word document.

9. From the Table menu, select Insert and then select Table. Notice that your new defaults have been applied.

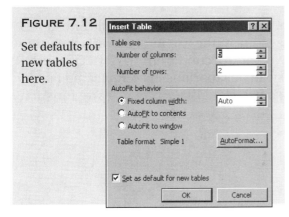

FIGURE 7.12

Set defaults for new tables here.

Why is my table getting cut off at the bottom of the page?

Text wrapping is the main reason for a table not spanning more than one page. Text wrapping is a great feature that allows you to put text right beside your table without using a text box. If your table is longer than one page, however, you must remove text wrapping. To do this, click in the table. From the Table menu, choose Table Properties. In the Table tab, under Text wrapping click None.

How can I center my table on the page without centering all the text in its cells?

If you don't have the entire table selected prior to centering, you will center the text rather than the entire table. To center a table without centering the text inside, make sure you have the entire table selected (from the Table menu, choose Select, and then choose Table), and then click your Center button on the Formatting toolbar. Voilá!

How can I perform mathematical functions on noncontiguous cells in my table?

If you have cells that don't touch each other but you still want to do table math, never fear. The cells in Word 2000 tables have secret numbers assigned to them that you already know if you've used a spreadsheet program before. If you count your table columns starting at the left side, they are referred to as columns A, B, C, and so on, just like in Excel. As you've guessed by now, rows work just like Excel, too: row 1, 2, 3, and so on.

Armed with this knowledge you can now create complex formulas like =sum(a1,b2) to add the value in the top left cell with the value in the cell second from the top and second from the left. Of course, counting rows and columns can be laborious in complicated tables, but you're probably using a program like Excel already for such things. Right?

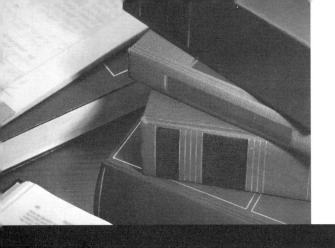

CHAPTER 8

SPELLING AND GRAMMAR

IN THIS CHAPTER

- ◆ Automatic spelling and grammar checking

- ◆ Spelling and Grammar dialog box

- ◆ Using the AutoCorrect feature with spelling

- ◆ Working with multiple languages

- ◆ Creating and using a custom dictionary

- ◆ Creating and saving an exclude dictionary

- ◆ Using thesaurus, hyphenation, and change case tools

Nothing says poor quality like a document filled with spelling and grammar errors. No need to worry: Word includes a set of powerful spelling and grammar checking tools to help you create a good impression by catching these errors before the client does.

Word 2000 also supports multilingual spelling and grammar checking. This feature is great if your firm has international offices or shares information with clients in different countries. You can use multiple languages in one document and have Word automatically check the text for you.

AUTOMATIC SPELLING AND GRAMMAR CHECKING

If, like the authors of this book, you are not a stellar typist, you may find your screen filled with red and green wavy lines beneath words. This is the result of Word's automatic spelling and grammar checking feature. Automatic spelling and grammar checking is turned on by default.

You don't need to do anything special to get this feature to work, just open a document and start typing. Of course, if you don't like the feature, you can always turn it off—but we'll discuss how to do this after you've had a chance to see how useful this feature can be.

CHECK SPELLING AND GRAMMAR ON THE FLY

1. Create a new Word document.

2. Type **Signed and sworn to by each of the affiants above**, and then press Enter. The word *affiants* is not in Word's built-in dictionary, so Word flags it as an incorrect spelling by placing a red wavy line beneath the word.

3. On the next line type **We wants to meet the filing deadline.**, and then press Enter. Grammatical errors are flagged by a wavy green underline.

As you type, perceived spelling errors appear as red wavy lines, and grammatical errors appear with the offending word or phrase underlined with a green wavy line.

NOTE

Word 2000 recognizes the names of countries, United States cities with medium to large size population, and major corporations.

CONTROLLING AUTOMATIC SPELLING AND GRAMMAR CHECKING

Legal documents are filled with long sentences and words that aren't part of everyday speech, which Word's grammar and spelling checkers may not recognize as appropriate to their context. If you have both automatic spelling and grammar turned on, your documents could look like a four-year-old was let loose with two colors of crayons. You can adjust the grammar rules and spelling dictionary to match your style and subject matter, which will reduce the amount of markup; the procedures appear later in this chapter. And if you find the Technicolor effect distracting, you can always turn it off entirely.

From the Tools menu, select Options and then select the Spelling & Grammar tab. This tab is shown in Figure 8.1. To toggle Check Spelling As You Type option on or off, select or clear the adjacent button. To toggle automatic grammar checking on or off, select or clear the option button next to Check Grammar As You Type. The following exercise takes you through the steps to control these settings.

FIGURE 8.1

You can toggle automatic spelling and grammar checking.

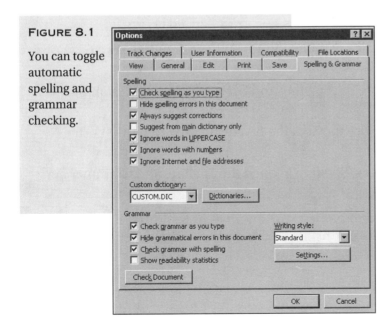

TURN AUTOMATIC SPELLING AND GRAMMAR CHECKING ON OR OFF

1. From the Tools menu, choose Options.

2. Select the Spelling & Grammar tab.

3. To start or stop the automatic spelling checker, select or clear the option button next to Check Spelling As You Type.

4. To start or stop the automatic grammar checker, select or clear the option button next to Check Grammar As You Type.

NOTE If you select automatic spelling or grammar checking, Word turns off the Hide Spelling Errors In This Document and Hide Grammar Errors In This Document check boxes respectively.

5. Turn on Check Spelling As You Type and Check Grammar As You Type, and then click OK.

CORRECT FLAGGED SPELLING AND GRAMMAR ERRORS

There are two great things about automatic spelling and grammar checking: first, the error is visible to you within the document, and second, making the correction is easy.

There are four primary ways to correct flagged errors:

- ◆ Alternate-click with the mouse on the offending word or phrase and select the correct word from the Shortcut menu.

- ◆ Double-click the Spelling and Grammar Status icon on the Status bar.

- ◆ Press Alt+F7 to move to the first error and open the shortcut menu.

- ◆ Choose Tools, Spelling to open the Spelling and Grammar dialog box.

Most people use the first option most of the time. But as with all Microsoft applications, there are multiple ways to accomplish the same thing.

CORRECT DETECTED SPELLING AND GRAMMAR ERRORS

1. Locate the word *affiants* that you typed into the document. If you did not go through the steps in the exercise titled "Check Spelling and Grammar on the Fly," type a misspelled word in a document and press the Spacebar.

2. Alternate-click with the mouse on the misspelled word.

3. Click the Ignore All button on the Spelling and Grammar dialog box.

4. Type the word **doog**.

5. Alternate-click the misspelled word and select "dog" from the shortcut menu.

6. Double-click the Spelling And Grammar Status icon on the Status bar. The icon looks like a book with an "x" or checkmark on the right page.

7. Select the correction if one appears on the shortcut menu.

You can also make the correction directly in the document.

CHECKING SPELLING AND GRAMMAR TOGETHER

Going through each flagged error in a document can be time-consuming, especially in a long document. When you want to check all spelling and grammar at the same time and have everything appear in a neat and tidy dialog box, activate Word's spelling and grammar checker by choosing Tools and then selecting Spelling And Grammar, by clicking the Spelling and Grammar button on the toolbar, or by pressing F7. The result is shown in Figure 8.2.

When Word finds a possible spelling or grammar error, the word or phrase is displayed in the Spelling and Grammar dialog box. You can make the changes in this dialog box or you can edit the error directly in the document and click Resume in the Spelling and Grammar dialog box to continue checking the document.

FIGURE 8.2

All spelling
and grammar
errors will
show up in the
Spelling and
Grammar dia-
log box.

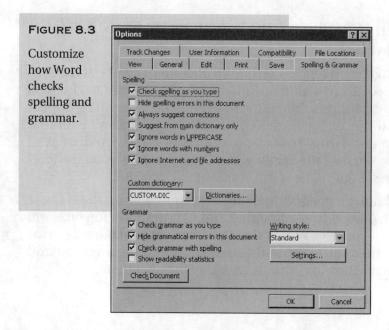

TIP

To check the spelling of hidden text, click the Show/Hide button on
the Standard toolbar and then start the spell checker.

SPELLING AND GRAMMAR OPTIONS

Although Word checks both spelling and grammar by default, if you
prefer to use only one of these tools, you will need to choose Options
from the Tools menu, select the Spelling & Grammar tab, and clear
the option that you wish to turn off. This tab is shown in Figure 8.3.

FIGURE 8.3

Customize
how Word
checks
spelling and
grammar.

There are many options that can be turned on or off to customize spelling and grammar checking to meet your needs.

SPELLING OPTIONS

If you use a mixture of alpha and numeric to create a client matter or other number, chances are you will want to set the option in spelling to ignore words that contain numbers. There are many other useful spelling options that can be customized on the Spelling & Grammar tab in the Options dialog box of the <u>T</u>ools menu. The following are options that can be set that affect spelling:

- **Check spelling as you type.** Enables automatic spell checking. Errors are flagged in the document with a red wavy line beneath the detected spelling error.

- **Hide <u>s</u>pelling errors in this document.** Turns off automatic spell checking.

- **Always suggest corrections.** Controls whether Word offers suggestions for misspelled words. This only controls the use of spelling and grammar checking through the dialog box and does not affect background checking.

- **Suggest from main dictionary only.** Suggests spelling corrections from the main dictionary only and not from any custom dictionaries you may have on your computer. You'll want to clear this option if you have a custom dictionary and wish to use it and the main dictionary during spell checking—a topic addressed later in the chapter.

- **Ignore words in uppercase.** The spelling checker does not detect words in all uppercase if this option is checked.

- **Ignore words with numbers.** The spelling checker does not detect words that contain numbers if this option is checked.

- **Ignore Internet and file addresses.** Check this option to have Word skip Internet, e-mail, and file addresses during a spell check.

- **Custom dictionary**. Although Word has a fairly powerful dictionary, you will want to add familiar words that may not be in Word's dictionary to a custom dictionary of your own. This prevents the word from being flagged as an error when you type it. Words such as your firm name or city that you work in are naturals for addition to a custom dictionary. This feature is covered later in this chapter.

If you edit a custom dictionary, Word turns off the automatic spelling checker. If you want the facility active when you go back to work on your regular document, you will need to return to the Spelling & Grammar tab on the Options dialog box of the Tools menu and reset the option.

If you forget what any option does, click the question mark button on the right side of the title bar and then click the desired option to open a context-sensitive help screen.

If you want Word to skip specific text during a spelling and grammar check, select the text not to be checked, and then select Tools, Language, Set Language. Then select the option Do Not Check Spelling Or Grammar and click OK.

GRAMMAR OPTIONS

Many law firms choose to turn off some grammar checking options before deploying Word to the user. For example, since long sentences are common to legal documents, flagging them as grammar errors may not be desired. The grammar options that are controlled on the Spelling & Grammar tab of the Options dialog box on the Tools menu include:

- **Check grammar as you type.** Enables automatic grammar checking as you type.

- **Hide grammatical errors in this document.** Turns off the display of grammatical errors.

- **Check grammar with spelling.** To check spelling but not grammar, clear this check box.

- **Show readability statistics.** Readability statistics provide information such as the number of words, characters, paragraphs, and sentences in the document. Additionally, Word calculates the average number of sentences per paragraph, words per sentence, and characters per word. Most important, it analyzes the percentage in which passive sentences are used and the grade level that can easily comprehend the text within the document.

FIGURE 8.4

Specify what rules Word should apply when checking grammar.

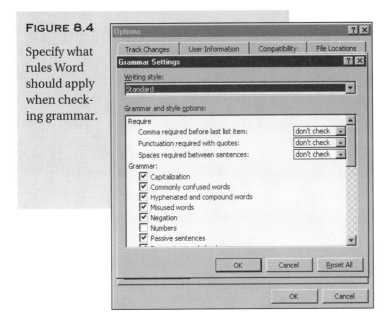

CHOOSING A WRITING STYLE

Legal documents have a more formal writing style than, say, the letters you write to your relatives. When you write a book or manuscript, a technical writing style is preferred. Word has a built-in feature that can adjust the rules to be applied for different writing styles.

Word includes five default writing styles, Casual, Standard, Formal, Technical, and Custom. You can apply one of these writing styles, create a new style, or customize an existing style. To customize a writing style, click the Settings button that appears on the Spelling & Grammar tab. The Grammar Settings dialog box shown in Figure 8.4 lists the different options.

USING AUTOCORRECT WITH SPELLING

When you first start using Word, you may think that your typing has vastly improved. You'll find fewer spelling errors in your document, and all of your sentences will start with capital letters. What's going on here? The AutoCorrect feature available in previous versions of Word has been made even more powerful for Word 2000. This feature corrects the most common typing errors. The AutoCorrect options are shown in Figure 8.5.

FIGURE 8.5

The AutoCorrect dialog box has numerous settings that improve your typing.

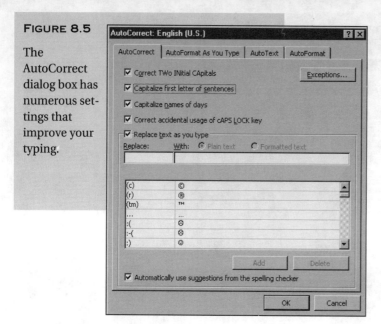

The following list describes the features in AutoCorrect:

- **Correct TWo INitial Capitals.** Corrects two initial capital letters at the beginning of a word. For example, if you type *YEsterday*, Word automatically corrects it to *Yesterday*.

- **Capitalize first letter of sentences.** Capitalizes the first letter of each sentence.

- **Capitalize names of days.** Corrects monday to Monday.

- **Correct Accidental usage of cAPS LOCK key.** Saves you time if you have accidentally pressed the Caps Lock key on your keyboard. As soon as you type *yESTERDAY*, Word corrects it to *Yesterday*.

- **Replace text as you type.** Corrects many common spelling errors. For example, if you type *beleive*, Word changes it to *believe*.

ADD MISSPELLED WORDS TO AUTOCORRECT

One thing that makes AutoCorrect so powerful is the opportunity to add your own characteristic typos and spelling mistakes to the AutoCorrect utility. You can customize AutoCorrect to deal with your specific typing habits and make Word work for you.

One of the easiest ways to use AutoCorrect is by integrating it with the automatic spelling feature. Every time a misspelled word appears on the screen with the red wavy underline, it can quickly be added to the AutoCorrect list.

NOTE To turn on automatic spell checking, choose Options from the Tools menu. Select the Spelling & Grammar tab, and then select Check Spelling As You Type.

ADD A MISSPELLED WORD TO AUTOCORRECT

1. Type **The Esteat of Jane Doe.**
2. The misspelled word *Esteat* shows up with a red wavy underline. Alternate-click the misspelled word.
3. Select AutoCorrect from the shortcut menu.
4. Select "Estate" from the list of suggestions. The misspelled word and its replacement are added to the AutoCorrect list.

Word 2000's AutoCorrect feature is not limited to the predefined list that appears in the AutoCorrect dialog box. Now Word uses the spelling dictionary to correct misspelled words, providing you with thousands of corrections automatically! For this feature to work, automatic spell checking must be turned on.

This feature is activated when Replace Text As You Type and Automatically Use Suggestions From The Spelling Checker are turned on. Both of these features are located on the AutoCorrect tab of the AutoCorrect dialog box. Make sure they are both selected before trying the next exercise.

USE SUGGESTIONS FROM THE SPELLING CHECKER WITH AUTOCORRECT

1. Type **I undrestand your concern.**
2. Notice that Word automatically corrected the misspelled word *undrestand.*
3. From the Tools menu, choose AutoCorrect.
4. Scroll through the list of misspelled words. Notice that *undrestand* is not in the list, yet Word corrected it automatically.

USING AUTOCORRECT TO QUICKLY INSERT TEXT

Another way to use AutoCorrect is to create shortcuts for long or complex phrases that you type often. For example, you might add the name of your firm as an AutoCorrect entry so that you don't have to type the complete name each time it shows up in a document.

ADD A COMMONLY USED PHRASE TO AUTOCORRECT

1. From the <u>T</u>ools menu, choose <u>A</u>utoCorrect.
2. Type **sjr** in the <u>R</u>eplace box.
3. Type **Smith Jones and Reed, PLLC** in the <u>W</u>ith box.

NOTE

You are limited to 255 characters of replacement text in the <u>W</u>ith box.

4. Click the <u>A</u>dd button.
5. Click the Close button.

USE AUTOCORRECT TO INSERT A PHRASE

1. In an open document, type **sjr** (the entry that you created in the preceding exercise).
2. Press the Spacebar. Word inserts the complete firm name.

NOTE

Never use a real word as the code for an AutoCorrect entry. For example, don't use *firm* as the code instead of *sjr*. If you do, then every time you type *firm* in a document, Word will replace it with your firm's name, which will look odd if you're talking about a firm reply or a firm mattress.

ADDING OR DELETING AUTOCORRECT ENTRIES

If AutoCorrect is capitalizing or correcting words and phrases that you do *not* want corrected, you can remove those options from AutoCorrect, and Word will no longer make the changes as you type. For example, the feature that turns (c) into a copyright symbol © is a nuisance for many firms. It's easy to remove unwanted AutoCorrect entries. In fact, if you don't like the idea of Word making any changes in the document without your permission, you can turn AutoCorrect completely off.

REMOVE AN ITEM FROM THE AUTOCORRECT LIST

1. From the <u>T</u>ools menu, choose <u>A</u>utoCorrect.
2. Click the AutoCorrect tab.
3. Locate the entry that replaces (c) with ©. Click the entry once to select it.
4. Click the <u>D</u>elete button to delete the entry.
5. Click Close.

To completely disable AutoCorrect, uncheck all the options listed on the AutoCorrect tab.

Automatic corrections can save writing and editing time because so many common typing mistakes are fixed for you. You may find a few of the automatic corrections in Word 2000 bothersome, however. The following examples relate to the Capitalize First Letter of Sentences feature.

When you are at the end of a letter and you type cc: to denote a carbon copy, Word will correct it to Cc: because it views your typing as the beginning of a sentence. Don't worry, you can quickly fix this problem without turning off the capitalization feature.

EXERCISE: ADD "CC:" AND "BCC:" TO AUTOCORRECT

1. From the <u>T</u>ools menu, choose <u>A</u>utoCorrect.
2. Click the AutoCorrect tab.
3. Type **Cc:** in the <u>R</u>eplace box.
4. Type **cc:** in the <u>W</u>ith box.
5. Click the <u>A</u>dd button.
6. Type **Bcc:** in the <u>R</u>eplace box.
7. Type **bcc:** in the <u>W</u>ith box.

8. Click the Add button.

9. Click the Close button.

AUTOCORRECT EXCEPTIONS

AutoCorrect may also cause problems with some abbreviations. If you type a sentence such as "Harris Ltd. Is my largest client," the *is* becomes capitalized because Word sees the period after "Ltd." and assumes that you are starting a new sentence. If you are addressing a letter to "CNA Insurance," "CNA" becomes "CAN" because Word assumes you are misspelling the word *can*.

You can solve these problems by adding items to the Exceptions list. Figure 8.6 shows the First Letter tab of the Exceptions list. There are three types of exceptions:

- **First Letter.** Add abbreviations to this list if you don't want to capitalize the first letter after the abbreviation. *Ltd.* and *seq.* are some common entries to add.

- **Initial caps.** Add words that are meant to have the first two letters capitalized, such as AEtna.

- **Other exceptions.** Add words that appear to be misspelled that Word is automatically correcting from the spelling dictionary.

TIP

You probably can't think of every abbreviation that you might use that is not included in the Exceptions list. If Word capitalizes a word or makes any other type of correction that you don't want, press Ctrl+Z (the Undo command) immediately following the correction, and Word will restore the word to its original state.

ADD "LTD." TO THE EXCEPTIONS LIST

1. From the Tools menu, choose AutoCorrect.

2. Click the AutoCorrect tab.

3. Click the Exceptions button.

4. Select the First Letter tab.

5. Type **Ltd.** in the Don't Capitalize After box. Click the Add button.

6. Click the OK button and then click the Close button.

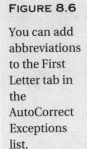

FIGURE 8.6

You can add abbreviations to the First Letter tab in the AutoCorrect Exceptions list.

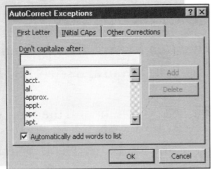

TIP

If you choose the Automatically Add Words To List option in the Exceptions dialog box, Word automatically adds an exception to the list each time you press Backspace and type over the correction.

WORKING WITH A CUSTOM DICTIONARY

Let's say your firm is Pretzelly Amos & Abolderbash. If you don't want to have the first and last words in your firm name flagged as spelling errors, you'll need to add them to a custom dictionary. The process sounds more difficult than it is—in fact, adding words to the custom dictionary is as easy as correcting any type of spelling error. Once you add words to your custom dictionary, they no longer show up as spelling errors.

ADD WORDS TO A CUSTOM DICTIONARY

1. Type **Pretzelly Amos & Abolderbash.**
2. Alternate-click the word *Pretzelly.*
3. Select Add from the shortcut menu.
4. Repeat Steps 3 and 4 for the word *Abolderbash.*

EDITING THE CUSTOM DICTIONARY

If you accidentally add a misspelled word to the custom dictionary, Word 2000 makes it easy to fix your mistake.

EDIT THE CUSTOM DICTIONARY

1. Misspell the word *registration* by typing **regstration**.

2. Alternate-click the misspelled word and select Add from the shortcut menu.

3. From the Tools menu, select Options and then the Spelling & Grammar tab.

4. Click the Dictionaries button.

5. Select the custom dictionary you are using, and click the Edit button.

6. A message appears reminding you to turn on automatic spelling and grammar checking when you have finished editing the custom dictionary. Click OK.

7. The custom dictionary opens. Delete the misspelled word you added in Step 2.

8. Save the document, and then close the file.

NOTE

The number of words that you can have in custom dictionaries in Word 2000 is limited to 10,000. The maximum custom dictionary file size is 366,590 bytes.

CREATE AN EXCLUDE DICTIONARY

You can create an exclude dictionary file that flags certain words as errors, even if they are spelled correctly.

CREATE AN EXCLUDE DICTIONARY

1. Create a new blank document.

2. Type words to include in the exclude dictionary, pressing Enter after each word.

3. From the File menu, choose Save As.

NOTE

In Microsoft Windows 95 or 98, save your exclude dictionary in either the C:\Windows\Application Data\Microsoft\Proof or the C:\Windows\Profiles\UserName\Application Data\Microsoft\Proof folder if you have user profiles enabled. In Windows NT it's C:\Windows\Profiles\UserName Folder. The exclude dictionary is stored in the same folder location as your main dictionary and has an EXC file extension.

4. Change Save As Type to Text Only.

5. Give the file the same name as your main language dictionary it's associated with but with the file extension .exc. The English (United States) dictionary is named Mssp3en.lex so if you are creating an associated exclude dictionary, name the file Mssp3en.exc.

6. Click Save and then click Yes to save the exclude dictionary in Text Only format.

7. From the File menu choose Close to close the exclude dictionary, and then exit out of Word. You will need to restart Microsoft Word to use the exclude dictionary.

RECHECKING THE DOCUMENT

Have you ever used the spelling checker for a document and noticed some misspelled words being skipped? It's possible that some words are marked as "ignored," which means the spelling checker will skip the words. If this is happening to you, don't panic! You can reset the document to have the spelling checker recheck words that were previously set to Ignore.

If you did the preceding exercise, you need to turn automatic spelling and grammar checking back on. From the Tools menu, choose Options and then select the Spelling & Grammar tab. Select Check Spelling As You Type and Check Grammar As You Type, and click OK.

RECHECKING A DOCUMENT

1. Open a document and type some misspelled words or grammatically incorrect sentences.

2. Alternate-click the green or red wavy underlines and select Ignore from the shortcut menu.

3. From the Tools menu, choose Options.

An easy way to access Spelling and Grammar options is to alternate-click the dictionary icon in the Status bar, and then select Options from the shortcut menu.

4. Select the Spelling & Grammar tab.

5. Click the Recheck Document button.

6. Click Yes to continue with the spelling and grammar check, or No to cancel.

7. Click OK.

8. Run a Spelling and Grammar check. Notice that the words you previously marked to Ignore are now being checked.

CHECKING SPELLING AND GRAMMAR IN ANOTHER LANGUAGE

The new multilingual support in Word allows you to have multiple languages in your document and automatically have them checked for spelling and grammar. The English-language version of Office 2000 contains proofing tools for English, Spanish, and French. You will need to purchase proofing tools for other languages from an authorized reseller.

If you're checking French language text, you can have the spelling checker accept and suggest accents for uppercase letters. From the Tools menu, choose Options and select the Edit tab. Select the Allow Accented Uppercase In French option and click OK.

NOTE

You can purchase additional proofing tools from Alki Software at their Web site, http://www.alki.com/.

Once the proofing tools are installed, you need to enable multiple language proofing.

ENABLE MULTIPLE LANGUAGE SUPPORT

NOTE

Before performing this exercise, you must have purchased and installed the proofing tools for the languages you are enabling. Also, you should save and close all files in open applications. The system needs to reboot after enabling multiple language support.

1. Click the Windows Start button.

2. Select Programs.

3. Select Microsoft Office Tools.

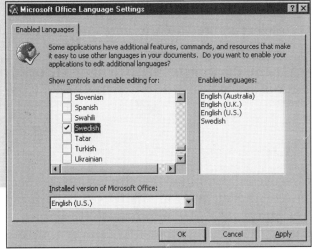

FIGURE 8.7

Turn on multiple language editing for your programs.

4. Select Microsoft Office Language Settings. The dialog box in Figure 8.7 appears.

5. Select the languages for which you have installed proofing tools.

6. Click OK.

7. Click OK again to shut down and restart the computer.

USING THESAURUS AND HYPHENATION

We like the Thesaurus so much that we used to teach our students how to add the Thesaurus command to the text shortcut menu. Having the command on the shortcut menu gave them handy access to the Thesaurus whenever they alternate-clicked any word.

We must not be the only ones who liked this command, because the Synonyms command automatically appears on the text shortcut menu in Word 2000. Now you can quickly get a list of synonyms for any word, and jump into the Thesaurus more easily.

USE THE THESAURUS

1. Type **Isn't this a great feature?**

2. Alternate-click the word *great*.

3. Select Synonyms from the shortcut menu.

4a. Click to select and replace the word *great* with any of the suggested synonyms. Or . . .

4b. Select Thesaurus from the shortcut menu to open the Thesaurus dialog box.

HYPHENATION

Many firms use fully justified text, that is, text spread out to fill the space between the left and right margins. If your firm uses justification, you may want to explore the hyphenation feature. Hyphenating the words in a justified paragraph keeps the document from having too much space between words.

You can manually hyphenate your document, or have Word do it for you automatically. To manually hyphenate text, press the hyphen key on the keyboard at the point where you want the word to split. Or, you can use an optional hyphen. An optional hyphen only prints if the word falls at the end of a line. You can insert an optional hyphen by pressing Ctrl+-, or by choosing an optional hyphen from the Special Characters tab on the Symbol menu.

TURN ON AUTOMATIC HYPHENATION

1. From the Tools menu, choose Language.

2. Select Hyphenation.

3. Select Automatically Hyphenate Document.

4. Select or clear the option Hyphenate Words In CAPS.

5. Increase or decrease the Hyphenation Zone from .25".

NOTE

The hyphenation zone is the amount of white space after the last word on a line and the right margin. Reducing the zone results in more hyphenated words, while increasing the zone results in fewer hyphenated words.

6. Select how many lines in a row can contain hyphens by typing a number in the Limit Consecutive Hyphens To box.

TIP

A good rule of thumb is to have no more than three consecutive hyphenated lines.

7. Click OK.

WORD COUNT

If you write articles or have a restriction on the number of words that you can have in a document, you'll find the Word Count feature in Word 2000 useful. By choosing <u>T</u>ools and then selecting <u>W</u>ord Count, you can display a dialog box that includes statistics such as the number of pages, words, characters (with and without spaces), and paragraphs and lines there are in the document. You can even choose whether or not to count words that appear in footnotes and endnotes. The Word Count dialog box is shown in Figure 8.8.

COUNT THE WORDS IN A DOCUMENT

1. Open a document with footnotes or endnotes.
2. From the <u>T</u>ools menu, choose <u>W</u>ord Count.
3. Notice the number of words. Clear the option to Include <u>F</u>ootnotes And Endnotes. If the document does not contain footnotes or endnotes, this option is unavailable.
4. Click Cancel to close the dialog box.

FIGURE 8.8

Analyze the content of documents from the Word Count dialog box.

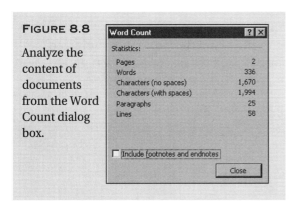

5. Select one paragraph in the document.

6. From the Tools menu, choose Word Count.

7. Notice the difference in the number of words. Click Cancel to close the dialog box.

CHANGING CASE

If you've ever typed a paragraph with the Caps Lock key accidentally pressed, you'll appreciate the Change Case feature in Word. Change Case allows you to select typed text and change the way it was typed.

To change case, first select the text you typed. Then choose Change Case from the Format menu. Select an option, and click OK. The Change Case options shown in Figure 8.9 include:

- **Sentence case** makes the first word of every sentence capitalized.

- **lowercase** makes all of the letters lowercase.

- **UPPERCASE** makes all of the letters uppercase.

- **Title Case** capitalizes the first letter of each word.

- **tOGGLE cASE** changes uppercase to lowercase, and vice versa.

TIP

Pressing Ctrl+F3 toggles between uppercase, lowercase, and sentence case.

CAUTION

Changing case *does not* change the character format for selected text. If you want all of your Heading text to be formatted in uppercase font, select the All Caps effect in the Font dialog box.

FIGURE 8.9

Change the case of selected text.

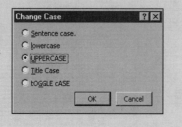

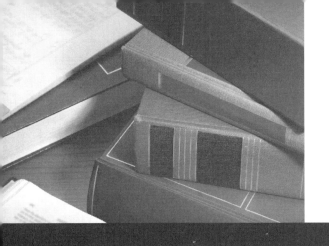

CHAPTER 9

MAIL MERGE

IN THIS CHAPTER

- ◆ Defining Mail Merge
- ◆ The four steps for Mail Merge
- ◆ Editing the data source
- ◆ Sorting and filtering the data source
- ◆ Creating envelopes
- ◆ Creating file folder labels
- ◆ Printing specific pages of a mail merge
- ◆ Using WordPerfect merges in Word
- ◆ Customizing the main document
- ◆ Creating lists with Mail Merge

DEFINING MAIL MERGE

What do you think of when you hear "Mail Merge"? Form letters? Mass mailing? Or even . . . junk mail? Hold that thought. Although Mail Merge *is* a great way to handle mass mailings and form letters, it's also one of the best ways to use your firm's existing database of information. Imagine being able to quickly gather information about all the clients in your firm, publish the results in lists, sort the information, and even merge it into letters, labels, or envelopes! These functions and more are available using Word's Mail Merge feature.

If you need to prepare a form letter, Mail Merge will save you time by eliminating the need to type the same information repeatedly. Mail Merge is a great way to communicate with clients, allowing you to send thank-you letters, invoices, and announcements, and even create mailing labels for holiday cards. If the firm's client information is stored in a database, the Mail Merge process is already halfway complete.

Performing a mail merge is a four-step process:

- ◆ Create or open a main document.
- ◆ Create or specify a data source.
- ◆ Link data source items to specific locations in the main document.
- ◆ Perform the merge.

Word makes Mail Merge easy. Even if you do not have a data source, Word gets you started with a few mouse clicks.

The following sections describe and demonstrate all steps of a mail merge: creating a main document, creating a data source, and merging them into a new document. You will begin a set of merge files in the first exercise and continue to use the same files in subsequent exercises. Following all the steps shows how the entire process is completed.

STEP 1: CREATE THE MAIN DOCUMENT

The first step of the mail merge process begins with the *main document*. Main documents generally contain the information that doesn't change from document to document. Another way of thinking about the main document is that it contains the boilerplate text. For example, the main document for a merge letter would be the body text of the letter.

The main document can be a form letter, mailing label, catalog, or an envelope. The following table lists each option and the results of the final merge.

TABLE 9.1 MAIN DOCUMENT OPTIONS AND RESULT

CHOOSE THIS OPTION . . .	TO CREATE . . .
Form Letters	A merged document consisting of multiple sections. Each section represents one merged document.
	For example, a letter that is merged with 20 addressees will create a merged document consisting of 20 different sections. Each section will contain the body of the letter and different addressee information.
Mailing Labels	A merged document consisting of labels. Don't be misled by the term *mailing*; you can create labels for file folders, floppy disks, name tags, and more. A mailing label merged document contains one record for each label—and as many records on a page as your defined page size allows.
	For example, if you merge address labels for a large mailing, each label will contain information for a different addressee, laid out to print on your label stock.
Envelopes	A merged document consisting of envelopes. Like form letters, envelopes are each created in a separate section within the merged document.
Catalog	A merged document consisting of multiple records on one page. This feature is similar to mailing labels in that multiple records of information appear on the same page. However, you are not limited to a label format.
	This is a great way to create lists or directories of information. For example, you might print a booklet of names and addresses from a contacts database for attorneys to carry with them when they travel.
Restore to Normal Word Document	This option is available only when you choose Mail Merge while you're in a main document. It removes any attached data source and restores the main document to a normal Word document.

CREATING A MAIL MERGE LETTER

One of the best uses of Mail Merge is to send a letter containing the same information to hundreds of people. One example might be letters mailed to all clients when a firm's office location changes or a new office is opened. You can create a main document by using a new blank document, a template, or an existing document.

CREATE A MAIN DOCUMENT

1. From the File menu, choose New and select the Letters & Faxes tab.

2. Select any one of Word's letter templates, or select your own firm's letter template if one exists. Click OK.

3. Customize information in the letter template for your firm. If you are using one of Word's default templates (templates that come with Microsoft Word), select and delete the instructional text in the body of the letter. Add the word "Dear" in the appropriate place for the salutation.

4. Type the following in the body of the letter, pressing Enter twice to put two blank lines between the address and the complimentary closing:

   We have recently moved to a larger, more convenient office location. We are sure this move will help provide better service to you. Please join us at our Open House on June 11th from 4-7 PM.
   Our new address is:
   2400 Imperial Towers
   345 Front Street
   Seattle, WA 98101
   Sincerely,

5. From the Tools menu, choose Mail Merge to open the Mail Merge Helper dialog box.

6. Click Create in the Main Document section. The Create options appear, as shown in Figure 9.1.

6. Select Form Letters from the list.

7. A message box appears, asking whether Word should use the document that is open or create a new document. Click Active Window to use the currently open document.

8. Leave the Mail Merge Helper open for the next exercise.

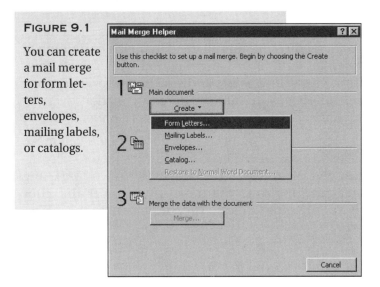

FIGURE 9.1

You can create a mail merge for form letters, envelopes, mailing labels, or catalogs.

STEP 2: SPECIFY THE DATA SOURCE

The second step of the Mail Merge process is to specify a *data source*. The data source contains the information that will be merged with the main document. In contrast to the main document, which contains information that *is common* to all the letters, the data source contains information that *is unique* to each letter. Some information commonly used in a data source is name, address, and company name.

A data source can be a Word document, an Excel spreadsheet, an Access database, or the Outlook or Schedule+ address book or contact list. You can even use documents from other software applications, such as WordPerfect, for the data source. If your firm stores information on a large database, such as SQL Server, Word can grab the information from there as well.

If you are familiar with WordPerfect terminology, Word's main document is the same as WordPerfect's primary file. Word's data source is the same as WordPerfect's secondary file.

CREATE A DATA SOURCE DOCUMENT

Data sources contain two types of information: data fields and data records. Data fields are individual pieces of information, and data records are collections of fields. For example, consider a client database. A data field is a piece of information, such as a last name or a Zip code. A data record contains all the data fields pertaining to one individual client. A data record might contain all of the following data fields: first name, last name, address, and phone number. Data sources are stored as Word tables where the header row contains the different data field names and each row is a data record.

When using Mail Merge, a little planning before you begin can make creating your data source a lot easier. What do you need to accomplish with it? How will the data source be used? Will you be using this information again? Do you want the option to sort and filter your data? These types of questions are very important to the design of your data source.

The more detailed your data, the more sorting, filtering, and creating options you will have. If you are creating the data source, it's a good idea to narrow the field names down to the smallest possible piece of information. For example, rather than using one field called Client, create three fields: Title, First Name, and Last Name. With the information organized in this fashion, you can create a letter that uses Title, First Name, and Last Name in the address line. Then you can reuse the First Name field or the Title and Last Name fields in combination in the salutation of the letter.

CREATE A DATA SOURCE

1. Return to the Mail Merge Helper from the last exercise. If you closed the dialog box, reopen it from the Tools menu by choosing Mail Merge.

2. Click Get Data in the Data section. The Data Source options appear, as shown in Figure 9.2. Several options are available for getting data; they are outlined in Table 9.2.

3. Select Create Data Source. The Create Data Source dialog box appears, as shown in Figure 9.3.

4. Commonly used fields are available in the Field Names In Header Row window. Scroll through the field names and select Country.

5. Click Remove Field Name.

6. Select and remove WorkPhone.

FIGURE 9.2

Create a new data source, open an existing data source, use the Address Book, or specify header options for a data source.

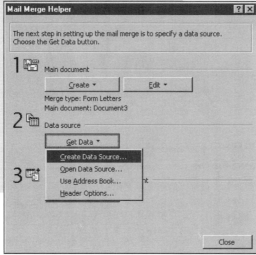

TABLE 9.2 DATA SOURCE OPTIONS

OPTIONS	RESULT
Create Data Source	Word opens a Data Form for you to enter information into the data source.
Open Data Source	Word retrieves existing data from another file.
Use Address Book	Word uses the Outlook Address Book or Contact List to populate the data source.
Header Options	Word identifies the top row that contains field names. The header can be attached to the data source. A header row is optional and is needed only when you attach several different data sources to the main document.

FIGURE 9.3

You can add and delete fields in the Create Data Source dialog box.

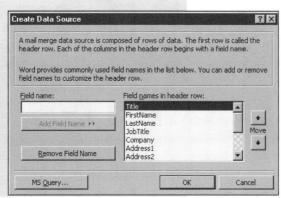

7. Select and remove HomePhone.

As you remove each item, it appears in the Field Name box. If you remove a field by mistake, click Add Field Name to add it back easily.

8. Click in the Field Name box. Delete the text that is currently there.

9. Type **Attorney**.

10. Click Add Field Name.

You can have a total of 63 fields in one data source. Field names must be unique and cannot contain spaces, but you can use underscores to separate words (for example, First_Name).

11. Click OK.

12. The Save As dialog box appears. Type **Client Addresses** in the File Name box and click Save.

13. Word displays a message box with two options available for continuing the merge, as shown in Figure 9.4.

14. Click Edit Data Source to open the Data Form.

15. Leave the data form open for the next exercise.

USING THE DATA FORM

The Data Form provides an easy interface for you to enter your data.

FIGURE 9.4

Word gives you the option to edit either the data source or the main document.

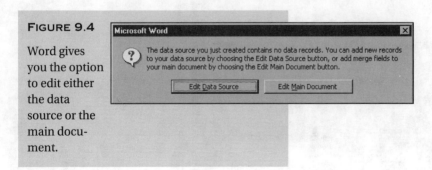

FILL OUT THE DATA FORM

1. Return to the data form from the previous exercise.

2. Figure 9.5 shows an example of a data record. Type the appropriate information into the fields on the Data Form. Press the Tab or Enter key to move between fields.

3. To add a new record, press the Enter key in the last field of the record, or click Add New.

4. Enter the following three records and click OK when you are finished.

> **Mr. Jim Lewison**
> **CEO**
> **The Lewison Group**
> **234 Front Street**
> **Suite 1200**
> **Portland, OR 97204**
> **Jane Attorney**
>
> **Mrs. Sally Johnson**
> **VP Marketing**
> **ABC Company**
> **1234 Fifth Avenue**
> **Suite 1100**
> **Seattle, WA 98101**
> **Jane Attorney**

FIGURE 9.5

Enter client information into the Data Form dialog box.

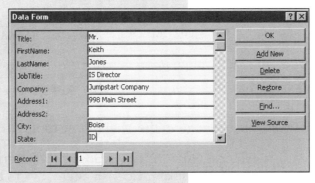

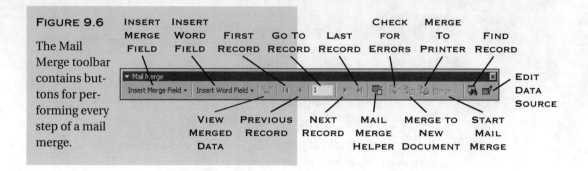

FIGURE 9.6

The Mail Merge toolbar contains buttons for performing every step of a mail merge.

Ms. Betty Potter
Administrator
Empower Industries
220 16th Street
Seattle, WA 98102
Fred Partner

Word returns to the main document. The Mail Merge toolbar is automatically displayed in the main document. See Figure 9.6 for a picture of the Mail Merge toolbar.

STEP 3: INSERTING MERGE FIELDS

Step 1 and Step 2 are now complete! The main document and the data source have been established. Now the merge fields need to be inserted into the main document. The easiest way to insert merge fields into the main document is by using the Mail Merge toolbar.

INSERT MERGE FIELDS IN THE MAIN DOCUMENT

1. Return to the Mail Merge main document.
2. Position the insertion point in the letter where the addressee's name is to be inserted.
3. Click Insert Merge Field on the Mail Merge toolbar. Select Title.

TIP

Keyboard users can press Alt+Shift+F to access the Insert Merge Field dialog box. The dialog box provides an alternative to the toolbar and allows keyboard users to insert merge fields without using a mouse.

4. Press the Spacebar after inserting the Title field.

NOTE

It is important to insert the correct spacing and punctuation when adding merge fields to a document, otherwise when the merge is complete, the text in the fields will run together.

5. Click Insert Merge Field, select FirstName, and then press the Spacebar.

6. Click Insert Merge Field, select LastName, and then press Enter.

7. Continue inserting Mail Merge fields to address the letter. See Figure 9.7 for a picture of a letter with merge fields inserted.

FIGURE 9.7

A main document with merge fields

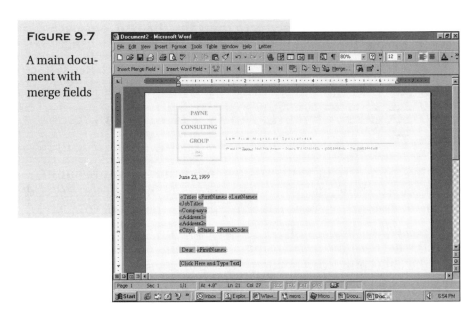

9. Click Insert Merge Field and select Attorney.

10. Continue to edit the letter as needed.

11. To preview the Letter, click View Merged Data (a button with the letters ABC) on the Mail Merge toolbar.

TIP

Previewing merged data is a good way to check for mistakes in the merged document. It's better to make changes before the merge, especially if you have a large number of records to be merged.

12. Click View Merged Data again to view the merge fields.

13. Save the main document as **Mail Merge Letter**. Leave it open for the next exercise.

Merge fields appear in a document with chevrons (<< >>) around each field. If Field Code view is activated, the merge fields appear in field code brackets: { }. Because they are *fields* and not text, merge fields must be inserted by clicking Insert Merge Field or by pressing Alt+Shift+F—you can't just type them in.

Merge fields may appear shaded on the screen. This shading is for display purposes only and does not print. To control the shading, from the Tools menu, choose Options and select the View tab. Select Always or When Selected to show the shading, or select Never to remove the shading from the screen.

STEP 4: MERGE THE DATA WITH THE DOCUMENT

You have completed the three most important steps of your mail merge: creating the main document, creating the data source, and linking them together. Now it is time to see the results of your work.

The last step of the Mail Merge process is to merge the information from the data source into the main document. All the information from the data source can be merged, or you can set query options to merge only selected records. For example, you might want to merge only those addressees that reside in a certain city or state. Query options are discussed later in the chapter.

You can choose to merge your information into a new Word document, send it directly to the printer, or, if your data source contains e-mail addresses, send the merge to the e-mail recipients. In this exercise, you will merge to a new document so that you can view the final result of the merge process.

Even if you plan to print your output, it's best to merge to a new document rather than directly to a printer. This way, you can check the formatting of the document and Merge fields before printing a large number of copies. You can print the merged document when the merge is complete and you have had a chance to review the formatting.

PERFORM A MAIL MERGE

1. Return to the mail merge main document (letter), open from the last exercise.
2. Click Merge To New Document on the Mail Merge toolbar. Keyboard users can press Alt+Shift+N.
3. Use the scroll bar to move through the document and view each of the letters created.

TIP

Notice that each letter is its own section. Word does this to ensure the correct page numbers are on each letter and help you find and print specific letters.

Congratulations! You've finished a mail merge! Word has placed the merged information into a new document named Form Letters1, although you can change that name when you save the document. You can save this document and edit it further or print it right away. When printing, you can print all or specific pages of your new Form Letters1 document. See "Printing Specific Pages" later in the chapter for more information. You can use the same data source to create mailing labels or envelopes—also described later in the chapter.

DATA SOURCE OPTIONS

What if the address of a particular client has changed? If the client information is loaded into a data source, it's easy to open the data source, locate the address, and change it. The next person who creates a letter or envelope for the client won't have to worry about changing the address because the data source will be up to date.

EDITING THE DATA SOURCE

Word provides two ways to update the data source. The first is to open the data source document, find and change the address, and then save the data source. The second is to open the Merge Letter document and then view the data source in a Data Form.

EDIT THE DATA SOURCE THROUGH THE DATA FORM

1. Open the Mail Merge Letter.doc that was created in the last exercise. Make sure you open the main document with the fields, not the merged document, Form Letters1.

2. Click Edit Data Source on the Mail Merge toolbar.

Keyboard users can press Alt+Shift+E to open the Data Form dialog box.

3. If the data source is small, locate the record by using the Previous and Next buttons next to the Record box. If the data source contains numerous records, locate the record by clicking the Find button. The Find in Field dialog box appears, as shown in Figure 9.8.

4. Type **Jones** in the Find What box. Select LastName in the In Field box.

5. Click Find First. After Word locates the record, it displays the record on the Data Form. If it is the correct record, close the Find in Field dialog box. Otherwise, click Find Next until the correct record is located.

6. To edit a record, click in the appropriate field and make the changes. Keyboard users can press the Tab key to move from field to field.

7. To save changes to the data source, click View Source to open the data source. Save the data source and then close it.

FIGURE 9.8

Search for any of the information contained in the data source by using the Find in Field dialog box.

FIGURE 9.9

Word warns
you if a data
source has
been changed
but not saved.

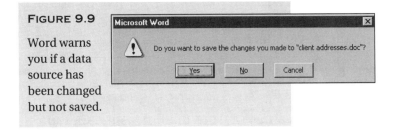

If the data source is not saved, the message shown in Figure 9.9 appears when the main document is closed. Click Yes to save changes to the data source.

NOTE

It's important to understand the difference between making changes in the data source and making changes in the resulting merged document. If changes are made in the resulting merged document, those changes affect that document only. The changes will be gone when the merge is performed again. To make permanent changes, edit the data source rather than the merged document.

ATTACHING A NEW DATA SOURCE

Once you have become a Mail Merge expert, you can set up a number of main documents and a variety of data sources to choose from. For example, say that last year you created a holiday greeting letter and this year, your data source has changed. Or each attorney may give you his or her data information separately. Rather than redo your entire letter, you can just attach a different data source.

The Mail Merge Helper makes this process very simple.

ATTACH A DIFFERENT DATA SOURCE

1. Open Mail Merge Letter.doc, which was created in the previous exercise.
2. From the Tools menu, choose Mail Merge. The Mail Merge Helper opens.
3. Click Get Data in the Data section.
4. Choose Open Data Source.
5. Open the data source document that you would like to use.

It's that easy. If you perform a merge to a new document, you will see the data from the newly attached data source.

CREATING A DATA SOURCE FROM DELIMITED TEXT

As mentioned earlier, you can use a Word table as your data source or create one using the Data Form. The information could also have been typed as a delimited file. A *delimited file* is a file in which a tab, comma, or some other identifier is placed between the data fields, as in the following examples:

TAB DELIMITED:

Client	Matter	Attorney
100	1	Jane Samuels
100	5	Roger Carlson
200	4	Jeff Williams

COMMA DELIMITED:

Client,Matter,Attorney

100,1,Jane Samuels

100,5,Roger Carlson

200,4,Jeff Williams

CHARACTER DELIMITED:

Client%Matter%Attorney

100%1%Jane Samuels

100%5%Roger Carlson

200%4%Jeff Williams

In delimited files, each record is separated by a return at the end of a line of data.

You might look at the preceding examples and wonder why anyone would create a comma- or character-delimited file, because it is so difficult to read. Some data management applications do not allow you to directly merge stored data into Word 2000. Instead, you must export the information from the data management application into some kind of delimited format so that Word can read the data for the merge. If you have a choice of using anything other than a comma when you export data, choose a character such as a tab or percent sign—safer alternatives because some data records may contain commas within the data. For example, company names such as Harrison, Jones and Rudder or Payne Consulting Group, Inc. contain commas within the company names. These extra commas may confuse Word as to where a string of data begins and ends, causing the data to merge incorrectly.

You can either open or copy the delimited file into Word. Since the fields are usually separated by a unique character (for example, a tab or percent sign) the file can easily be converted into a table format. This makes it ideal as a data source, making it easier to view, read, and sort. For more information about converting delimited text into table format, see Chapter 7, "Using Tables in Legal Documents."

CREATING MAILING LABELS AND ENVELOPES

Now that you know how to use Mail Merge to create a form letter, you can follow the same steps to create mailing labels or envelopes. Which is better? That depends on the number of records in the data source and the type of printer available.

Choose an envelope when you're printing a small number of records, or when you're printing a large number of records and have an automatic envelope feeder available. Choose a mailing label if the envelope is oddly sized or difficult to feed through the printer. No one wants to stand in front of a printer for hours feeding envelopes, so if no automatic envelope feeder is available for the printer, mailing labels can make life a lot easier.

CREATE AN ENVELOPE MERGE

1. Create a new blank document.
2. From the Tools menu, choose Mail Merge to open the Mail Merge Helper dialog box.
3. Click Create in the Main Document section to see the main document options.
4. Select Envelopes.
5. A message box appears, asking whether Word should use the document that is open or create a new document. Click Active Window to use the currently open document.
6. Click Get Data in the Data Source section.

7. Select Open Data Source.

8. Locate and double-click Client Addresses.doc. This is the contact list created earlier in the chapter.

In the preceding example, you created addresses in a data source. If you already have client addresses in an Outlook Address Book or Contact List, select Use Address Book in the Data Source section of the Mail Merge Helper. If your client addresses are located in an address book in another software program, export the addresses to a file and then select Open Data Source in the Data Source section of the Mail Merge Helper.

9. Click Set Up Main Document. The Envelope Options dialog box appears, as shown in Figure 9.10.

10. Select the correct size from the Envelope Size drop-down list.

11. Click OK. The Envelope Address dialog box appears.

12. Click Insert Merge field in the Envelope Options dialog box.

13. Select Title and press the Spacebar.

14. Continue inserting the fields necessary for an envelope by clicking Insert Merge Field and selecting the appropriate fields.

Remember to use spaces and punctuation between the fields if you want spaces and punctuation to appear on the envelope.

FIGURE 9.10

Choose the envelope type, address fonts, and printer feed options in the Envelope Options dialog box.

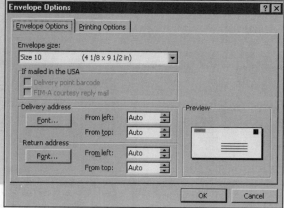

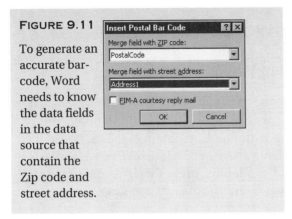

FIGURE 9.11

To generate an accurate bar-code, Word needs to know the data fields in the data source that contain the Zip code and street address.

15. Click Insert Postal Bar Code to insert a barcode. The Insert Postal Bar Code dialog box appears, as shown in Figure 9.11.

16. Select PostalCode in the Merge Field With ZIP code box.

17. Select Address1 in the Merge Field with Street Address Code box, and click OK. A line now appears in the Create Envelope dialog box that reads, "Delivery point barcode will print here!"

NOTE

Placing a barcode on a label or envelope can speed up the delivery of your letter. Barcodes are valid only for addresses within the United States.

18. Click OK when you have finished inserting Merge fields onto the envelope.

19. Click Merge in the Mail Merge Helper. The Merge dialog box appears.

TIP

The Merge dialog box contains an option called Don't Print Blank Lines When Data Fields Are Empty. If a field in the data source is blank, Word will not print a blank line on the envelope. For example, many of the records may not have a second address line, or an entry for Job Title. If the option Don't Print Blank Lines When Data Fields Are Empty is selected, your envelopes will come out perfectly.

20. Click Merge. Word merges the records in the data source with the envelopes and creates a new merged document called Envelopes1 with a different section for each person in the data source.

21. Edit the individual envelopes or the entire document, if necessary

22. Close all of the documents without saving.

The U.S. Postal Service recommends addressing mailing labels or envelopes in uppercase letters with no punctuation (See U.S. Postal Service Publication 221, available from `http://www.usps.gov/`). To quickly change the case of the labels, press Ctrl+A to select all the labels, and from the F̲ormat menu choose Change Cas̲e.

CREATING FILE FOLDER LABELS FROM A PLEADING INDEX

Don't be tricked into thinking that Mail Merge is just for contact information for letters, envelopes, and mailing labels. Anything that you need to create in bulk can be done quickly with a mail merge. For example, you are probably already using Pleading Indexes to keep track of all the documentation for a specific case or cases. When you need to create file folder labels for the client and matter numbers listed in the Pleading Index, Mail Merge can make the process a snap!

In the next exercise, you are going to create a basic Pleading Index and then use that Pleading Index to generate labels.

CREATE A PLEADING INDEX DATA SOURCE

1. Create a new blank document.

2. From the T̲able menu, choose I̲nsert, T̲able. Insert a table that has 4 columns and 4 rows.

3. In the first cell, type **Date** and press Tab, type **Client/Matter** and press Tab, type **Name** and press Tab, and type **Document** and press Tab.

4. Fill in the rest of your table with the following information:

Date	Client/Matter	Name	Document
5/7/99	100-2	ABC Company	Motion to Suppress
6/3/99	100-3	ABC Company	Letter
5/18/99	200-1	Jones, Inc.	Brief

5. Save this document as **Pleading Index**. (Remember the location where you saved it.)

6. Close the document.

NOTE

The data source does not need to be open when you perform a merge. However, you can perform a merge with it open. If your system is low on resources, or if the data source document is extremely large, you may want to close it so that you don't risk running out of system resources.

Now that you have created a Word table, you can use it as a data source. In the preceding exercise, you created a Pleading Index. If you already had a Pleading Index created, you would just need to know where it is stored on your computer or network to be able to use it in your Mail Merge.

In the next exercise, you are going to merge the Client/Matter Column into file folder labels.

USE THE PLEADING INDEX IN THE MERGE

1. Create a new blank document.
2. From the Tools menu, choose Mail Merge to open the Mail Merge Helper dialog box.
3. Click Create in the Main Document section to see the main document options.
4. Select Mailing Labels.
5. A message box appears, asking whether Word should use the document that is open or create a new document. Click Active Window to use the currently open document.
6. Click Get Data in the Data Source section.
7. Choose Open Data Source.
8. Locate and open Pleading Index.doc that was created in a previous exercise.
9. Click Set Up Main Document. The Label Options dialog box appears.
10. Choose the Label Product and Number that corresponds to your labels. (To follow along with this exercise, choose Avery 5066.)
11. Click OK.
12. Click Insert Merge field in the Label Options dialog box.
13. Select the ClientMatter field.

NOTE

Even though your data source has multiple fields, you only use the ones that you need.

14. Click OK.
15. Click <u>M</u>erge in the Mail Merge Helper. The Merge dialog box appears.
16. Click <u>M</u>erge. Word merges the records in the data source with the labels and creates a new merged document called Labels1. Notice that the document is formatted as a table, so you can use the table skills that you learned in Chapter 7 to edit the document.

CAUTION

Do not change the width or size of the cells or table. The table was designed to match the label size that you selected. Changing the dimensions of the table can cause the labels to print incorrectly.

PRINTING A SINGLE LABEL OR ENVELOPE

When you want to print a single label or envelope, you probably won't want to go through all the steps of a Mail Merge. Word has a much easier way to print single labels and envelopes.

PRINT LABELS

1. Create a new blank document.
2. From the <u>T</u>ools menu, choose <u>E</u>nvelopes And Labels.
3. Select the <u>L</u>abels tab.
4. Type the name and address in the <u>A</u>ddress window. If you store addresses in the Outlook address book, click the Address Book icon and locate the desired name and address.
5. Select Delivery Point <u>B</u>arcode to print a barcode on the label.
6. In the Print section, select <u>F</u>ull Page Of The Same Label or Si<u>n</u>gle Label.

TIP

If <u>F</u>ull Page Of The Same Label is selected, you can print the labels by clicking <u>P</u>rint, or add the labels to a new document by clicking New <u>D</u>ocument. Add the labels to a new document if you want to modify the labels by centering the text or changing the case. Many people use this feature to create return address labels.

7. If Single Label is selected, type the Row and Column of the label. Identifying the row and column allows you to print from sheets of labels that have been partially used. Figure 9.12 shows a completed Label dialog box.

8. Click Print to print the labels.

TIP

If you frequently print envelopes and labels, you can add the Envelopes And Labels button to a toolbar, or assign a shortcut key. See Chapter 1 for more information.

Many firms using WordPerfect 5.x have a macro to print envelopes. When your firm switches to Word, you won't need a macro any longer because Word makes it easy to create an envelope.

NOTE

WordPerfect for Windows has its own specialized envelope routines that are very similar to Word.

There are two ways to create envelopes. If you are typing a letter, Word locates the address in the letter and creates an envelope. You can also choose Envelopes And Labels from the Tools menu and type the envelope address in the Envelope dialog box.

FIGURE 9.12

Word can print single labels in specific parts of a page, or entire sheets of labels.

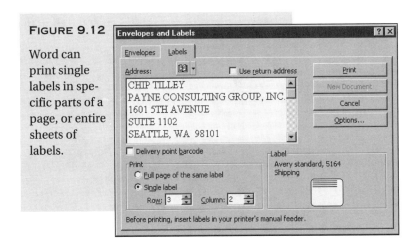

PRINT AN ENVELOPE

1. Open a letter with an address.

2. From the Tools menu, choose Envelopes And Labels. The Envelope and Labels dialog box appears.

3. Select the Envelopes tab.

4. Word locates the address in the letter and displays it in the Delivery Address window, as shown in Figure 9.13.

Sometimes you will need to select the address text in the letter before choosing Envelopes And Labels from the Tools menu. If Word cannot correctly locate the address, or if there are multiple addressees, you will need to select the address in the letter before choosing Envelopes And Labels from the Tools menu.

5. The Return Address window may have a return address displayed. If you are using preprinted envelopes, select Omit so that the return address will not be printed on the envelope.

If no address appears in the Return Address window, no address information is entered into the computer. From the Tools menu, choose Options and select the User Information tab. Type a return address in the Mailing Address box and click OK.

6. Click Options to access additional options. The Envelope Options dialog box appears, as shown in Figure 9.14.

FIGURE 9.13

Identify a delivery address and a return address in the Envelopes and Labels dialog box.

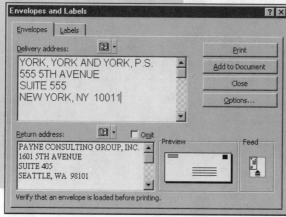

FIGURE 9.14

Several
options are
available for
printing
envelopes.

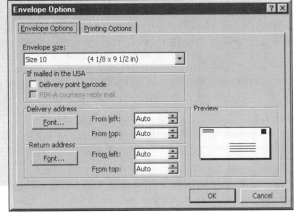

7. Select the type of envelope in the Envelope Size box.

8. Select Delivery Point Barcode or FIM-A Courtesy Reply Mail in the If Mailed In The USA section.

9. Change the font of the delivery address by clicking Font in the Delivery Address section. Change the font of the return address by clicking Font in the Return Address section.

To permanently change the font of the delivery address and return address, open the Normal template and modify the Envelope Address or Envelope Return style. For more information about modifying styles, see Chapter 6, "Styles."

10. Change the placement of the delivery address by changing the From Left or From Top measurements in the Delivery Address section. Change the placement of the return address by changing the From Left or From Top measurements in the Return Address section.

11. Select the Printing Options tab to see the available printing options.

12. Change the orientation of the envelope in the Feed Method section, or change the paper tray in the Feed From section.

13. Click OK.

14. Click Print to print the Envelope, or click Add To Document to place the envelope permanently at the top of the letter.

In the previous exercise, all the envelope options were explored. However, using the default options is usually acceptable. Under most circumstances, printing envelopes is just a two- or three-click process!

If the Add To Document option is selected, an envelope is automatically added to the top of the document. Scroll through the document and notice that the envelope is page zero and the letter begins on page one. To print just the envelope, from the File menu, choose Print and type the number **0** (zero) in the Pages box. To print the letter without the envelope, from the File menu, choose Print and type **1-** in the Pages box. Typing **1-** will print from the first page of text to the end of the document.

QUERY OPTIONS

You have two query choices when performing a merge: sort or filter. Let's say you can use bulk rate postage for mailing to clients in Seattle but have to pay regular postage for your international clients. You can sort your records so the Seattle addresses come out of the printer before the other cities. Or perhaps you do not need to perform a merge for all of the records in the data source. Instead, you can choose specific records in the data source by certain criteria. For example, say your notice of rate increases only affects the clients in a specific state—there's no need to generate copies of the notice for everybody else. This selection process is called *filtering*.

SORTING THE DATA SOURCE

Currently there is really no logical order to your data source. Or maybe it was sorted by client's last name. Now, suppose all the attorneys want to sign their own letters once they are printed. By adjusting the Mail Merge Letter.doc to group all the letters by attorney's name, you can quickly distribute the letters to each attorney. The next exercise shows you how to sort records in a data source.

SORT RECORDS IN A DATA SOURCE

1. Open Mail Merge letter.doc created earlier in the chapter.
2. From the Tools menu, choose Mail Merge. The Mail Merge Helper opens.
3. Click Query Options.

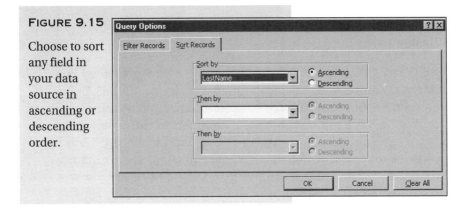

FIGURE 9.15

Choose to sort any field in your data source in ascending or descending order.

4. Select the Sort Records tab. The Query dialog box appears, as shown in Figure 9.15.

5. Choose Attorney in the Sort By field.

TIP

Word gives you up to three keys to sort by. For example, you have more than one attorney with the last name "Smith," your second sort key could be "First Name."

6. Click OK to save your Sort information.

7. Close the Mail Merge Helper.

8. Click the Merge To New Document button on the Mail Merge toolbar.

9. Use the scroll bar to move down through the document and view each of the letters created. Notice that the letters are now in order by Attorney.

10. Close the document without saving. Leave the Mail Merge Letter open.

FILTERING YOUR DATA

Queries are not limited to just changing the order of your data. You can also specify certain criteria that the data must meet in order to be merged. This is very powerful, allowing you to use essentially the same simple procedure if you need to send information to only the clients in one state or you have a letter for a specific attorney's clients. In the next exercise, you'll create a filter that will only merge Seattle clients.

NOTE

Setting Query Options is different from using Microsoft Query in a Mail Merge. You activate Microsoft Query by clicking the MS Query button on the Open Data Source or Create Data Source dialog box. Microsoft Query is a separate program designed to extract information from external databases, such as Excel, Access, or SQL Server. Microsoft Query is not installed with a typical installation of Office 2000. For information about installing and using MS Query, search Word's help for "Use Microsoft Query to retrieve data from an external data source."

SET QUERY OPTIONS

1. Mail Merge Letter.doc should still be open from the last exercise. If it isn't, open it.

2. Click Merge on the Mail Merge toolbar.

3. Click the Query Options button and select the Filter Records tab. The Query Options dialog box appears, as shown in Figure 9.16.

4. Click the drop-down arrow next to the Field box and select City. Windows applications refer to this control as a *drop-down* because when you click it, a list "drops down" to display more options from which to choose.

FIGURE 9.16

Word allows multiple selections in the Query Options dialog box.

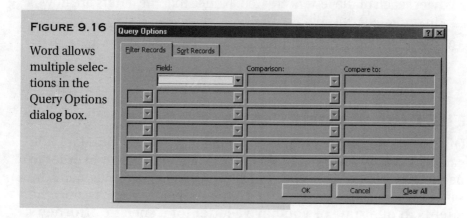

5. Click the drop-down arrow next to the Comparison box and select Equal To.

6. Type Seattle in the Compare To box.

NOTE

The value you type into the Compare To box must match the data source exactly. For example, if you used WA in the state field for Washington in the data source, you must type WA in the Compare To box. If you misspell or select an option that does not exist, Word will give you a message that says no data records exist for your query.

7. Click OK and then click <u>M</u>erge on the Mail Merge Helper.

8. Click <u>M</u>erge in the Merge dialog box to complete the merge.

Word creates a letter for each record that had Seattle as the city, which matched your filter.

NOTE

Every time that Word performs a mail merge from a template, two new documents are created. The main document will be DocumentX and the result of the merge will be Form LettersX, where *X* is a sequential number. The Form Letters document is the document that should be saved, although you can change the name when you do. The main document named DocumentX can be closed without being saved.

PRINTING SPECIFIC PAGES OF A MAIL MERGE

When Word performs a mail merge, it places the merged information in separate sections. If you merge 200 names and addresses into a one-page form letter, Word places each letter in a separate section. Because each individual letter is marked as Page 1, a command to print Page 1 would print all 200 pages of the merge.

So, how do you print just the third, fourth, and sixth letter? You must tell Word to print specific sections of the document. For more information about sections and section printing, see Chapter 5, "Page Setup and Layout."

FIGURE 9.17

You can print specific pages or sections of a merge.

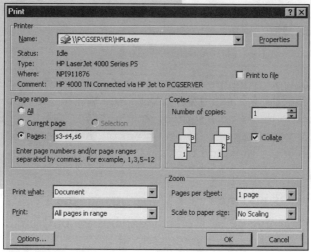

PRINT SPECIFIC SECTIONS OF A MERGE

1. Open a document with several sections of merged data.

2. From the File menu, choose Print. Keyboard users can press Ctrl+P.

3. Type **s3-s4,s6** in the Pages box to print Sections 3, 4, and 6. Figure 9.17 shows the Print dialog box.

TIP

Have you ever printed a large merged document without meaning to? If you need to cancel a print job, double-click the printer icon that appears on the Word Status bar (not the Windows taskbar) while Word is sending the print job to the printer.

4. Click OK to print.

USING WORDPERFECT MERGES IN WORD

If your firm is converting from WordPerfect, there are probably several merged letters you would like to convert. Word easily converts WordPerfect primary and secondary files, so you won't have to follow all the steps outlined earlier in the chapter to set up the merge.

The first step is to open the WordPerfect primary file in Word. From the <u>T</u>ools menu, choose Mail Me<u>r</u>ge and then select Form <u>L</u>etters as the main document. Word generally can find the secondary file after you have specified the primary file. If Word can't find it, click the <u>G</u>et Data button and then choose <u>O</u>pen Data Source. Locate the WordPerfect secondary file and click to open the document.

Each *fieldname~* in the WordPerfect file will be converted to a Word field with an equivalent name. If the WordPerfect field names are numbered, Word will convert them as F1, F2, and so on.

NOTE

Field names in Word cannot begin with numbers. Word places the letter F in front of each numeric name so that the field name begins with a letter.

CUSTOMIZING THE MAIN DOCUMENT

Just because you are creating a form letter doesn't mean that every letter has to look exactly the same. There are numerous ways to add customizations to a merged document so that your clients feel as if they are receiving a personalized letter.

USING IF . . . THEN FIELDS

If . . . Then fields are a great way to tell Word to act one way in a certain situation and another way in a different situation. For example, maybe you want to write a form letter using <<Title>> and <<LastName>> fields in the salutation to create "Dear Mr. Doe." In situations that have no Title for an individual, you may want the salutation to say "Dear John." Using If . . . Then fields allows you to easily control this type of scenario. With If . . . Then fields, Word can use Title and Last Name in the salutation *if* the record has a title. Otherwise, Word uses the First Name in the salutation.

The following example inserts the correct closing based on the contents of the Attorney field in the data source.

ADD IF . . . THEN FIELDS TO A MERGE PLEADING

1. Open the Mail Merge Letter.doc created earlier in the chapter.
2. From the <u>T</u>ools menu, choose Mail Me<u>r</u>ge.
3. In the main document, delete the word *Sincerely* near the bottom of the letter.

FIGURE 9.18

Use an If . . .
Then field to
specify condi-
tional infor-
mation in a
merged docu-
ment.

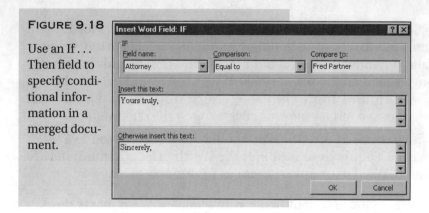

4. Click the Insert Word Field button on the Mail Merge toolbar.

5. Select If . . . Then . . . Else. The Insert Word Field:IF dialog box appears.

6. Select Attorney in the Field Name box.

7. Select Equal To in the Comparison box.

8. Type **Fred Partner** in the Compare To box.

9. In the Insert This text box, type **Yours Truly**.

10. In the Otherwise Insert This Text box, type **Sincerely**. Figure 9.18 shows a completed Insert Word Field: IF dialog box.

11. Click OK.

12. Merge the letter with the data source by clicking Merge To New Document. Keyboard users can press Alt+Shift+N.

CREATING CATALOG LISTS WITH MAIL MERGE

The last type of Mail Merge is called a catalog merge. The term *catalog* can be misleading. A catalog merge does not have to be used to produce catalogs; you can use it for lists, directories, and more.

The basic difference between a catalog merge and a form letter merge is the location of the record in the merged document. In a form letter merge, Word places each record on a separate page. In a catalog merge, Word fills each page with records.

Suppose that an attorney would like an address list of all the clients in the Client Addresses document. This next exercise does just that. It will list each client, one right after another on the same page.

CREATE A CATALOG MERGE

1. Create a new blank document.
2. From the Tools menu, choose Mail Merge.
3. Click Create to display the options for a main document.
4. Select Catalog.
5. A message box appears, asking whether Word should use the document that is open or create a new document. Click Active Window to use the currently open document.
6. Click Get data.
7. Select Open Data Source. (If you select Use Address Book, you will have the option of using the Contacts in Microsoft Outlook, your Personal Address Book or Schedule + Contact List. See Chapter 16, for information on how to generate a mail merge from within Outlook 2000.)
8. Locate Client Addresses.doc created earlier in this chapter, and double-click the document to open it.
9. Word displays a message box saying that there are no Merge fields in the main document. Click the Edit Main Document button.
10. Click the Insert Merge Field button, select Title, and press the Spacebar.
11. Follow the same steps to put in the rest of the address fields, with the correct punctuation. Do *not* insert the Attorney field.
12. Press Enter twice after inserting the last field (PostalCode).
13. To merge all of the clients from the data source into the merged document, click the Merge To New Document button on the Mail Merge toolbar. All the records appear on the same page in list format as shown in Figure 9.19.

FIGURE 9.19

A catalog merge places all the records on the same page.

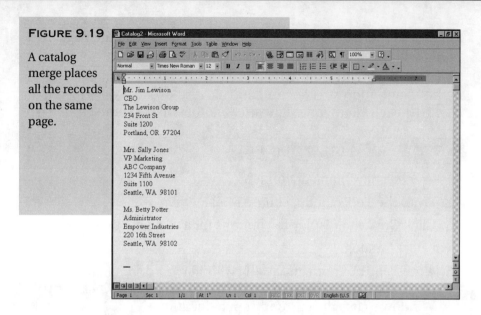

In this chapter we explored many of the powerful options that Mail Merge offers. Remember that you are not limited to names and addresses. Take any data that you have (case lists, office locations, billing amounts, or whatever) and perform queries or sorts, or create special if-then comparisons using one or multiple fields within the list to get a variety of unique documents.

ANSWERING COMMON QUESTIONS

Is there a way to spell out numeric text in a mail merge?

Let's say you want to send letters to volunteers who helped with during a firm-sponsored charity drive. In order to personalize the form letter, you wish to acknowledge the time contribution given from each participant. A general rule when working with numbers is to spell out numbers under ten and use numeric expression for numbers 10 and over. Using a field switch along with merge fields, converts numbers to text. To apply this switch, alternate-click on the merge field that has a numeric equivalent and choose Toggle Field Codes from the shortcut menu. Click after the field code and type * CardText. The *\ CardText switch changes the number to text. For example, if a merge field is named hours, your modified field code would appear as { MERGEFIELD Hours * CardText }.

Can I select multiple names and addresses in my document and create envelopes and labels like I could in WordPerfect?

If there are multiple addressees, you will need to select each address in the letter individually, before choosing Envelopes And Labels from the Tools menu. Payne Consulting Group has developed an add-in called the Address Assistant that allows a user to select multiple names and addresses in a document and quickly generate envelopes and labels without having to use mail merge. You can even look up and retrieve information from Outlook and Groupwise. For more information go to `http://www.usps.gov/`.

Why are the merge fields printing on the envelopes?

If merge fields print instead of the resulting information, it means you probably have the option to print field codes set. To check this, from the Tools menu, choose Options and select the Print tab. In the Include With Document section, uncheck Field Codes.

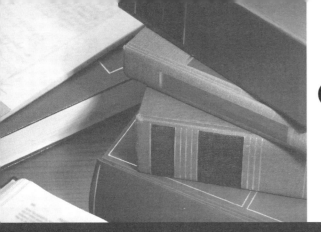

CHAPTER 10

CREATING LEGAL TEMPLATES

IN THIS CHAPTER

- ◆ Creating effective legal templates
- ◆ Learning about workgroup templates
- ◆ Using the Legal Pleading wizard to create a legal pleading template
- ◆ Learning about template storage and add-ins
- ◆ User profiles
- ◆ Customizing a toolbar for legal pleading templates
- ◆ Creating a global template to store AutoText entries
- ◆ Using the Organizer to copy custom settings between templates

Before you jump into the heart of this chapter, take the time to read the introductory section. Even if you are in a hurry to get to the core of the "how to" parts of the chapter, reading the entire introduction will benefit you. Especially if you are new to Word or if you are upgrading from an earlier version of Word and don't know how Word 2000 stores and uses templates and user profiles. Save yourself time and energy by learning the different types of templates, their function and location, and how they will relate to the needs of your firm.

INTRODUCING TEMPLATES

Can you imagine setting up a pleading from scratch every time you needed one? You'd have to set the margins, add line numbers, use court-specified font and page formats; the process would take, oh, about five times longer than it should. A better use of your time is to create a boilerplate for the document—also known as a template. Templates are set up once for repeated use.

When you use a template to create a new document, you get predefined settings for the document, specifying things such as margins, boilerplate text, headers, and footers. A pleading template can include the caption, line numbers, and a signature block as well. Pleading templates can contain all of the necessary formatting for a specific court's rules. If you work in several courts, districts, states, or countries, you can create multiple pleadings, each specific to the rules of a different court.

Templates are not limited to pleadings. You can create templates for form letters, memorandums, contracts, and other necessary documents. Templates can contain fields that allow users to quickly insert necessary information as well. For example, you might use a fill-in field to prompt users to input the judge's name in a pleading. Using preset formatting, fields, and styles not only saves time but also ensures consistency between departments and offices.

The fact is, you cannot get away from templates when using Word. Every document that you create in Word is based on a template. Even blank documents are based on Word's most important template, Normal (more about the Normal template in a moment).

Once a template is created, each time you use it, the correct formatting and boilerplate text are already there so you can concentrate on creating the contents without having to worry about how the document is laid out. For example, your letter template would contain all the basic letter elements and formatting and you would just need to add the necessary addressing information and the body of letter. This saves a lot of time because you don't have to repeat unnecessary steps.

You may well be thinking: Why not just open a letter I wrote last week and change the text? Word does allow you to work this way, and a lot of people do it. But consider the possible dangers. If you reuse old documents, you must copy the original document or perform a Save As to create a new document. If you forget this important step, you run the risk of overwriting and losing an existing document. You (and your clients) won't be too pleased if this happens. (Remember, you cannot undo the Save command!) Also, you have to make sure you remove every bit of text that relates to the original document and doesn't apply to the new one, or you may find yourself sending out misleading or even confidential material.

Another reason to use templates is to maintain consistency. Consistency between documents and offices is quite important. Consistent documents are easier to read and digest because clients don't have to take time to familiarize themselves with the format. A document should be easily recognizable as coming from your firm, regardless of the department or office that prepared it. Many firms spend thousands of dollars on new software and extensive training, only to find that everyone "does their own thing." Take this opportunity to standardize firmwide documents and explore setting up consistent templates for your firm.

Remember that consistency also reduces training and support time. If styles are used to format text correctly, a user from one practice group can assist with overflow work from another practice group. For example, a corporate secretary can assist in creating litigation documents as long as the templates and styles are defined correctly. The secretary would not need 100 percent knowledge about litigation to provide support. The same thing holds true for temporary or floating employees. If they are familiar with legal documents and understand how to use Word templates and styles, they should be able to produce the necessary documents for any given practice group.

Consider creating a style manual for your firm—a binder filled with all different document types, indicating which specific template to base each document on, and what formatting and styles to use throughout.

You can also reduce employee training time because users do not have to spend as much time learning how to format legal documents. After they learn which templates to use and what styles are required, they can produce practically anything!

TEMPLATE TYPES

There are three types of templates that can be used within Word: Normal, Attached, and Global. You can use Word's built-in templates, or you can create your own. You can even set up a location on your network and access workgroup templates from this location.

THE NORMAL TEMPLATE

Each time you create a document by clicking the Blank Document icon, you are using the Normal template. But the Normal template has much more powerful uses than just creating blank documents. Basically, this template is so important that it is required for Word to run.

If Word cannot locate a Normal template, it creates a new one. The Normal template is always open when Word is running, even if you do not have a blank document open.

The Normal template is also where user customizations are stored. For example, if users create AutoText entries, keyboard shortcuts, or any other customization, those customizations are stored by default in the Normal template on the user's computer.

Items such as AutoText entries stored in the Normal template are global, meaning that they are available in all documents on the computer where the Normal template resides. We recommend using the Normal template to store user-level customizations, not firmwide customizations. In other words, if a user creates an AutoText entry, it is saved to the Normal template and available only on that user's computer. Firmwide customizations should be stored in global templates, which you'll learn about in the next section.

Although it is the default, users do not have to save customizations in the Normal template. Customizations made to templates can be stored in specific templates. For example, you might modify the toolbar for a letter template and want those changes to only appear in letters rather than in all documents you create. In a case such as this, you can save the modification in a letter template rather than in the Normal template, and the customization will appear only in letters based on that specific letter template. You'll learn how to do this later in the chapter.

The default location for the Normal template on a computer using Windows 95 or 98 is C:\Windows\Application Data\Microsoft\ Templates\Normal.dot. On a computer running Windows NT or with user profiles enabled, the default is C:\WINDOWS\profiles\ <USER-NAME HERE>Application Data\Microsoft\Templates\Normal.dot.

ATTACHED TEMPLATES

Every document that is created in Word has a template attached to it. For example, if you create a letter using a letter template, the letter template is attached to your document so that you can use any styles, AutoText, or toolbars located in that template. You attach a template to a document in one of two ways: by creating a document based on that template, or by opening a document and manually attaching the template to it.

Attached templates come from various sources: a default Word template that installs with Word, a custom template set up by a user, or a Workgroup template designed for a group of users.

WORD USER TEMPLATES

Word comes with a number of templates (and wizards) that are installed during Setup. To create a new document based on a template, from the File menu, choose New. At this point, Word looks for the location of your user templates and workgroup templates, and displays them to you in a series of tabs. Each tab represents a folder in the Templates folder on your computer. Within the templates folder, you can create additional folders to organize how templates appear in the New dialog box.

Wizards are a special type of template; they are discussed later in the chapter.

Figure 10.1 shows the New dialog box. Each tab located in the dialog box is a folder within the templates directory. Creating folders for each template type is a great way to organize templates so that users can easily find what they need.

FIGURE 10.1

You can create tabs in the New dialog box by creating folders in the templates directory.

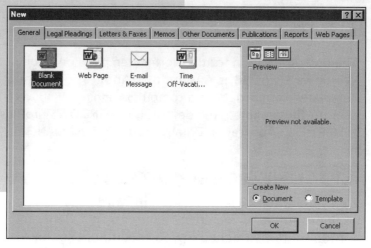

If a folder within the template directory is empty, it will not appear as a tab in the New dialog box.

NOTE

CREATE A NEW LETTER BASED ON A WORD LETTER TEMPLATE

1. From the File menu, choose New. The New dialog box appears
2. Select the Letters & Faxes tab, as shown in Figure 10.2.

FIGURE 10.2

Microsoft Word comes with several useful templates.

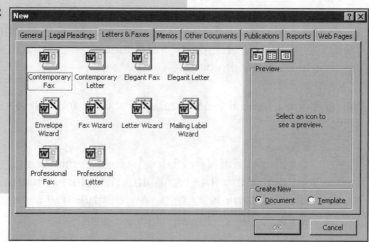

3. Select Professional Letter, and then click OK. A new letter based on the Professional Letter template appears.

4. Click where indicated to complete the letter. Keyboard users can press F11 to move to the next field or Shift+F11 to move to the previous field.

If a template is not installed during Setup, it installs automatically the first time you choose to run it. Table 10.1 lists all the templates provided with Word and indicates which ones are installed automatically and which ones install on first use.

You'll find additional templates and wizards on Microsoft's Web site. From the Help menu, select Office On The Web. Your Web browser will take you to a location where Microsoft includes templates, wizards, and other goodies that you can access or download. Select Downloads in the Word section to see the available files.

TIP   You can use Word 97 templates in Word 2000.

TABLE 10.1   TEMPLATES PROVIDED WITH WORD

INSTALLED WITH A TYPICAL SETUP	INSTALLED ON FIRST USE
Memos	Agenda
Letters	Batch Conversion Wizard
	Brochure
	Calendar
	Directory
	Faxes
	Manual
	Pleading Wizard
	Reports
	Resumes
	Thesis

CUSTOM USER TEMPLATES

Custom user templates are ones that you create or purchase specifically for your firm. You can create custom templates from scratch, from a blank document, or by basing a new template on an existing one. You can modify any of the following items in custom templates:

- Text
- Formatting
- Styles
- AutoText entries
- Toolbars and menus
- Macros
- Shortcut keys

The default location for the custom user templates on a computer using Windows 95/98 is C:\Windows\Application Data\Microsoft\Templates\. On a computer running Windows NT or with user profiles enabled, the default is C:\WINDOWS\profiles\<USERNAME HERE>Application Data\Microsoft\Templates\.

WORKGROUP TEMPLATES

Workgroup templates are similar to user templates in that they hold formatting, styles, toolbars, AutoText, and more. The difference is that Workgroup templates are stored in a location specified on the File Locations tab in the Options dialog box. Firms often set up a workgroup templates location as read-only so that users can access these templates but not make changes. Using a workgroup template location is a great way to share firmwide templates while leaving the standard user templates folder intact. This approach will help prevent conflicts with other Office applications and any Word 2000 add-in programs that your firm may want to use. The next section discusses add-in programs.

Like the user template folder, any folders created within the workgroup template folder appear as tabs in the New dialog box. Workgroup templates can be stored on a local computer or network drive.

Any templates residing in the workgroup template location appear on the General tab of the New dialog box. If they reside in folders within the workgroup template location, they appear on their own tabs in the New dialog box. Word will recognize workgroup templates only if the Workgroup Templates file location is set in the Options dialog box. Like user templates, tabs for workgroup folders will not appear in the New dialog box if the folders are empty. You will learn how to set up a workgroup template location later in this chapter.

NOTE Using a network-based template directory can have a few drawbacks. For example, traveling and home users may not have access to those templates when they are not connected to the network. Similarly, if the network goes down, users will not be able to access these templates for creating new documents.

The decision about whether to use a workgroup template folder, and where to locate such a folder, should be discussed during the planning stages of your upgrade to Word 2000. Your decision will depend upon the needs and size of your firm and systems department.

GLOBAL TEMPLATES

Like those in the Normal template, customizations stored in global templates are available in every type of document. These templates add only customized settings to Word. Users do not use them to create new documents, as they will not show up in the New dialog box. Global templates are stored in the Startup directory and are automatically loaded each time Word starts.

NOTE Many law firms set up several global templates, each with a specific purpose:

- AutoText Template

- Macro Template

- Toolbar and Menu Customization Template

- Keyboard Shortcut Template

If your firm has a large number of global customizations, organizing them at the template level can make finding items that need to be modified easier. If you have a small number of customizations, you may find that one global template is sufficient for all items.

Global templates are where you should store firmwide customizations. This allows users to use their Normal template for personal customizations without interference.

If you store firmwide customizations in the Normal template, every time you make a change to one of the customizations, you will be required to distribute an updated Normal template to each user. If you do this, you will overwrite the existing Normal template belonging to each user. Users who have stored any of their own macros, keyboard shortcuts, or AutoText entries there will lose them and have to recreate them. As you can imagine, this causes quite a bit of frustration, as well as being inefficient. Storing firmwide customizations in a global template allows you to update and distribute them without overwriting user customizations each time.

The default directory for global templates is C:\Windows \Application Data\Microsoft\Word\Startup on Windows 95 and 98 or C:\Windows\Application Data\Microsoft\Word\Startup in Windows NT or when user profiles are enabled. However, you can specify a different local or network drive by modifying the global template file location. You'll find instructions for changing the Startup file location in the section called "Creating Global Templates" later in this chapter.

You can create as many global templates as you like; however, too many global templates may slow down the startup of Word 2000. You may also run into memory issues with a large number of global templates, depending upon the amount of memory available on a given machine.

WHAT ARE WIZARDS?

You may have heard the term *wizards* used along with templates. Wizards make creating documents easier because they walk you through the steps required to set up the document just the way you want it. A good example of this is the Calendar wizard. If you had to set up a table with the correct number of days in it and then put the appropriate date in the monthly calendar, it could take a while. Instead, use the Calendar wizard, and the process takes less than a minute.

USE THE CALENDAR WIZARD

1. From the File menu, choose New. The New dialog box appears.

2. Select the Other Documents tab.

3. Double-click Calendar Wizard.

FIGURE 10.3

Select options for the calendar.

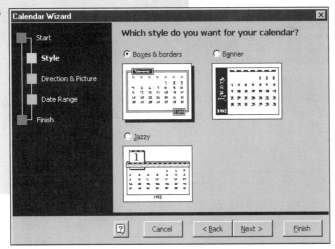

4. Click Next to move to the first step of the wizard as shown in Figure 10.3.

5. Select a style for the calendar and click Next.

You don't have to walk through every step in the wizard. If you want to skip one or more steps, click the flow chart diagram in the dialog box and you move to this step in the process.

6. Select options for the layout of the page and click Next.

7. Select the Month and Year to start and end the calendar and click Next.

8. Click Finish. The finished result is shown in Figure 10.4.

One of the most important wizards for law firms is the Legal Pleading wizard. The Legal Pleading wizard guides you through the process of creating a pleading. It sets up the caption and line numbering automatically, and then prompts you for specific information to create the caption and signature block. Later in this chapter you will use the Legal Pleading wizard.

FIGURE 10.4

The Calendar wizard creates a calendar in a matter of moments.

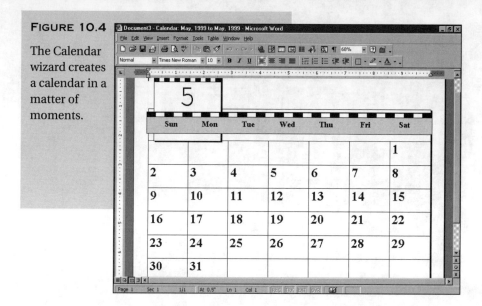

Word ships with eleven Wizards to aid in the creation of documents.

- Agenda
- Calendar
- Envelope
- Fax Cover Sheet
- Legal Pleading
- Letter
- Mailing Label
- Memo
- Newsletter
- Resume
- Web Page

ADD-IN PROGRAMS

Add-in programs are additional programs that you can purchase to work with Word or other applications. Most add-ins are stored in the Startup directory.

Several types of Office and Word 2000 add-ins are on the market. For example, users might use a document management system, a contact information manager, or another type of program that works specifically with Office or Word 2000. Add-ins can be programs (.exe files), dynamic link libraries (.dll files), templates containing macros (.dot files), or a combination. The Legal Numbering macro provided by Payne Consulting Group is an example of a template add-in file.

Visit the Payne Consulting Group Web site at `http://www.payneconsulting.com/` for more information about the Legal Numbering add-in or the Forms Assistant that provides automated solutions for your firm templates.

Visit Alki Software Corporation for a legal dictionary add-in at `http://www.alki.com/`.

Visit Avery Dennison for a label generator add-in at `http://www.avery.com/`.

It is vitally important to use styles in legal templates. Styles are not covered in this chapter because they are thoroughly documented in Chapter 6. Combining styles with templates is probably the most useful and important aspect of Word 2000. Please take time to read the "Styles" chapter to familiarize yourself with the power of Word 2000.

OK! That's it! Now that you understand the different types of templates and how they are used, you can get started creating some helpful legal templates.

CREATING LEGAL TEMPLATES

Templates are so important in the legal environment that it's a good idea to practice creating more than one template. This will allow you to really dig in and get comfortable with the process. The next exercise shows you how to create a simple fax template. When you have the basics down, you can move on and create a more complex pleading template. After the templates are created, you'll see how to add some fill-in fields to automate them and then create a custom menu.

If you're interested in global templates, feel free to skip this section and go right to the section on creating global templates.

CREATING A FAX TEMPLATE

When you create a template, you can start with a blank document, but it is easier to base it on an existing template. For this exercise, you'll use the Professional Fax template that is installed with Word 2000. If you don't have the template available, you can install it (see "Word User Templates" earlier in this chapter for installation instructions), or you can open a different template.

When you're making the decision whether to base a new template on an existing one or to create a template from scratch, one important thing to consider is what styles and other customizations you want in the new template. For example, you might want to create all of your pleading templates based on an existing template that contains line numbering, styles, and other items specific to pleadings. This way, you won't have to take time recreating or copying those items. This advantage is especially important for templates that will contain a large number of styles or complex layouts.

CREATE A NEW FAX TEMPLATE BASED ON THE PROFESSIONAL FAX

1. From the File menu, choose New. The New dialog box appears.
2. Select the Letters & Faxes tab.
3. Select the option to create a Template in the Create New section of the dialog box.
4. Select Professional Fax, and then click OK. A new template based on the Professional Fax appears, as shown in Figure 10.5. If you have never created a fax document before, you may receive a message stating that the fax template needs to be installed.
5. Once the document is open, choose Save As from the File menu. The Save As dialog box appears with the user template directory folder.

NOTE

When you save a template for the first time, Word automatically defaults to the user template folder. If you save the file at this location, it will appear on the General tab of the New dialog box. To place the template on another tab, open a folder within this location before saving the file.

FIGURE 10.5

The Professional Fax is one of several templates that ship with Word 2000.

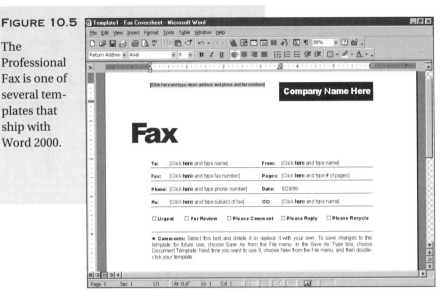

6. Double-click the Letters & Faxes folder to open it.

7. Type **My Fax** in the File Name box. If you want to name the file something different, that's OK; just make certain that it isn't the same name as an existing fax template, or Word will overwrite that template.

You don't have to type **.dot** after the name of the template. Word inserts it for you automatically. The .dot file extension differentiates a template from a Word document (.doc) file type.

8. Click Save to save the template. Leave it open for the next exercise.

You can also create a template from scratch starting at a blank document. If you choose to use this method, choose Document Template from the Save As Type drop-down list in the Save As dialog box.

MODIFYING THE FAX TEMPLATE

After you have created a template, you probably want to modify it to make it consistent with other firm templates. Just as with documents, you can open templates to apply editing and formatting changes. You can add customizations to a template manually, or you can use the Organizer to copy styles and other items from an existing template to the new one. Using the Organizer is covered later in this chapter.

MODIFY THE FAX TEMPLATE

1. Return to the Fax template created in the last exercise.
2. Select the text "Company Name Here" and type your firm name.
4. Click in the field at the top of the fax labeled "Click Here and Type Return Addresses and Phone and Fax Numbers" and type the appropriate information.
5. Click in the field next to "From" and type your name.
6. Delete the paragraphs that display instructional text after the word "Comments."
7. Save and close the fax when you have finished making changes. The fax should look similar to the one shown in Figure 10.6.

FIGURE 10.6

You can customize a template to match your firm's style.

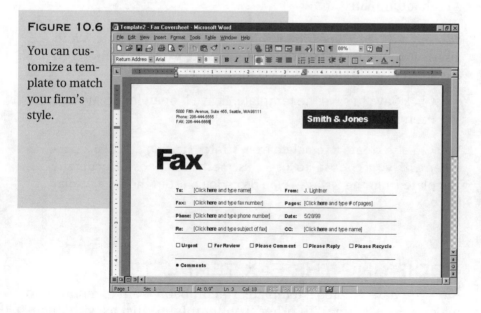

NOTE

When customizing templates for your firm, you may want to alter margins, styles, and other settings in the template.

USING THE FAX TEMPLATE

After you have created a template, you can use it to create new documents. Like all templates, the template will appear in the New dialog box.

CREATE A NEW FAX BASED ON THE FAX TEMPLATE

1. From the File menu, choose New. The New dialog box appears.
2. Select the Letters & Faxes tab to view the available faxes.
3. Select "My Fax" (or whatever you called the template) and click OK. A new fax appears on the screen.

NOTE

If you saved the fax template in a different folder, it may appear on a different tab in the New dialog box. If it does not appear anywhere, it's likely that you accidentally saved it outside of the template folder. Use Windows Explorer to relocate the file into the template folder, or repeat the previous exercise, making certain to save the file in the correct location. For help on using Windows Explorer, click Start, and then click Help. Select the Index tab and type **Windows Explorer** in the Type In The Keywords To Find box.

4. Edit the new fax document.
5. Click where indicated to complete the fax recipient information.
6. Press Ctrl+End to move to the last paragraph in the fax and type the desired text.

In these few short steps, you have created, modified, and used your first template. Now that you understand how it works, you can go on to create a legal pleading template.

CREATING A LEGAL PLEADING TEMPLATE

Whether your firm is large or small, you will probably need to create pleadings. Some firms are so specialized, they need only one type of pleading for the work they do. Others are so diverse that they require several types of pleading templates. You can create as many pleading templates as necessary for different courts, districts, states, and even countries.

NOTE

Because readers of this book have different needs when it comes to pleadings, the exercise walks you through creating a very generic pleading. You can then add styles and other formatting specific to your firm's needs on your own, based on what you've learned.

Because pleading templates require complex formatting for captions, footers, and line numbering, it's best to use Word's Legal Pleading wizard to create the first one. This helps you get started with a pleading that you can customize for the district in which you file.

NOTE

The Pleading Wizard is installed on first use by default. If you do not see the wizard in the New dialog box, you may need to install it.

CREATE A PLEADING TEMPLATE USING WORD'S LEGAL PLEADING WIZARD

1. From the File menu, choose New. The New dialog box appears.
2. Select the Legal Pleadings tab.
3. Select Pleading Wizard and click OK. The Legal Pleading wizard appears, as shown in Figure 10.7.

FIGURE 10.7

Use the Legal Pleading wizard to create a pleading template.

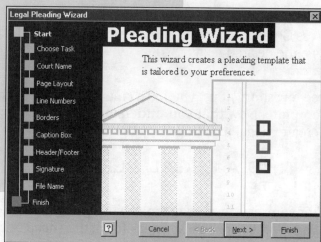

TABLE 10.2 LEGAL PLEADING WIZARD OPTIONS

BUTTON	ACTION
Cancel	Close the Legal Pleading wizard without creating a pleading. Keyboard users can press the Esc key.
Help (displayed as a button with a question mark)	Access Help for the Legal Pleading wizard.
Next	Move to the next screen. This button is not available on the last screen.
Back	Move to the previous screen. This button is not available on the first screen.
Finish	Create the pleading and close the Legal Pleading wizard.
Any button on the flow chart on the left	Move to the selected screen.

NOTE If you select the option to create a new Template in the New dialog box, the Pleading Wizard will give you an error message. Running the Pleading Wizard creates the new template.

4. You can move through the Legal Pleading wizard using any of the methods described in Table 10.2.

5. Move through each screen, inputting and selecting the necessary information for the pleading.

TIP If you need to change any of the information you have typed, click the Back and Next buttons to navigate through the set of screens.

6. When you have finished setting up the pleading, click the File Name option on the wizard flow chart to the left of the wizard. Name this pleading **Temporary Pleading**.

TIP This template is not the final template. It will be used in the next exercise to build the final template. Naming it **Temporary Pleading** will make it easy for you to differentiate it from the final template when you're working with both files.

7. Click Finish to complete the pleading template.

8. Word creates a new pleading template with the information that you have just typed. A new wizard screen appears for you to fill in specific case information. For now, click Cancel to

close the second wizard without creating a pleading. The new blank template appears on screen.

9. Save the template.

The process is now 50 percent complete. Before continuing, however, you need some background on the current process and what is happening with the template.

Word has created a blank pleading template. You can use this blank template, but it will require you to enter information such as a firm name, address, and so on *every time* you create a new pleading. Rather than use the blank template, you can customize it further to have standard information included each time you create a new pleading.

CUSTOMIZE THE PLEADING TEMPLATE

1. From the File menu, choose New. The New dialog box appears.

2. Select the Legal Pleadings tab and locate the Temporary Pleading template that you created in the previous exercise.

3. Select the template and click OK.

4. The Legal Pleading wizard appears. Move through the screens and enter the information that you want to appear on the pleading template.

5. If this template will be used by multiple users and for multiple cases, be sure to exclude specific information such as plaintiff, defendant, and attorney names. Instead of entering specific names, it's a good idea to insert tip text indicating to the user where to insert the names. For example, type **PlaintiffName** in the plaintiff name box, and so forth. Eliminating spaces from the tip text will enable users to select the entire tip text with a double-click instead of having to click and drag to select both words. Typing will then replace the selected text with the new information automatically.

NOTE

Don't worry too much about this now. Later in this chapter, you will see how to insert fields that prompt users for this information.

6. When you have entered all the information on each screen, click Finish to close the wizard and create a new pleading.

7. From the File menu, choose Save As.

8. Select Document Template (*.dot) from the Save As Type drop-down list. Word will default to the user template folder automatically.

9. Double-click the Legal Pleadings folder to open it, or select a workgroup folder for the template. Workgroup templates are covered later in this chapter.

10. Enter a name for the new pleading template in the File Name box and click Save. Word automatically converts the document to a template.

11. Make any additional modifications that you want to the pleading template.

12. Save and close the pleading template.

AUTOMATING A TEMPLATE

In the previous exercise, you created a legal pleading template that contains standard information. It would be nice, however, to automate the pleading template to prompt a user for the information that changes each time a pleading is created.

In this exercise, you will use fill-in fields to automate the pleading template you just created.

USE FILL-IN FIELDS TO AUTOMATE THE PLEADING TEMPLATE

1. Open the pleading template created in the preceding exercise.

2. Move the insertion point to the location of the judge's name. If a name appears there, delete it.

NOTE

If you don't see the location for the judge's name, it could be for one of the following reasons:

♦ You are in Normal view. The judge's name is inserted into a text box. To see the text box, you must be in Print Layout view. You can access Print Layout view on the View menu.

♦ You did not select the option to insert a judge's name in the Legal Pleading wizard. This option is not a default in the wizard; you must select it if you want the name inserted. If you wish, you may add a text box in the appropriate place.

3. From the Insert menu, choose Field. The Field dialog box appears, as shown in Figure 10.8.

4. Select Fill-in from the Field Names list.

5. Enter a prompt in the Field Codes box to make the field and prompt appear as follows:

FILLIN "Enter the Judge's name:"

6. Add the Upper switch after the prompt to force the name to appear in UPPERCASE format. The text in the Field Codes box should appear as follows (for more information about switches, see Chapter 11, "Creating Legal Forms"):

FILLIN "Enter the judge's name:" * Upper

7. Click OK to insert the field. A fill-in box appears on screen.

8. Leave the box empty and click OK. Because the judge's name can vary, it is left blank in the template.

9. Repeat Steps 3 through 8 in the appropriate locations for the attorney, plaintiff, and defendant names. You can also add a fill-in field for the Case Number, Title, Attorney Bar Number, and any other necessary information.

10. When you have finished inserting fields, save and close the template.

11. Create a new pleading using the updated template to test the changes that you made.

FIGURE 10.8

Insert fill-in fields in templates to prompt users for information automatically when new documents are created.

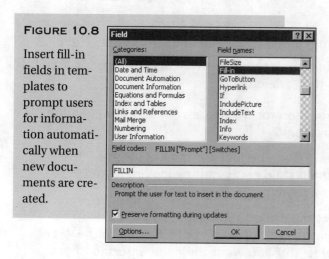

NOTE If you see the field codes rather than the text that you entered on-screen, it means that Field Code view is activated. Turn this off from the Tools menu by choosing Options. Select the View tab and then clear the Field Codes option. If you turn off Field Code view in the template, new documents based on the template will not have the view activated.

USING THE ORGANIZER TO COPY CUSTOM SETTINGS BETWEEN TEMPLATES

The Organizer is a tool that allows you to copy customizations between templates. You can use the Organizer to copy macros, toolbars, AutoText entries, and styles. This is especially helpful when you're developing templates that require many of the same customized items.

When a pleading template is created using the Legal Pleading wizard, a special toolbar is created that references a set of legal macros that are available in the template. When you created the automated pleading in the previous exercise, however, those helpful modifications were lost. In the next exercise, you will use the Organizer to copy the toolbar and macros from the temporary pleading to the automated one.

COPY A TOOLBAR AND MACROS FROM ONE PLEADING TEMPLATE TO ANOTHER

1. Open the pleading template that you automated in the previous exercise.
2. From the Tools menu, choose Templates And Add-Ins. The Templates and Add-Ins dialog box appears.
3. Click Organizer. The Organizer dialog box appears, as shown in Figure 10.9.

NOTE Figure 10.9 shows the Organizer dialog box with the automated and temporary pleadings displayed. When you first open the Organizer dialog box, the automated pleading template will appear on the left side of the dialog box, and the Normal template will appear on the right.

FIGURE 10.9

The Organizer allows you to copy custom items from one template to another.

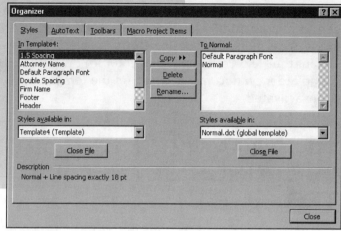

4. Click Close File below the Normal template to close it. The button changes to read Open File.

5. Click Open File. The Open dialog box appears.

6. Select the Temporary Pleading template in the Legal Pleadings directory.

7. Click Open to open the file and return to the Organizer dialog box. The Temporary Pleading is now displayed on the right side of the Organizer dialog box.

8. Select the Toolbars tab. One toolbar will appear in the In Temporary Pleading.dot list box.

9. Select the Temporary Pleading toolbar and click Copy. The toolbar is copied to the automated pleading.

10. Select the Macro Project Items tab. Three macro projects should appear in the In Temporary Pleading.dot list box.

11. Select the three macros and Copy them to the automated pleading template.

You can select multiple items in a list by clicking the first item and then Shift+Click the last item. To select noncontiguous items in a list, Ctrl+Click each item that you want selected.

12. Click Close to close the Organizer.

FIGURE 10.10

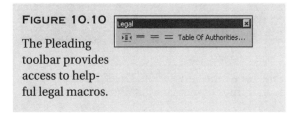

The Pleading toolbar provides access to helpful legal macros.

13. If the Pleading toolbar is not displayed onscreen, alternate-click any toolbar and select it from the shortcut menu. Keyboard users can select a toolbar from the View menu by choosing Toolbars. Refer to Figure 10.10 for a picture of the Pleading toolbar.

NOTE Don't be alarmed if the Pleading toolbar on your screen looks a little different from what you see in Figure 10.10. The toolbar has been resized to make it easier to place labels in the picture. Usually, the Pleading toolbar appears with the Table of Authorities button below the other buttons, sort of like a two-tier toolbar. You can resize the toolbar to make it look like the one in Figure 10.10 by dragging the sides of the toolbar.

14. Save and close the automated pleading template.

EXPLORING THE LEGAL TOOLBAR AND MACROS

The legal toolbar and macros that you have copied to the automated pleading template allow you to quickly perform five actions while working in a pleading.

Table 10.3 describes the options that are available on the Pleading toolbar.

CAUTION The Pleading toolbar does *not* apply styles to block quotes. Also, if Normal or Body Text style is being used for double or single spacing in a pleading, using the toolbar buttons to modify or reset spacing does not reapply the original style. If users rely on styles for fast updating of documents, you may want to use toolbar buttons that apply the correct styles. Adding a button to a toolbar that applies a style is covered in the next section of this chapter.

TABLE 10.3   PLEADING TOOLBAR BUTTONS

BUTTON	FUNCTION
Block Quotation	Format selected paragraphs for a block quotation. Does not apply a style. Click the button several times to increase left and right indents.
Single Space	Format selected paragraphs to single space. Applies "Single Space" style.
1.5 Space	Format selected paragraphs to 1.5 space. Applies "1.5 Space" style.
Double Space	Format selected paragraphs to double space. Applies "Double Space" style.
Table of Authorities	Opens Index and Tables dialog box with Table of Authorities tab selected.

NOTE

The first time that you use the Pleading toolbar, Word may be slow to respond. This is because it must load the legal macros into memory. Word responds more quickly after the first time.

EXPLORE THE PLEADING TOOLBAR

1. Create a new pleading based on the automated pleading template.

2. Display the Pleading toolbar if it is not visible. You can display a toolbar by choosing Toolbars from the View menu.

3. Position the insertion point in the body text area of the pleading.

4. Click the Block Quotation button on the Pleading toolbar. The paragraph is indented for a block quote.

5. Click the Block Quotation button again to further indent the paragraph.

6. Click the other buttons on the toolbar to see how they function.

7. Close the document without saving it.

CUSTOMIZING TOOLBARS FOR LEGAL TEMPLATES

One of the great things about Word 2000 is the flexibility available when it comes to customizing the work environment. Like most things in Word 2000, toolbars are fully customizable. You can even create your own toolbars if you don't want to customize any of the existing ones! Instructions for creating a new toolbar are in the "Creating a Legal Toolbar" section in Chapter 1.

The main reason for modifying or creating a toolbar is to make Word more convenient for working with legal documents. For example, you can modify the pleading toolbar that you explored in the preceding exercise so that it applies styles to selected text.

You are not limited to styles when you add buttons to a toolbar. You can add macros, built-in Word commands, AutoText entries, and more.

ADD HEADING STYLES TO THE PLEADING TOOLBAR

1. Create a new pleading using the automated template.
2. Position the insertion point in the body text area of the pleading.
3. Display the Pleading toolbar if it is not already visible.
4. From the Tools menu, choose Customize. The Customize dialog box appears, as shown in Figure 10.11.

TIP

Mouse users can alternate-click any toolbar and then from the shortcut menu, select Customize to access the Customize dialog box.

NOTE

The Pleading toolbar will disappear when the Customize dialog box opens. Select the pleading template from the Save In list and the toolbar will reappear. Make certain that you select the template and not the document.

5. If the dialog box and pleading toolbar overlap, drag them to different locations onscreen so that you can see each clearly.
6. Select All Commands in the Categories list. Available commands appear in the Commands list.

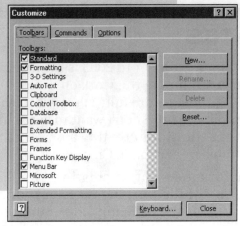

FIGURE 10.11

The Customize dialog box allows you to customize tool-bars.

NOTE

If you select Styles in the Categories list, the heading styles may not appear. This is because they have not yet been used in the document. You must either choose All Commands to see the styles, or apply the styles temporarily within the document before accessing the Customize dialog box.

7. Drag the Heading 1 style from the Commands list onto the Pleading toolbar. Repeat this process for the Heading 2 and Heading 3 styles. Don't worry if the toolbar wraps around. You can drag the sides to resize it after you close the Customize dialog box.

TIP

If you want to rename the toolbar buttons, alternate-click them while the Customize dialog box is still open and edit the Name entry. If you closed the dialog box already, just reopen it and then alternate-click the buttons that you want to rename.

To specify a keyboard shortcut, place an ampersand (&) before the character you want to use as the shortcut key. For example, the name &Undo Underline would designate the letter U as the hot key for accessing this command.

8. Click Close to close the Customize dialog box.

9. Close the document. You do not need to save changes to the document, but make sure that you answer Yes when asked whether you want to save changes to the template.

TEST THE TOOLBAR BUTTONS

1. Create a new pleading using the automated template.
2. Display the Pleading toolbar if it is not already visible.
3. Position the insertion point in the body text area of the pleading.
4. Click Heading 1 on the Pleading toolbar to switch to Heading 1 style.
5. Type a heading and press Enter.
6. Click Heading 2 on the Pleading toolbar.
7. Type a heading and press Enter.
8. Click Heading 3 on the Pleading toolbar.
9. Type a heading and press Enter.
10. Close the document without saving it.

TIP

If you want to remove buttons from a toolbar, go to the Tools menu and choose Customize to open the Customize dialog box. Drag the buttons off the toolbar (into the document window) to delete them. A shortcut for removing a button from a toolbar is to hold down the Alt key and then drag the button off the toolbar. If you use the shortcut method, you may not know what template you are altering (the Normal or document template). To make the change to a specific template, use the Customize dialog box so that you can select the template that you want to modify.

NOTE

Deleting buttons from a toolbar does not delete them from the system. You can find them in the Customize dialog box and add them back to the toolbar at any time.

When you add or delete toolbar buttons, make certain that you select the correct template in the Save In list in the Customize dialog box. If you fail to do this, the changes will appear in the wrong templates. For example, changes made to toolbars while Normal.dot is selected will appear in all Word documents.

USING WORKGROUP TEMPLATES

As you learned earlier in this chapter, Word allows you to create folders within the template location folder so that templates can be grouped by type, practice group, department, or any other way that you want to organize user templates. Word allows you to create and use a workgroup template directory in the same manner.

NOTE

If you are not familiar with workgroup templates, and if you have not yet read the chapter introduction, take a moment to go back to the beginning of this chapter and read the workgroup template introduction for important considerations about using workgroup templates.

When a user creates a new file, the templates in the workgroup location show up in the New dialog box in the same manner as user templates. Folders within the workgroup folder appear as tabs in the New dialog box. No matter which type of templates you use, there is no difference between how the templates appear in the New dialog box.

SET THE WORKGROUP TEMPLATE FILE LOCATION

1. From the Tools menu, choose Options. The Options dialog box appears.
2. Select the File Locations tab.
3. In the list of File Types, select Workgroup Templates.
4. Click Modify. The Modify Location dialog box appears.
5. Select a location for workgroup templates and then click OK.
6. Click Close to close the Options dialog box.
7. From the File menu, choose New to show workgroup and user templates in the New dialog box.

CREATING GLOBAL TEMPLATES

Global templates are used to store customizations that are available in all Word documents. If you have a small number of firmwide customizations, you can store them all in the same template. If you have a large number of firmwide customizations, it's better to organize them in separate global templates. For example, you might have one global template for AutoText entries, another for macros, and still another for toolbar and keyboard customizations. Organizing customizations in several templates makes locating items easier when updates are necessary. It also makes file sharing easier. For example, you might want to share your AutoText entries with an affiliate, but not your macros or keyboard shortcuts. If the AutoText entries are stored separately, you can send a copy of the AutoText template without worrying about the other customizations.

During your upgrade planning, it's a good idea to determine which customizations need to be available in all documents, and which ones should be stored at the document template level. For example, AutoText entries for storing letter notations (such as Via Messenger, Via Facsimile, and so on) would be appropriate for storage in letter templates. AutoText entries that can apply to all kinds of legal documents (such as Confidential, Draft, and specific legal boilerplate clauses) are good candidates for global templates because they will be needed in several types of documents.

When you store customizations in a global template, the global template must be open. If you want to create the customizations in a file other than the global template, you can use the Organizer to copy them from the template in which they were created to the global template. See "Using the Organizer to Copy Custom Settings between Templates" in this chapter for information about the Organizer.

You can redirect Word to a Startup directory on any local or network drive. However, remember that if you change the location of the Startup directory, you may need to manually move and customize other global templates and add-ins provided by outside vendors. Refer to this chapter's introduction for more information about global template storage.

CAUTION Do not set the Startup directory to the same location as the user template directory. Doing so will generate errors because Word 2000 will attempt to load the Normal template twice.

EXPLORE THE STARTUP FILE LOCATION

1. From the Tools menu, choose Options. The Options dialog box appears.
2. Select the File Locations tab. The File Locations options appear, as shown in Figure 10.12.

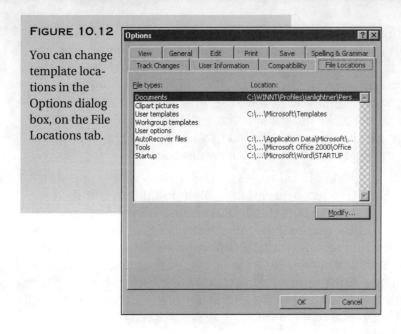

3. In the File types list, select Startup.

4. Click Modify. The Modify Location dialog box appears, as
shown in Figure 10.13.

5. Accept the current folder or select a new one.

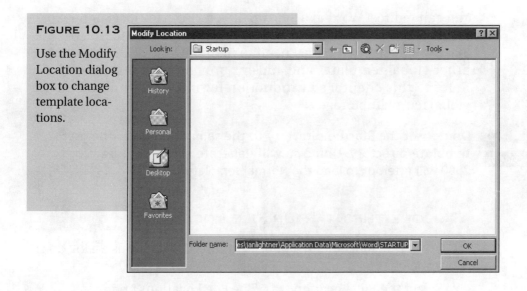

6. Click OK to close the Modify Location dialog box.

7. Click Close to close the Options dialog box.

After you have determined a Startup file location, you can begin using global templates.

CREATE A GLOBAL AUTOTEXT TEMPLATE

1. From the File menu, choose New.

2. Select the Blank Document template on the General tab.

3. Select Template in the Create New section of the New dialog box.

4. Click OK. A new blank template appears.

5. Type **DRAFT** and then insert a date and time field from the Insert menu by choosing Date And Time.

Make certain that the Update Automatically option is selected in the Date and Time dialog box. Otherwise, the date and time will be inserted as text rather than as an automatically updating field.

6. Select the text, including the paragraph mark.

7. From the Format menu, choose Font and make the following changes to the text:

   Color: Red

   Font: Arial

   Font Style: Bold

   Size: 18

8. Select the formatted text and paragraph mark.

Select the paragraph mark of an AutoText entry when you want to include the paragraph mark—and the formatting included in it—as part of the entry.

9. From the Insert menu, choose AutoText.

10. Choose AutoText. The AutoCorrect dialog box appears with the AutoText tab selected, as shown in Figure 10.14.

Do not choose New, because the entry will likely be stored in the Normal template if you choose this option. To make certain that an AutoText entry is stored in the correct template, you should always insert entries from the AutoText tab in the AutoCorrect dialog box.

FIGURE 10.14

You can control where AutoText entries are stored by selecting a template from the Look In list in the AutoCorrect dialog box.

11. Leave the suggested name, or enter a new name in the Enter AutoText Entries Here box.

12. Select the global template in the Look In list. This option determines where the AutoText entry will be stored.

13. Type a name for the AutoText entry in the Enter AutoText Entries Here box.

NOTE

When you select a template in the Look In list, the original Auto Text entry name is cleared from the Enter AutoText Entries Here box.

14. Click Add.

15. From the File menu, choose Save As. The Save As dialog box appears.

16. Locate the Startup folder that you set in the previous exercise.

17. Type a name for the global template and click Save.

18. Add additional AutoText entries as desired.

19. Save and close the template.

The global template will not load until you exit and restart Word. Templates located in the Startup folder are loaded automatically each time that Word starts. To manually load a new global template, from the Tools menu, choose Templates And Add-Ins, and then select the template that you want to load.

Word 2000 follows rules of hierarchy when it encounters duplicate customizations. For example, an AutoText entry in a document template could have the same name as one in a global template. As with all rules, however, this has exceptions, especially concerning macros and AutoText entries. For detailed information about the Word 2000 template hierarchy and how it works, refer to Chapter 17, "Introduction to Visual Basic for Applications." as well as the next section, "Template Hierarchy."

TEMPLATE HIERARCHY

Since you can have numerous templates loaded at once, how do you determine which template has priority? Word uses a simple hierarchy system in determining priority.

1. Attached templates

2. Normal template

3. Global templates (in alphabetical order)

4. Add-Ins

DEMONSTRATE TEMPLATE HIERARCHY

1. Type "Spot" and select the text. Insert Spot as an AutoText entry named "dog" in the Normal.dot.

2. Now open a template (not Normal.dot) and type "Goldie." Insert Goldie as an AutoText entry named "dog" into the open template, by selecting Insert, AutoText, AutoText and changing the Look In list box to the currently opened template.

3. Create a new document based on the template you chose in step 2. Insert the "dog" AutoText entry. The word Goldie is inserted.

4. Create a new blank document (leave the current document open).

5. Insert the "dog" AutoText entry. In this new blank document, Spot is inserted.

AUTOMATED AUTOTEXT ENTRIES

You can enhance global AutoText templates by adding automated AutoText entries. Automated AutoText entries use fill-in fields that prompt users for input when inserting the entry. For example, you might create an AutoText entry that prompts the user to input party names, attorney names, and more. To keep this example simple, we show you how to create a one-line AutoText entry that prompts users for a date.

Because you just saw how to create an AutoText entry in the last exercise, this one gives you more general instructions for creating the entry. If you get lost, just review the last exercise.

USE A FILL-IN FIELD AND CREATE AN AUTOTEXT ENTRY IN THE GLOBAL AUTOTEXT TEMPLATE

1. Open the global AutoText template that you created in the last lesson, if it's not already open.

2. Type the following text, inserting fill-in fields as indicated:
   Dated this {FILLIN "Enter day (e.g., 1st, 3rd, etc.):"} day of {FILLIN "Enter Month and Year (e.g., October, 1999):"}

   If you can't remember how to insert fill-in fields, refer to the automated pleading exercise earlier in this chapter.

NOTE

The text appears to wrap in this example, but it should be on one line in your document.

3. Select the text that you entered and then create an AutoText entry in the global AutoText template.

4. Delete the text from the template.

5. Test it by inserting it into the template. Word should automatically prompt you to enter the field information.

TIP

To insert an AutoText entry, type the name of the entry in the document and then press the F3 key to insert it.

6. Delete the text that was inserted into the template.

7. Save and close the global AutoText template.

Remember that the global template will not be activated until you close and restart Word. In the future, the template will automatically load. To prevent the template from loading, remove it from the Startup folder.

ANSWERING COMMON TEMPLATE QUESTIONS

My pleading line numbers don't print but they appear onscreen.

When you use the Pleading Wizard to create a pleading, the line numbers are placed in a text box in the header and footer layer. Text boxes are considered a drawing object. What has most likely happened in this case is that the option to print drawing objects has been disabled. To change this, from the Tools menu, choose Options, select the Print tab, and check Drawing Objects.

When I try to save a document, Word only lets me save it as a template.

When Word forces you to save all document types as templates, this is a sure sign that you have been infected with a macro virus. Viruses created to attack Word documents often infect Word by adding macros to the Normal template. Once Word is infected, the virus can replicate—that is, when you have a virus and work on a document, the virus attaches itself to that document. You can't see it, but if you send the document to someone else and they open it, their computer also gets infected. While some viruses are fairly harmless, others can completely wipe out your computer, or the files on a network. The virus named Concept—the most common virus that causes a file to be saved as a template—is just an annoying one.

Make sure that you have the latest virus protection software installed on your computer.

A good article on macro viruses is available on the Microsoft Web site at `http://support.microsoft.com/support/kb/articles/q187/2/43.asp`.

Two good resources for virus and virus protection information are `http://www.symantec.com/` for Norton AntiVirus, and Cheyenne's InocuLAN, which is available at `http://www.cheyenne.com/`.

TIP

AutoOpen, AutoNew, and AutoClose macros run automatically when you open, create, or close a file respectively. Sometimes people who create or distribute viruses put the virus in one of these three macros.

How can I attach a template to the active document?

From the Tools menu, choose Templates And Add-Ins. Click the Attach button, and click OK.

How much automation can I add to a template?

Templates can be very elaborate or very simple. The most important thing to remember is that they are designed to help speed up the process of creating documents of the same type. Many firms choose either to develop very automated templates in-house or to purchase them from a vendor so that the users only have to fill in the blanks in a dialog box. When they click OK, the information fills into the correct location for them and formats with the appropriate style. Figure 10.15 shows an example of what can be done in the way of automating law firm templates. This template is one that Payne Consulting Group created as a part of our template and macro package. For more information visit `http://payneconsulting.com/`.

FIGURE 10.15

An automated letter template

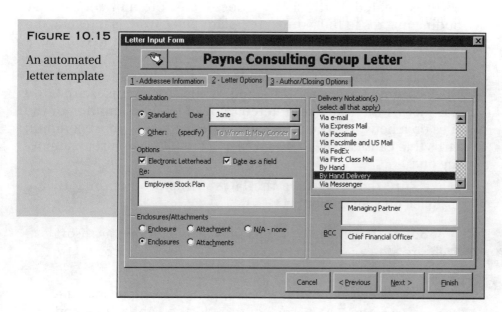

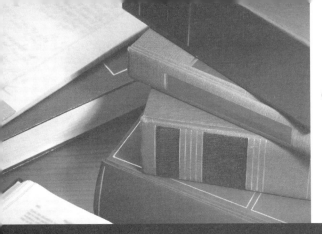

CHAPTER 11

CREATING LEGAL FORMS

IN THIS CHAPTER

- Creating helpful forms for the legal office
- Using and distributing forms
- Inserting and updating form fields
- Formatting and deleting form fields
- Using fill-in fields in forms
- Creating customized Help for a form
- Running a macro within a form field
- Other useful fields

Form creation and usage is an important and useful part of word processing in law firms. Think of the legal or administrative forms required in the daily routines of your firm: you can save a lot of time and expense by making these forms available electronically from within Word. You can increase these savings even more by having users submit forms in e-mail! Whether you want to set up a paper-less office or just want to make completed forms more consistent, Word's forms will help you meet your goal.

With a special toolbar to provide the necessary field codes and tools to generate a basic form, Word makes forms design fun and easy! Although complex forms may require programming, you can complete many of the forms that you use daily without any knowledge of or need for programming.

TIP

For an example of a complex form created in Visual Basic for Applications, download the free Office Services Request Form template from the Payne Consulting Group Web site at `http://www.payneconsulting.com/`.

As this chapter will demonstrate, Word makes creating forms easy and intuitive. Form functionality is another way in which Word simplifies everyday tasks in the legal office.

INTRODUCING FORMS

Forms are documents that contain fields or placeholders for users to enter information. The most important thing to understand about forms is that they are just like any other document that you create in Word. Forms are usually set up as templates that users can access from the New file dialog box. The only difference between a form template and a regular document template is that form templates are a little more restrictive. Forms are protected so users can enter only the options available to them on the form; they cannot modify or edit the text or layout of the form in any way.

A form is created by inserting form fields into a document. Form fields are a special set of fields that allow users to put check marks in boxes, pick items from lists, and insert text into a form.

If you know how to write macros, you can even create forms that automatically run macros based on user input. If you don't know how to write macros, you can use the Record feature in Word to record simple macros that you might want to use in your forms. See Chapter 17, "Introduction to VBA," if you want help getting started with creating macros. But don't let the thought of using macros make you nervous—you don't have to use macros to create forms.

Now that you have an idea of how forms work, you can get started exploring this exciting and powerful feature.

CREATING FORMS

As noted, forms are documents or templates that consist of text and form fields. It is important to remember that forms are protected (locked). Therefore, there must be form fields inserted into the document in every location where users will need to input information into the form.

Form fields are inserted from the Forms toolbar (see Figure 11.1).

USING THE FORMS TOOLBAR

Before you create a form, you need to display the Forms toolbar.

DISPLAY THE FORMS TOOLBAR

1. If the Forms toolbar is not already visible on the screen, from the <u>V</u>iew menu, choose <u>T</u>oolbars.

2. Select Forms from the list of available toolbars.

Mouse users can alternate-click any toolbar and then select Forms from the shortcut menu. To learn more about toolbars, see Chapter 1, "Getting Started."

The Forms Toolbar contains nine buttons. Table 11.1 shows each button and its function.

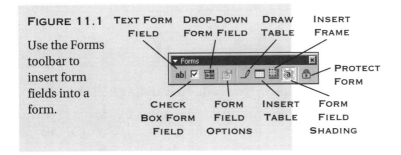

FIGURE 11.1

Use the Forms toolbar to insert form fields into a form.

TABLE 11.1   FORMS TOOLBAR BUTTONS

BUTTON	FUNCTION
Text Form Field	Inserts a text form field where you can enter text.
Check Box Form Field	Inserts a check box into your document that users will either check or uncheck.
Drop-Down Form Field	Inserts a drop-down form field that provides the user with a predefined choice of what can be selected.
Form Fields Options	Displays the properties (settings) for each form field in the document. In a text form field, these include default text, text format, maximum length, macros to run on entry and exit of the field, and more.
Draw Table	Displays the Tables and Borders toolbar that allows you to draw and configure your own table directly in the document easily.
Insert Table	Inserts a table with a specific number of rows and columns where the cells are all the same height and width.
Insert Frame	Inserts a box (or frame) in a specific area of the document that is used to position an item. Although the frame resembles a text box, it is not. To change a frame, first select it and then, from the Format menu, choose Frame.
Form Field Shading	Toggles gray shading on form fields.
Protect Form	Locks the layout and content of the form, and opens the fields for user input.

CREATING A FORM TEMPLATE

When the Forms toolbar is displayed, Word is ready for you to begin entering text and form fields into the form.

The first step is to create a new document or template. If you want users to be able to select this form from the New file dialog box, you will need to create the form as a template. The following exercise demonstrates how to create a template. (See Chapter 10 for more information about templates.)

CREATE A FORM TEMPLATE

1. From the File menu, choose New. The New dialog box appears.
2. Select any template on which you want to base this form. If you want a blank document, Blank Document (on the General tab in the New file dialog box) is usually the default.

FIGURE 11.2

Use the New file dialog box to create a new form template.

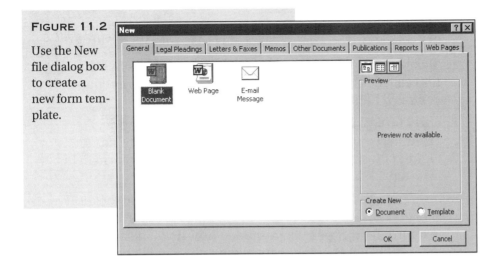

3. Select the Create New Template option (see Figure 11.2).

4. Click OK. A new template appears.

5. From the File menu, choose Save As to save the new template. Make certain to give the template a name that will be easy for users to recognize. For example, if the form will be used to request time off, name the form Time-Off and Vacation Request Form.

NOTE

If you forgot to select the Create New Template option in the New file dialog box, don't worry. Simply select Document Template (.dot) in the Save As Type list in the Save As dialog box. Word will automatically convert the document to a template.

INSERTING TEXT FORM FIELDS INTO A FORM TEMPLATE

The text form field is a special field that enables users to type text into a form. For example, most forms require users to enter their name along with other information, such as an extension or office location. You can insert text form fields to allow users to input text into a form.

This field is also used for inserting dates, calculations, and numbers with special formats such as dollar signs.

INSERT TEXT FORM FIELDS INTO A FORM TEMPLATE

1. Make certain that the Forms toolbar is displayed. See the section called "Using the Forms Toolbar" earlier in this chapter if you need help displaying the Forms toolbar.

2. Enter text asking the user for the desired information. For example, you might enter text asking for the user's name. Figure 11.3 shows an example of a form with text form fields inserted.

3. Insert a text form field into the form at the desired location by clicking the Text Form Field button on the Forms toolbar. The text form field appears as a shaded box. If you have the display of nonprinting characters turned on, five small circles (non-breaking spaces) will appear within the box.

4. Insert as many text form fields as you need for the form.

TIP

If you need to insert a large number of form fields, you might use Copy and Paste, or create an AutoText entry that automatically inserts the form fields. With either method, make certain to set the form field options first so that the newly inserted fields will have the same attributes (see the following section).

FIGURE 11.3

Text form fields enable users to enter text into a form.

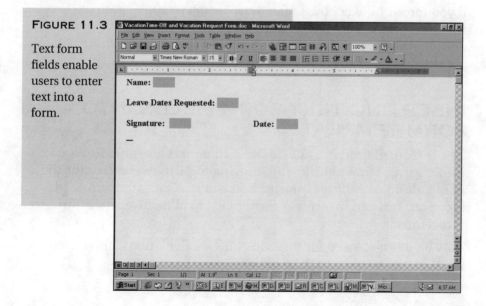

TABLE 11.2   TEXT FORM FIELD OPTIONS

OPTION	PURPOSE
Type	Controls the type of input allowed. Select from the following options:
	Regular Text—allows the user to enter any type of information.
	Number—restricts the entry to numeric data.
	Date—requests a user-entered date.
	Current Date—plugs in the system date.
	Current Time—plugs in the system time.
	Calculation—puts in the results of calculating from data in other fields.
Default Text	Insert default text into the text form field.
	Using default text when appropriate can save users time by reducing the need to enter text. For example, you might use a default value such as the name of the city for an office location field.
Maximum Length	Limit the number of characters that users can type into the text form field.
	A text form field can be unlimited, or you can enter a number between 0 (zero) and 32,767. Entering a value of zero sets the field to "Unlimited."
Text Format	Control the look of the text entered into the field.
	These options will vary depending upon the selected option in the Type list. For example, Regular Text can be formatted in UPPERCASE or in First Capital format. Dates can be formatted with slashes, dashes, or they can be spelled out.

SETTING OPTIONS FOR TEXT FORM FIELDS

After you insert text form fields, you will often want to set options that control how the fields work on the form. Table 11.2 shows the options that are available for text form fields.

SET OPTIONS FOR A TEXT FORM FIELD

1. Double-click the field that you want to modify. The Text Form Field Options dialog box appears (see Figure 11.4).

TIP

If you have trouble double-clicking items, you can alternate-click the field to make a Shortcut menu pop up. Click Properties and the Text Form Field Options dialog box appears.

FIGURE 11.4

The Text Form
Field Options
dialog box
enables you to
set options for
controlling
user input.

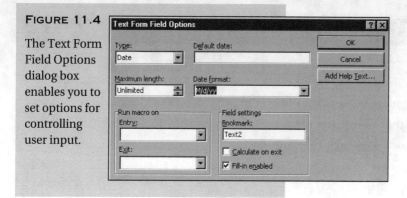

NOTE Keyboard users can access the Form Field Options dialog box by selecting the field, pressing Shift+F10, and then choosing Properties from the shortcut menu.

2. Select the options that you want. Refer to the table of options (Table 11.2) shown earlier in this section.

3. Click OK to close the dialog box when you finish with it.

INSERTING CHECK BOX FORM FIELDS INTO A FORM TEMPLATE

The check box form field is a field that allows users to select from one or more options on a form. For example, you might use check boxes on your time-off form for an employee to indicate whether the time will be leave of absence, vacation, or sick days. If you create a survey form, you can have users check all that apply using check box form fields.

INSERT CHECK BOX FORM FIELDS INTO A FORM TEMPLATE

1. Make certain that the Forms toolbar is displayed.

2. Insert a check box form field into the form at the desired location by clicking the Check Box Form Field button on the Forms toolbar. The check box form field appears.

NOTE

The field is called a check box form field because the button on the Forms toolbar has a check mark. When you select a check box in a form, however, you will see an X rather than a check mark. It's part of Word's design and cannot be changed, so don't spend time trying to find an option for a check mark rather than an X.

3. Insert as many check boxes as you need for the form.

TIP

As with text form fields, you can use Copy (Ctrl+C) and Paste (Ctrl+V) or use AutoText to insert a large number of check boxes.

SETTING OPTIONS FOR CHECK BOX FORM FIELDS

Check box form fields have fewer options available than text form fields do. Table 11.3 describes options that you can set for a check box in the Check Box Form Field Options dialog box.

SET OPTIONS FOR A CHECK BOX FORM FIELD

1. Double-click the field that you want to modify. The Check Box Form Field Options dialog box appears (see Figure 11.5).

2. Select the options that you want. Refer to the table of options shown earlier in this section.

3. Click OK to close the dialog box when you finish with it.

TABLE 11.3 CHECK BOX FORM FIELD OPTIONS

CHECK BOX OPTION	PURPOSE
Check Box Size Auto	Insert a check box in the same point size as the current text.
Check Box Size Exactly	Insert a check box in the specified point size (which must be entered in the adjacent spin box).
Default Value Not Checked	Have the check box clear (unselected) when the user creates a new form.
Default Value Checked	Have the check box selected when the user creates a new form.

FIGURE 11.5

The Check Box
Form Field
Options dialog
box enables
you to set
default
options for
check boxes.

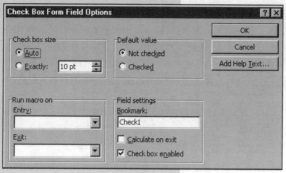

TIP

When the form is protected, users will be able to check and
uncheck the check box form field by pressing either the Spacebar
or the X key.

INSERTING DROP-DOWN FORM FIELDS INTO A FORM TEMPLATE

The drop-down form field lets users select one item from a list of
options on a form. For example, you might use a drop-down list to
allow employees to indicate the city in which their office is located.

Drop-down lists are helpful when you have a large number of items
and you want to conserve space, or when you want to limit users to
selecting only one option (with check boxes, users can select more
than one item).

INSERT DROP-DOWN FORM FIELDS INTO A FORM TEMPLATE

1. Insert a drop-down form field into the form at the desired location by clicking the Drop-Down Form Field button on the
Forms toolbar. The drop-down form field appears.

2. Insert as many drop-down form fields as needed for the form.

TIP

As with text and check box form fields, you can use Copy and Paste
or AutoText to insert a large number of drop-down fields.

SETTING OPTIONS FOR DROP-DOWN FORM FIELDS

Drop-Down form fields have only one specialized option available in the Drop-Down Form Field Options dialog box. The Drop-Down Item option enables you to insert items into and remove items from the drop-down list box. See Figure 11.6 for a picture of the Drop-Down Form Field Options dialog box.

INSERT ITEMS INTO A DROP-DOWN LIST BOX

1. Double-click the drop-down form field that you want to update. The Drop-Down Form Field Options dialog box appears.

NOTE

You can set options in text and check box form fields to specify preferences for each field. The options for text and check box form fields are truly optional. In other words, the fields will still work properly even if you don't set any options. Drop-down form fields, on the other hand, must have options set in order to function properly.

2. Enter the first list item into the Drop-Down Item box.

TIP

If you want the drop-down list to appear a little less cluttered, add two or three spaces after your longest entry to expand the width.

3. Click the Add button to add the item to the Items In Drop-Down List box, or press the Enter key. The item appears in the list.

FIGURE 11.6

The Drop-Down Form Field Options dialog box enables you to insert items into and remove items from a drop-down list box.

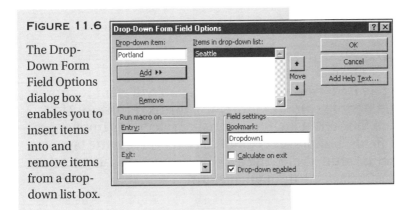

4. Add additional items.

5. To remove an item from the list, select the item in the Items In Drop-Down List box, and then click Remove.

6. To move an item within the list, select the item in the Items In Drop-Down List box, and then click the up or down arrow buttons to move the item.

The order of the items within the Items list is the same order in which the user will see the choices displayed in the drop-down field on the form. Word will not alphabetize the list. The first item in the list will appear as the "default" choice on the form.

If you do not want one of the choices to be displayed by default, you can add a blank item by holding down your Spacebar, or add an option that says "Choose location" (or whatever suits the content of the list).

7. When you finish adding items to the list, click OK to close the dialog box.

If you want to try out the new field, make certain that you protect the form first. If you don't protect the form, the field will not function properly. Protection is covered in the next section.

If you click the Cancel button to close the dialog box, Word does not save the items that you entered.

Figure 11.7 shows all three types of fields inserted into a Vacation Request form.

USING FORMS

Before you release forms for general use, you will want to protect them so that people cannot modify the forms. *Protecting* forms enables users to insert data into and make selections from appropriate form fields, but prevents them from modifying the layout or text of the actual form. Protecting a form also allows users to use the Tab key to easily navigate through the form.

FIGURE 11.7

This example of a time-off request form uses all three types of form fields available in Word.

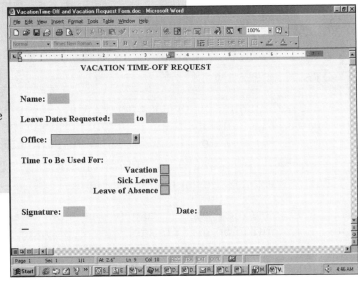

Plan to spend a little time deciding how to implement your firm's forms. Placing them in a Workgroup Template directory on a network might be best, so that forms can be updated regularly and still remain accessible to users (as long as they have network access). If you have a large number of forms, you might want to place them in directories based on practice group or type of form so that users can find the form they want without spending a long time hunting through the template lists. Be sure to read Chapter 10, "Creating Legal Templates," for information about organizing templates.

PROTECTING AND UNPROTECTING FORMS

Protecting forms is easy with Word 2000. You can protect forms with or without a password. If you want to be certain that users cannot modify the forms, you should use a password along with form protection.

A form will not function properly until it is protected. Therefore, even if you do not want to prevent users from modifying the form, you must still protect it. Protect the form without a password if you want to allow users to unprotect it and make changes.

When you tell Word to protect a form, it clears the undo stack of all the steps you took during the development process. This means that you cannot use the Undo command to reverse any edits after a form has been protected. For more information about the Undo command, see Chapter 2, "Working with Text."

PROTECT A FORM

1. Make certain that the form is open in Word. If you have created the form as a template, then the template should be open, rather than a new document based on the template.

2. From the Tools menu, choose Protect Document. The Protect Document dialog box appears (see Figure 11.8).

NOTE

You cannot access the Protect Document dialog box by clicking the Protect Form button on the Forms toolbar. If you want to assign a password, you must go through the Tools menu (as shown in Step 2).

3. Select the Forms option. If the form has multiple sections, the Sections button becomes active. For more information about document sections, see "Inserting Section Breaks" in Chapter 5.

4. By default, all sections of a multisection form are protected. To unprotect specific sections, click Sections. The Section Protection dialog box appears (see Figure 11.9). Clear the options for any sections that you want to unprotect, and then click OK.

5. If you want to protect the form with a password, enter a password in the Password box.

6. Click OK to save the settings and exit the dialog box.

7. If you entered a password, the Password Confirmation dialog box will appear. Enter the password again and click OK.

FIGURE 11.8

The Protect Document dialog box allows you to protect all or part of a form.

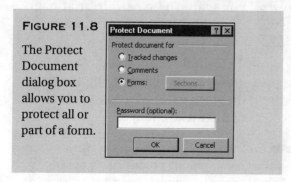

FIGURE 11.9

The Section Protection dialog box enables you to unprotect specific sections of a multisection form.

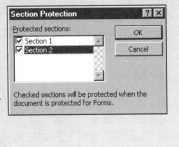

CAUTION

Remember that passwords are *case sensitive*. This means that you must always enter a password in the same case as the original or your entry will be invalid. Keeping a record of passwords in use, along with the names of the documents in which they have been used, might be wise. An alternative is to keep an original copy of the document or template that is not protected so that Word can recover the document if the password is lost. There is no easy way to recover a lost password in Word.

After you have protected a form, you must unprotect it to make modifications to the form.

UNPROTECT A FORM

1. From the Tools menu, choose Unprotect Document.
2. If the document is protected with a password, the Unprotect Document dialog box will appear. Enter the password into the Password box.
3. Click OK. The form is unprotected. If an incorrect password is entered, Word notifies the user that the password is incorrect and the form remains protected.

NOTE

If a document has been protected, but no password assigned, then choosing Unprotect Document from the Tools menu will simply unprotect the form without prompting for a password.

TIP

Mouse users can quickly protect and unprotect forms by clicking the Protect Form button on the Forms toolbar. This button is especially helpful when you're designing forms because you do not enter a password to protect the form. You can quickly protect the form for testing, and then unprotect to continue modifying the form.

COMPLETING A FORM

After you have designed and protected a form, it is ready to be used. When you open a protected form or create a new document from a protected form template, the first field in the form will be selected and you can begin filling out the form.

MOVING THROUGH A FORM WITH THE KEYBOARD OR MOUSE

Keyboard users should press the Tab key to move forward from one field to another. To move backward, press Shift+Tab. You can also use the Up Arrow and Down Arrow keys on the keyboard to position the insertion point within the various fields. If you try to use the arrow keys while a drop-down list is displayed, however, Word will scroll through the items in the list rather than move you to the next or previous field. Mouse users can move from field to field by clicking the field they want to access.

Keyboard users can display items in a drop-down list by pressing Alt+Down Arrow (notice that the arrow is underlined on the drop-down form field). Use the Up Arrow or Down Arrow key to move through the items on the displayed list. To select an item, press Enter. Mouse users can display items in a drop-down list by clicking the down arrow on the drop-down form field. To select an item, click it with the mouse. Pressing Enter makes a selection in a drop-down list.

Keyboard users can select or clear a check box by pressing the Spacebar or the letter X while the check box form field is selected. Mouse users can select or clear a check box by clicking it with the mouse.

To insert text into a text form field, simply type the desired text. You can insert a Tab into a text form field by pressing Ctrl+Tab. Pressing Enter or Shift+Enter in a text form field will create a paragraph or new line, respectively.

If a field has been limited in length, Word will not allow any characters to be entered after the limit has been reached.

Users can continue to press the Enter key in a limited field, even after the limit has been reached. This may expand the size of the field to a point where the form runs off of the page.

If you have added Status bar Help text to the form fields, the Help text will appear on the Status bar as you move from field to field. Other Help text may appear if a user presses F1 while a field is selected. Adding Help text to form fields is covered later in this chapter.

Word has a feature called Form Field Shading. You might find turning this option on while you're completing a form useful so that you can easily see each form field. You can activate Form Field Shading by clicking the Form Field Shading button on the Forms toolbar.

COMPLETE A FORM

1. Create a new document based on a form template that you have created. If you have created a document rather than a template, open the document.

If the first field of the form is not selected, the form has not been protected. Turn on document protection so that the form functions correctly. See the "Protecting and Unprotecting Forms" section earlier in this chapter for help with protecting a form.

2. Complete the selected field by entering text, selecting or clearing a check box, or selecting an item from a drop-down list.
3. Press the Tab key to move to the next field.
4. Continue to fill out the form until it is completed.
5. After you complete the form, you can save it like any Word document.

MODIFYING FORM FIELDS

Word provides many ways to customize forms so that they are easier to use and read. You already learned how to set options for fields earlier in this chapter. You can also format, name, and disable fields.

FORMATTING FORM FIELDS

You can format form fields as easily as you format text. Just select the field that you want to format and then apply the desired formatting. For more information about formatting text, see Chapter 3.

Keep in mind that employees will not be able to format fields in a protected form. You must apply formatting while you are creating the form, or allow users to unprotect the form to apply formatting.

FORMAT FORM FIELDS

1. Select the field that you want to format.

2. Apply the desired formatting from the Format, Font menu or Formatting toolbar. Keyboard users can use any of the available formatting shortcut keys.

For a complete list of formatting methods and options, see Chapter 3, "Formatting Text."

NAMING FORM FIELDS

Naming fields makes them easier to locate on large forms. It also allows you to specify fields when you're using macros or calculating fields. For example, you might have several fields in a travel reimbursement form that you want to calculate. Naming the fields enables you to easily perform mathematical functions with the values entered by the user. Calculating fields is covered later in this chapter.

When you insert a field, Word automatically assigns it a bookmark name. Default bookmark names are fairly generic. For example, text form fields are named Text1, Text2, Text3, and so on as they are inserted. You can rename fields, though, to make the names more intuitive and helpful.

If you insert fields using Copy and Paste, Word does not assign a default bookmark name.

If you insert fields using an AutoText entry, the bookmark name will always move to the newly inserted field. For example, if you insert a text form field with the name "Text1," and then select that entry and create an AutoText entry based on it. When you then insert the new text form field by using AutoText, the bookmark name of "Text1" will be assigned to the newly inserted field. The original field will no longer have a name.

NAME A FIELD

1. Double-click a field in an unprotected form to activate the Form Field Options dialog box for that field.

NOTE

If double-clicking a field does not open the Form Field Options dialog box, make certain that the form is unprotected.

2. Enter a bookmark name in the Bookmark box.
3. Click OK to save the new name and close the dialog box.
4. To quickly move to a named field, choose Go To from the Edit menu. Keyboard users can press Ctrl+G.
5. In the Enter Page Number box, type the name of the field and then click Go To. The field is selected.

TIP

If you can't remember the name of the field, select Bookmark from the Go To What list. Then select the name from the Enter Bookmark Name list.

6. Click Close to close the dialog box. Keyboard users can press the Esc key.

Later in this chapter, you'll see how to use named fields in a calculation.

DISABLING FORM FIELDS

Sometimes you may want to prevent users from entering data or selecting a form field. You can disable form fields to prevent users from accessing them. You can set a default value for a disabled field, or leave the field clear.

If a field is disabled, a user cannot move to or select the field when the form is protected.

DISABLE A FORM FIELD

1. Double-click the field that you want to disable to open the Form Field Options dialog box (the form must be unprotected or the dialog box will not appear).

2. Clear the option that enables the field. The dialog box will offer these options based on the type of field selected:

   ◆ Text field   Fill-In Enabled

   ◆ Check box   Check Box Enabled

   ◆ Drop-down field   Drop-Down Enabled

3. Click OK to close the dialog box and save the selected option.

DELETING FORM FIELDS

As forms are updated and modified, and as your firm changes the way it does business, you may want to remove fields from a form. You can delete form fields as easily as text.

DELETE FORM FIELDS

1. Select the field that you want to delete.

2. Press the Delete or Backspace key.

NOTE

If you attempt to delete a form field that is not selected, Word will select the field rather than remove it. Pressing the Delete or Backspace key a second time will then remove the field from the form.

CLEARING FORM FIELDS

If you test a form in the form template, the values that you input remain visible after you unprotect the form. They will automatically clear the next time that you protect the form. You may want to manually clear all (or selected) fields without reprotecting the document, however. You can use the Update Field command to clear the existing form field entries in a form.

CLEAR FORM FIELDS

1. Make certain the form is unprotected.

2. Select the entire form, or select just the portion that you want to clear.

3. Press the F9 key. All fields are returned to their default values.

CALCULATING FIELDS

One of the most powerful and useful form features is the capability to perform calculations. Imagine how helpful such a feature can be when you're creating expense report forms or other forms that include totals and calculations.

You can calculate any values on a form or document. For example, you can calculate numbers in a table or numbers entered into named form fields. If you have a large number of fields to calculate, you will probably find using a table easier.

Both methods are described in the next two exercises.

CALCULATE NAMED FORM FIELDS

1. Insert two or more text form fields into a form. These fields will hold the values entered by the user.

2. Set the Form Field Options for each of the fields, making them Number type fields with Calculate On Exit selected, and enter a unique bookmark name for each field.

When you name form fields, use names that are easy to remember, because you will need to recall each name when you insert calculation fields. If you have a large number of fields, you might find writing down the name of each field helpful.

The Calculate On Exit option forces Word to update the calculated total field when the user moves out of any field included in the calculation. If you do not select this option, users will not see the updated total onscreen.

You may choose to select this option only for the final field so that the total is not updated until the user inputs the final number. If the user moves back to an earlier field and makes changes, however,

Word will not reflect the new total until the user enters and exits the final number field. This feature can be confusing and cumbersome for users because they must Tab into and out of the final field each time they change a field that is used in the calculation. It also causes forms to be incorrect if the user fails to enter and exit the final field.

3. Insert another text form field into the form. This field will hold the total of the values entered by the user.

4. Double-click the field that will contain the total. The Form Field Options dialog box appears for that field.

5. From the Type list, select Calculation.

6. In the Expression field, enter a calculation using the normal mathematical operators and the named form fields that you want to calculate. Figure 11.10 shows an example of a calculation.

NOTE

The Expression box does not appear until Calculation is selected in the Type list.

TIP

You can use the Sum function for entering calculations. For example, entering:

=Meals+Tickets+Parking is the same as entering
=Sum(Meals,Tickets,Parking)

This function is even more helpful when you're working with numbers in a table. See the next exercise for more information and examples.

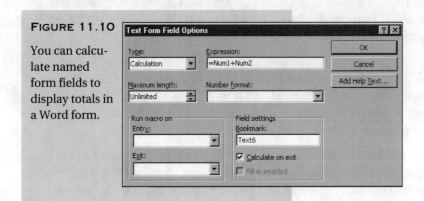

FIGURE 11.10

You can calculate named form fields to display totals in a Word form.

7. If desired, select a format for the total from the Number Format list.

8. Click OK to save the settings that you have entered and close the dialog box.

After you have inserted the calculation field, test the form. The numbers should calculate automatically. If the total field is not updated as you move through each field, make certain that you have selected the Calculate On Exit option for each field included in the calculation, as mentioned earlier.

CALCULATE FORM FIELDS IN A TABLE

1. Set up a form that contains text form fields in a table. Make certain that you set the fields so that users can enter only numbers, and so that the total is calculated on exit (see the preceding exercise if you need help setting these options).

   Figure 11.11 shows an example of a protected form with text form fields in a table. If your form is not protected, it will look different.

TIP

Setting the field type to Number prevents users from accidentally entering text into a field that will be used in a calculation.

NOTE

You do not have to set a name for form fields when you calculate fields in a table. If you want to calculate specific, noncontiguous fields in a table, however, you may find using named form fields easier.

2. Set up the calculation field in the table cell that will hold the total.

3. If the fields used in the calculation all appear in the same column or row, you can use the Sum function to insert the total. Table 11.4 lists the behavior of functions in the Expression box.

For more information about the mathematical functions available in Word, explore Word's Help and search on the topic Math.

FIGURE 11.11

Placing form fields in a table makes calculating them easier.

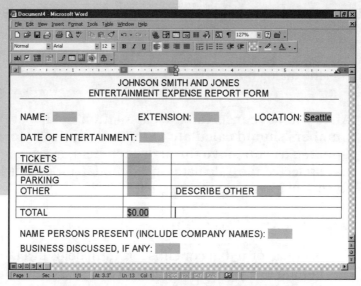

  Even with tables, you must set the fields used in the calculation to Calculate On Exit in the Form Field Options dialog box; if you don't, the totals will not appear when you complete the form.

CREATING PROFESSIONAL-LOOKING FORMS

There are a number of ways in which you can give forms a professional appearance. Features such as fill-in fields, reference fields, and Help text can make complex forms easier to use.

TABLE 11.4   CALCULATING IN THE EXPRESSION BOX

TO TOTAL . . .	ENTER . . .
An entire column	=Sum(Above)
An entire row	=Sum(Left)
A Specific set of cells	=Sum(A1:C1) or =Sum(A1,C1,E1)

Users who are familiar with Excel spreadsheet formulas will be familiar with these commands. For more information about this feature, consult Word's Help.

You may find calculating named fields easier in some instances.

USING FILL-IN FIELDS

Fill-in fields are special fields in Word that you can use to prompt users for information. The really neat thing about fill-in fields is that they are automatically activated whenever someone creates a new form using a form template. For example, if you create a form template and want a user to enter the name and address of a contact or client on each new form, you can use a fill-in field to prompt the user for the information.

Users can press Enter to insert returns directly into a fill-in field.

Keep to a minimum the number of fill-in fields that you use in a form. Remember that you can use text form fields for the majority of information needed on a form. Fill-in fields are best used when multiple lines of information are required (for example, a client's name and address). Using a large number of fill-in fields can frustrate users because they cannot skip over them.

After users insert the fill-in field text into a protected form, they cannot modify that information if they make a mistake. The only way to update the information is to unprotect the form. You can write a macro to enable field updating in a protected document. For more information about macros, see Chapter 17, "Introduction to VBA," or contact Payne Consulting Group for information on classes on Word and Visual Basic for Applications (VBA).

INSERTING FILL-IN FIELDS INTO FORMS

To insert a fill-in field into a document, use the Field dialog box.

INSERT A FILL-IN FIELD INTO A FORM

1. Position the insertion point in the form template where you want the fill-in field to appear.

2. Choose Field from the Insert menu. The Field dialog box appears (see Figure 11.12).

3. In the Field Names list, select Fillin. If you don't see Fill-in in the Field Names list, check to make sure that (All) is selected in the Categories list.

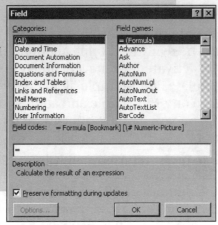

FIGURE 11.12

Use fill-in fields to automatically prompt users for multiple lines of information.

4. In the <u>F</u>ield Codes box, enter a prompt for the field and any switches that you want to add to the field. Table 11.5 shows how the field should appear in the <u>F</u>ield Codes box with and without switches. You can replace the information shown in quotation marks with anything that you want to say to the user (see examples in the table).

NOTE

The prompt is what the user will see when the fill-in field appears onscreen.

TABLE 11.5 FILL-IN FIELD SAMPLES

ENTER . . .	TO PRODUCE THIS RESULT . . .
FILLIN "Enter the client name and address:"	A fill-in box asking the user to enter the client's name and address.
FILLIN "Enter the name of the firm:" \d "Johnson, Smith and Porter".	A fill-in box asking the user to enter name of a firm, with the fill-in box defaulting to "Johnson, Smith and Porter."
FILLIN "Enter the name of the firm:" \d "Johnson, Smith and Porter" * UPPER.	A fill-in box asking the user to enter name of a firm, with the fill-in box defaulting to "JOHNSON, SMITH AND PORTER". Whatever the user types will also appear in UPPERCASE.

You do not have to use the \d switch (default text) to use a capitalization switch. For example, the following fill-ins would produce the examples shown:

FIELD TEXT . . .	RESULT . . .
FILLIN "Enter your name:" * UPPER	SALLY PORTER
FILLIN "Enter your name:" * LOWER	sally porter
FILLIN "Enter your name:" * CAPS	Sally Porter
FILLIN "Enter your name:" * FIRSTCAP	Sally porter

5. When you have completed the field code text, click the OK button to insert the field.

6. Word displays the fill-in box. Click the OK button to close the box without entering text. Keyboard users must press Tab to select the OK button, and then press Enter. This is because you can use the Enter key in the fill-in box area to insert new lines.

If you accidentally press the Enter key in the text area of the fill-in box, press the Backspace key to remove the new line.

If you enter text in the fill-in box at design time, that text will appear in the box each time someone uses the form to create a new document. If you want the box to be empty, be sure to leave it empty at design time, or add a switch for the default to be blank, such as **\d ""**.

7. Word inserts the field. If there is a default value, or if you entered text when prompted, the result will appear onscreen. If you left the box empty, no result will appear onscreen.

If Field Code view is activated, you will see the field code rather than the result on the screen. To turn Field Code view on or off, from the Tools menu, choose Options, and then select the View tab. Select the Field Codes option to see field codes onscreen, or clear the option to see field code results. Keyboard users can press Alt+F9 to toggle Field Code view off and on.

If you want to leave a fill-in box empty but still be able see it onscreen without turning on Field Code view, enter a space into the fill-in box when prompted. The space will be visible on the screen, but when users are prompted in a new form, no default text will appear except the space. Default text is automatically selected within the fill-in box, so when you type a value, Word deletes the space.

8. To test the final version of the form template, create a new document based on the form template. The fill-in boxes appear automatically when you create the new document.

When you protect a form, Word automatically updates all fields. As a result, you are prompted once again with all of the form's fill-in boxes.

If you print a form and the fill-in fields prompt you for answers again, Field Updating may be turned on in the Print Options. To turn Field Updating off, from the Tools menu, choose Options, and then select the Print tab. Clear the Update Fields option in the Print Options section.

If you want to update a fill-in field at design time, select the field (or fields) that you want to update and then press the F9 key.

USING REFERENCE FIELDS TO REPEAT INFORMATION IN A FORM

Sometimes you will need to repeat user input elsewhere in a form. Rather than require users to input the same information multiple times, you can use bookmarks and reference fields to enable them to repeat the information throughout the form.

Word gives you multiple ways to set bookmarks in forms. The following exercise shows one method that works for both form and fill-in fields. For information on additional methods for setting bookmarks for fields, refer to Word's help.

NAMING FILL-IN FIELDS

Before you can repeat information, you must name the field for which you want to repeat the value. The following exercise shows you how to name a fill-in field. For information about naming form fields, see the "Naming Form Fields" section earlier in this chapter.

NAME A FILL-IN FIELD

1. Select the fill-in field that you want to name.

NOTE If you cannot see the field onscreen, turn on Field Code view. To do this, from the Tools menu, choose Options. Select the View tab and then select the Field Codes option.

2. From the Insert menu, choose Bookmark. The Bookmark dialog box appears. Keyboard users can press Ctrl+Shift+F5.

3. Enter a name for the field in the Bookmark Name box. Bookmark names cannot contain spaces.

4. Click Add.

REFERENCING NAMED FIELDS

After you have named a field, you can use a reference field to repeat the value of the field elsewhere in a form.

NOTE If you want to reference a form field, in the Form Field Options dialog box, you must set the field that you want to reference to Calculate On Exit. This forces Word to update the reference each time a user exits the field.

INSERT A REFERENCE FIELD

1. Position the insertion point in the form where you want to repeat information.

2. From the Insert menu, choose Cross-Reference. The Cross-Reference dialog box appears.

3. Select Bookmark in the Reference Type list. All available field names will appear in the For Which Bookmark list. If you have other bookmark names in the form, they will also appear in the For Which Bookmark list.

4. Select the bookmark that you want to reference in the For Which Bookmark list.

5. Select Bookmark Text in the Insert Reference To list. For forms, you can clear the Insert As Hyperlink option because users cannot use this feature in a protected document.

If you are working on a large or complex form, you can leave the Insert As Hyperlink option selected to quickly locate a source field during the design process. To use this feature, simply click the reference field in the document, and Word will move the insertion point to the fill-in or form field being referenced.

6. Click the Insert button to insert the reference field into the form.

7. The Cross-Reference dialog box remains onscreen so that you can click back in the document and insert additional reference fields. To close the box, click Close.

If your cross-references are not automatically updating when the form is completed, the cause could be one of the following:

If you are using fill-in fields, your cross-references might not be updating because Word updates fields in the order in which they appear in a document. Although references should automatically update when a new file is created regardless of where they are positioned, I have heard of instances when reference fields did not update when they appeared before the fill-in fields in the document. Make certain that you place reference fields after the fill-in boxes that provide their contents.

If you are using form fields, you must set the form field that you want to reference to Calculate On Exit in the Form Field Options dialog box. Doing so forces Word to update the reference each time that a user exits the field.

ADDING HELP TEXT TO FORM FIELDS

You may want to add Help text to forms to make them easier to use. Users may not always understand what information should be entered in specific fields. Providing Help text for each form field eliminates the need for users to pick up the phone and call for help when they are uncertain how to proceed.

Form fields offer an extensive set of Help text options. You can display Help text on the Status bar as well as by the use of the F1 key (the standard method for executing Help in Windows applications). You can type Help text directly into a Form field, or you can reference AutoText entries for Help text. AutoText entries are helpful when you have several fields that use the same Help text.

ADD HELP TEXT TO A FORM FIELD

1. Double-click the form field for which you want to add Help text. The Form Field Options dialog box appears.

2. Click Add Help Text. The Form Field Help Text dialog box appears see Figure 11.13).

3. Select the Status Bar tab to insert Help text that will appear on the Status bar. Select the Help Key (F1) tab to insert Help text that will appear when the user presses the F1 key.

If you want to create Help text for both the Status bar and the F1 key, create the Help text as an AutoText Entry and reference the entry on both tabs in the dialog box.

4. If you have created an AutoText entry for the Help text, select the AutoText Entry option and then select the entry from the list of available entries.

5. If you are not referencing an AutoText entry, select the Type Your Own option and then enter the Help text into the box below that option.

FIGURE 11.13

The Form Field Help Text dialog box enables you to embed advice to users in a form template or document.

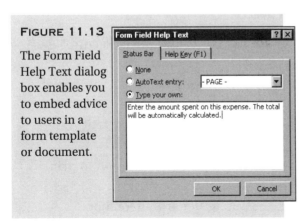

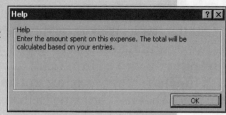

6. Click OK to save the settings and close the Form Field Help Text dialog box. The Form Field Options dialog box appears.

7. Click OK to close the Form Field Options dialog box.

8. Test the changes by protecting the form and tabbing through the form fields. Status bar Help text will appear when a form field is selected. To test F1 key help, press the F1 key when the form field is selected. Figure 11.14 shows an example of a Help dialog box that appears when you press the F1 key.

ADDING MACROS TO A FORM

By adding a macro to a form, you can automate the form in several ways. A macro can be attached to the template your form is based on so the user always has access to it. Once the macro has been created, you can assign it to a form field.

You can use macros to take the information a user stores in a particular field and assign it to other fields in the form.

CREATE A SIMPLE MACRO

1. From the Tools menu, point to Macro, and select Record New Macro.

2. Name the macro **PrintForm,** and save it in documents based on your Investment Options template.

3. Click OK. The macro recorder is now recording each of your actions.

4. From the File menu, choose Print, and then click OK to print the document.

5. Click the Stop button on the Macro Recording toolbar.

ATTACH A MACRO TO A FORM FIELD

1. Insert a new Text field at the bottom of your form. In the Text field properties, set the default text to read **Thank you for your contribution! Click here to print the form.**

2. In the "Run Macro on Entry" area, select PrintForm.

3. Click OK.

4. Protect the form and see your macro in action.

For information on macros, see Chapter 17, "Introduction to VBA."

OTHER USEFUL FIELDS

Word 2000 has many fields, far more than what is available on the Forms toolbar. While form fields discussed previously in this chapter require the form to be protected, non-form fields do not.

Some common fields are the DATE and TIME fields, PAGE, which is inserted automatically when you add page numbers to a document, and USERNAME, which inserts the name you specify. To specify a username, choose Tools, Options, then select the User Information tab and type a name in the Name box.

THREE KINDS OF FIELDS

Word offers more than 70 fields that can be divided into three categories: *Result fields*, *Marker fields*, and *Action fields*.

RESULT FIELDS

The fields you'll use most frequently are result fields. Result fields retrieve a particular piece of information and place it in the document. When you enter the DATE field, for example, it retrieves the current date from your computer's system clock and enters that date at the field position. Similarly, the FILENAME field retrieves the name of the document and places that information at the field position.

MARKER FIELDS

A marker field does not return a result. Rather, it supplies information to Word. For example, you can use the XE (Index Entry) field to mark entries for an index. The Index Entry field provides the information that Word uses to compile an index.

ACTION FIELDS

Unlike result and marker fields, action fields tell Word to perform an action. For example, the FILLIN field tells Word to prompt the user for information and to store that information in the document. Some action fields tell Word to perform the action only when you update the fields; others tell Word to perform the action automatically.

INSERTING FIELDS

A field can be inserted using the <u>F</u>ield command on the <u>I</u>nsert menu or by pressing Ctrl+F9. If you are familiar with the field and its syntax it may be quicker to insert it manually, if not the Field dialog box provides information and simplifies the process.

FIELD DIALOG BOX

Most fields are inserted from the field dialog box shown in Figure 11.15. You can open this dialog box by choosing <u>F</u>ield from the <u>I</u>nsert menu.

INSERT A FIELD FROM THE FIELD DIALOG BOX

1. From the <u>I</u>nsert menu, choose <u>F</u>ield.
2. Select Date and Time from the <u>C</u>ategories list.
3. Select Time from the Field <u>N</u>ames box.

FIGURE 11.15

To view Help on a specific field, select it in the Field Names box, and press F1.

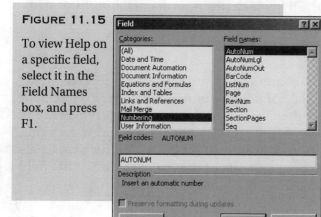

4. Click Options to see formats that you can apply to the field.

5. Select h:mm:ss AM/PM and click Add to Field and click OK ad then OK again to close the Field dialog box. The current time is inserted into the document with the format: hour:minutes:sections AM/PM.

6. Alternate-click on the field and choose Toggle Field Codes to see the inserted field code.

7. Alternate-click on the field and choose Toggle Field Codes again to display the field code result.

8. Update the field code by placing your insertion point within the field and pressing F9.

INSERT A FIELD MANUALLY

Field characters can be quickly inserted by pressing Ctrl+F9. Once the characters are inserted it is simply a matter of typing in the field type, whichever instructions are required, and the desired switches. One of the best uses of manually inserting field codes is simple math calculations. For example, press Ctrl+F9 and type =98*9 and when you press F9, you get the result of multiplying 98 by 9–784.

MANUALLY INSERT A FIELD

1. Create a new blank document.

2. Save the document with the name **fields**.

3. Press Ctrl+F9 to insert a field into the document.

4. Type **filename** within the field brackets.

5. Press F9 to update the field. The name of the document is inserted at the insertion point.

6. Alternate-click on the field and choose Toggle Field Codes from the shortcut menu.

7. Enter a space and a **\p** after filename and press F9 to update the field. The full path of the document displays as the field result.

PREVENTING A FIELD FROM BEING UPDATED

To lock a field and prevent updates until it is unlocked press Ctrl+F11. The field can be unlocked by pressing Ctrl+Shift+F11. To unlink the field and permanently convert the current result to normal text press Ctrl+Shift+F9 or Ctrl+6 (not the 6 on the numeric keypad).

INSERTING FIELDS AS A TEXT PLACEHOLDER

One field that is useful to law firms is MACROBUTTON. This field runs a macro when a user double-clicks the field or presses Alt+Shift+F9.

Another use for this field is to create "Click Here and Type" or text placeholder fields where the user selects the field and replaces the field with information. You can insert any message that you want to display to users when creating the field.

To insert a field such as this, press Ctrl+F9 to insert the field. Type **MACROBUTTON NOMACRO Enter the Judge's Name** in the field. Press F9.

If you use this type of field to create firm wide templates, make sure to set field shading to always so the field gets set apart from normal text. To do this, from the Tools menu, choose Options and select the View tab. Under Field Shading: select Always.

ANSWERING COMMON FORMS AND FIELDS QUESTIONS

Can I print just the data in a form?

If your firm has preprinted forms and you just want to print the information that has been filled into form fields, from the Tools menu, choose Options. Select the Print tab and check the Print Data Only For Forms option.

How can I save just the data entered into the form?

In the Save As dialog box, from the Tools menu, choose General options. Select the Save Data Only From Forms option.

I see the field name instead of the result. How can I find out what's in the field?

A great thing about fields is that they can be toggled to show the field name or the result of what was entered into the field. While the field name is great for troubleshooting or creating new fields, it makes the form virtually useless for the one who has to fill it out or use the data. If your field names are showing instead of the value, from the Tools menu, choose Options. Select the View tab and uncheck Field Codes.

CHAPTER 12

WORKING WITH LONG DOCUMENTS

IN THIS CHAPTER

- ◆ Creating a table of contents
- ◆ Creating a table of authorities
- ◆ Working with indices
- ◆ Adding footnotes and endnotes
- ◆ Marking bookmarks
- ◆ Locating cross-references
- ◆ Counting words
- ◆ Formatting captions
- ◆ Creating a table of figures
- ◆ Using hyperlinks
- ◆ Troubleshooting long documents

Have you ever been trying to meet a filing deadline, only to realize that someone forgot to mark the entries for the table of contents? Or perhaps you've received a document with cross-references, and upon review, you notice that the paragraph numbers referred to are incorrect and out of date. The features described in this chapter can help you manage those long, complex documents that you work with every day.

Producers of long documents need to be able to rely on their word processor to quickly and accurately create tables of contents, tables of authorities, footnotes, cross-references, and other features for organizing complex documents. Without automated methods for organizing long documents, you can easily become frustrated and run the risk of missing critical deadlines. In this chapter, you'll learn how to use the built-in tools available in Word for managing long documents. These tools include Table of Contents, Table of Authorities, cross-references, indices, and more.

TABLE OF CONTENTS

When you use Word's styles to create documents, generating a table of contents is quick and painless. With only a few mouse clicks, you can have Word find the paragraphs in the document that are formatted with heading styles, indent each level appropriately, and assign tab leaders, page numbers, and other formatting. In just a few seconds, you can generate an accurate table of contents!

Of course, the Table of Contents feature does not have to use Word's heading styles. You can customize the Table of Contents feature so that it references any style in a document, or you can manually mark table of contents entries using field codes. Whichever you choose, updating and maintaining the table of contents is a snap. You can even click the page numbers in the table of contents to quickly jump to that location in the document. Figure 12.1 shows a typical table of contents.

NOTE

In Normal and Print Layout view, table of contents appear as a hyperlink with the page number of the entry displayed. When you click the hyperlink, you go to that page. If you display the table of contents in Web Layout view, the page numbers disappears.

FIGURE 12.1

The table of contents in this agreement is formatted using the Formal format, one of six formats available in Word.

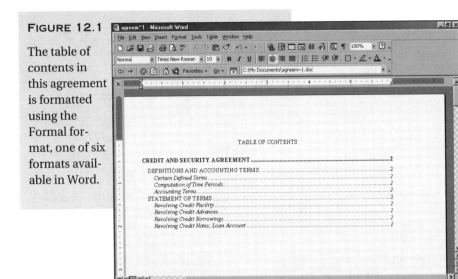

GENERATE A TABLE OF CONTENTS USING WORD'S BUILT-IN STYLES

You can generate a table of contents using Word's built-in styles, such as Heading 1, 2, and 3, or by creating and using your own custom styles. If you have a document with no style formatting, the first step is to select the headings and other paragraphs in the document that need to be in the table of contents, and then apply the appropriate styles to the paragraph. See Chapter 6, "Styles," for more information about applying styles.

If the document already contains styles, you need to decide which styles to use in the table of contents. One way to visually determine which styles are being used in the document is to activate the Style Area. The Style Area appears in a pane on the left margin of the screen. It lists the style for each paragraph next to the paragraph it is applied to. The Style Area is available in Normal or Outline view. From the Tools menu, choose Options, and then select the View tab. In the Outline and Normal options section, change the Style Area width from 0 to 1 inch. Switch to Normal or Outline view to see the styles in the document.

INSERT A TABLE OF CONTENTS

1. Open a document and apply Heading 1, 2, and 3 to paragraphs that you want to appear in the table of contents.

TIP

To quickly apply Heading 1 style, place the insertion point in the paragraph and press Alt+Ctrl+1. Press Alt+Ctrl+2 for Heading 2, or Alt+Ctrl+3 to format the paragraph with Heading 3 style.

2. Place the insertion point in the document where you want to insert the table of contents.

3. From the Insert menu, choose Index And Tables, and then select the Table of Contents tab. The Table of Contents tab appears on top of the stack, as shown in Figure 12.2.

4. Click the drop-down arrow in the Formats list box and select a format. Notice how the Print Preview window changes to reflect the format you have selected.

NOTE

If you select the From Template format, Word builds the table of contents using the TOC styles defined in the template the document is based on. You can modify these styles if you need to make changes to the formatting of the table of contents. This topic is covered later in this chapter, in "Modifying Table of Contents Styles."

5. Clear the Show Page Numbers option if you want to remove page numbers from the table of contents.

6. Clear the Right Align Page Numbers option if you want to place the page numbers directly next to the headings.

FIGURE 12.2

The Table of Contents tab of the Index and Tables dialog box.

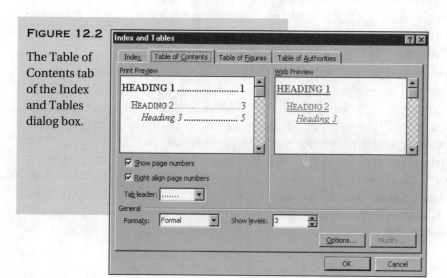

7. Click the spin box arrows next to Show <u>L</u>evels to specify which levels of heading styles should be included in the table of contents. Keyboard users can type a number directly into the Show <u>L</u>evels box.

8. Choose (none) in the Ta<u>b</u> Leader box if you want to remove tab leaders from the table of contents, or select a tab leader that you wish to use. Remember that tab leaders disappear in Web Layout view.

9. Click OK to insert the table of contents.

BUILDING A TABLE OF CONTENTS USING CUSTOMIZED STYLES

What if you don't want to use Word's built-in heading styles for a table of contents? Perhaps you have created your own styles, such as OutlineLevel 1, OutlineLevel 2, or OutlineLevel 3, and you wish to use these styles in the table of contents. You can use a combination of built-in and user-defined styles when generating the table of contents.

GENERATE A TABLE OF CONTENTS USING CUSTOM STYLES

1. Open a document that has been formatted with customized styles.

2. Place the insertion point in the document where you want to insert the table of contents.

3. From the <u>I</u>nsert menu, choose In<u>d</u>ex And Tables, and then select the Table of <u>C</u>ontents tab.

4. Click <u>O</u>ptions. The Table of Contents Options dialog box appears (see Figure 12.3).

5. Locate the customized styles in the list of available styles and assign each a TOC level by typing a number in the TOC <u>L</u>evel box.

FIGURE 12.3

Determine whether the table of contents is built from styles, marked table entry fields, or both.

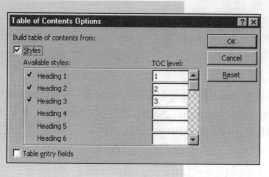

NOTE

In the Table of Contents Options dialog box, you can select Word's built-in styles as well as customized styles that you have created.

6. Click OK to close the Table of Contents Options dialog box. The Index and Tables dialog box appears.

7. Click OK to insert the table of contents.

NOTE

If the page numbers for the table of contents pages need to be numbered differently from the rest of the document (for example, i, ii, and iii), remember to place section breaks around the table of contents. See Chapter 5, "Page Setup and Layout," for more information about section breaks and page number formatting.

The Table of Contents feature generates a field, not actual text; this may make the table of contents appear shaded. The shading is displayed onscreen and does not print. To remove the shading, from the Tools menu, choose Options, and then select the View tab. Select Never from the Field Shading drop-down list to remove any shading in the document, or select When Selected to have the shading appear only when you click in the table of contents.

On some occasions, you may not see the table of contents, but instead see some strange characters that look like {TOC \o "1-3"}. When this happens, you're seeing the field codes that create the table of contents, not the results of the field codes. To view the table of contents again, press Alt+F9 to toggle the field codes in the document.

UPDATING A TABLE OF CONTENTS

As you continue to edit your document and add headings, you'll periodically need to update the table of contents. As noted in the preceding section, the table of contents is a field, meaning that Word created it for you based on the styles in your document. Word gives you four ways to update a table of contents; choose the method that works best for you:

- **Shortcut menu**. Alternate-click anywhere in the table of contents and choose Update Field from the shortcut menu.

- **Keyboard**. Click anywhere in the table of contents and press the F9 key on the keyboard.

- **Update selected text**. Select the text you want to update, and then press F9 to update all fields in the selected region. This method works well when you have additional fields in the document, such as cross-references, indices, and other tables.

- **Update when printing**. From the Tools menu, choose Options, and then choose the Print tab. Select Update Fields in the Printing Options section. This updates the table of contents as well as all other fields every time you print the document.

Regardless of how you choose to update the table of contents, Word opens an Update Table of Contents dialog box. You have two choices when you update the table of contents:

- **Update Page Numbers Only**. Word repaginates the document and updates any page numbers that have changed during editing. Any manual editing or formatting in the table of contents is preserved.

- **Update Entire Table**. Word updates the table of contents headings and the page numbers. If you have manually edited the table of contents by adding or deleting text, the manual changes in the table of contents are lost.

CAUTION

If you made changes to headings within the document during editing, make certain that you update the entire table, or the new table of contents will not reflect those changes.

Figure 12.4 shows the Update Table of Contents dialog box.

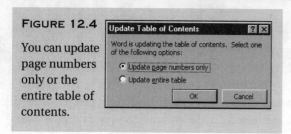

FIGURE 12.4

You can update page numbers only or the entire table of contents.

DELETING OR REPLACING A TABLE OF CONTENTS

To delete the table of contents, double-click at the beginning of the field to select the entire table and then press the Delete key on the keyboard.

You may want to replace a table of contents with a new one rather than delete it. There are several reasons you might want to replace an entire table of contents:

- **Change in formats**: You have inserted a table of contents with one format, and you want to replace it with a table of contents of another format.

- **Change in styles**: You built the original table using Heading 1, 2, and 3 styles, and now you need to include Heading 4 style.

- **Change in methods**: You built the original table of contents using marked table entry fields, and now you want to include styles.

You can replace the current table of contents with a new one from the Insert menu by choosing Index And Tables. Select the Table of Contents tab and choose the new formatting and style options that you want. Click OK to receive a dialog box asking whether you want to replace the current table of contents. Click OK, and the new table of contents replaces the previous one.

MODIFYING TABLE OF CONTENTS STYLES

Do you find that you are continually adjusting the formatting of your table of contents? Perhaps you always change the tab settings or spacing. If you are making the same adjustments to a table of contents each time you update or replace it, you can save a great deal of time by modifying the table of contents styles. Changing the styles preserves the formatting changes when you update or replace the table of contents.

You can even save changes to table of contents styles to the document template so that each new document you create has a table of contents formatted exactly the same.

Word provides nine table of contents styles, named TOC 1 through TOC 9. These styles are used every time you create a table of contents. Word marks each style as an Automatically Updating style, meaning that if you make a change to one paragraph that is formatted with the TOC 2 style, all TOC 2 styles in the document update to reflect the modifications.

You can modify the TOC styles at the same time that you insert the table of contents into your document. The next exercise shows you how.

MODIFY TOC STYLES

1. Open a document that has headings formatted with styles.
2. Place the insertion point in the document where you want the table of contents to appear.
3. From the Insert menu, choose Index And Tables, then select the Table of Contents tab.
4. In the Formats box, select From Template.
5. Click Modify.
6. In the Styles list, select the TOC style that you want to modify and then click Modify.
7. Click Format. Change any attributes of the style as desired.

NOTE

For more information about modifying styles, see Chapter 6.

8. To add the modified styles to the template, select Add To Template in the Modify Style dialog box.
9. Click OK or Close until all open dialog boxes are closed.

CREATE A TABLE OF CONTENTS BY MARKING THE ENTRIES

If you do not want to use styles to create a table of contents, you can manually mark each entry that you want to include in the table of contents. Although this is more labor intensive than using styles, it may sometimes be necessary. For instance, if you do not want the text in the heading paragraph repeated word for word in the table of contents, then you can manually mark text for the table of contents.

You may also want to use manually marked entries when you work with documents that have been converted from other software programs. These documents may already have table entry fields, and you might need to know how to build a table of contents using these fields. For example, documents converted from WordPerfect often have table entry fields.

You can manually mark a table of contents entry in one of two ways. The following exercise demonstrates how to mark table of contents entries with a keyboard shortcut. The tip that follows describes how to add a toolbar button to manually mark your table of contents.

MARK TABLE ENTRIES MANUALLY

1. Open a document in which you want a table of contents.
2. Select the text of the first table of contents entry.
3. Press Alt+Shift+O on the keyboard to open the Mark Table of Contents Entry dialog box (refer to Figure 12.5).
4. The selected text appears in the Entry box. Modify the text of the entry if you want it to appear differently in the table of contents.
5. The default Table Identifier is C. If you only have one table in your document, leave this setting on C. If you have multiple

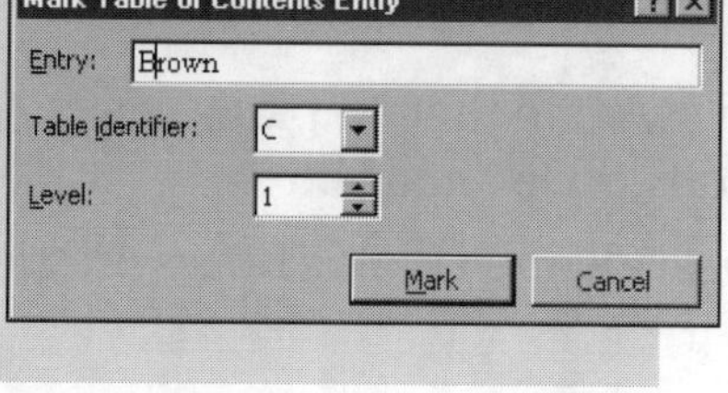

FIGURE 12.5

The Mark Table of Contents Entry dialog box

tables in a document, such as a table of figures or a table of illustrations, you can establish a different Table Identifier for each table.

6. The Level designation in the Table of Contents Entry dialog box represents the hierarchy of entries, with 1 being the most important, or highest, level. Level 1 would be equivalent to a paragraph styled Heading 1.

7. Click Mark to mark the entry.

8. Repeat Steps 2 through 7 until all entries are marked. After selecting each new entry, click in the Entry box to update the information in the Entry box.

TIP

There is another method to mark table of contents entries. The command does not currently appear on any menus, but you can add it to the menu bar or any toolbar. To add the command, from the Tools menu, select Customize. Click the Commands tab and select Insert from the list of Categories. Now scroll through the Commands list until you reach Mark Table Of Contents Entry. Click the command and drag it to one of the existing toolbars, and then close the Customize dialog box. To use the command, select some text and click Mark Table Of Contents Entry.

When you mark a table of contents entry, Word inserts a TC field code next to the selected text. This code is formatted with hidden text, so it appears on the screen but does not print. After you have marked the table of contents entries, you can generate the table of contents. The following exercise shows you how to complete this process.

GENERATE A TABLE OF CONTENTS FROM MARKED ENTRIES

1. Open a document with manually marked table entries.

2. Place the insertion point in the document where you want the table of contents to appear.

3. From the Insert menu, choose Index And Tables, and then select the Table of Contents tab.

4. Click Options.

5. In the Build Table Of Contents From area, clear the option for Styles and select the option for Table Entry Fields.

6. Click OK until all open dialog boxes are closed.

You can build a table of contents based on styles, table entry fields, or both. This flexibility is helpful when you inherit a document with table entry fields and you want to use styles for additional headings. Simply select both options (Styles and Table Entry Fields) in the Table of Contents Options dialog box.

Keep in mind that the text in the document and the TC field code are not linked or connected in any way. If the text in the document changes, you also need to change the text marked in the TC field code. Updating the table of contents does not automatically change marked table entry fields in the document.

MODIFY TABLE ENTRY FIELDS

1. Open a document with manually marked table entries.

2. If the TC field codes are not displayed, click the Show/Hide button to display hidden text.

3. Change some document text that appears in the table of contents. Notice that the marked text in the TC field code does not change.

4. Click inside of the TC field code and edit the text for the table of contents.

The text that appears in the table of contents is surrounded by quotes in the TC field code. Do not delete the beginning or ending quotes, or you will have unwanted text in the table of contents.

5. Alternate-click the Table Of Contents field, and select Update Field from the shortcut menu.

6. Choose Update Entire Table and click OK.

TABLE OF AUTHORITIES

Marking a document for citations to generate a table of authorities is very similar to marking table of contents entries. Word can even search the document for you, looking for terms commonly used in a table of authorities. Word can build a table of authorities for cases, statutes, rules, treatises, constitutional provisions, or any other authority you designate.

MARKING CITATIONS

The following exercise describes the steps necessary for building a table of authorities. You must mark each citation that belongs in the table of authorities.

MARK TABLE OF AUTHORITIES ENTRIES

1. Open a document that you want to mark up for a table of authorities.

2. From the Insert menu, choose Index And Tables, and then select the Table of Authorities tab.

3. Click Mark Citation to open the Mark Citation dialog box, as shown in Figure 12.6.

4. Click Next Citation.

5. Word searches for the first citation in your document. When Word locates a citation that should be included in the table of authorities, click back in the document and select the text containing the full citation. For example, *Brown* v. *Board of Education,* 273 US 177, 93 F2d 14 (1953).

FIGURE 12.6

Keyboard users can press Alt+Shift+I on the keyboard to open the Mark Citation dialog box.

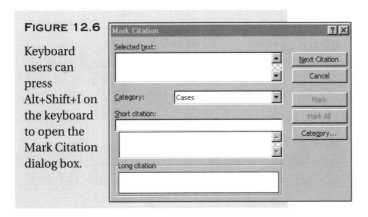

NOTE Word looks for the following terms when it searches for a citation: in re, v., Id., Supra, Ibid, Infra, Cong. (for Congress), Sess. (for Session), § (Section symbol), 18XX) (to find 19th-century dates in parentheses; X can be any number), and 19XX) (to find 20th-century dates in parentheses; X can be any number).

CAUTION Since the product is called Word 2000, you would assume that it could automatically locate dates in or after the year 2000. Guess what—it doesn't.

6. After you select the text, click in the Selected Text area of the Mark Citation dialog box. Word takes what appears in the Selected Text area and marks it as the full citation in the document.

TIP You can apply formatting with keyboard shortcuts in the Selected Text box to change the formatting of the entry. For example, perhaps the case is underlined in the document and you want it italicized in the table of authorities. Select the case in the Selected Text box and press Ctrl+U to remove the underline. Then press Ctrl+I to italicize.

7. Select the Category for the citation.

8. Edit the text as it appears in the Short Citation box to match the short citations in the document. For example, *Brown* v. *Board of Education*.

NOTE If you are not the original author of the document, it pays to take a few minutes to review the document before marking cites. If you specify "*Brown* v. *Board of Education*" as the short citation, Word will not find a reference in the document listed as "the Brown case." However, if you specify "Brown" as the short citation, Word also marks "Mr. Brown" and "the Brown Case" as table of authorities short citations. Spend a few moments familiarizing yourself with the document so you know how to mark the short citations.

9. Click Mark to mark this citation, or Mark All to search through the document and mark all long and short citations that match this entry. After selecting Mark, the long citation is filled in with the selected text in the box above.

10. Repeat Steps 4 through 9 until you have completely marked all the citations in the document. Click Close to close the Mark Citation dialog box.

GENERATING A TABLE OF AUTHORITIES

After you have marked the document for a table of authorities, you insert the table of authorities into the document. The following exercise shows you how to generate the table of authorities.

GENERATE A TABLE OF AUTHORITIES

1. Open a document marked with table of authorities entries.

2. Place the insertion point where you want the table of authorities to appear.

3. From the Insert menu, choose Index And Tables, then select the Table of Authorities tab, as shown in Figure 12.7.

4. Select the different formats in the Formats box and notice how the Print Preview window changes.

5. Clear the Use Passim option to turn passim off. If you use passim, any table of authorities entry with five or more page numbers will be listed as "passim." If you do not use passim, any table of authorities entry will list each page number, regardless of how many there are.

6. Clear the Keep Original Formatting option to have the table of authorities formatted according to the table of authorities style. If you select this option, any formatting (such as underlining) that you have applied to the citation in the document

FIGURE 12.7

Use the Table of Authorities tab to create and format tables of authorities.

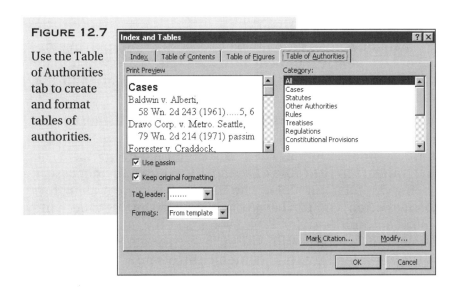

remains with the citation when you insert it into the table of authorities.

7. Select a Category for the table of authorities. Select All to have the table of authorities built for all categories, or select one category to have the table of authorities generated for a single category, such as cases.

8. Select (none) in the Ta<u>b</u> Leader box to turn off tab leaders, or select a desired style from the list (dotted, dashed, or underlined).

9. Click OK to insert the table of authorities into the document.

NOTE

If you want the pages in the table of authorities to be numbered differently from the rest of the document, place the table of authorities in a section by itself. You can then change the page number format for that section. See Chapter 5 for more information about section breaks and page number formatting.

UPDATING A TABLE OF AUTHORITIES

After you have inserted a table of authorities into the document, you can easily update it. If you have added new citations to the document, simply repeat the steps necessary for marking table of authorities entries. If you have added more short citations for a long citation already marked in the document, select the long citation, press Alt+Shift+I, and click Mark <u>A</u>ll.

You can manually modify the table of authorities by applying formatting or by typing text directly into the table. When you update the table of authorities, however, you lose any manual formatting or edits that you have applied.

Instead of editing text in the table of authorities, edit the text in the TA field code. To show the TA field codes, click the Show/Hide button on the Standard toolbar. The text surrounded by quotes is the text that appears in the table of authorities. Make the necessary edits, being careful not to delete the quotes. If you are making format changes often, you can save yourself some time by modifying the table of authorities styles. When you insert the table of authorities, click <u>M</u>odify on the Table of Authorities tab. You can then access the TOA Heading style (which controls how the Category Name appears), or the Table of Authorities style (which controls how the entries in the table of authorities appear). For more information about modifying styles, see Chapter 6.

INDICES

Now that you know how to mark table of authorities entries, you can easily apply that knowledge to the next task: marking index entries. Word can build an index based on the entries that you have marked within a document, or by using a concordance file.

MARKING INDEX ENTRIES

The procedure for marking index entries is exactly the same as for marking table of contents or table of authorities entries. Select the text that you want Word to index, and then press Alt+Shift+X to open the Mark Index Entry dialog box. If you prefer to use menu commands, select the text and choose In_dex And Tables from the _Insert menu. Select the Inde_x tab and click Mar_k Entry to open the Mark Index Entry dialog box.

MARK INDEX ENTRIES

1. Open a document that you want Word to index.
2. Select the first instance of the text to be indexed.
3. Press Alt+Shift+X to open the Mark Index Entry dialog box (see Figure 12.8).

FIGURE 12.8

The Mark Index Entry dialog box has options for numerous customizations for index entries.

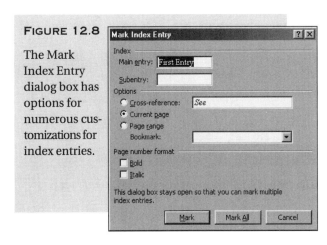

TABLE 12.1 INDEX ENTRY OPTIONS

SELECT . . .	TO . . .
Cross-Reference	Refer to another indexed entry in the document. For example, an entry marked "Extra Hours" might read "See Overtime Policies."
Current Page	Refer to the page number of the marked index entry.
Page Range	Refer to a range of pages spanned by a bookmark. For example, Pages 5–10. You'll learn more about using bookmarks later in this chapter.

4. The selected text appears in the Main Entry box. Edit the entry if you want it to appear differently in the index.

5. Add a Subentry if you need one in the index. For example, if you were indexing an employee handbook, a main entry might be Leave Policies, whereas subentries under that category would be Family Leave, Sabbaticals, and so on.

6. Select an option for the index. Index entry options are shown in Table 12.1.

7. Click Mark to mark this index entry, or Mark All to search through the document and mark all text that matches this entry.

Index entries are case sensitive. If you click Mark All, the text in the document must match *exactly* in order for the Index entry to be created. For example, if the Main Entry is "Style," Word will not mark the text "style." Word also will not mark "Styles" because it does not match exactly. Keep in mind that Word only marks the first instance of the text in any paragraph.

8. Repeat Steps 2 through 7 until all entries are marked. Click Close to close the Mark Index Entry dialog box.

INSERT AN INDEX

1. Open a document marked with index entries.

2. Position the insertion point in the document where you want the index to appear.

3. From the Insert menu, choose Index And Tables.

4. Click the Index tab (see Figure 12.9).

FIGURE 12.9

The Index tab in the Index and Tables dialog box has several built-in formats for an index, or you can define your own format with the options available.

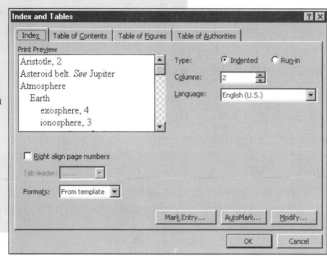

5. Select a Type: Indented or Run-in. Indented indices place subentries on separate lines; run-in indices place subentries on the same line, separated by semicolons.

6. Click the arrows in the Columns spin box to change the number of columns for the index. Keyboard users can type a number directly into the Columns box.

7. Select a Language for the index.

8. Select Right Align Page Numbers to change the alignment of the page numbers.

9. Select (none) in the Tab Leader box to turn off tab leaders, or select a tab leader style.

10. Select the different formats in the Formats box to see the different options in the Print Preview pane.

Tab leaders are available only if you select the option for Right Align Page Numbers, or select the Formal format.

11. Click OK to insert the Index. Word automatically places continuous section breaks at the beginning and the end of the index. This allows you to have the index formatted with multiple columns.

If you mark text that contains a colon or quotation marks, Word inserts a backslash before the colon or each quotation mark in the resulting index entry. This tells Word to print the colon or quotation marks as part of the index entry.

USING A CONCORDANCE FILE

If you are indexing the same information in numerous documents, you can use a concordance file to save time and guarantee consistency in your indices. A *concordance file* is a document containing a two-column table. The first column contains the text in the document to be indexed; the second column contains the index entries for the text.

Because index entries are case sensitive, you may want to turn off the feature that automatically capitalizes the first letter of sentences while you are creating the concordance file. Otherwise, every entry you type in the concordance file will start with a capital letter. From the Tools menu, choose AutoCorrect, and then deselect Capitalize First Letter Of Sentences.

After you create and save the concordance file, from the Insert menu, choose Index And Tables, and click AutoMark on the Index tab. When the Open Index AutoMark File dialog box appears, select the concordance file to have Word search through a document for the text that you specified.

UPDATING THE INDEX

Updating an index is easy. Alternate-click the index to bring up the shortcut menu, and then select Update Field. Keyboard users can click anywhere in the index and then press F9.

To ensure correct pagination, remember to hide the index entries before you generate the index. You can hide the index entries by clicking the Show/Hide button on the Standard toolbar.

FOOTNOTES AND ENDNOTES

People who work in a law firm must eventually use footnotes and endnotes in their legal documents. Luckily, Word makes automatic numbering and insertion of footnotes and endnotes into a document easy. You can edit and format the footnotes and endnotes whenever you wish, and they automatically renumber if you have to add, move, or delete notes. Even better, you can view footnotes and endnotes by holding the mouse pointer directly over the reference number in the document—there's no need to open a separate pane just to see what a note says.

The footnote number in the document is called the *Footnote Reference*; the endnote number in the document is the *Endnote Reference*.

Footnote text appears at the bottom of a page or the end of text; endnote text appears at the end of a document or section. The document pictured in Figure 12.10 shows the ScreenTip that appears for viewing footnotes when you hold the mouse pointer over the footnote reference mark.

NOTE

This chapter discusses footnotes for most of the examples regarding footnotes and endnotes. The two features function almost identically. Where differences occur, you'll get distinct instructions and options.

FIGURE 12.10

Footnotes appear on the screen when you hold the mouse pointer over the footnote reference mark.

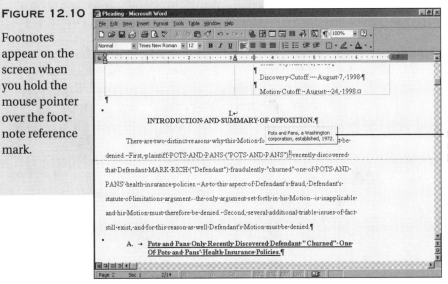

SCREEN TIP
FOR VIEWING
FOOTNOTES

INSERT A FOOTNOTE INTO A DOCUMENT

1. Open a document in which you would like to insert footnotes.

2. Switch to Normal view by choosing <u>N</u>ormal from the <u>V</u>iew menu or by pressing Alt+Ctrl+N.

NOTE

Footnotes appear differently, depending on which view is active. In Normal view, Word opens a Footnote pane, which allows you to split the screen while you add footnotes, so you can view the document and the footnote simultaneously.

3. Place the insertion point at the end of a sentence where you would like the footnote reference mark to appear.

4. Choose Foot<u>n</u>ote from the <u>I</u>nsert menu to open the Footnote and Endnote dialog box, as shown in Figure 12.11. This dialog box provides choices for inserting footnotes or endnotes, changing the style of numbering, or changing where footnotes or endnotes are displayed in the document.

5. Select <u>F</u>ootnote to insert a footnote, or <u>E</u>ndnote to insert an endnote.

TIP

If you choose <u>F</u>ootnote and later need to convert it to an endnote, don't worry. Word gives you the option of converting footnotes to endnotes and vice versa.

6. Select <u>A</u>utoNumber to have Word automatically number the footnotes. Click <u>C</u>ustom Mark to insert your own marks, such as *, **, or ***. You can choose <u>S</u>ymbol from this dialog box to open the Word symbol menu. You can use any symbol as a footnote or endnote reference mark.

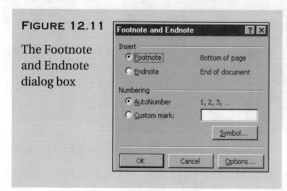

FIGURE 12.11

The Footnote and Endnote dialog box

FIGURE 12.12

The Note Options dialog box contains choices for the starting number, the type of number, and the placement of the number in the document.

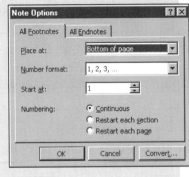

CAUTION
If you choose to use a custom mark, the marks do not automatically update or renumber when you insert or remove footnotes.

7. Click Options to change the number format or the placement of the footnote. Figure 12.12 shows the available options. Table 12.2 provides an explanation of each footnote and endnote option.

TABLE 12.2 FOOTNOTE AND ENDNOTE OPTIONS

SELECT . . .	TO . . .
Place At	Determine where the footnote or endnote appears.
	Options for footnotes are bottom of page or beneath text; options for endnotes are end of document or end of section.
Number Format	Sets the type of number used.
	Options include: Arabic (1, 2, 3); upper- and lowercase alphabetic (A, B, C); upper- and lowercase roman numerals (i, ii, iii); or a series of symbols (*, †, ‡, §).
Start At	Set the starting number for a footnote or endnote.
Numbering	Set an option for numbering:
	Continuous continues the numbers from the previous page.
	Restart Each Section restarts numbering in each new section.
	Restart Each Page restarts the numbering on each new page.

Keyboard users can press Alt+Ctrl+F to immediately open the footnote pane and type the footnote, or Alt+Ctrl+D for an endnote. (Word 97 users may remember pressing Alt+Ctrl+E for an endnote. But in Word 2000, Alt+Ctrl+E inserts the currency symbol for the Euro). Word applies default numbering and placement options to the footnote or endnote.

8. Click OK after you have set the footnote or endnote options. The Footnote and Endnote Options dialog box closes and the Footnote and Endnote dialog box appears.

9. Click OK to close the Footnote and Endnote dialog box and enter the note pane.

10. Type the footnote and click Close on the note pane, or press Alt+Shift+C to close the note pane.

VIEWING AND EDITING FOOTNOTES AND ENDNOTES

Word provides several ways to locate footnotes and endnotes in a document, and viewing and editing them couldn't be easier.

VIEW AND EDIT FOOTNOTES AND ENDNOTES

1. Switch to Normal view by choosing Normal from the View menu or by pressing Alt+Ctrl+N.

2. Choose Footnotes from the View menu.

The View menu includes the Footnotes command even if you have only endnotes in the document. If you have both footnotes and endnotes, a dialog box appears asking which you would like to view.

3. The note pane opens at the bottom of the screen. To view all footnotes, from the Footnotes list, select All Footnotes. To view all endnotes, from the Footnotes list, select All Endnotes.

4. Edit the footnote or the endnote.

5. Click Close on the note pane.

TIP

Keyboard users can press the F6 key while in the note pane to jump between the note pane and the note reference mark in the document.

BROWSING BY FOOTNOTES

After staring at a computer screen all day long, those little reference marks in the document seem to get smaller and smaller. Don't reach for the magnifying glass! Word provides a tool for browsing through documents, one footnote or endnote at a time. Let Word find those tiny numbers and save you some eyestrain.

BROWSE BY FOOTNOTES OR ENDNOTES

1. Click the Browse Object or press Alt+Ctrl+Home.

2. Click the Browse By Footnote icon or the Browse By Endnote icon on the Browse By menu. Each picture represents a different Browse By object. To find out what each one is, place your mouse pointer over the pictures. Figure 12.13 shows the Browse Object.

3. Click the double-headed arrows above or below the Browse Object to move to the next or previous footnote. Keyboard users can press Ctrl+Page Up or Ctrl+Page Down to move to the next or previous footnote or endnote.

TIP

After you have set the Browse Object to browse for footnotes or endnotes, you will not be able to use it for Page Up or Page Down. To reset the Browse Object, click it and select the Browse By Page icon.

FIGURE 12.13

The Browse Object has options for scrolling through the document by footnote or by endnote.

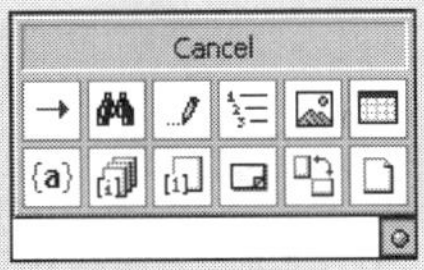

DELETING FOOTNOTES OR ENDNOTES

If you no longer need a footnote or endnote in a document, don't open the footnote pane and delete the text of the footnote. Instead, delete the footnote or endnote reference mark in the document. When you delete a footnote or endnote, the remaining notes in the document automatically renumber.

CONVERTING FOOTNOTES AND ENDNOTES

You've slaved over a long document, getting all the footnotes in the right place, on the correct page. At the last minute, someone tells you that the footnotes were supposed to be endnotes. What can you do? Just take a few seconds to tell Word to convert all the footnotes to endnotes.

CONVERTING ALL NOTES

1. Switch to Normal view from the View menu by choosing Normal, or by pressing Alt+Ctrl+N.

2. From the Insert menu, choose Footnote to open the Footnote and Endnote dialog box.

3. Click Options.

4. To convert all footnotes to endnotes, select the All Footnotes tab and click Convert. To convert all endnotes to footnotes, select the All Endnotes tab and click Convert.

5. When the Convert Notes dialog box appears, select Convert All Footnotes To Endnotes, Convert All Endnotes To Footnotes, or Swap Footnotes And Endnotes.

You don't have to convert all the notes in a document in one fell swoop. Selected notes can be converted one at a time.

CONVERTING SELECTED NOTES

1. Open the note pane from the View menu and choose Footnotes.

2. Select the footnote to be converted.

3. Alternate-click the footnote to be converted, or press Shift+F10.

4. Select Convert To Endnote from the shortcut menu. If you are converting an endnote, the shortcut menu offers Convert To Footnote.

BOOKMARKS

Everyone's used a bookmark before; they're a handy way to mark your place so that when you close the book and then open it later, you can pick up right where you left off. Word uses bookmarks the same way. You can mark any spot in a document and easily jump right back to it. You can even use Word bookmarks as a way to jump to a specific spot in another document.

INSERTING A BOOKMARK

You insert bookmarks into a document by using the Bookmark dialog box. You might insert a small number of bookmarks, however, to easily move back and forth between two or more locations within the document.

You can insert a bookmark anywhere in a document. If you select text and assign the bookmark to the selected text, Word automatically selects the text when you move to that bookmark.

INSERT A BOOKMARK

1. Open a document.
2. Navigate to a page where you would like to insert a bookmark.

TIP

A quick way to get to a specific page is to press the F5 key. Choose Page in the Go To What list; then type the page number in the Enter Page Number box. Press Enter to move to the page specified, and then press the Esc key to close the dialog box.

3. Select a paragraph on the page.
4. Choose Bookmark from the Insert menu. Keyboard users can press Ctrl+Shift+F5. The Bookmark dialog box appears (see Figure 12.14).
5. Type a name for the bookmark in the Bookmark Name box.

FIGURE 12.14

Bookmark names can be up to 40 characters long.

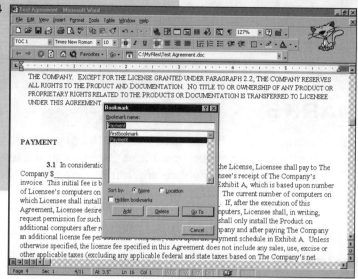

NOTE

You can have numbers in bookmark names, but bookmark names cannot begin with a number. Spaces are not allowed, but you can use the underscore character.

6. Click Add.

USING A BOOKMARK

Now that you have bookmarks in a document, how do you use them? Moving to a bookmark is easy. Simply press F5 or choose Go To from the Edit menu. From the Go To What list, select Bookmark. A drop-down list of all of the bookmarks becomes available in the Enter Bookmark Name list. Choose the bookmark that you want and click Go To; Word takes you to the bookmark. If the bookmark was assigned to text (as in the previous exercise), the text is selected.

You do not have to select Bookmark in the Go To What list. If Page is selected in the list, simply type the bookmark name in the Enter Page Number box and then click Go To. Word moves to that location in the document.

TIP

Word has some built-in bookmark locations in the document. You can use the GoBack command to move to the previous locations where editing occurred. To access this command, press Shift+F5.

Continue pressing Shift+F5 to go back to the previous editing locations.

ADVANCED BOOKMARK FUNCTIONS

If you don't have a caption bank available in your firm, bookmarks are a great way to start one. Every time you create a pleading for a client, you use the same information repeatedly: case number, judge's name, plaintiff, and defendant. You can bookmark all that information and retrieve it for insertion into a new pleading when you need it.

BOOKMARK A CAPTION IN A PLEADING

1. Open an existing pleading that contains a caption.
2. Select the entire text of the caption.
3. From the Insert menu, choose Bookmark. Keyboard users can press Ctrl+Shift+F5.
4. Type **caption** in the Bookmark Name box. Click Add.
5. Save and close the pleading.

After you have marked a caption with a bookmark, you can use it repeatedly. You need to bookmark a caption only once, and then you can retrieve it whenever necessary. If you like this idea, consider marking the pleading template with a caption bookmark. For more information about templates, see Chapter 10, "Creating Legal Templates."

Word allows you to retrieve a portion of an existing document and insert it into a new document by referring to a bookmark name. In the following exercise, you see how to insert a caption from an existing pleading into a new one.

USE A BOOKMARK NAME TO RETRIEVE A PLEADING CAPTION

1. Create a new pleading.
2. Position the insertion point in the document where you would like Word to insert the caption.
3. From the Insert menu, choose File to open the Insert File dialog box (see Figure 12.15).

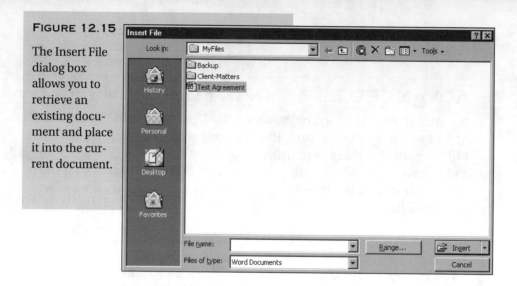

4. Navigate to the pleading that contains the bookmark. Click the pleading document once to select it.

5. Click Range and type the name of the bookmark in the Range box. Click OK to return to the Insert File dialog box.

6. Click Insert. The text of the bookmark appears in the new document.

CROSS-REFERENCES

Legal documents use cross-references in many situations. Cross-references are a valuable way to direct readers to a more detailed area of a document without having to restate the same information. For example, a loan agreement might state the terms of the agreement in one paragraph and then refer to it later with the statement, "See paragraph II.A.2 for Terms of Loan."

Anyone can type "See paragraph II.A.2 for Terms of Loan." But what if you move that paragraph? It may become paragraph II.B.1. It takes a sharp eye to locate all the cross-references in a document and continually check them to guarantee accuracy. Luckily, Word can do this automatically when you use the cross-reference feature.

INSERT A CROSS-REFERENCE

1. Open a document in which you would like to place cross-references.

2. Position the insertion point in the document where you would like a cross-reference to appear.

3. Type **See paragraph** and press the Spacebar.

4. From the Insert menu, choose Cross-Reference to open the Cross-Reference dialog box (see Figure 12.16).

5. Select the type of reference from the Reference Type box. You can cross-reference numbered lists, headings, bookmarks, footnotes, endnotes, equations, figures, or tables.

6. If you do not want the reference to be a hyperlink, clear the Insert As Hyperlink option. If the cross-reference is a hyperlink, readers can click the cross-reference to quickly jump to that portion of the document.

TIP

Inserting hyperlinks can be helpful when you are editing long documents. Hyperlinks enable you to quickly move to the location of a reference by clicking the cross-reference in the document.

7. Select the numbered item, heading, bookmark, footnote, endnote, equation, figure, or table to be referenced in the For Which box.

8. Select information about the reference in the Insert Reference to box. The contents of this box change, depending on what you select in the Reference Type box.

FIGURE 12.16

Numbered items, headings, bookmarks, footnotes, endnotes, equations, figures, and tables can all be cross-referenced.

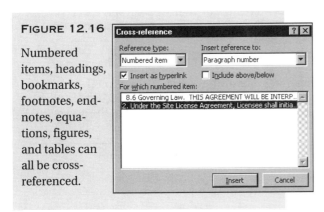

NOTE

If you are referring to a numbered paragraph and you want to reference the paragraph number, you have several choices: Paragraph Number, Paragraph Number (no context), and Paragraph Number (full context). Table 12.3 describes these options.

9. Select the Include Above/Below option to include the words *above* or *below* in the cross-reference. For example, with this option selected, a cross-reference to a numbered paragraph might read "See paragraph II.A.1 above."

10. Click Insert.

The Cross-Reference dialog box stays open until you close it, so you can scroll through the document and insert multiple cross-references. To close the Cross-reference dialog box, click Close.

TABLE 12.3   PARAGRAPH NUMBER OPTIONS FOR CROSS-REFERENCES

SELECT . . .	TO . . .
Paragraph Number	Insert a reference to the paragraph number relative to the current paragraph.
	For example, if you are inserting a cross-reference in paragraph II.A and you are referring to Paragraph II.A.1, the cross-reference reads "Paragraph 1."
	If you are in paragraph II.A and you are cross-referencing Paragraph III.B.1, the cross-reference reads "III.B.1."
Paragraph Number (no context)	Insert a reference to the paragraph number without regard to the position of the paragraph.
	The cross-reference always reads "Paragraph 1" regardless of its placement in the document. This choice can be confusing, as there may be many Paragraph 1's in the document and the reader may not be sure which one is being referenced.
Paragraph Number (full context)	Always list the full location of the paragraph.
	The cross-reference always reads "Paragraph II.A.1" regardless of where it is located. This choice is best as it avoids any confusion about the location of the cross-reference.

VIEWING AND UPDATING CROSS-REFERENCES

If you have inserted cross-references as hyperlinks, you can click a cross-reference to immediately jump to the referenced location in the document. Cross-references may appear on the screen with gray shading. The gray shading is determined by the Field Shading: selection found on the View tab of the Options dialog box. To locate this option, from the Tools menu, choose Options. Field shading does not print.

When a paragraph or heading changes, the cross-reference does not automatically update to reflect the change. Cross-references are *fields*, which means that you didn't type the information that appears in a cross-reference—Word retrieved it for you. Several ways to update fields are available; we discussed these options previously in this chapter in the "Updating a Table of Contents" section. You can also Print Preview the document to update cross-references.

COUNTING WORDS

After you have done all the work to create a long pleading, you may need to count the words in the text. Many courts place a limit on number of words, and it may save you some time to do the count now, instead of having the court return your document!

COUNTING WORDS IN A PLEADING

1. Open a pleading.
2. Place the insertion point anywhere in the document.

To count the words in a portion of the document, select the text that you want to count.

3. From the Tools menu, choose Word Count. Word opens the Word Count dialog box, as shown in Figure 12.17.
4. Select Include Footnotes And Endnotes to include the text of footnotes and endnotes in the word count.
5. Click Close.

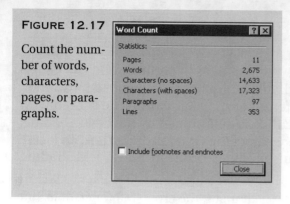

FIGURE 12.17

Count the number of words, characters, pages, or paragraphs.

CAPTIONS

Law offices and word processing packages use different terminology, so a caption may not be what you think it is. Captions in Word are different from captions in pleadings. A Word caption is a descriptive label applied to a table, figure, equation, or other item in a document that Word treats as an object. Captions are very effective for identifying and keeping track of such objects in the document.

If you have only one table in a document, typing a label for the table is OK. But what if you have 20 tables? Do you want to keep track of each table and renumber all of them each time you move, insert, or delete one? Of course not! That's why you use a word processing application. Word's Captions feature automatically numbers objects in a document so that you don't have to.

INSERT A CAPTION ON A TABLE

1. Open a document that contains a Word table. For more information on tables, see Chapter 7, "Using Tables in Legal Documents."

2. Click anywhere in the table.

3. From the Insert menu, choose Caption to open the Caption dialog box, as shown in Figure 12.18.

4. Word is clever: because you are in a table, the Caption automatically reads "Table 1." You can type more information after the label if necessary, such as **Summary of Damages**.

FIGURE 12.18

The Caption dialog box allows you to automatically number objects such as tables, figures, and equations in a document.

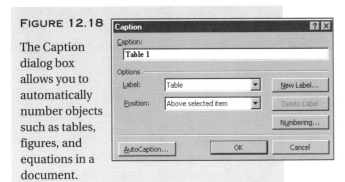

5. The Label list box has "Table" selected because a table was selected when you activated the dialog box. Click the Label drop-down arrow to see additional options. Click New Label to create a new label.

6. Select a position for the label from the Position list box. You can place the label above or below the selected object.

TIP

It's usually a good idea to choose "Above Selected Item" as the position so that Word automatically applies Keep With Next formatting to the caption. That way, the caption and the object are never separated by a page break.

7. Click Numbering to change the format of the caption numbering. You can choose Arabic, alphabetic, or Roman numerals for the captions.

8. Click OK to close the Caption Numbering dialog box. The Caption dialog box appears.

9. Click OK to close the Caption dialog box and insert the caption into the document.

UPDATING CAPTIONS

If you insert another object above the current captioned object, Word automatically renumbers the captioned object for you. If you move or delete objects, however, you must update the captions manually. Refer to the "Updating a Table of Contents" section earlier in this chapter for information about updating fields.

If you regularly insert certain types of objects, such as tables, you can turn on a feature called AutoCaption. This causes Word to automatically insert a caption each time that you insert an object. You

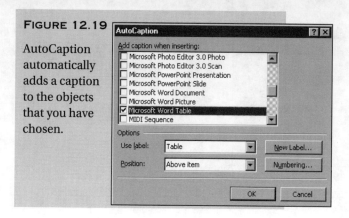

FIGURE 12.19

AutoCaption automatically adds a caption to the objects that you have chosen.

can turn AutoCaption on from the Insert menu by choosing Caption and then clicking AutoCaption. This opens the AutoCaption dialog box, as shown in Figure 12.19.

When you activate AutoCaption, the Caption dialog box does not appear. The label and number are automatically inserted above or below the object. Click the caption and type any text necessary for the label.

A style named Caption determines the appearance of a caption. If you find that you always change the formatting of a caption, modifying the caption style may be easier. See "Modifying Styles" in Chapter 6 for more information about changing a style.

TABLE OF FIGURES

One of the advantages of using captions in a document is that you can automatically generate a table of figures. A table of figures guides the reader to all the captioned objects in the document. For example, your document can have a table of illustrations, a table of figures, or a table of tables. These are all referred to as tables of figures.

INSERT A TABLE OF FIGURES

1. Open a document with captioned objects.
2. Position the insertion point in the document where you want the table of figures to appear.

FIGURE 12.20

Tables of figures
can be built on
any captioned
objects, such as
figures, equa-
tions, or tables.

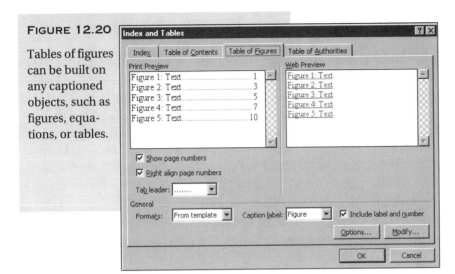

3. From the Insert menu, choose Index And Tables, and then select the Table of Figures tab to open the Table of Figures dialog box (see Figure 12.20).

4. Clear the Show Page Numbers option if you want to remove page numbers from the table of figures.

5. Clear the Right Align Page Numbers option if you want to place the page numbers directly next to the captions.

6. Select (none) in the Tab Leader list if you want to remove tab leaders from the table of figures, or select a desired format for tab leaders.

7. Select the various formats in the Formats box and notice how the Print Preview window changes.

8. Select the objects that have captions in the Caption Label box.

9. Clear the Include Label And Number option to show only the text of the caption.

10. Click OK to insert the table of figures.

You can update, delete, or modify the table of figures using the same techniques outlined earlier in this chapter (see "Updating Table of Contents," "Deleting Table of Contents," or "Modifying Table of Contents").

HYPERLINKS

You may have used them before, but do you know what, exactly, hyperlinks are? Hyperlinks are just an easy way to move from one spot in a document to another. You can even use hyperlinks to jump from one document to another. Think of them as replacements for those long and boring network paths. Rather than send someone a memo saying "Take a look at the agreement I drafted. It's in the F:\myname\clients\agreements directory and is named Loan Agreement.doc," you can insert a hyperlink that reads "Click Here to see the agreement" right in the document!

Hyperlinks are also a great way to leave notes for people who are unfamiliar with your system. Say that a temporary employee will be sitting at your desk while you are on vacation. The temporary employee, who is not familiar with your firm's network, may have trouble locating documents. Or maybe you have a highly complex directory structure on your own hard drive and you know it is difficult for others to navigate it. You can leave one document with hyperlinks pointing to the most important documents that may be needed while you are away.

Another useful feature of hyperlinks is that they can jump you to locations on the World Wide Web or your firm's Intranet. Think how handy it would be for someone to receive a letter via e-mail from you, and then be able to view your firm's Web page just by clicking the URL (Web address) in the e-mail message.

INSERT A HYPERLINK

1. Create a new document.

2. From the Insert menu, choose Hyperlink, or press Ctrl+K. The Hyperlink dialog box appears (see Figure 12.21).

3. Select one option in the Link To area. See Table 12.4 for the four link options when inserting hyperlinks.

4. Type the text you want to appear as the hyperlink in the Text To Display box.

5. Click ScreenTip and add some text to display when the mouse pointer pauses over the hyperlink.

6. Fill in the remaining fields for the hyperlink (the fields are different depending on which Link To option you selected) and click OK.

FIGURE 12.21

Hyperlinks can jump the insertion point to another spot in the current document, a different document, or to the World Wide Web.

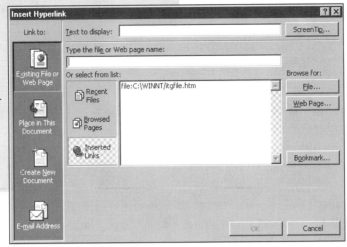

Hyperlinks normally appear with a blue font and underline formatting. To change how hyperlinks appear in the document, modify the Hyperlink style. See "Modifying Styles" in Chapter 6 for more information about modifying a style.

VIEWING HYPERLINKS

To jump to a hyperlink, just click the hyperlink anywhere. Word jumps you directly to the link, whether it is another location in the current document or one in a completely different document. If Word takes you to another document, the original document remains open. To get back to it, click its icon on the Windows taskbar. Keyboard users can press Ctrl+F6 to toggle through all open documents.

TABLE 12.4 HYPERLINK OPTIONS

LINK TO	RESULT
Existing File Or Web Page	Inserts a hyperlink in the current document to another document or Web page.
Place In This Document	Inserts a hyperlink to another location in the current document. The other location can be Headings or Bookmarks.
Create New Document	Inserts a hyperlink to a new document. You can edit the new document immediately, or work on it later.
E-mail Address	Inserts a hyperlink to an e-mail address.

After someone has viewed a hyperlink, Word formats it onscreen with a violet font. This indicates to users that they have already viewed the contents of that hyperlink. To control the color of viewed hyperlinks, modify the Followed Hyperlink style.

NOTE

To follow hyperlinks to Web addresses, the user reading the document must have browser software (such as Microsoft's Internet Explorer or Netscape Navigator) installed, as well as access to the Internet. To use hyperlinks with e-mail addresses, readers must have e-mail software installed on their system.

To use hyperlinks to other server locations, readers must have been given permission to access files on the designated server or the link will not connect and will act like a "dead" link.

If the hyperlink takes you to the Web, Word is minimized while the Web browser software is active. To get back to Word, click the Windows 95/98 or Windows NT taskbar to maximize Word, or press Alt+Tab to toggle through the open programs.

COMMON QUESTIONS ON LONG DOCUMENTS

Can I generate a table of contents from another document?

Using the Reference Document field (RD), you can tell Word to go to another document and get table of contents entries and then generate them in another document.

REFERENCE ANOTHER DOCUMENT FOR A TABLE OF CONTENTS

1. Create a new blank document.
2. Click the Show/Hide button to show non-printing characters if they are not already displayed.
3. Press Ctrl+F9 to insert a field into the document.
4. Inside the field, type **RD "C:\\My Documents\\FileName.doc"** where My Documents is the folder that you want to look in, and FileName is the document name that you want to generate a table of contents from. Make sure that the reference document has heading styles applied or table of contents entries marked.

5. Press Enter to move to the end of the line and then press Enter twice. Now you're going to insert a table of contents.

6. From the Insert menu, choose Index and Tables, select the Table of Contents tab and click OK. The table of contents from the referenced document appears in within the other document.

NOTE

The pathname must include double backslashes unless the reference document is in the same folder as the document that you are inserting the table of contents into. If the file is in the same folder as the current document, the RD field would instead be: { RD "filename.doc" }.

I want the beginning of a numbered paragraph to appear in the table of contents, but not the entire paragraph.

This is one of the biggest issues for our legal clients. Many agreements and other business documents use automatically numbered paragraphs with styles. In order to select part of a paragraph, and still include the paragraph number, you need to "trick" Word.

Many third-party software vendors have table of contents generators available for law firms to purchase.

If you don't want to use a third-party add-in to fix this problem, your only other option is to place a hidden paragraph mark after the heading text you want to appear in the table of contents. Format the following paragraph with a style that is *not* used in the table of contents. You can format a paragraph mark as hidden by selecting it and pressing Ctrl+Shift+H, or choosing Font from the Format menu, and then selecting Hidden.

Why do some paragraphs other than the heading paragraphs appear in the table of contents?

The Show Levels box on the Table of Contents dialog refers to the Outline level of the paragraph. The default for a table of contents is to include all paragraphs with Outline levels 1, 2, or 3. Word's built-in styles have Outline levels set automatically. For example, Heading 1 and Title styles are Level 1, and Heading 2 and Subtitle styles are Level 2.

The Outline level of a paragraph is specified in the Format, Paragraph dialog box, in the Outline Level list box. Note that Word doesn't allow you to change the Outline levels of any of the Heading styles, but you can change the Outline levels of other styles. If you change the Outline level of a paragraph to Body Text, it does not automatically appear in the table of contents.

Why are the page numbers in the table of contents or table of author-ities incorrect?

Table of contents and table of authorities fields appear in the document as hidden text. If numerous entries exist, they may begin to affect the pagination of the document. Before generating the table of contents or table of authorities, turn off the display of hidden text by clicking the Show/Hide button on the Standard toolbar.

Isn't there an easier way to generate a table of authorities?

Word's Table of Authorities feature is a bit labor intensive, since you need to manually mark all of the citations. Several products are available for automatically creating a table of authorities in your document.

FullAuthority from LEXIS-NEXIS is one product that often comes in handy for law firms. Visit the LEXIS-NEXIS Web site at `http://www.lexis-nexis.com/` for more information, or contact LEXIS-NEXIS Legal Toolbox Sales at 800-528-1891.

CiteLink, from the West Group, finds legal citations in the document and creates hyperlinks to the full text of the documents on Westlaw. The CiteLink software is free and available on the Internet at `http://www.westlaw.com/`, or you can call 800-WESTLAW. West Group also has other products that make checking cites and working with legal documents easier.

When I click the Show/Hide button, the field codes remain on the screen.

You may have the Hidden Text option turned on, which means that the Show/Hide button is not toggling the display of hidden characters. From the Tools menu, select Options, and then choose the View tab. Uncheck the option for Hidden Text in the Formatting Marks section, and click OK. Hidden text is applied in the Font dialog box. From the Format menu, choose Font. Check or uncheck Hidden under Effects.

Why does the footnote reference mark appear on one page while the footnote appears on another?

This was a common problem in Word 97. You'll be happy to know that it has been fixed in Word 2000, so that when you are creating new documents, your footnote reference mark and the footnote itself will always appear on the same page. However, if you open a

Word 97 document in Word 2000, you may see the problem crop up again.

To fix the footnote, from the Tools menu, choose Options, and then select the Compatibility tab. Uncheck Lay Out Footnotes Like Word 6.x/95/97, and click OK.

Payne Consulting Group has created some additional enhancements for footnotes, such as the ability to convert numbered footnotes to asterisks. Check out the Footnote Assistant, available as a free download from `http://www.payneconsulting.com/`.

What is Table of Contents in Frame?

Word 2000 includes a new way to generate a table of contents within a frame on the left side of the document. This sounds great and it is, if you intend the document for use as a Web document either online or on a firm Intranet. Before you use this feature however, make sure to read this entire section and follow the following exercise. There are some unexpected results when using the Table of Contents in Frame feature.

INSERT A TABLE OF CONTENTS IN FRAME

1. Open a long document that has built-in heading styles applied.
2. Press Ctrl+A to select the entire document.
3. Copy the contents by pressing Ctrl+C and create a new blank document.
4. Press Ctrl+V to paste the contents into the new document.
5. From the File menu, choose Save. Name the document **Frames**.
6. To generate a table of contents in a frame, from the Format menu, choose Frames and select Table of Contents In Frame. The table of contents appears in a frame on the left side of the document as shown in Figure 12.22. The frames toolbar shown in Figure 12.23 also appears.

If you look at the title bar, notice that Word created a new document when inserting the table of contents in a frame. So what happened to your other document? When the frame is inserted, the original document is closed without warning!

[2]Using a Concordance File
[2]Updating the Index
[1]Footnotes and Endnotes
[2]Viewing and Editing
Footnotes and Endnotes
[2]Browsing by Footnotes
[2]Deleting Footnotes or
Endnotes
[2]Converting Footnotes and
Endnotes
[1]Bookmarks
[2]Inserting a Bookmark
[2]Using a Bookmark
[2]Advanced Bookmark
Functions
[1]Cross-References
[2]Viewing and Updating
Cross-References
[2]Counting Words
[1]Captions
[2]Updating Captions
[1]Table of Figures
[1]Hyperlinks
[2]Viewing Hyperlinks
[1]Troubleshooting Long
Documents

FIGURE 12.22

The table of contents in a frame is made up of hyperlinks.

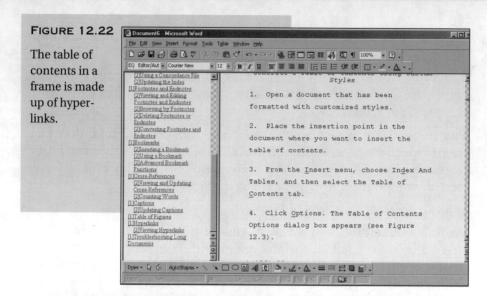

FIGURE 12.23

The Frames toolbar

TABLE OF CONTENTS IN FRAME   NEW FRAME RIGHT   NEW FRAME BELOW   FRAME PROPERTIES

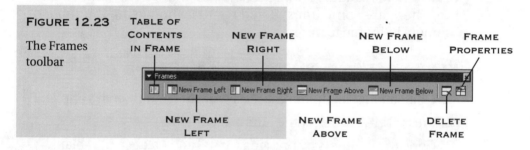

NEW FRAME LEFT   NEW FRAME ABOVE   DELETE FRAME

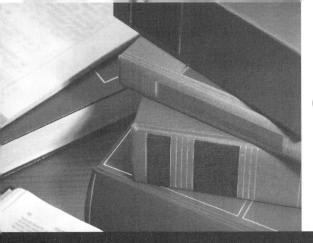

CHAPTER 13

SHARING LEGAL DOCUMENTS

IN THIS CHAPTER

- Sharing documents
- Using the Reviewing toolbar
- Using Comments
- Using the Track Changes feature
- Comparing documents
- Merging, versioning, and protecting documents
- Using master and subdocuments
- Online collaboration

Most legal documents are worked on by more than one person. Sometimes this is a secretary and an attorney, other times, the document goes back and forth between attorney and client. In any scenario, Word's features for sharing documents will make the process easier. This chapter includes information on how to send a document to someone else, how to track changes, compare documents, insert comments, collaborate online, and more. This chapter pulls no punches—if a feature is something to look out for, we tell you so.

SHARING DOCUMENTS

In some law firms, sharing documents takes place every day. One attorney may prepare a contract and then ask another attorney to review the contract. Either attorney can make changes before the contract is sent to the secretary or to word processing to be put into final form. The client may then request that additional changes be made.

When so many different people work on the same contract, it becomes difficult to tell who made which changes, what version is the most current, and whether all necessary changes have been incorporated into the final version. Word 2000 has numerous features that will help you manage documents that require collaboration.

Documents are shared in several ways. You can share documents over your firm's network, a firmwide internal intranet, by e-mail, via the Internet, and by floppy disk.

COPYING A FILE TO DISK

To share files, you need to know how to manage them. One of the best-kept secrets regarding this task is Word's Open dialog box. From this location, you can open, explore, cut, copy, paste, rename, sort, search, and delete documents. You can even send a copy of a file to a floppy disk (or other storage formats like Jazz or Zip drives) without ever leaving the Word window.

SEND A COPY TO FLOPPY DISK

1. Create, save, and close a document.
2. Place a floppy disk in your computer's floppy drive.
3. From the File menu, choose Open.
4. Locate the file to be copied onto the disk and alternate-click the file name.

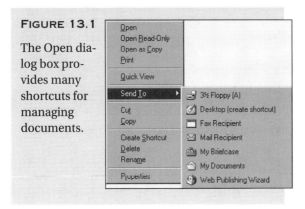

FIGURE 13.1

The Open dialog box provides many shortcuts for managing documents.

5. Select the Send To command and then click 3 ½ Floppy (A:). This command is shown in Figure 13.1.

NOTE

If your firm uses a document management system, you may need to check out and export the document to the floppy drive instead of using this method.

E-MAIL A DOCUMENT FROM WORD

There are three ways to e-mail a document without leaving the Word window—if your firm has an e-mail application that is compatible with Word. From the File menu, choose Send To. The following options are available for e-mailing your document.

 ◆ **Mail Recipient.** This includes the document as the body of the message. When the recipient opens the message, the document is not an attachment; it is the message itself. This feature is new in Word 2000.

CAUTION

It's not obvious how to take the e-mail message header off of the document if you change your mind about sending the file to someone as a mail recipient. Clicking the close button (X) in the upper-right corner of the window actually closes the document and not the message. I found this out the hard way the first time I tried it—and lost my document. If you change your mind about sending the message and want to return to Word without the e-mail addressing window, click the E-mail button on the Standard toolbar. This removes the e-mail message header and cancels the operation.

SEND TO MAIL RECIPIENT

1. Create a new blank document.

2. Type **I'm going to mail this to myself**.

3. From the <u>F</u>ile menu, choose Sen<u>d</u> To and select <u>M</u>ail Recipient. An e-mail header like the one shown in Figure 13.2 gets added to the document.

4. Type your e-mail address in the To box.

5. Enter a subject in the Subject box.

6. Click the Send a Copy button.

7. Create a new blank document.

8. Click the E-mail button on the Standard toolbar to turn on the message header.

9. Click the E-mail button again to cancel the process.

10. Close the document without saving.

FIGURE 13.2

The Mail Recipient feature lets you send the document within an e-mail message without leaving Word.

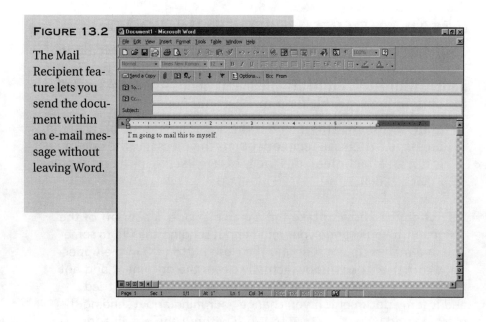

Mail Recipient (as Attachment) inserts the active document in an e-mail message as an attachment. Routing Recipient lets you define who receives the document and in what order. A routing slip also includes options for protecting and managing the document being routed. These options are covered in detail later in this chapter.

ADD A ROUTING SLIP FROM WORD

1. Open a Word document that you want to route to someone else.

2. From the File menu, choose Send To and then select Routing Recipient. Figure 13.3 shows the Routing Slip dialog box.

3. Click the Address button to define who should receive the document. After you have added names for the routing slip, click OK to close the Address Book dialog box and return to the Routing Slip.

TIP

You can control the order in which the recipients receive the routed document by changing the order of recipient names in the list. Move a name up or down in the list by selecting the recipient that you want to move and then clicking the appropriate arrow above or below the word *Move*.

FIGURE 13.3

The Routing Slip dialog box includes additional options, beyond sending a document via e-mail.

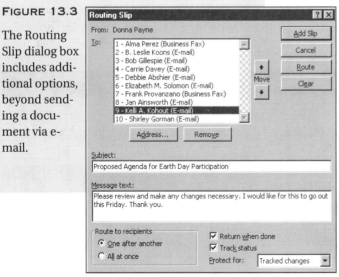

4. If you want to fill out the Subject and Message Text boxes, you can, although doing so is not required for the routing slip to work correctly.

5. In the Route To Recipients section of the Routing Slip dialog box, select whether to route the document to the recipients One After Another or All At Once.

6. Select the Return When Done option to automatically return the document to you after the last recipient closes it. Return When Done works if you specify One After Another or All At Once in the Route to Recipients section of the dialog box.

7. Select the Track Status option if you want to receive an electronic message each time the document is passed to the next person on the routing slip. This option is not available if you route to All At Once.

8. The final option on the Routing Slip is for protection. You can choose to protect the routed document to restrict any changes made. Table 13.1 shows each protection option and its function.

9. To route the document, click Route.

NOTE   Each recipient of a routed document receives an e-mail message with the document attached. The e-mail message will inform recipients that the document is a routed document, and give them instructions on routing the document to the next recipient.

TABLE 13.1   ROUTING SLIP PROTECTION OPTIONS

SETTING	FUNCTION
None	Does not protect the routed document. Any changes made by the reviewer are not tracked.
Tracked Changes	Revision marks are turned on and cannot be turned off by the reviewers.
Comments	Reviewers can insert comments into the document but are not permitted to change any of the document's contents.
Forms	The recipient is permitted to fill out the form but not make any changes to the form itself.

If the <u>O</u>ne After Another routing option is selected, when the first recipient is ready to forward the document to the next person on the routing slip, the first recipient chooses <u>F</u>ile, then Sen<u>d</u> To, and then <u>N</u>ext Routing Recipient.

To close the dialog box without routing the document, click the <u>A</u>dd Slip button. When you're ready to route the document, all you need do then is open the document, choose Sen<u>d</u> To on the <u>F</u>ile menu, and then <u>N</u>ext Routing Recipient.

USING THE REVIEWING TOOLBAR

Word's Reviewing toolbar is designed specifically to help you work with and share documents with other people. It includes options for adding and editing comments, tracking changes, highlighting text, creating Outlook tasks, saving a version, and sending to an e-mail recipient. Because not everyone shares documents, the toolbar is turned off until you need it. Figure 13.4 shows the Reviewing toolbar, and Table 13.2 runs through the buttons in detail.

To turn on a toolbar, just alternate-click any toolbar button and select the toolbar that you want to enable.

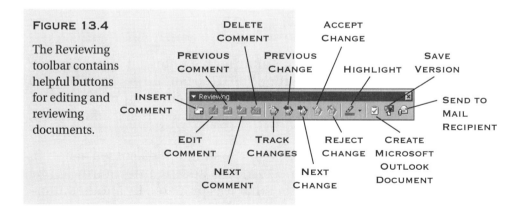

FIGURE 13.4

The Reviewing toolbar contains helpful buttons for editing and reviewing documents.

TABLE 13.2 REVIEWING TOOLBAR BUTTONS

TOOLBAR BUTTON	FUNCTION
Insert Comment	Inserts a comment at the insertion point
Edit Comment	Displays all comments made by reviewers in the Comment window
Previous Comment	Moves to the previous comment in the document
Next Comment	Moves to the next comment in the document
Delete Comment	Deletes the selected comment from the document
Track Changes	Enables the Track Changes feature within Word and keeps a record of all changes made by each reviewer
Previous Change	Moves to the previous change within the document
Next Change	Moves to the next change within the document
Accept Change	Accepts the current change and removes the revision marks from it
Reject Change	Rejects the current change and removes the revision marks from it
Highlight	Highlights text to make it stand out from the rest of the text in the document
Create Microsoft Outlook Task	Creates a task in Microsoft Outlook
Save Version	Saves and maintains different versions of the same document in one file
Send to Mail Recipient	Sends the current document as an attachment in an e-mail message

USING COMMENTS

A comment, by default, is a nonprintable note that appears when you're viewing a document online. You can, however, choose to print the comments from a document. A comment provides a visible reference in the document that pertains to missing information, a question, or a suggestion.

The comment feature is ideal for the situation discussed earlier in this chapter, in which an attorney is adding information to be included in a client's contract that was prepared by another attorney. Rather than scribble on the printed contract or type over the original information, you can insert a comment directly into the document without changing the original text of the document.

A comment can appear as a ScreenTip that comes up when the mouse pointer is paused over a highlighted area. The comment can also be an embedded sound object. That's right: if your firm has sound cards and microphones installed in the computers, you can record your own voice comment and embed it into a Word document. The embedded sound object appears as a horn icon that, when double-clicked, plays a recording of your voice and comment about the document. Please note, however, that your message will be both useless and frustrating if you send it to someone whose computer doesn't have a sound card and speakers—the recipient will see the horn icon, but won't be able to hear anything.

Attorneys and staff tend to react to this feature quite differently. Attorneys generally like the idea of being able to dictate into a Word document and have it play back like a tape-recorded message. The people who have to deal with these messages, on the other hand, understand that there is no way to slow down or fast-forward the recording and fear having this feature used in place of a dictation device. Spoken commentary also has some side effects if it is overused. For instance, each time that you create a sound recording, more disk space is required because sound recordings increase the file size substantially. To keep the file size manageable, you should use text-based comments rather than sound comments.

INSERT A COMMENT

You can insert a comment in one of three ways: by choosing Comment from the Insert menu, by clicking the Insert Comment button on the Reviewing toolbar, or by pressing Alt+Ctrl+M.

NOTE

You don't need to be working with anyone to get value from the comments feature in Word. Adding comments is a great way to keep notes for yourself within the document.

INSERT A COMMENT USING MENU COMMANDS

1. Create a new Word document.

2. Type **Due to the gross negligence of the defendant, the lowest amount of settlement that we're looking for is 2.5 million dollars.**

3. Select 2.5 million.

4. From the Insert menu, choose Comment. A Comments pane appears at the bottom of the screen.

FIGURE 13.5

The Comments pane reveals all the comments inserted into the document.

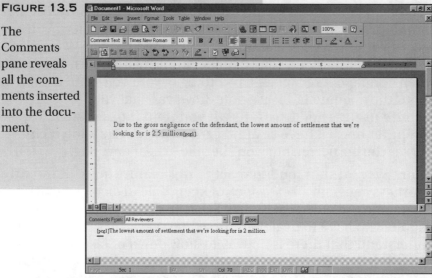

5. Type **The lowest amount of settlement that we're looking for is 2 million.** (see Figure 13.5).

6. Click <u>C</u>lose to close the Comments pane. Keyboard users can press Alt+Shift+C to close the Comments pane.

Comments appear onscreen as shaded text with a light-yellow background. The text that is highlighted depends on where the insertion point is when you insert the comment. If you select text when you insert the comment, the entire selection is highlighted. When nothing is selected, the word to the left of the insertion point is highlighted.

If comments do not appear as highlighted text on the screen, the ScreenTips option may not be activated. From the <u>T</u>ools menu, choose <u>O</u>ptions and then select the View tab. In the Show section, select the Scr<u>e</u>enTips option.

REVIEWER SCREENTIPS

When the mouse pointer rests over the highlighted area, a ScreenTip pops up with the reviewer's name and contents of the comment. This information comes courtesy of a setting accessed by choosing the <u>O</u>ptions command from the <u>T</u>ools menu and then selecting the User Information tab. The <u>N</u>ame is placed in the comment ScreenTip, and the <u>I</u>nitials are placed in the text of the document, directly next to the comment.

TIP

If you're working at someone else's computer, make sure to change the user information to your name so as to track your comments correctly. Just remember to put the regular user's name back when you finish.

Turn on the Show/Hide button on the Standard toolbar and you'll see the reviewer's initials and the sequential number of the comment in brackets next to the highlighted comment area. This text is not visible when you print the document. If you print just document comments, the reviewer's initials are printed next to that person's comments.

VIEW A COMMENT

You can view comments by pausing the mouse pointer over the highlighted area, without clicking.

VIEW COMMENTS

1. Place the mouse pointer over the highlighted portion of the text **2.5 million** that you typed in the previous exercise. The exposed comment is shown in Figure 13.6.

2. Move the mouse pointer away from the comment and the ScreenTip disappears.

If you have received a long document and you are wondering whether it has any comments, from the <u>V</u>iew menu, choose <u>C</u>omments. This command activates the Comments pane. You can display the comments from all reviewers, or just view the comments from selected reviewers.

TIP

You can use the Find and Replace dialog box to go to comments. If you do so, you have a special option not available with other methods. You can go to comments by any reviewer or a specific reviewer—but the nifty benefit to this method is that you can type **+4** and go to the fourth item of this type, and you can use negative numbers to move backward. To do this, from the <u>E</u>dit menu, choose <u>G</u>o To (or press Ctrl+G or F5) and select Comment under the Go To What section.

FIGURE 13.6

A ScreenTip appears when the mouse pointer pauses over a comment.

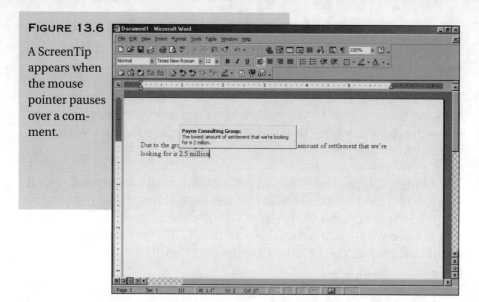

BROWSING BY COMMENT

The Browse Object located on the vertical scroll bar will allow you to browse through a document by comment. Click the Browse Object and then select Browse By Comment, represented visually by a yellow sticky note. This activates the Browse Object for comments. Clicking the double-headed arrows above or below the Browse Object then takes you to the next or previous comment in the document.

EDITING AND DELETING COMMENTS

The easiest way to edit or delete a comment is to alternate-click the highlighted comment area and then choose Edit Comment or Delete Comment from the shortcut menu.

TIP

If the Show/Hide toolbar button is activated to reveal all nonprinting characters, you can double-click the initials and number in brackets to open the Comments pane. You can work with the Comments pane open. To move between the document and the pane, just click in each area.

EDIT A COMMENT

1. Alternate-click the comment within the document.
2. From the shortcut menu, choose Edit Comment.
3. Change some of the text of the comment.
4. Click Close to close the Comment pane.

DELETE A COMMENT

1. Alternate-click the comment within the document.
2. Select Delete Comment from the shortcut menu.

DELETING ALL COMMENTS AT ONCE

After you've finished reviewing and editing a document, you should strip out all the comments before delivering it to the client. This eliminates potentially embarrassing situations for yourself and the firm. Stripping comments from a document is required only if you are sending the client an electronic version of a document.

DELETING ALL COMMENTS FROM A DOCUMENT

1. From the Edit menu, choose Replace to open the Find and Replace dialog box, as shown in Figure 13.7.

FIGURE 13.7

You can replace special characters, formatting, and comments from within the Find and Replace dialog box.

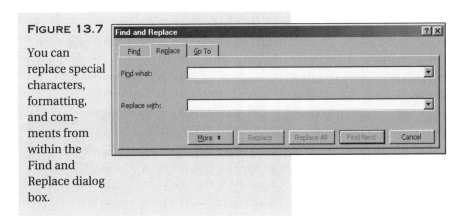

2. Click the <u>M</u>ore button to display the bottom portion of the dialog box. When the Find and Replace dialog box is fully expanded, the <u>M</u>ore button turns to <u>L</u>ess.

3. Click in the Fi<u>n</u>d What box and delete any text that appears. Click the Sp<u>e</u>cial button. Select Comment M<u>a</u>rk from the Special list.

4. Click in the Replace Wi<u>t</u>h box and make certain that it has no words or characters in it. If words appear under the box, click the No Forma<u>t</u>ting button.

5. Click Replace <u>A</u>ll and then OK to accept the changes.

6. Click the Close button to close the Find and Replace dialog box.

NOTE

If you accidentally choose Co<u>m</u>ment from the <u>I</u>nsert menu and find yourself in the Comments pane, even if you press Esc or click Close, a blank comment is still inserted into the document. That's why it's important to know how to edit and delete comments. When in doubt, alternate-click the comment and you will be able to choose <u>E</u>dit Comment or Delete Co<u>m</u>ment from the shortcut menu.

PRINTING COMMENTS

By default, comments in a document do not print, although you can print comments by changing an option in the Print dialog box. To print all comments in the document, from the <u>F</u>ile menu, choose <u>P</u>rint and select Comments from the Print <u>W</u>hat list.

Changing the Print options affects only the current document. You can have Word print comments for all documents by choosing <u>O</u>ptions from the <u>T</u>ools menu and then selecting the Print tab. In the Include With Document section, select <u>C</u>omments, and then click OK.

When comments are inserted, a PAGE field is inserted into your document that lets you know what page of the document the comment appears on. This field automatically updates when you print to include the most current information. To see this feature in action, try the following exercise.

SEE THE PAGE FIELD INSERTED WITH COMMENTS

1. Insert several comments into a Word document.

2. From the View menu, choose Comments and notice that no page numbers appear with the comments. Close the Comments pane.

3. From the File menu, choose Print.

4. From the Print What drop-down list, select Comments.

5. Click OK.

6. From the View menu, choose Comments and note that page numbers are now associated with each comment.

7. Click the word Page once, and press Shift+F9 to display the field code.

8. Press Shift+F9 again to toggle the field back to displaying the field result instead of the field code.

9. Close the Comments pane and then close the document without saving.

USING THE TRACK CHANGES FEATURE

In Word, you can use the Track Changes feature to keep a record of any modification to a document. This is extremely useful when multiple parties are working on a document. You can protect the document before giving it to another person to keep track of what they've changed. Whether the revision marks are visible or hidden, once you turn on Track Changes it continues to work in the background.

NOTE

Whether you like Word's Track Changes feature, or you decide to use a third-party product like CompareRite by LEXIS-NEXIS, you will still need to know how to tell if your changes are being tracked or if there are any residual changes that should be cleared before giving the document to the client or opposing counsel. This information is covered in this chapter.

Representatives from Microsoft have stated that the Track Changes and Compare Documents features in Word will improve in future versions. For now however, if you have complex legal documents to compare or redline, you may want to use CompareRite™.

CompareRite is available from LEXIS-NEXIS. Visit their Web site at `http://www.lexis-nexis.com/` or call 800-528-1891.

Track Changes allows you to dispense with the manual marking of documents and instead makes and reviews all changes electronically. The Track Changes feature in Word actually encompasses two separate features: you can compare two documents using the Compare Documents command, or you can view edits in a document as you make changes. Comparing two documents is often referred to as "redlining" and is covered in the next section.

TRACK CHANGES OPTIONS

Track Changes allows you to make edits and have the changes appear on the screen as you type. Changes that appear on the screen are marked with different types of formatting, such as underlining or strikethrough, depending on the options you have selected. The formatting options for revisions are located under the Tools, Options, Track Changes tab (see Figure 13.8) and are described in Table 13.3.

FIGURE 13.8

The Track Changes options allow different types of formatting for revised text.

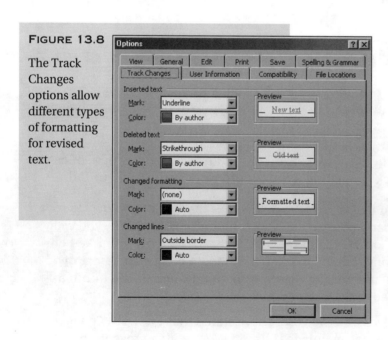

TABLE 13.3 TRACK CHANGES OPTIONS

TYPE OF EDIT	OPTIONS
Inserted Text	The default mark for inserted text is an underline. You can also format inserted text with bold formatting, italics, or a double underline. You can specify a color for inserted text. Choosing By Author marks the first eight reviewers' comments with different colors. Selecting Auto marks all inserted text with the default color, and selecting a specific color marks inserted text the chosen color.
Deleted Text	Deleted text can be formatted as hidden, which would allow it to be shown or hidden on the screen with the Show/Hide button on the Standard toolbar. Strikethrough formatting can be applied to deleted text, which allows the deleted text to appear on the screen with a line through the text. If you do not want the deleted text to appear on the screen, select the ^ or # symbol for deleted text.
Changed Formatting	To show differences in formatting between documents, select bold, italic, underline, or double-underline formatting.
Changed Lines	Every paragraph that has a change shows a revision mark next to the paragraph. These revision marks can be displayed on the left border of the paragraph, the right border, or the outside border.

TURNING ON TRACK CHANGES

Word provides four ways to enable Track Changes. If you look on the Status bar, you will see the Track Changes status represented by the letters TRK. When Track Changes is off, TRK appears dimmed. Double-clicking TRK enables Track Changes. Double-clicking again turns off Track Changes. You can also choose Track Changes from the Tools menu and then choose Highlight Changes to open the Highlight Changes dialog box. Select the Track Changes While Editing option.

Another way to turn on Track Changes is by displaying the Reviewing toolbar, which is covered in the next section, "Viewing Tracked Changes." If you prefer keyboard shortcuts to mouse clicks, the last way to turn on Track Changes is Ctrl+Shift+E. Pressing this combination a second time toggles off the feature.

USE TRACK CHANGES

1. Open a document in which you would like to use Track Changes.
2. Double-click TRK in the Status bar to enable Track Changes.

3. Delete some text from the document and then add some new text.

4. Hover the mouse pointer over the changes in the document to see when they were made and by whom.

NOTE

If your name does not appear on the ScreenTip, check <u>T</u>ools, <u>O</u>ptions, User Information, and then add your name in the <u>N</u>ame box.

5. Save the document.

VIEWING TRACKED CHANGES

When you receive a document with changes, you have several options for viewing the changes and accepting or rejecting each change that has been made. First, turn on the Reviewing toolbar by alternate-clicking any toolbar and selecting Reviewing. Figure 13.9 shows the Reviewing toolbar and all the commands for Track Changes.

If you pause the mouse pointer over any marked change on the screen, a tip appears, telling you who made the change, when it was made, and what was changed. If you do not see the tips, make sure that you have them activated. On the <u>T</u>ools menu, choose <u>O</u>ptions, select the View tab, and then Sc<u>r</u>eenTips.

If you find the marked changes on the screen distracting, you can turn them off. To see the changes without redline formatting, from the <u>T</u>ools menu, choose <u>T</u>rack Changes, and then choose <u>H</u>ighlight Changes. Clear the Highlight Changes On <u>S</u>creen option. To print a clean copy of the document—with none of the redline formatting visible—clear the Highlight Changes In <u>P</u>rinted Document option.

FIGURE 13.9

The Reviewing toolbar has all the commands necessary for reviewing documents marked with changes.

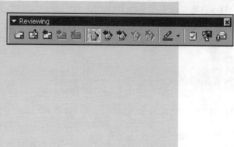

You can still view the original document even if you have received the document with marked changes. From the Tools menu, choose Track Changes and then choose Accept or Reject Changes. In the View section, select Original to view the original document without marked changes.

REVIEWING MARKED CHANGES

To review each change in the document, click the Next Change or Previous Change button on the Reviewing toolbar. As each change is selected (that is, highlighted), click the Accept Change or Reject Change button, depending on how you want to handle the change.

If you don't want to go through the document one change at a time, you can easily accept or reject all the changes in the document. To do this, from the Tools menu, choose Track Changes, and then Accept Or Reject Changes. Click the Accept All or Reject All button. When you do this, you receive a message asking whether you want to accept or reject all remaining changes without reviewing them. Answer Yes to accept or reject all changes, or No to continue viewing the changes one at a time.

TIP

You can click and edit the document even with the Accept or Reject Changes dialog box open.

Many attorneys have found that they are receiving documents from clients or from attorneys at other law firms with Track Changes enabled. If you receive a document with Track Changes enabled, leaving it turned on and making your changes electronically is best.

If you do not want your changes marked, you can turn Track Changes off by double-clicking the TRK on the Status bar. If you double-click the TRK status and find that you can't turn it off, the document has been protected with a password.

You can ensure that all reviewers will have their changes marked by protecting the document and adding a password to it.

PROTECTING A DOCUMENT FOR TRACKED CHANGES

1. Open a document that you want to protect for Tracked Changes.

2. From the Tools menu, choose Protect Document.

3. Select Tracked Changes, type a password in the Password box, and click OK.

4. Confirm the password by typing it again when the Confirm Password dialog box appears.

5. Click OK.

PRINTING TRACKED CHANGES

By default, Word prints the document with revision marks showing. To print a document without the Track Changes markup, from the Tools menu, choose Track Changes and select Highlight Changes. Clear the Highlight Changes In Printed Documents option and click OK. When you print the document, it includes what you would get if all changes were accepted, but the original text is still available in the file.

STRANGE TABLE AND TRACK CHANGES BEHAVIOR

Editing a table with Track Changes turned on can produce results different from what you get with regular text. If Word detects that you are attempting to work with text within the table, the text is marked as a change. If Word detects that you are attempting to change the structure of a table, a message will appear letting you know that the change will not be marked. If you proceed, the section of the table and all the text within it will be deleted and will no longer be visible as a change. If you choose this option, there is no way to retrieve that deleted information once the document is saved. Unfortunately, what Word interprets as your intention may not be what you had in mind.

WORK WITH TABLES AND TRACK CHANGES

1. Create a new document.

2. Insert a table with three rows and three columns.

3. Type something in each cell.

4. Turn on Track Changes.

5. Edit the contents in the first cell.

6. Select the second row and press Delete. No problems there.

7. Click Undo on the Standard toolbar.

8. Select the same row and press Backspace. You get a message that the action will not be marked as a change and asks if you wish to continue.

9. Click OK. The row and all its contents are deleted and not marked as a change.

10. Close the document without saving.

COMPARING DOCUMENTS

Track Changes works while you are making changes to an original document, but what if you already have the changed document and Track Changes was not enabled? Word can handle this scenario as well. The Compare Documents feature allows Word to look at two separate documents and mark the differences between the documents. The result of the comparison, often referred to as a "compared" document, can be printed or saved.

When you compare two documents, the changes appear on the screen in the current document. To save the changes in a separate document, from the File menu, choose Save As. If you do not need to save the changes, print the document with the redlining and then close it without saving changes.

When you compare documents, Word does not generate a third document that contains all of the comparisons. This is different from CompareRite and may be confusing if you have worked with this product. To create a third, redlined document, from the File menu, choose Save As, and save the document as a new document with a different name.

The following exercise walks you through creating and editing a document, and then comparing the edited version to the original version.

If you are printing and faxing a document with redlining, you should set the color of inserted and deleted text to Auto or Black. If you are printing to a black-and-white printer or a fax modem, certain colors, such as red, may be printed in a light shade of gray that is difficult to read.

COMPARE DOCUMENTS

1. Open a new blank document and type **This is the original agreement.**

2. Save the document as **Original Agreement.doc.**

3. In the document, change the word *original* to **edited.** Add this new sentence to the end of the paragraph: **Changes have been made to reflect the client's revisions.**

4. From the File menu, choose Save As and name the document **Revised Agreement.doc.**

5. With Revised Agreement.doc open, from the Tools menu, choose Track Changes and then choose Compare Documents. The Select File to Compare With Current Document dialog box appears, as shown in Figure 13.10.

6. Double-click Original Agreement.doc.

7. The changes appear in the document. Choose Save As from the File menu.

8. Save the document as **Agreement Compare.doc**.

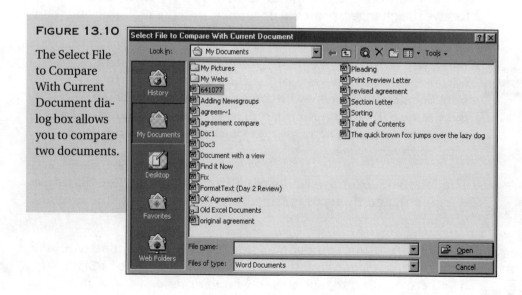

FIGURE 13.10

The Select File to Compare With Current Document dialog box allows you to compare two documents.

In this exercise, you compared the newest version of the document against the original, which is the most common way of comparing two documents. You could have opened the original first and compared it to the newest version also.

Generally, the two documents you are comparing must have different file names. What if they have the same name? For example, you may have the original file stored on the network and then receive a disk from the client with the same file name. As long as the files are in two separate folders, you can compare two documents with the same name, but it is not a good idea to do so as it can be confusing; try to avoid doing so.

MERGING DOCUMENTS

Imagine asking several people to review a document for you, and then being able to quickly incorporate all of their suggestions into the original document. With Merge Documents, you can do just that. Merge Documents is a powerful feature that allows you to merge changes from revised copies of a document back into the original document.

The Merge Documents feature should not be confused with Mail Merge. Information about Mail Merge is available in Chapter 9, "Mail Merge."

Merge Documents marks each author's revision in a different color, up to the first eight reviewers. After eight reviewers, Word begins to reuse previously used colors. After you have merged all of the changes into the original document, you can review the original document with all the changes, and accept or reject each reviewer's changes.

To make Merge Documents work properly, you must first protect the document for tracked changes. You do this from the Tools menu by choosing Protect Document. Select the Tracked Changes option and add a Password if you like. Do you need a password? It depends. If you do not add a password, the reviewers can choose the Tools menu and then Unprotect Document, which means that their changes will not be tracked. A password is a good idea if you want to guarantee that everyone's changes are tracked appropriately. Remember that passwords are case sensitive! Keep a list of passwords you use in a safe place just in case you forget what password you have used for a document.

After a document has been protected, you can notify others that it's available for review. The best way to notify others and make the document readily available to them is to route or e-mail the document. You can do this from the File menu by choosing Send To. If you are not connected to other reviewers via e-mail, you can route the document by saving it to a floppy disk and sending the floppy disk to the other reviewers. For more information about routing and e-mailing documents, see "Sharing Documents" earlier in this chapter.

After the reviewers have made changes, you can merge their changes into the original document. Open the original document and choose Merge Documents from the Tools menu. Figure 13.11 shows the Select File to Merge Into Current Document dialog box.

In the Select File to Merge Into Current Document dialog box, double-click one of the documents that contain changes. Repeat this step with each changed document until all the changes have been merged into the original document.

When you are finished merging all the changes, you will have the original document with all of the reviewers' changes marked with revision marks. You can review each change and choose to accept or reject each change. From the Tools menu, choose Track Changes, and then click Accept or Reject Changes. Use the Find arrow keys to navigate to each change, and the Accept or Reject buttons to incorporate the changes into your original document.

FIGURE 13.11

The Select File to Merge Into Current Document dialog box allows you to choose documents with changes to merge into an original document.

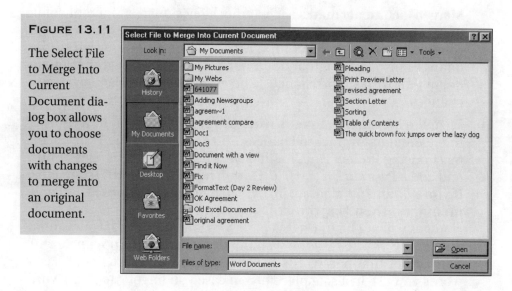

For more information on accepting or rejecting changes, see "Reviewing Marked Changes" earlier in this chapter.

VERSIONING

If you have ever worked with document management software, you know how convenient versioning is. Versioning allows you to save changes to a document as different versions. Word allows you to review, edit, print, or delete previous versions. Versioning allows you to save multiple versions of a document with the same name.

Unlike most document management software products, Word does not keep each version of the document in a separate file. Word keeps only one document, and when you open the document, you automatically receive the most recent version. Although there is only one document, it can contain multiple versions.

Word gives you two ways to know whether you are working in a document that has versions. If the document has versioning enabled, the Status bar displays a small icon of three folders. If you double-click the icon, it opens the Versions dialog box. Another way to determine whether versions exist in a document is to choose Versions from the File menu. If versioning has been turned on, the versions of the document appear in the Existing Versions box.

SAVE A DOCUMENT WITH A VERSION

1. Create a new blank document.

2. Type **This is the original version**.

3. From the File menu, choose Versions.

4. Click Save Now.

5. Type a Comment in the Versions dialog box.

When you add comments to the Versions dialog box, use meaningful comments that accurately describe the version being saved. These comments will aid you in locating a specific version at a later date.

6. Click OK.

7. When the Save As dialog box appears, save the file as **My version.doc**.

FIGURE 13.12

The Versions dialog box lists all existing versions and has buttons with commands for working with versions of the document.

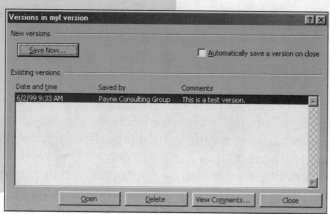

Notice that the document has the Versions icon in the Status bar. If you double-click the Versions icon, the Versions dialog box appears, and you can see when the document was saved and by whom. The Versions dialog box is shown in Figure 13.12.

The Versions dialog box has several buttons that allow you to manipulate each version of the document. Table 13.4 explains these buttons.

Two other ways exist to save versions of a document. One is in the Save As dialog box where from the Tools menu, you can choose Save Version. If you click Save Version, the Save Version dialog box appears, and you can enter comments.

TABLE 13.4 VERSIONS DIALOG BOX BUTTONS

CLICK THIS BUTTON . . .	TO . . .
Open	Open the version that is selected in the Existing Version list.
Delete	Delete the version that is selected in the Existing Version list.
	To delete multiple versions, hold down the Ctrl key as you click versions in the Existing Version list, and then click Delete.
View Comments	Click View Comments to view the full contents of the comments for a selected version.
Close	Close the Versions dialog box.

USE THE SAVE AS DIALOG BOX TO SAVE A VERSION

1. Open the My version document that you created in the previous exercise.
2. From the File menu, choose Save As.
3. Click Tools and choose Save Version.
4. Enter a Comment for the version.
5. Click OK.

The last way to save a version is to have Word automatically save a new version each time you save changes to the document.

AUTOMATICALLY SAVE VERSIONS

1. From the File menu, choose Versions.
2. Select the Automatically Save A Version On Close option.

The language on the Versions dialog box is misleading. The instructions say "Automatically save a version on close." Word actually saves a new version each and every time that you *save* the document, however, not just when you close the document. The Help file is also misleading on this topic. If you save the document frequently, you run the risk of the file growing larger than the allowable file size in Word (32 megabytes). This can cause the document to become corrupt, resulting in loss of all or a portion of the text. Before deciding whether or not to use the Versions feature in Word, be sure to read the next section, "Problems with Versioning."

3. Click Close.
4. Make some changes to the document.
5. From the File menu, save changes by choosing Save.
6. Now, from the File menu, choose Versions. Notice that Word automatically saved a new version of the document.
7. Close the Versions dialog box.

When Word automatically saves a version, the comments read "automatic version."

PROBLEMS WITH VERSIONING

Law firms should be aware of two issues that arise with versioning. The first is that you cannot easily compare two versions of a document against one another. If you are used to working with a document management system and CompareRite, you know how easy it is to compare version 1 against version 2. In Word, version 1 and version 2 are contained in the same document, and you must rename one of the versions to use the Compare Documents feature.

To save a version with a different name, open the document from the File menu, and then choose Versions. Select the version of the document that you need and then click Open. Now choose Save As from the File menu and save the document with a different name. Now you can compare the two documents against each other.

The second versioning issue to be aware of is the file size problem, which is serious enough to warrant repetition here. If Automatically Save Changes On Close has been selected, Word saves a new version *every time* the document is saved. If you spend an hour editing a document, and you conscientiously save every 10 minutes, that would result in six different versions. Each time you save a version, the file grows bigger. To prevent a marked increase in file size, it is best to save specific versions by choosing Versions from the File menu, or by choosing Save Version in the Tools menu of the Save As dialog box. Remember, if a document exceeds the file size limitation in Word (32 megabytes), the file can become corrupt, resulting in a loss of all or a large portion of the document.

Most law firms remove Versions from the File menu before deploying Word to users, or strongly discourage their staff from using the feature. If you choose to use the Versions feature you can reduce file size by going into the Versions dialog box, selecting a version that is no longer needed, and click the Delete button.

Another potential problem with law firms using Versions is the potential for escape of a preliminary version of a document including things that turned out to be better said in different terms or not at all.

PROTECTING DOCUMENTS

You've spent the entire week on a report for a new client. The report is due Monday at noon and you've finished in time to relax and enjoy the weekend before Monday's meeting. You ask a couple of colleagues to log on to the network and read over what you've done. When you return to the office on Monday morning, you open the document and find that entire sections of the document have been deleted. You have no backup copy.

When a document is important to you or is sensitive in nature, you'll want to protect it. You can protect a document from being opened or modified, or you can suggest that anyone opening it do so in read-only mode. If you know how to save a document, you can learn to protect it. And you should *always* keep a backup, no matter how much you trust those who have access to your files.

PROTECT A DOCUMENT

1. From the File menu, choose Save As.

2. Click Tools and then choose General Options. Figure 13.13 shows the Save dialog box that appears.

3. Under File Sharing Options for the document, enter passwords to apply the different levels of protection. If you type a password, you will be asked to confirm it. Table 13.5 shows the different levels of password protection.

FIGURE 13.13

Passwords are case sensitive.

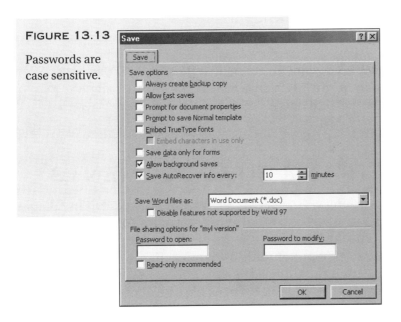

TABLE 13.5   PASSWORD PROTECTION OPTIONS

PASSWORD TYPE	RESULT
Password to Open	The highest level of password protection. Requires a password to open the file. If you forget the password, the document cannot be opened.
Password to Modify	The next level of password protection. A password must be entered in order to change the document. If a password is not entered, the document can be opened as read-only. The file must be saved with a different name.
Read-only Recommended	The lowest level of protection. No password is required. The document will open with a message telling the user that the document should be opened as read-only. The user can accept the suggestion by clicking Yes, or ignore the suggestion by clicking No.

Writing down the password to a file and keeping them in a safe place is important. If you forget a password for a document, you cannot recover the document without spending a lot of money. If you know the password for a file but receive incorrect password errors, make sure that the Caps Lock key is not pressed on your keyboard. Passwords are case sensitive.

4. Click OK and Save to save the file.

If you are saving this document for the first time, you need to enter a new file name in the File Name box. If the file already has a name, leave the existing name in the File Name box and save the document.

USING MASTER AND SUBDOCUMENTS

When you're working with a very large document, you can break up the document into several smaller documents to make it more manageable. The smaller documents are linked, but you can still edit and create a table of contents and index on the document as a whole. The feature that allows this operation is called Master and Subdocuments. This technique reduces file size and makes the document load, save, and close faster than it would if it were one large document.

Examples of legal documents for which master and subdocuments might come in handy are an Employee Policy Manual or an Employment Law Handbook. Or you might place the entire text of a state law into a Word document and make each section a subdocument.

CREATE A MASTER DOCUMENT

1. Create a new document and type the information shown in Figure 13.14.

It's useful to work in Normal view and set the Style Area width to 1" to help you know which styles to apply to each line of text.

2. From the View menu, choose Outline.

In previous versions of Word, there was a Master Document command on the View menu. In Word 2000, Master Document view is built into Outline view and is controlled by the Outline toolbar.

3. Save the document as **Firm Policy Manual** to the My Documents folder on your computer.

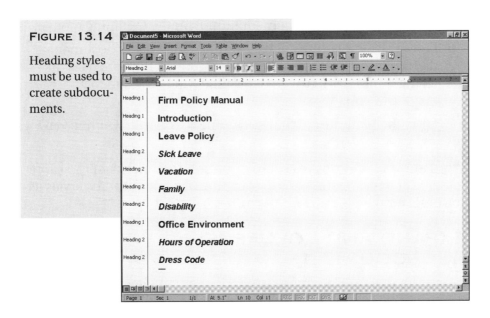

FIGURE 13.14

Heading styles must be used to create subdocuments.

FIGURE 13.15

Section breaks are inserted between each pair of subdocuments.

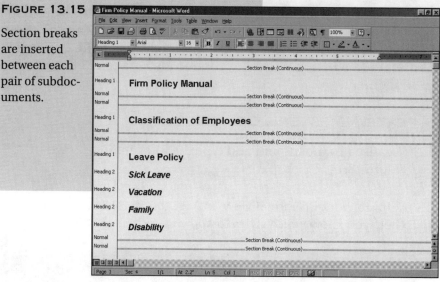

You can use the Outline toolbar buttons to promote or demote styles to different heading levels.

4. Press Ctrl+A to select all text within the document.

5. Click the Create Subdocument button on the Outlining toolbar.

6. From the View menu, choose Normal. The master document is divided into sections, as shown in Figure 13.15. Word uses the changes in styles in use to determine where the subdocuments begin and end.

7. From the View menu, choose Outline to return to Outline view.

Word automatically saves each of the subdocuments in the same folder as the master document, using the text with heading styles as the basis for the file names.

EXPAND AND COLLAPSE SUBDOCUMENTS

When the master document is open, you can view the subdocuments in two ways: expanded or collapsed. The expanded view is the default, and all headings and text are visible and may be edited from within the master document. The other view is collapsed. In the collapsed view, the subdocument is shown as a hyperlink to each individual subdocument file name. When you click the hyperlink, the subdocument opens as its own separate Word document.

EXPAND AND COLLAPSE SUBDOCUMENTS

1. On the Outlining toolbar, click Collapse Subdocuments to display each subdocument as a hyperlink.
2. Click the second subdocument, \\Classification of Employees.doc to open the Classification of Employees document.
3. Close the Classification of Employees document and return to the master document.
4. Click Expand Subdocuments on the Outlining toolbar.

ADD SUBDOCUMENTS TO A MASTER DOCUMENT

Occasionally, you'll want to use existing documents for subdocuments. Clicking Add Subdocument on the Outlining toolbar enables you to insert an existing document as a subdocument.

INSERT A SUBDOCUMENT

1. Create a new document.
2. Type **Solicitation, Security, and Safety** and press Enter.
3. Format the text as the Heading 1 style.
4. Save this document as **Security** in the My Documents folder on your computer's hard drive. Then close the file.
5. Return to the Firm Policy Manual document in Master Document view.
6. Press Ctrl+End to go to the end of your document.
7. Click Insert Subdocument on the Outlining toolbar. The new document will be inserted at the insertion point.
8. In the Insert Subdocument dialog box, select the file named Security, and click Open to insert the document as a subdocument in your master document.

DELETING A SUBDOCUMENT

To delete a subdocument, you need to make sure that you are in the section to be deleted. Then click the Remove Subdocument button on the Outlining toolbar.

DELETE A SUBDOCUMENT

1. Click Classification Of Employees in the Firm Policy Manual document.
2. Click Remove Subdocument on the Outlining toolbar.

NOTE

This procedure still leaves the text of the subdocument in the master document; however, it is no longer considered a subdocument. To remove the subdocument completely from the master document, press Delete and remove the text as you would any text.

OTHER BUTTONS ON THE OUTLINING TOOLBAR

The Outlining toolbar contains other buttons that are useful for working with long documents. Buttons on this toolbar are shown in Figure 13.16 and described in Table 13.6.

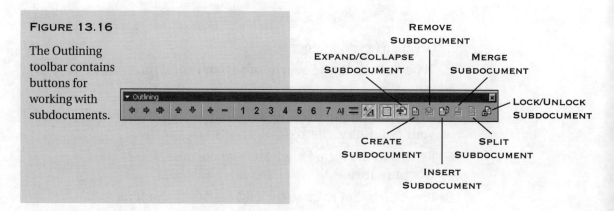

FIGURE 13.16

The Outlining toolbar contains buttons for working with subdocuments.

TABLE 13.6 OUTLINING TOOLBAR BUTTONS

TOOLBAR BUTTON	FUNCTION
Expand/Collapse Subdocument	Toggles between expanding and collapsing subdocuments. Expand shows the document within the master document; collapse shows the subdocument as a hyperlink.
Create Subdocument	Converts the selected text in a master document to subdocuments based on the first selected heading style.
Remove Subdocument	Removes the selected subdocument from the master document. When you remove a subdocument from a master document, the subdocument file remains in its original location. If you want, you can delete this subdocument file.
Insert Subdocument	Inserts an existing file as a subdocument at the location of the insertion point.
Merge Subdocument	Combines selected subdocuments into one subdocument. When you save the master document, Word saves the combined subdocuments with the file name of the first subdocument.
Split Subdocument	Splits a subdocument into two subdocuments.
Lock/Unlock Subdocument	Lock prevents modification of a subdocument; Unlock allows it to be modified.

LOCKING SUBDOCUMENTS

A padlock symbol appears next to the subdocument when the subdocument is locked: you can view the document but you can't modify it. A subdocument is locked when another user is working on the subdocument, or when the subdocument is set to read-only access. When you display subdocuments in the collapsed view, all subdocuments appear locked. To unlock the subdocument for editing, click the Expand Subdocuments button on the Outlining toolbar. When you open a locked subdocument in a separate window, "read-only" appears in the title bar.

USING MASTER AND SUBDOCUMENTS ON A NETWORK

A real benefit to large law firms is the ability to set up the master document on a network and let various people in the firm work on their own subdocuments simultaneously. Imagine several employment law attorneys preparing an employee handbook for a client. If the employee handbook is a single document, only one attorney can access any part of the handbook at a time. If the employee handbook is a master document located on the firm's network, each attorney can access a different subdocument with no trouble.

Another benefit is the consistent formatting that you can maintain by using master and subdocuments. Because the master document controls the styles in all the subdocuments, any style changes made to the master document automatically update all the subdocuments.

ONLINE COLLABORATION

Word 2000 also includes a way for you to collaborate simultaneously with others online. Online Collaboration uses a Web server to store the document in one location and then collect and present it in a chat room or discussion thread interface that is easy to read and use. Don't let the name "Online Collaboration" fool you, however. You can only leave messages or comments about the document, you cannot edit the document with others at the same time.

To access Online Collaboration, from the Tools menu, choose Online Collaboration, and then choose Web Discussions. The interface appears at the bottom left portion of the window. It's a bit difficult to detect initially—look for the discussion button just above the page number on the Status bar.

Not everyone will want to use Online Collaboration—it has some pretty stiff requirements. However, if you are a part of a large law firm and think that this feature may be of interest, you may want to contact your Information Systems department. Online Collaboration requires the following arrangements:

- Internet Information Server (IIS) 4.0 or higher running on Windows NT (Service Pack 3) or higher.
- Office Server Extensions (OSE) installed.
- Version 3 or later of Microsoft Internet Explorer or Netscape Navigator.
- User accounts set up.

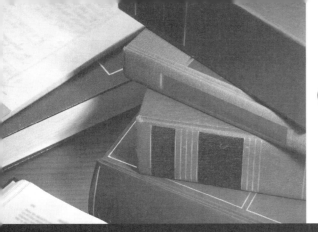

CHAPTER 14

DOCUMENT CONVERSION

IN THIS CHAPTER

- ◆ Converting legal documents with Word
- ◆ Converting your WordPerfect documents
- ◆ Cleaning up converted documents
- ◆ Converting to previous versions of Word
- ◆ Using the Batch Conversion wizard

Conversion! You probably have heard your fair share of warnings about this issue. Or maybe this is a new topic for you. Either way—whether you consider yourself an expert or a beginner—this chapter will introduce you to important information that you need to know to get a non–Word 2000 document into Word. It is important that you understand the process completely so you can estimate how long the conversion process should take and what steps are involved to return the best results.

This chapter begins by discussing what types of documents you can import into Word as well as what you can export in other formats. You will then discover areas to watch out for when converting documents between Word 2000 and other word processing applications.

CONVERSION: THE REAL STORY

Many people think that the complete conversion process consists of opening and saving a document created in a different word processing package directly into Word 2000. They get this impression because upon opening the document, the Status bar reads "Converting Document." When this "conversion" is complete, at first glance, the documents do appear to come over fairly well—however, what you don't see is all of the remaining junk buried beneath the surface that will cause corruption if it isn't removed. And eventually, a corrupt document simply won't open no matter what you do. It's better to do the cleanup early; then you don't have to worry.

Microsoft Word's built-in converter does a pretty good job of performing literal translations of WordPerfect features to Word. However, not everything converts well. Leftover codes, tabs, indents, and legal style (outline numbering) can be especially nasty. In effect, the document becomes an orphan without an associated word processing program. It's no longer in the format it was created in, and it's not a true Word document yet.

The full conversion process takes two steps: Convert and Clean Up. Converting is easy, the cleanup (removal of codes and reformatting) is what usually takes the time and effort. You may be tempted to take shortcuts, but resist! Dealing with a document that has become corrupt is far more time-consuming and frustrating than protecting it from corruption up front.

To help get you started on the cleanup process, this chapter will focus on different scenarios:

- **Quick and Dirty**. This method gives you the basic steps for what to do if you have a time crunch and need to get a document out the door to meet a filing deadline.

- **Spic and Span**. Here you look at using features built into Word such as Find and Replace, clearing tab stops, and page formatting to create clean, useable documents.

- **Spring Cleaning**. This is the only method that is safe for documents you are planning to use as a base for additional documents you're developing.

ROUND-TRIPPING

Round-tripping is the continual converting of documents back and forth between two or more word processing programs. A document that is converted back and forth between different software applications has a very good chance of corruption. Round-tripping should not be used very often—if at all. Realistically, however, unless everyone in the world uses the same software program and the same version of the software, some amount of round-tripping may be necessary.

If your document falls into this category, there are a few things that may reduce your chances of a corrupt document:

- Have at a least one version of the second software application available at your firm.

- Keep the document in both formats.

- Have a backup copy of the document (just in case).

The first two items may seem redundant, but once you have read through this chapter you will realize that it's easier to maintain two copies of a document (one in each application) than it is to clean up a document each time it gets converted.

FILE TYPES THAT WORD CAN CONVERT

If you need to share documents between Word 2000 and Word 97, you'll be happy to know that it is extremely easy to convert documents between the two versions. Both use the same file format, which means you don't need a converter to open or save documents as Word 97. Even better, Word 97 users don't need to do anything special to read Word 2000 files. Of course, there are some new Word 2000 features that don't exist in Word 97, but you can disable those features if you are sharing documents with Word 97 users.

Word recognizes many file formats from common word processing applications and can usually open their files with little or no difficulty. If you do a complete installation of Word 2000, you'll have more than 20 different text converters that allow you to open or save a document as different file types. Some common file types are Word documents, templates, previous versions of Word (including Word for the Macintosh), text, WordPerfect (different versions), Microsoft Works, and HTML.

Word 2000 has a new feature called *Install on First Use*. Install on First Use (sometimes also called Install on Demand) installs the converters that you need when you attempt to open a file. You can imagine how useful this feature could be! For example, say you receive an e-mail message with an attached WordPerfect 6.1 document. When you attempt to open the attachment, Word automatically installs the WordPerfect 6.1 converter so you can read the file. Converters installed by default are Recover Text and the Word 6.0/95 export converter. All other text converters are installed on first use.

TIP

If you don't see the type of file formats that you're looking for, rerun Word 2000 Setup and click Add Or Remove Features. Select Converters And Filters, and then select Text Converters. Notice the converters with a 1 listed next to their name. These converters are configured to install on first use. To install the converter immediately, click the converter name, and then select Run From My Computer. Click the Update button and Word installs the converter for you.

In case you need to convert documents from Lotus Word Pro, you should know that no converter is available. The best approach for these types of documents is to open the document in Word Pro and save to a format (such as WordPerfect) that Word can convert easily. For more information and ideas about converting documents from Word Pro to Word 2000, see the Microsoft Knowledge Base article `http://support.microsoft.com/support/kb/articles/Q139/7/92.asp`.

Microsoft organizes converters into two categories: import converters and export converters. Import converters are used when you open a different file format. Export converters are used when you save a document in a different format. To find out whether a specific text converter is installed on your computer, try the following exercise.

VIEW INSTALLED TEXT IMPORT CONVERTERS

1. Open Word.
2. From the File menu, choose Open.
3. Click the arrow next to Files Of Type and scroll through the list of available converters. If you see the file type, the text converter is installed, or will be installed on first use.

TIP

To view the export converters, from the File menu, choose Save As and click the arrow next to Save As Type. Scroll through the list of available converters.

Some text converters are not included with Word 2000. Microsoft offers a free set of supplemental text converters that work with Word 2000:

* Lotus Ami Pro 3.x
* RFT-DCA
* Windows Write 3.0 or 3.1
* Microsoft Word 3.x, 4.x, 5.x, and 6.x for MS-DOS
* WordStar 3.3–7.0 for MS-DOS and WordStar for Windows 1.0–2.0 (importing only)
* WordStar 4.0 or 7.0 for MS-DOS (exporting only)

If you don't see the converter you need and you are certain that you have installed all of the converters, the format that you need may not be supported. For more information on the text converters that are available during the Word 2000 installation, look up the topic "File format converters supplied with Microsoft Word" in Help.

THE CONVERSION PROCESS

When you open a non–Word 2000 document, Word automatically determines what type of file is being opened and uses the correct converter. If you want Word to display a message and ask what type of converter to use, choose Options from the Tools menu and select the General tab. Select Confirm Conversion At Open to open the Convert File dialog box, as shown in Figure 14.1.

Most of the converters are not installed until the first time you use them. Therefore, when you open a non–Word 2000 document, Word displays a message that the document cannot be imported because the feature is not installed. This is an important option because it gives you the opportunity to decide whether you truly need the converter before it is installed. If you click Yes, Word installs the necessary converter and opens the document. If you click No, the document is not opened.

When you open a document created in an application other than Word, the document is temporarily converted to Word format so that Word can display the file correctly onscreen. As the document is being opened, a message on the Status bar indicates the progress of the conversion. This conversion is for display purposes only; the document has not truly been converted to Word format. Understanding this fact is really important! At this point, many people start working in the document, and click the Save button to save changes. Then they wonder why their document doesn't have the proper formatting when they open the file again later.

To ensure your changes are saved in Word 2000 format, you must choose Save As from the File menu and change the Save As Type option to Word Document (*.doc).

FIGURE 14.1

In the Convert File dialog box, select the type of converter that Word should use.

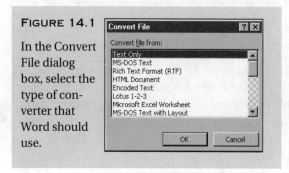

CONVERT A DOCUMENT TO WORD 2000

1. From the File Menu, choose Open.

2. Change Files Of Type to look for All Files. This step is important because the default is to show only Word documents.

3. Navigate to where a non–Word 2000 file is stored and double-click it to open it. Figure 14.2 shows the Open dialog box with all file types displayed.

If you look at the Status bar while opening the document, you'll see the message that Word is converting the document. You can press the Esc key if you want to cancel the conversion and not open the file.

The document usually takes a few moments to open while Word is converting it. Don't worry if the document looks strange when it is first opened; you'll learn how to fix this later in the chapter.

4. From the File menu, choose Save As.

5. Click the arrow next to Save As Type and then choose Word Document.

6. Click Save.

FIGURE 14.2

The Open dialog box with all file types displayed.

CONVERTING FROM WORDPERFECT

In the last section, you saw how easy it is to open a non–Word document. When you open a WordPerfect file, Word 2000 does an excellent job of converting the text. But since WordPerfect uses a different logic when creating documents, Word may not convert all of the WordPerfect codes. This section describes many of the items that do not convert or convert incorrectly.

Be aware that not all of these items will be found in every converted document and there may be additional items that are not discussed here. Since each document is formatted differently, it converts differently. This section describes the most common stumbling blocks and what causes them; in the next section, you will see how to clean up or fix them.

Read through this section so as to be prepared for the next steps in the WordPerfect conversion process, which is covered in the "Cleaning Up Converted Documents" section later in the chapter.

PRIVATE FIELDS

Word uses Private fields to store information about the converted file's native format. These fields appear most often in documents converted from WordPerfect 5.1 or earlier versions. When converting from more recent versions of WordPerfect, Private fields appear less often. Private fields are formatted as hidden text, which means they appear on the screen but do not print. To toggle the display of Private fields onscreen, click the Show/Hide button on the Standard toolbar.

TIP

If the Private fields do not disappear from the screen when you click the Show/Hide toolbar button, Word may be set to always display hidden text. From the Tools menu, choose Options, and then select the View tab. Clear the Hidden text option in the Formatting marks section.

If you won't be using the document in WordPerfect again, you can delete the Private fields altogether. If you think that you might later save the document in a WordPerfect file format, however, leave the Private fields there; Word uses them to store formatting information required to return the document to its original file format. Private fields can be scattered throughout the document, as shown in Figure 14.3.

FIGURE 14.3

A converted
WordPerfect
file contains
Private fields.

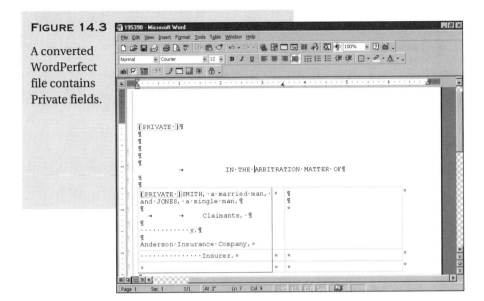

FIGURE 14.3

A converted
WordPerfect
file contains
Private fields.

COMPATIBILITY OPTIONS

Once you have converted a document, it's a good idea to take a look at the Compatibility settings. Although you have saved the document as a Word document, Word retains some settings related to the original file type. When you see odd formats on your screen— say, the top part of your text is cut off or the table borders aren't there—this could be the result of Word being set for the wrong document type.

Compatibility options include the recommended settings for converting 10 different types of file formats and one custom file format setting. Figure 14.4 shows the Compatibility tab where these settings are stored.

VIEW COMPATIBILITY OPTIONS

1. From the Tools menu, choose Options.

2. Select the Compatibility tab.

3. Select WordPerfect 6.x for Windows from the Recommended Options For list and note that 15 boxes are checked.

4. Select WordPerfect 5.x from the Recommended Options For list. Now 13 boxes are checked.

5. Click Cancel to close the Options dialog box.

FIGURE 14.4

Compatibility options determine how Word handles formatting in the document.

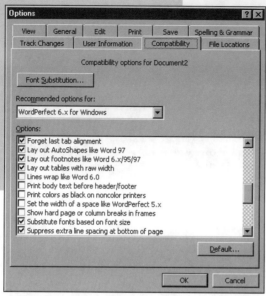

If you want the document to be a true Word 2000 document, change the Recommended Options For box to Microsoft Word 2000. This forces Word to treat the document as a native Word 2000 document, without any special settings.

NOTE To read what each Compatibility option does, visit Microsoft's Support Web site at `http://support.microsoft.com/support/kb/articles/Q166/0/16.asp`. The article describes Compatibility settings so you can understand what formatting Word is trying to maintain in the document.

SECTION BREAKS

In more complex legal documents, you will notice that an abundance of section breaks may appear once the document is converted from WordPerfect.

Formats such as page margins, headers and footers, and indents are treated very differently in WordPerfect and Word. For example, each time WordPerfect made a change in a header and footer or margin, Word puts in a section break as it converts the file. It's not uncommon for a converted long document to have 22 or more section breaks because of changes in headers, footers, or margins.

VIEW LARGE NUMBER OF SECTION BREAKS

1. Open a WordPerfect document.

NOTE

To get the best example of this, be sure to open a complex document that has different headers and footers.

2. Press Ctrl+End to move to the end of the document.

3. Compare the number of pages to number of sections on the Status bar as shown in Figure 14.5. The document shown only has three sections; however, it's not uncommon to have 10 or 20 sections in a more complex converted legal document.

4. Close the document without saving.

Since the page formatting options are so very different in Word 2000 when compared to WordPerfect, it's both easier and safer to simply remove all of the section breaks and recreate the headers and footers. This is demonstrated in the "Cleaning Up Converted Documents" section later in this chapter.

FIGURE 14.5

Many section breaks are added once a document is converted.

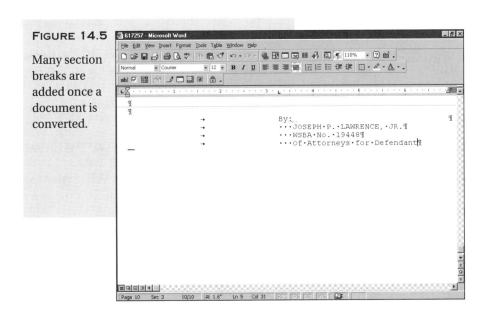

QUOTATIONS AND APOSTROPHES

Word's AutoFormat As You Type feature includes the Replace "Straight Quotes" With "Smart Quotes" option. This is great stuff—unless the document is coming from another application where this feature was either turned off or not available. Your converted document will end up with a combination of straight and smart quotes or apostrophes, which looks very unprofessional. Even worse, if the incoming document uses different smart quote characters from the ones your system is looking for, you can get the most amazing garbage—dead characters, @ signs, even letters of the alphabet.

FIELD CODES

Word uses field codes to generate tables of contents, tables of authorities, cross-references, and so on. When a document is converted, the field codes sometimes convert into usable codes and sometimes they don't. Table of contents codes convert smoothly, for example, but table of authorities codes do not work at all.

CONVERTING NUMBERED PARAGRAPHS

You have several options for converting numbered paragraphs from WordPerfect to Word, depending on what you intend to do with the document.

If you are converting from WordPerfect versions 5.x and earlier, numbered paragraphs will be converted to Sequence fields in Word. *Sequence fields* give you a way to keep track of numbers in a document automatically. Sequence fields do an excellent job of taking the WordPerfect numbering system and converting it to Word.

In more recent versions of WordPerfect, the conversion of numbered paragraphs depends on how the numbered list was set up. Usually the first level converts fairly well. The second level seems to lose the connection to the first level if it comes over at all and the third level could convert a sequence field or a manual number.

HEADER AND FOOTER MARGINS

The default margins for a header and footer are set to 0.5" from the edge of the page. In converted documents, this value may change to 1", which can cause the pagination of the document to change.

WIDOW AND ORPHAN CONTROL

In Word 2000, all new documents have Widow and Orphan control turned on by default. This prevents a single line of a paragraph from being left by itself at the top or bottom of a page. In WordPerfect, you had to set this option by choosing the Keep Text Together option. Word 2000 converts the WordPerfect Keep Text Together option to Widow and Orphan control in Word. If you become comfortable with Widow and Orphan control, you may want to turn it on for the rest of the converted document.

UNUSUAL TAB SETTINGS

You may notice many tabs or odd tabs set on the ruler at negative positions. This affects your new Word document if you are trying to change indents or tab settings. Clearing tabs is covered later in this chapter.

PARALLEL COLUMNS, TABLES, AND BORDERS

Word 2000 does not have a Parallel Column feature. When a document that contains a set of parallel columns is converted to Word, the parallel columns convert to a table. Word does extremely well converting tables from one application to another. There is one area that you will want to be aware of, however: occasionally, a converted table's borders may not print. This usually happens at the bottom of a page.

In WordPerfect tables, you would only apply borders to either the top or bottom of a cell because if you applied both, your border would end up looking thicker than the rest of the borders. When the cell gets to the bottom of a page and there is not a bottom border applied, the cell will be missing the bottom border in Word 2000.

CLEANING UP CONVERTED DOCUMENTS

Just when you think your document is completely converted and you are home free, guess what? It's time for Step 2—Clean Up! The term *clean up* here means to remove codes and to reformat your document. This is the most critical part of the conversion process. Taking shortcuts here can damage your newly converted documents.

You have variety of choices for how to clean up a document. The steps you choose will depend on how quickly the document is needed or how important the document is. For example, you would want to spend a lot more time on a precedent document (a document used as the basis for other documents) than you would on a letter that you may use only once. Before diving into the how-to, it is important to understand the background.

WHY CLEAN UP?

The earlier section discussed some of the formatting codes that remain in the document after converting to Word. Every time you work in a document that contains codes, the codes are converted. After a while, there is a chance that important codes will be lost and the document will become corrupt.

A corrupt document may start acting strangely when you are working in it. In the worst case, Word will not allow you to open the document at all. Below, you will see some of the most common codes that are left over and how to clean them. Since each document can be uniquely formatted, the codes will show up differently from one document to another.

Cleaning up a document can be time-consuming, but the use of Styles will help the reformatting of a document go a lot quicker. If a document contains complex formatting, however, you might find it easier to copy the text from the converted document and paste it into a new document based on the desired template. For example, pleadings contain a pleading caption and line numbering. Rather than try to manipulate the caption and line numbering in a converted document, it is sometimes easier to copy the body of the pleading from the converted document and paste it into a new pleading that contains the caption, line numbering, and styles required. Before you do this, though, read these tips to help make things easier:

- *Never* copy the final paragraph mark in a document when you're copying the text to a new document. The final paragraph mark contains formatting codes and other information about the document. Copying it from one document to another can cause the new document to become corrupt, resulting in the loss of the document.

- *Always* keep a copy of the original file for reference and backup purposes. Keep a printed copy of the original file as well—that will show you what the author intended the document to look like.

- ◆ To completely remove all codes and formatting from the original document, see "Using Paste Special" in the "Spring Cleaning" section later in this chapter.

- ◆ Use Find and Replace as much as possible to apply new formatting. See "Using Find and Replace to Strip Out Unwanted Codes" later in this chapter for ideas on how to take advantage of this feature.

QUICK AND DIRTY (LESS THAN AN HOUR)

This chapter talks about many steps required to convert and clean up a document but it would be naive to expect you to follow them every time. You won't always be able to indulge in the luxury of stripping out all the codes and reformatting an entire document. If the document was supposed to be out yesterday or the filing date is now, you can perform a few very quick steps to get the document out the door in a hurry.

NOTE

We want to strongly warn you that this method should not be standard practice each time you open the document. While it may seem like every document is a "rush" job, if you cut corners, you will end up causing yourself a lot more work in the long run—when your documents become corrupt. Follow these steps as a temporary measure, and if this document needs to be used again, go back when things are a little less hectic and do a proper cleanup.

INSERT FILE

If you're in a hurry and need to get the text into a Word document quickly for *one-time* use, and you don't have time to perform the cleanup procedures, you can insert the file directly into Word. This command puts all of the text and formatting into a new Word document with the correct Compatibility settings, which should allow the document to be printed correctly.

For information on these settings, see the "Compatibility Options" section earlier in this chapter.

INSERT A WORDPERFECT FILE INTO A WORD DOCUMENT

1. Open a new blank document.
2. From the Insert menu, choose File.
3. Navigate to and insert the WordPerfect file or non–Word 2000 file. If you need to print or look at the file only once, this is a good method.

LOCK FIELDS

Fields such as table of contents, cross-references, and table of authorities are very prominent in Word. As mentioned earlier, some of these fields convert over to working fields in Word and some do not.

Considering that you do not have a lot of time, you do not want to worry about your document's being full of error messages where fields are not updating correctly. To prevent this from happening, you will want to lock all the fields in the document. This preserves the field contents from the original document.

NOTE

Locking fields is a solution for a quick cleanup only. If you have made many changes to your document, your tables and cross-references will need to be regenerated to ensure accuracy.

LOCK FIELDS

1. Press Ctrl+A to select the entire text of the document.
2. Press Ctrl+F11 to lock the fields.

Your document should be in pretty good shape now. Just remember—if you are planning to use this document again, be sure to follow one of the more detailed cleanup regimens described in the following sections.

SPIC AND SPAN

If you plan on using a document throughout the year, making minor changes here and there, you will need to do a much more thorough job of cleaning. This is the time to remove the leftover WordPerfect codes and reformat your document in Word.

Following this cleaning routine removes the more obvious codes and still leaves in basic text formatting such as bold, underlined, centered, and so on. Most of the stripping of codes can be done with Find and Replace and reformatting can be done easily with styles. See Chapter 6, "Styles," for more information.

NOTE

This cleanup method removes most of the codes in your document but since every document is uniquely formatted, it is not 100 percent guaranteed to remove everything. See the "Spring Cleaning" section later in this chapter for the most thorough (and recommended) cleanup option.

TIP

When working with important or complex documents, you always want to have a hard copy of the document as a reference to allow you to reformat to match the original.

Start with the same first step as the quick-and-dirty method—that is, insert the file into Word and save it as a Word document. Next you will use Find and Replace to remove most of the residual codes.

USING FIND AND REPLACE TO REMOVE UNWANTED CODES

Word's Find and Replace feature will become one of your best friends while cleaning up documents, providing a quick and easy way to strip out unwanted formatting. For example, with a document that converts with straight quotation marks and you add new Word "smart" (curly) quotation marks, your document will end up looking disconnected and unprofessional. With Find and Replace you can make all the quotation marks smart—just like you!

CHANGE STRAIGHT QUOTES TO SMART QUOTES

1. Start with a blank Word document.
2. From the File menu, choose Insert.
3. Navigate to and insert the WordPerfect file.
4. From the File menu, choose Save As. Save the file as a Word 2000 document.

5. From the <u>E</u>dit menu, choose R<u>e</u>place. Keyboard users can press Ctrl+H. The Find and Replace dialog box appears with the Re<u>p</u>lace tab selected.

6. Delete any text from the Fi<u>n</u>d What box. If formatting options have been set, click No Forma<u>t</u>ting to clear the options. Type in a quotation mark (").

7. Delete any text from the Replace W<u>i</u>th box. If formatting options have been set, click No Forma<u>t</u>ting to clear the options. Type in a quotation mark (").

8. Click Replace <u>A</u>ll to replace your quotes in the document.

9. Leave this document open for the next exercise.

You can follow these exact steps, substituting an apostrophe (') for single quotes.

You are not finished with Find and Replace yet! You can also use this feature with invisible characters as well. For example, you can use the feature to remove {PRIVATE} codes, extra tabs, and more.

REMOVE FIELD CODES

1. From the <u>E</u>dit menu, choose R<u>e</u>place. Keyboard users can press Ctrl+H. The Find and Replace dialog box appears with the Re<u>p</u>lace tab selected.

2. Click <u>M</u>ore to expand the dialog box if it is not already expanded.

3. Delete any text from the Fi<u>n</u>d What box. If formatting options have been set, click No Forma<u>t</u>ting to clear the options.

4. Click Sp<u>e</u>cial to expand the list of special characters.

5. Choose Fiel<u>d</u>.

To save time, you can type ^**d** directly into the Fi<u>n</u>d What box. The caret (^) character can be inserted by pressing Shift+6.

6. Delete any existing text from the Replace W<u>i</u>th box. If formatting options have been set, click No Forma<u>t</u>ting to clear the options.

7. Click Replace <u>A</u>ll to remove all fields from the document.

NOTE

Since the ^d code is not unique to any single type of field, you may want to just choose Replace (instead of Replace All) and be selective on what fields to remove and which ones to keep, especially if you want to retain your table of contents markers. Later in this section you'll see how to update a table of contents.

TIP

You can also easily remove all Sequence numbering. Just make sure you are viewing the Field Codes (press Alt+F9) before you complete the Find and Replace.

There are many other special characters that you can use to clean up a document. Table 14.1 shows you some of the more common ones.

Certain settings can be applied to the entire document and therefore do not need to be fixed with Find and Replace. It is important to complete the find and replace tasks first to remove all the excess codes (such as section breaks) and then apply other formats.

AUTOMATIC PARAGRAPH NUMBERS

What to do with the numbers in a converted document depends on your needs. The following list describes your three basic options:

- If you intend to add and make changes to the document, you may decide that removing all the sequence codes and applying styles to the document is best. This option takes some time because you must manually apply the styles, but it's the best alternative if the document requires extensive editing. In some

TABLE 14.1 COMMON FIND AND REPLACE TECHNIQUES FOR CONVERTED DOCUMENTS

FIND WHAT	REPLACE WITH	RESULT
^t	[leave blank]	Removes tab characters
^p^p	^p	Replaces double paragraph marks with a single paragraph mark
^b	[leave blank]	Removes all Section Breaks
^#.^t	[leave blank]	Removes manual numbers followed by period and tab
^#^#.^t	[leave blank]	Removes double digit manual numbers followed by period and tab

cases, you can use Word's Find and Replace feature to remove Sequence fields as shown in the previous section.

♦ Convert the WordPerfect numbers as text. You can do this using the Paste Special option in the "Spring Cleaning" section or in the Batch Conversion wizard described at the end of this chapter.

♦ If the document has sequence codes and you have a thorough knowledge of sequence fields, simply maintain the sequence codes and continue working with the document. You can add and update the existing codes.

♦ If the first level of a numbered list converts well, it usually has a style attached to the paragraphs as well and you can attach one of Word's Outline numbering formats to that style and then reformat the other levels.

USING SEQUENCE FIELDS

To use Sequence fields, you need to thoroughly understand how they work. If you add, delete, or move a numbered paragraph, you must manually update all the remaining sequence fields in the document to reflect the new numbers.

The format for a sequence field is as follows:
{SEQ Identifier [Bookmark] [Switches]}

The Sequence Identifier is the name assigned to a series of numbered items. The name must start with a letter and is limited to 40 characters, but it can include letters, numbers, and underscores. For example, the name for a series of numbered paragraphs might be one of the following: Level1, Level2; Outline1, Outline2; Interrogatory; or RequestforProd. In the following exercise, Word separately numbers each set of sequence fields. You can add the switches listed in Table 14.2 to a sequence field to control the way it works.

TABLE 14.2 SWITCHES FOR SEQUENCE FIELDS

FIELD SWITCH	FUNCTION
\c	Repeats the previous sequence number. This is useful for Section numbers that must repeat the previous Article Number.
\h	Hides the field result.
\n	This is the default switch that inserts the next sequence number.
\rx	Used to reset the sequence number to the number specified as x. For example, { SEQ rog \r7 } starts interrogatory numbering at 7.

INSERT SEQUENCE FIELDS

1. Type **INTERROGATORY** and press the Spacebar.
2. Press Ctrl+F9 to insert a field.
3. Type **SEQ rog** inside the field brackets.
4. Press F9 while the insertion point is still inside the field, to automatically update and toggle the view of the field. The number 1 should appear after INTERROGATORY.
5. Select "Interrogatory 1" and press Alt+F3 to name it as an AutoText Entry.
6. Type **rog** in the Create AutoText dialog box.
7. Practice inserting the rog AutoText entry by typing **rog** and then pressing the F3 key.

NOTE

Sequence fields do not automatically update. If you move or delete the interrogatories, the numbers remain as they were originally inserted. Press Ctrl+A to select all the text in the document, and then press F9 to update the fields.

Use sequence fields for different lists of numbers that are interspersed throughout the document. For example, create an AutoText entry using the preceding steps for requests for production and requests for admission. As long as each group of numbers has a different identifier in the SEQ field, the different numbered lists are maintained.

UPDATING A CONVERTED TABLE OF CONTENTS

Tables of contents from WordPerfect convert very well. WordPerfect Table Of Contents entries convert automatically to Word TC field codes. If you have chosen not to strip out all of the field codes in your document (as shown in the "Using Find and Replace to Remove Unwanted Codes" section of this chapter), you can regenerate the table of contents by updating the TC field.

If you choose to apply styles—which is a quick way to reformat your document—it would probably be easier to pull all the manual field codes out of the document and use styles to generate a new Table of Contents. For more information on styles, see Chapter 6, "Styles."

UPDATE TABLE OF CONTENTS

1. Open a WordPerfect file that contains a generated table of contents. If you don't have a WordPerfect file, open a Word document with a table of contents.

2. Place the insertion point anywhere in the table of contents.

3. Press F9 or alternate-click the table of contents, and then select Update Field from the shortcut menu to update the table of contents.

RESET HEADER AND FOOTER MARGINS

Once the section breaks have been removed from the document, you will need to go in and reset the Header and Footer margins back to 0.5". From the File menu, choose Page Setup and be sure to have the change apply to the entire document.

APPLY WIDOW AND ORPHAN CONTROL

Select all the text in the document. From the Format menu, choose Paragraph and select the Line and Page Breaks tab. Deselect all options except for Widow And Orphan. Ensure this option is checked (not gray).

CLEARING TAB SETTINGS

To quickly remove all excess tab settings, select the entire document and choose Clear All from the Tab dialog box. See the section on tabs for more information.

TABLE BORDERS

Although it does not happen with all tables, the bottom border of your table may be missing. You can correct this by reapplying Word borders. Select the entire table and turn off all the original WordPerfect borders and then reapply "all" borders in Word.

REFORMATTING THE DOCUMENT

The majority of codes in your document should be removed at this point. Now it's time to reformat the document. This is where having the hard copy of the original document is important. Following are the areas that want special attention:

◆ Headers and footers

◆ Automatic paragraph numbering

◆ Regenerating table of contents and cross-references

◆ General paragraph formatting (indents, tabs, and so on)

The best way to do most of these reformats is to use styles. If you already have styles you like stored in a different document or template, see the "Using the Organizer" section later in this chapter.

SPRING CLEANING (PRECEDENT DOCUMENTS)

If you have a document that is going to serve as the basis for other documents, the best bet would be to make it a template. For more information on templates, see Chapter 10. Whether you choose to do this or leave it as a document and continue to make copies of it, you will want the document to be as clean as possible.

NOTE

This is definitely not a place to take shortcuts. If the document will be used to create others, it must be stable. If not, not only this main document but all of those based on it will have a very high chance of becoming corrupt.

USING PASTE SPECIAL

This is it! The best solution for converting without retyping the entire document. This method removes all formatting codes in one step so all you have to do is reformat without the task of stripping the codes first. But *be* warned: when you use this option, you remove *all* formats—even bold, underlining, and other character-level formats that would convert perfectly well automatically. This is the safest way to clean up a document, since the document will no longer have any old codes left over, but it does require some careful handwork to finish the job.

You would think that using copy and paste should be a very easy task. Typically this is true, but if you use a regular paste to insert the text from a WordPerfect document into a Word document, you bring over all the codes as well as the text; this could be disastrous to your new Word document, unexpectedly changing the formatting of existing text. Word's Paste Special command allows you to bring the text over without the codes coming along.

TIP

Paste Special isn't just for entire documents; there are times when it can be very handy for document fragments as well. For example, you may want to use paragraphs three through ten from one WordPerfect document and then paragraphs five and six from another in your Word document. Using Paste Special/Unformatted Text is just as effective in this instance as it is for entire documents.

TRY IT FOR YOURSELF: USE PASTE SPECIAL

1. Create a letter using the letter template.
2. Open the WordPerfect document. If you don't have a WordPerfect document, any document will do.
3. Select and Copy the text in the WordPerfect (or other) document.
4. Switch to the letter document.
5. Put your insertion point where you want the text to be in the Word document.
6. From the Edit menu, choose Paste Special. (Don't use Paste!) The dialog box shown in Figure 14.6 appears.
7. Choose Unformatted Text. Make sure that you don't select Formatted Text (RTF), this pastes all of the codes that you are trying to get rid of!
8. Click OK.

FIGURE 14.6

The Paste Special dialog box allows you to choose how your copied text is inserted.

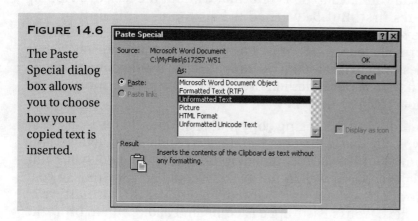

COPYING STYLES WITH THE ORGANIZER

Your document is now clean of codes but it is also clear of any formatting. Using styles is the fastest method to reformat the document. Word's Organizer allows you to access all styles in a template and copy them into the current document. After you convert a WordPerfect document, this is an excellent way to move all the styles from an existing Word template to the converted document.

USE THE ORGANIZER

1. Open a copy of a letter created in WordPerfect.
2. From the Tools menu, choose Templates And Add-Ins.
3. Click the Organizer button. On the left side of the Organizer window, Word displays all styles of the converted document. On the right side are styles in the Normal template.
4. Click the Close button under the Normal template. The Close button will change to an Open button.
5. Click Open and choose your letter template.
6. Select all the styles that you want to copy.
7. Click Copy.
8. Close the Organizer.

Once the styles are available in the converted document, you can apply them to paragraphs to obtain the correct formatting.

REMOVING PARAGRAPH AND CHARACTER FORMATTING

The Organizer is a great way to make firmwide styles appear in a converted document. Sometimes paragraphs formatted with the same style look different from one another. You might have two paragraphs that are in the Normal style, but one is double-spaced and the other is not. If they were formatted manually in WordPerfect, you'll need to remove the manual paragraph formatting. To do this, select the paragraph, including the paragraph mark, and press Ctrl+Q. Doing so removes manually applied paragraph formatting to make the selected paragraph match the selected style. Paragraph formatting includes tabs, indents, and spacing.

Press Ctrl+Spacebar to remove or apply character formatting such as bold, italic, underline, font, and font size formatting.

REMOVE CHARACTER AND PARAGRAPH FORMATTING

1. Select a paragraph, including the paragraph mark, and press Ctrl+Spacebar. All character formatting for the selected paragraph is removed.
2. Click anywhere in the paragraph and press Ctrl+Q. Any additional paragraph formatting that was applied in WordPerfect is removed.

TIP

Ctrl+Spacebar and Ctrl+Q do not remove formatting associated with the applied character or paragraph style. For example, if you press Ctrl+Spacebar in a heading paragraph, and if the applied heading style contains bold formatting, the bold formatting is not removed. Likewise, if the paragraph is not bold but the style calls for bold formatting, the bold format is applied when you press Ctrl+Spacebar. See Chapter 6, "Styles," for more information about character and paragraph styles.

CONVERTING OUTGOING FILES

Convenient as it would be if the whole world worked in Word 2000, that just isn't the case. The people who receive your files may not be able to work with them in Word 2000, and it is much safer to do the conversion yourself than to leave it to the recipients in the hope that they will get it right. Thus it is sometimes necessary to produce files formatted for other word processing systems.

CONVERTING TO PREVIOUS VERSIONS OF WORD

Microsoft's effort to make Word 2000 fully compatible with Word 97 has really paid off. In fact, in Word 2000, you don't need to save a document in Word 97 format. File formats are the same in Word 2000 as they are in Word 97. Some of the features that are available in Word 2000, however, are not supported in Word 97.

If you are concerned that the document may lose formatting or otherwise cause problems when opened in Word 97, you can disable

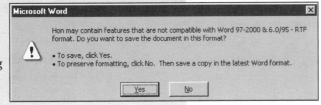

FIGURE 14.7

Word 97
Disabled
Features dialog
box

the new features and have Word 2000 save the document in a format that is fully supported by Word 97. From the Tools menu, choose Options, then select the Save tab. Click the check box next to Disable Features Not Supported In Word 97. When this option is turned on, Word 2000 will limit itself to what Word 97 can do. If you apply features not supported in Word 97, Word displays a message as shown in Figure 14.7.

Table 14.3 lists some features that are not supported in Word 97 or that are only partially supported. For partially supported features, read Word 2000 help for more information, under the topic "What Happens When I Save a Document As Word 97?"

While Word 2000 offers several features that are unsupported in previous versions of Word, most of the formatting is maintained. The unsupported features are those that are new to Word 2000. If you know that you will be converting a document to a previous version of Word, turn on the Disable Features Not Supported In Word 97 option to guarantee correct formatting in Word 97.

TABLE 14.3 PARTIAL LIST OF FEATURES NOT SUPPORTED IN WORD 97

FEATURE	RESULT IN WORD 97
Decorative underlines	Changed to single underlines
Text with colored underlines	Underline color becomes the same as the text color
Customized font colors	Changed to the closest matching font color
Text-wrapping breaks	Changed to manual line breaks
Top gutter position	Changed to Left gutter position
Nested tables	Inner tables converted to paragraphs within cells
Diagonal lines in tables	Disappear in Word 97

You can also save documents to other versions of Word, such as Word 6.0/95, Word 2.x for Windows, or Word for the Macintosh.

SAVE A DOCUMENT AS A WORD 6.0/95 DOCUMENT

1. Open a document that you want to save in Word 6.0/95 format.

2. From the File menu, choose Save As.

3. Select Word 6.0/95 (*.doc) from the Save As Type list.

4. Enter a file name and select a location in which you want to save the document.

5. Click Save. The file is saved in the correct format.

CAUTION If you want to keep a document saved as a Word 2000 document, be sure to use a different name for the Word 6.0/95 version; otherwise, the original file is overwritten.

AUTOMATIC NUMBERING AND OTHER FEATURES

One of the most important features in legal documents is automatic numbering. You'll be happy to know that Word 2000 documents with outline numbered styles retain their numbering format when opened in Word 97. However, if a Word 2000 document is saved as a Word 6.0/95 document, some problems with outline numbered styles may occur. For example, at least at the time of this writing, if you save a paragraph formatted with the Heading 2 style numbered as "Section 1.01," the "Section 1.0" is deleted, leaving just .1.

If you want to work on a document in Word but keep it in its original format, choose Save from the File menu. Not all word processing applications support the same functionality, so any formatting specific to Word 2000 may be lost or modified.

When you save a document in a non–Word format, Word displays a message that some features may not be supported in another file format. Word 2000 also shows you exactly what formatting you lose when exporting to Word 6.0/95 or HTML, and how many times the formatting was used in the document. Figure 14.8 shows the dialog box you see when saving a document with embossed formatting in Word 6.0/95 format.

FIGURE 14.8

The Save As warning dialog box

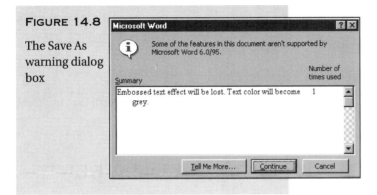

If you intend to keep a document in a format other than Word, it's a good idea to try to use formatting options that you know are supported in the other application. To continue with the save, click Continue.

SAVE A DOCUMENT IN A DIFFERENT TYPE OF FILE FORMAT

1. Create a new Word document.

2. Type **What will happen to my double wave underline?**

3. Select the text "double wave underline" but not the question mark.

4. Apply the double wave underline format from the Format menu by selecting Font, and choosing Double Wave Underline in the Underline Style list.

5. From the File menu, choose Save As, and select Word 6.x/95 from the list.

6. A warning dialog appears that explains which features will be lost if you continue. Click Continue to continue saving the file in Word 6.0/95 format.

Once a document has been saved in a different file format, features not supported in the chosen format are disabled. For example, if you save a file in Word 6.0/95 format and then try to apply engraved formatting, you see the dialog box shown in Figure 14.9.

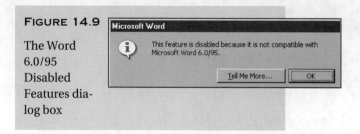

Microsoft Word

This feature is disabled because it is not compatible with Microsoft Word 6.0/95.

Tell Me More...   OK

SAVING A DOCUMENT TO A DIFFERENT FILE FORMAT

You can save Word 2000 documents in many different file formats. Be aware that some of the formatting may be lost, depending on the format selected. The following sections describe some of the file formats available to you.

TEXT ONLY

Saving a file as Text Only causes the document to lose all formatting. Page and section breaks convert to paragraph marks and are lost. Because you lose all formatting, you should choose the Text Only format only when you're distributing information that does not require formatting. For example, you might want to save a document such as a ReadMe file in text format when you are distributing it to a large number of people. All users, regardless of the word processing application or computer available to them, can read text files. These files are also much smaller than formatted files.

MS-DOS TEXT ONLY

This is similar to the Text Only format but is designed specifically for conversion to MS-DOS–based programs such as WordPerfect 5.1.

MS-DOS TEXT WITH LAYOUT

Indents, tables, line spacing, paragraph spacing, and tab stops are maintained if you save a document in MS-DOS Text with Layout file format. These settings may not match the exact settings from the converted document, however.

RICH TEXT FORMAT (RTF)

Rich Text Format saves the most formatting because it converts formatting codes into instructions that other programs can read and interpret. If you need to save a document to a format that is not supported by Word, save the document in Rich Text Format. It's likely that the destination application supports this format as well, so the formatting is retained when the file is opened.

SAVE IN A DIFFERENT FILE FORMAT

1. Open the file that you want to save in a different format.
2. From the File Menu, choose Save As.
3. Select the desired file type from the Save As Type list.
4. Enter a name for the file and then select a location in which to save the file.
5. Click Save. The file is saved in the selected format.

When Word documents are saved with a file name extension other than the default extension for that file type, Word adds the default extension to your file name (*.doc). To save a document with an extension other than the default extension, enclose the entire file name in quotation marks. An example of this is a WordPerfect file named brief.wp. To preserve the (*.wp) extension, name the file **"Brief.wp"** (with the quotation marks).

CONVERTING FROM WORD TO WORDPERFECT

Discussions of conversion tend to focus on converting from WordPerfect to Word. Once you have mastered that part of the conversion, there may be a need to take a Word document and convert it to WordPerfect format, if a client or the court is not using Word.

Earlier in this chapter, you read about Word's import converters that allow Word to read other word processing formats. The export converters allow Word to send the Word documents into other formats. Although Word 2000 has the ability to open all WordPerfect formats, it is only equipped with an exporter to WordPerfect 5.x and lower.

This means that if you need to save a Word document in WordPerfect format, the document needs to be saved down to WordPerfect 5.1. If the client you are sharing documents with has a more recent version of WordPerfect, much of the formatting in the document will be lost. To reduce the amount of lost formatting, consider the following:

- WordPerfect 8 users should be able to open the Word document without difficulty. WordPerfect 8 has a built-in converter for Word 97 and earlier versions of Word.

- For WordPerfect 6 and 7 users, Corel released a free convert utility that allows conversion between Word 97 or earlier versions of Word and WordPerfect 6 or 7. Your document needs to be saved in Word 97 format in order for the converter to work correctly. The converter can be found at `http://www.corel.com/support/ftpsite/pub/wordperfect/wpwin/70/cwps7.htm`.

NOTE

The converter is not supported by Corel.

CONVERT A WORD 97 DOCUMENT TO WORDPERFECT FORMAT

1. Download the free converter utility from Corel's Web site. Double-click the downloaded file to run the program.

2. Start cvwin80 from the location it was installed in. The WordPerfect Convert dialog box opens.

NOTE

The default location is c:\corel\convert.

3. In the From field, type the location and name of the file you wish to convert.

NOTE

This conversion utility requires that you type in the extension of the file. If you do not type in the extension, it will not find the file.

4. Choose the File type from the Type drop-down list. For example, Word 97.

5. In the To field, type in the location and name of the file you wish to convert.

6. Choose the new type from the Type field. For example, WordPerfect 6/7/8.

7. Click Convert. Your client can now open your document in WordPerfect.

CONVERTING SEVERAL DOCUMENTS SIMULTANEOUSLY

Microsoft Office includes a Batch Conversion wizard that walks you through the steps for importing batches of documents from another application to Word, *or* for exporting Word documents to a different file format.

NOTE

The Batch Conversion wizard only performs the first step of the conversion process: opening the file and saving it as a Word document. You still need to perform the second step to clean up the converted document.

You access the Batch Conversion wizard on the Other Documents tab, from the File New dialog box. The first time you run the wizard Word 2000 installs it for you. The file name of the conversion wizard is Batch Conversion.wiz. If you don't see this file on your computer, rerun Word 2000 Setup and click Add Or Remove Programs. Expand Microsoft Word for Windows, and then expand Wizards and Templates. Select More Wizards and click Update to install. If you don't have access to the Word 2000 Setup file, contact your Systems Help Desk for assistance.

RUN THE CONVERSION WIZARD

1. From the File menu, choose New.
2. Select the Other Documents tab.
3. Double-click the Batch Conversion Wizard icon.
4. The simple Start screen for the Batch Conversion wizard appears (see Figure 14.10). Click Next to begin.

The Batch Conversion Wizard dialog box has a flow chart on the left side that contains information about the process. A set of navigation buttons on the bottom of the dialog box will walk you through steps of the Wizard. After reading through and completing the required information on each screen, click the Next button to move through the process in the Wizard.

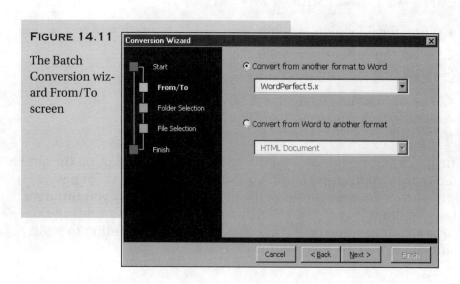

FIGURE 14.10

The Batch
Conversion wiz-
ard Start screen

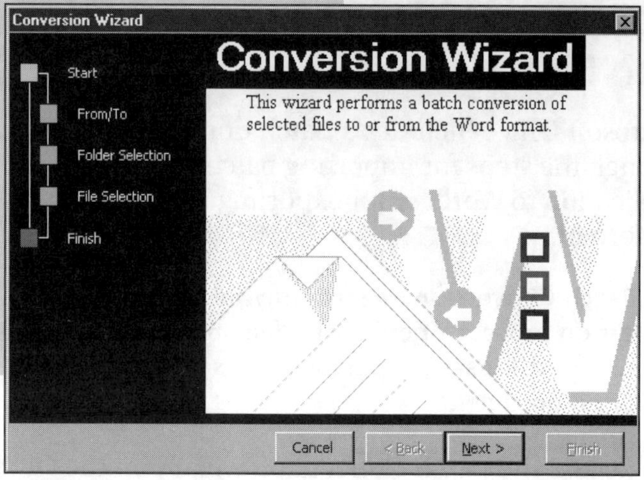

FOLLOW THE CONVERSION WIZARD

1. The Batch Conversion wizard asks if you want to convert files
   to Word format or convert files from another format to Word.
   (see Figure 14.11).

2. Select the Convert From Another Format To Word option. Click
   the down arrow to select the type of files to convert.

FIGURE 14.11

The Batch
Conversion wiz-
ard From/To
screen

3. Click Next.

4. In the Source Folder section, click the Browse button to select the location of the files that you want to convert. In the Destination Folder section, click the Browse button to select a destination for the converted files.

If you are converting documents where the file extension doesn't change (example: Word 6/95 to Word 2000) and you want to preserve the original files as well as create converted copies, specify a different destination folder. Otherwise, the original files are overwritten in the new format.

5. Click Next to move to the next step in the Conversion wizard.

If you want to show all file types in the File Selection dialog box, change the Type option from (*.doc) to (*.*).

6. Select one or more files and then click the Next button.

7. Click Finish to begin the batch conversion process.

8. Click No to close the Conversion wizard dialog box.

TROUBLESHOOTING COMMON CONVERSION ISSUES

Since people don't all create documents alike, the conversion and cleanup process that you face will be different from the ones faced by others working with different types of documents. This section discusses some troubleshooting issues that you may encounter when converting and cleaning up documents.

My document is not converting very well. It doesn't look right on the screen.

Word 2000 includes Compatibility settings that help you convert documents between WordPerfect and Word 2000. You may need to play with turning on and off different settings under Tools, Options, Compatibility to get the best result. The following settings may help with some of the conversion:

◆ **Suppress extra line spacing like WordPerfect 5.x.** This setting makes sure that the layout of converted WordPerfect documents formatted with automatic line height are close to the way they were in the original document.

- **Set width of a space like WordPerfect 5.x.** WordPerfect and Word calculate the width of proportional fonts differently. This option sets the width of a space as it was in WordPerfect 5.x.

Some of the formatting options are grayed out on menus.

If some options are not available and you are not doing anything out of the ordinary, perhaps the Disable Features Not Supported In Word 97 option is enabled. This option is set from the Tools menu by choosing Options and clicking the Save tab.

I have a lot of tabs on my ruler and some of them appear before the indent. I didn't set these; how did they get there and how do I remove them?

One sign that you're working with a converted document is that many tabs are put into the document during the conversion process. It's a dead giveaway when tabs appear before the indent—it would be hard for you to set these tabs manually. To clear all tabs, from the Format menu, choose Tabs and click Clear All.

Are there any products that do the conversion for me?

Some of Payne Consulting Group's clients are using the product DocXchange from Microsystems for converting and cleaning up their legacy documents. For information, check out `http://www.microsystems.com/` or phone 630-261-0111; for Sales, phone 201-947-2045.

Other third-party conversion products are Conversions Plus from Dataviz (`http://www.dataviz.com/`) 1-800-733-0030, and Pro ACE from Jenai Software Engineering (`http://www.jenai.com/`).

Is there a way for a client who does not have Word installed to view the document in Word?

You can save the document in HTML format which can be accessed by anyone with an up-to-date Web browser, or they can use the Microsoft Word Viewer that is a free download available from (`http://officeupdate.Microsoft.com/downloadcatalog/dld-word.htm`). There are two versions of the Word 2000/97 Viewer (both are for Windows operating system, not Macintosh or UNIX). On version is for Windows 95/98/NT, the other for Windows 3.x. The Word Viewer should be used primarily on a computer where Word is not installed. Users can access files, but cannot make any changes.

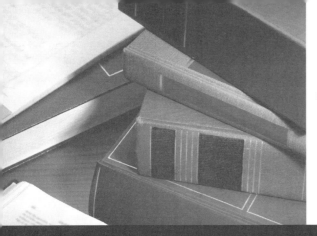

CHAPTER 15

PUBLISHING DOCUMENTS TO YOUR INTRANET

IN THIS CHAPTER

◆ The need for an Intranet

◆ Using Word to create a Web page

◆ Adding text

◆ Inserting hyperlinks

◆ Using the Web toolbar

◆ Converting a document to HTML

◆ Applying different formats

When we wrote the last version of our book, *Word 97 for Law Firms*, law firms were just beginning to explore the capabilities of the Web. Now we see sophisticated Web sites and Intranets at many firms, and every day lawyers ask us about creating Web pages or doing research on the Internet. With the advent of e-filing, soon we will all find ourselves creating HTML or other types of online documents. Luckily, Word 2000 makes it easy to create these documents without learning complicated HTML codes or features.

Many documents formerly distributed in paper form are now being stored on law firm Intranets. These documents include commonly used forms, employee handbooks, policy manuals, timesheet templates, attorney bios, and even conference room schedules. Because such documents must be available to many people within a firm, and must be kept up to date, an Intranet is an excellent place to store them. Another advantage of using an Intranet is that the documents can be accessed with a simple mouse click. There is no need to know the document number or its storage location on the network.

This chapter shows you how to use Word to set up a Web page and how to format documents, modify them, and link them to the Web page. You can follow along with the exercises even if your firm has not yet implemented an Intranet.

DON'T YOU MEAN INTERNET?

Most people are familiar with the Internet. It's an online meeting place where people from all countries, backgrounds, and persuasions can communicate. You access the Internet with a "browser," such as Microsoft Internet Explorer or Netscape Navigator, which you instruct to "Go" to a certain Web page using a Uniform Resource Locator (URL). While you're at each site, you can view content, post messages or e-mail, print, or download information.

An Intranet is similar to the Internet except that the information you access and share is limited to others in your law firm, or to clients or subcontractors with permission to access your site. The information is usually kept on a server maintained by a data administrator or webmaster you employ or a data company you hire.

An Intranet uses the same Web browser as the Internet, and you retrieve information in the same manner. If you know how to use the Internet, you will have no trouble using an Intranet.

THE NEED FOR AN INTRANET

An Intranet facilitates communication between employees of the firm and provides a one-stop place to find firmwide information. Documents such as employee handbooks, policy manuals, and conference room schedules can be stored and accessed from an Intranet site. You can also use the Intranet for different practice groups and departments within the firm as a place to share information easily. An Intranet makes it possible for attorneys to share and discuss information from a case with others in the firm, even if they are located in another office.

An Intranet is like a huge room full of people, books, and documents. When you enter, you can talk with someone else, read a book, and access documents. The only difference is that with an Intranet, you access these resources online. Table 15.1 outlines the benefits of having an Intranet.

CREATE A WEB PAGE

Creating a Web page document with Word 2000 is easy! From the File menu, you can choose Save As Web Page to turn existing documents into online documents. You can also create a Web page from templates and wizards that come with Word 2000.

NOTE

You create Web documents by saving your files in HTML (HyperText Markup Language) format. Browsers can read and display information from HTML documents. Other Office 2000 programs, such as Excel and PowerPoint, can save documents in HTML format for display on the firm's Intranet as well.

TABLE 15.1 BENEFITS OF AN INTRANET

BENEFIT	BY
One-Stop Access	Firmwide documents are stored in one location.
Simplify Updating	When information changes in one of these documents, you change it in one location. People who have subscribed to the page automatically receive updates.
Save Money and Resources	Online documents do not have to be copied or put in binders, reducing both the materials and labor cost of disseminating the information and generating further economies by shortening the time required to access it when it is needed.

We use the term *Web page* interchangeably with *document.* Also keep in mind that Web pages don't necessarily have to be located on the World Wide Web; they can also be located on the Intranet in your firm.

BASING A WEB PAGE ON A WEB TEMPLATE

Word makes it easy to create a Web page, by allowing you to base the page on a template. Do this by choosing New from the File menu, as you would to access any other template within Word.

CREATE A WEB PAGE BASED ON A TEMPLATE

1. From the File menu, choose New.
2. Select the Web Pages tab shown in Figure 15.1.
3. Double-click any of the Web Page templates.
4. Modify some of the text on the page to create a personalized Web page.
5. Save the document and close it. You will use it in the next exercise.

FIGURE 15.1

Word comes with built-in templates and wizards for creating a Web page.

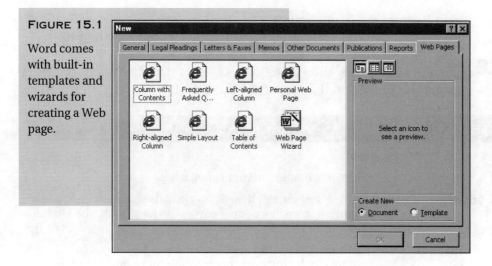

NOTE

Because you started from a Web template, Word automatically saves the document in HTML format.

USING THE WEB PAGE WIZARD

A Web site is a collection of Web pages that are linked together. With the new Web Page wizard, you can create an entire Web site with multiple Web pages. The wizard walks you through the process of creating a Web site step by step; you can create new pages or add existing pages to the site. You determine how the pages are formatted, and how the user navigates from one page to another. Using the Web Page wizard, you can create a professional-looking Web site in minutes.

USE THE WEB PAGE WIZARD

1. From the File menu, choose New.
2. Select the Web Pages tab.
3. Double-click Web Page Wizard. Click Next to specify the Title and Location for the Start page of the Web site. Figure 15.2 shows the Title and Location dialog box for the Web Page wizard.

FIGURE 15.2

Enter the title and location for the Web page.

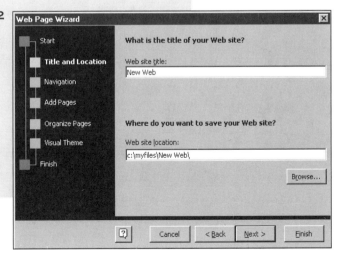

4. Type a title for the page in the Web Site Title box and type or select a location to store the page in the Web Site Location box. The Web site title appears on the title bar in the Web browser.

5. Click Next. The Navigation dialog box appears, as shown in Figure 15.3.

6. Select a type of navigation. For a description of each, click the option for a particular type of navigation and read the description.

If you select Vertical Frame or Horizontal Frame, the links to other pages appear on the same page as the content of the page. Some older versions of browsers do not support frames.

7. Click Next. The Add Pages dialog box appears, as shown in Figure 15.4.

8. Click Add New Blank Page to add a new page to the site.

9. Click Add Template Page to select a type of template, as shown in Figure 15.5. Click OK to return to the Add Pages dialog box.

10. Click Add Existing File and select the Web page you created in the previous exercise. Click OK.

FIGURE 15.3

Choose which navigation style to use for the Web page.

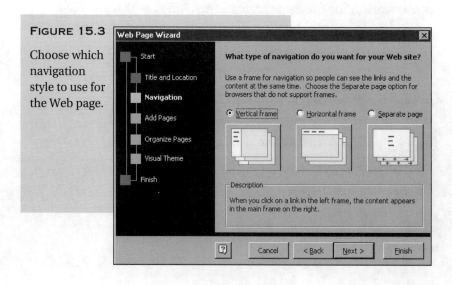

FIGURE 15.4

You can add new pages or use existing pages when creating your Web site.

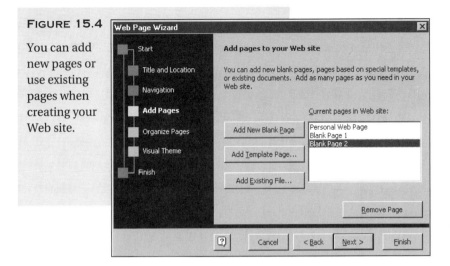

FIGURE 15.5

Click once on each type of template to preview the style.

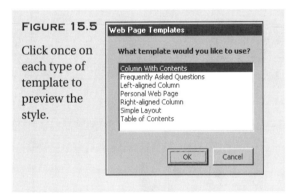

11. Click Remove Page to delete a selected page from the Web site.

12. Click Next. The Organize Pages dialog box appears, as shown in Figure 15.6.

13. To change the position of any Web page in the site, select the page and click Move Up or Move Down.

The order of the pages determines how they are listed on the Start page of the Web site.

NOTE

14. To change the name of any Web page, select the page and click Rename.

15. Click Next. The Visual Theme dialog box appears, as shown in Figure 15.7.

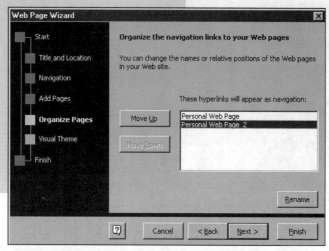

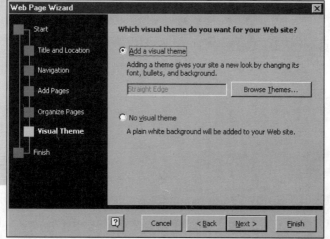

16. Select Add A Visual Theme and click Browse Themes to see a preview of available themes, as shown in Figure 15.8. Select a theme and click OK.

NOTE

If you select a theme that has not yet been installed, a message appears saying that the theme needs to be installed. Click Install to install the theme and see a preview.

17. If no theme is desired, click No Visual Theme.

18. Click Finish to complete the wizard and create the site. A completed Web site is shown in Figure 15.9.

FIGURE 15.8

Word offers you these choices of themes, but you're not limited to them—you can create your own themes if you have Microsoft FrontPage.

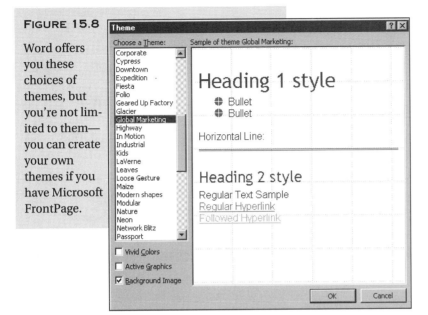

FIGURE 15.9

Click the links on the page to jump to other Web pages.

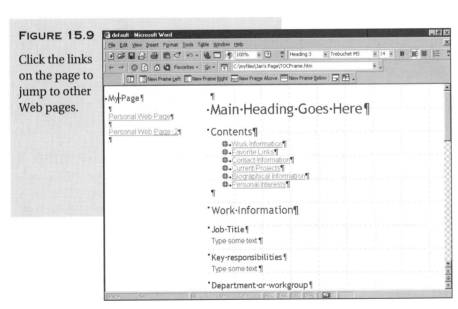

NOTE

The Frames toolbar may appear automatically when you have created a Web page. You can dock it on the side of the screen for now. Frames are discussed later in this chapter.

ADDING TEXT TO THE WEB PAGE

Now that the basic structure of the Web page is complete, it's time to make the text more meaningful. If you take a look at your Web site, you will see placeholder text in several locations. You may see phrases such as *Type some text, Insert a Hyperlink Here,* or *Add an Interest.* These are text placeholders that you should replace with your own text. If you don't want any text to exist in these locations, you can delete the text placeholders just as you can any other text in Word.

ADD TEXT TO THE WEB PAGE

1. Select some placeholder text and type information specific to your firm or practice (feel free to replace the text with anything that you want).

A shortcut for selecting an entire sentence is to hold down the Ctrl key while you click on the sentence.

2. Save the Web page document.
3. Keep the Web page open for the next exercise.

INSERTING HYPERLINKS

If you've used the Internet, you've seen a hyperlink. A hyperlink is just a shortcut for jumping to a different location, whether it's another document, a different place in the current document, a video or sound clip, another Web page, or a preaddressed e-mail form. After you create hyperlinks for file names, network paths, or Internet paths, you no longer have to remember them.

If you click a hyperlink, you move to that particular, predefined location. A hyperlink is formatted differently from text. Depending on which visual theme you selected, your hyperlinks may be formatted differently from the pictures in this book. Try to use the same formatting for all of your hyperlinks so users visiting your Web pages know what to click in order to move to the next location.

When you insert a hyperlink in the Web page, it is formatted with a color. Once you choose a hyperlink, its text color changes. This indicates which hyperlinks have been visited.

You can modify the default colors of hyperlinks by modifying the Hyperlink or the Followed Hyperlink style. See Chapter 6, "Styles," for more information.

Another result of clicking a hyperlink is that the Web toolbar appears. The Web toolbar is covered later in this chapter.

CREATE A MISSION STATEMENT AND HYPERLINK IT TO A WEB PAGE

1. Create a new Web Page by choosing <u>N</u>ew from the <u>F</u>ile menu.
2. Select the General tab.
3. Double-click the Web Page icon.

If you are already in a Web document, the New button on the Standard toolbar changes to a New Web Page button. Click New Web Page to quickly create a new blank Web Page.

4. Type the following:

    Firm Mission Statement

    The mission of our law firm is to offer clients the best legal representation possible. In addition, our commitment extends to each attorney and staff member. Our mission fails if our employees are not reasonably happy.

5. Choose <u>S</u>ave from the <u>F</u>ile menu and name the file **Mission Statement**. Save it on your computer in the Web page folder.

When you created a Web site using the wizard, a new folder was automatically created for each Web page in the site.

6. Close the Mission Statement.
7. On the Start page of your Web site, select some text labeled *Insert Hyperlink Here*.
8. Choose Hyper<u>l</u>ink from the <u>I</u>nsert menu. The Insert Hyperlink dialog box, shown in Figure 15.10, appears.

Other ways to insert a hyperlink include clicking Insert Hyperlink on the Standard toolbar or pressing Ctrl+K on the keyboard.

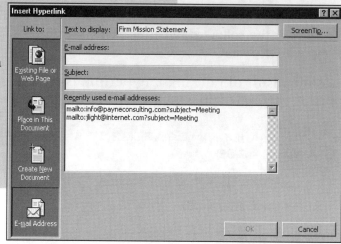

<blockquote>
FIGURE 15.10

You can link to a file or Web address and to a bookmark within a file.
</blockquote>

9. Type **Firm Mission Statement** in the Text To Display box.

TIP

To create a ScreenTip for the hyperlink, click ScreenTip and type some text to appear as a tip. The ScreenTip will appear when the mouse pointer hovers over the hyperlink.

10. Click Recent files and select the Mission Statement file from the list.

NOTE

Click File or Web Page to browse and locate a file or Web page that doesn't appear in the list. If you want the hyperlink to jump to a particular location in a document, click Bookmark and select the section or heading you want to link to in the selected document.

11. Select a location for the hyperlink by selecting a frame in the Click The Frame Where You Want The Document To Appear list box.

12. Click OK to return to the Web page.

Test out your new hyperlink by clicking the link. The screen displays the Firm Mission Statement file. It's that easy to create a hyperlink to a document! To return to the Start page where you inserted the hyperlink, click the Back button on the Web toolbar, or press Alt+Left Arrow. The next exercise shows you how to create a hyperlink to another Web page.

CREATING A LINK TO A WEB PAGE

If you have Internet access, you can create a link between your documents and the Web. Many of our clients use these types of hyperlinks to point to recent State or Supreme Court decisions, or to other helpful legal Web sites.

LINK TO A WEB PAGE

1. Select the text to be the hyperlink.
2. Choose Hyperlink from the Insert menu.
3. Type the text you want to appear in the Text To Display box.
4. Type the Web address in the Type The File Or Web Page Name box. Or click Browsed Pages to select from a list of recently browsed Web pages.
5. Click OK to insert the hyperlink.

CREATING A HYPERLINK TO E-MAIL

You can also use hyperlinks to send e-mail to specific individuals. Suppose that you're planning a multifirm event and want the RSVP to go to someone working on the project in another firm. You can create the Web page describing the event, publish the page on your firm's Intranet, and then create an e-mail hyperlink that addresses mail to a specific recipient when clicked.

CREATE A MAIL HYPERLINK

1. Type the text **Contact Webmaster** in the Web page.
2. Select the text you typed and then choose Hyperlink from the Insert menu.
3. Select E-mail Address in the Link To bar, as shown in Figure 15.11.
4. Type an e-mail address in the E-mail Address box, or select an address from the list of Recently Used E-mail Addresses.

The text **mailto:** automatically appears in the E-mail Address box when you start typing. Do not delete this text, as it is necessary for the hyperlink to work correctly.

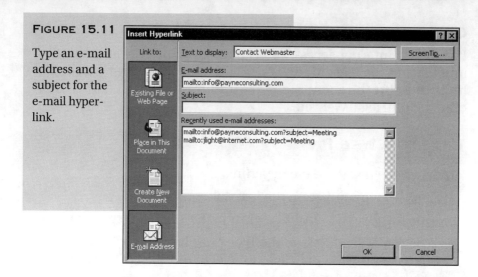

FIGURE 15.11

Type an e-mail address and a subject for the e-mail hyper-link.

5. Type a subject for the e-mail message in the Subject box.

6. Click OK to insert the e-mail hyperlink.

USING THE WEB TOOLBAR

Now that you're familiar with some of the terms used when creating Web pages, take a closer look at some of the tools on the Web tool-bar (see Figure 15.12). Each of the ten buttons helps you navigate between links to documents and Web pages. Table 15.2 describes each button's functions.

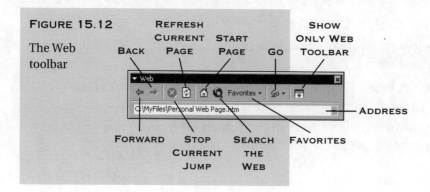

FIGURE 15.12

The Web toolbar

TABLE 15.2 WEB TOOLBAR BUTTONS

BUTTON	FUNCTION
Back	Retraces each step to the current page.
Forward	Moves to the next page.
Stop Current Jump	Discontinues the jump to another location. Use this button if you are connecting to a Web page that is taking an unusually long time to load.
Refresh Current Page	Refreshes the current page by reloading it.
Start Page	The Start page is the first page that loads when you start the Web Browser software. You can define the Start Page by clicking Go and choosing Set Start Page.
Search the Web	Opens the Search page so that you can search for words or phrases. You can define a Search page by clicking Go and choosing Set Search Page.
Favorites	Provides a way to store locations for commonly accessed sites.
Go	Provides a way to move to different locations.
Show Only Web Toolbar	Hides all toolbars except the Web toolbar.
Address	If you know the address of the place that you want to access, you can type it here and then press the Enter key to move to the desired location. A record of recently accessed locations is stored for your convenience.

SAVING A DOCUMENT IN HTML FORMAT

If your firm already has an Intranet, you can turn any existing Word document into an online document by saving it in HTML format. To do this, from the File menu, choose Save As Web Page. When you turn a document into an HTML document, some Word features are no longer available—they don't have Web equivalents.

Some things that don't convert are:

- ◆ Animated text
- ◆ Character borders
- ◆ Diagonal cell borders
- ◆ Margins
- ◆ Text wrapping around tables

The Help topic "Results of saving Word 2000 documents in other file formats" has complete information about which features are lost when saving a Word 2000 document as a Web page. To see this topic, from the Help menu, click Microsoft Word Help and type **Results of saving**, click Search, and then pick the topic above.

SAVE A DOCUMENT AS HTML

1. Open a Word document you have previously created.
2. From the File menu, choose Save As Web Page.

When you select Save As Web page, Word automatically selects HTML as the Save As Type.

3. Name the document and click Save.

WEB PAGE GOODIES

The only requirement for publishing a document to the firm's Intranet is saving the document in HTML format. After you've created a Web page you can access many goodies, such as sound, video, clip art, forms, scrolling text, and frames, that can make the page more exciting and easier for the reader to understand. You can even change the background or the theme for the page after it has been created. While this book isn't able to cover all the great features you can add to Web pages, the next section gives you a good preview.

CHANGING BULLET STYLES

You may not realize it, but the bullet symbol on the Web page is actually built into Word, as part of Word's ClipArt feature. Like all Word bullets, you can change the style to jazz up your document. First, select and delete the existing bullet, and then choose Bullets And Numbering from the Format menu to access different bullets. Click Picture to open the Picture Bullet dialog box, as shown in Figure 15.13.

Once you have located a bullet you like, click once to select it, and then select Insert Clip from the drop-down menu of commands.

FIGURE 15.13

Select Pictures
or Motion Clips
for bullets and
click OK.

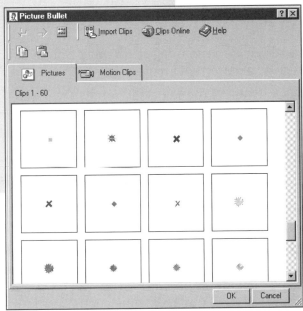

CHANGING THE BACKGROUND OR THEME OF THE PAGE

When you designed your Web site, you selected a theme to tie together all the visual elements of the pages. You can change the theme if you like, or, for more control of the page, change and customize the background.

To change the theme, from the Format menu, choose Theme. Select a different theme, and then click OK. To change the background of the page, from the Format menu, choose Background. From there, you can specify a color or a fill effect.

NOTE

If you change the theme, all pages in the Web site change. If you change a background, only the background of the current page changes.

CHANGE THE THEME OF YOUR WEB SITE

1. From the Format menu, choose Theme.
2. Select a theme in the Choose A Theme list. A preview of the theme appears in the Sample box.
3. Select Vivid Colors to make the text and table borders brighter.

4. Select Active <u>G</u>raphics to display animated graphics if you have inserted them in the Web page.

5. Turn off <u>B</u>ackground Image to display a plain background instead of a patterned image.

6. Click OK to apply the selected theme to the Web site.

INSERTING SCROLLING TEXT

If you want to draw attention to a particular item on your Web page, you can create scrolling text. This feature draws attention, but be aware that a little goes a long way. Generally, one line of scrolling text per page is plenty.

I stumbled onto a worst-case example of a Web page that overused this feature; every line of text was scrolling in opposite directions. Let me see if I can describe this for you: the page title bounced back and forth like a Ping Pong ball while each line of text below started and moved in opposite directions. What a disaster! The person who created the Web page was trying to draw my attention, but instead I got a headache trying to read all that moving text and quickly switched to a different Web page.

INSERT SCROLLING TEXT

1. Choose <u>T</u>oolbars from the <u>V</u>iew menu.

2. Select the Web Tools toolbar.

3. Select some heading text in the Web Page document.

4. Cut the text by pressing Ctrl+X.

5. Click Scrolling Text on the Web Tools toolbar.

6. Click in the Type The Scrolling <u>T</u>ext Here box and press Ctrl+V (the keyboard shortcut for Paste).

7. Change any other option in the Scrolling Text dialog box and click OK.

NOTE

If the page is viewed in a browser that doesn't support scrolling text, the text appears without the scrolling.

8. To stop the text from scrolling, alternate-click the scrolling text and choose Stop.

ADDING FRAMES

When you created the Web site in the beginning of this chapter, you may have noticed a Frames toolbar appear automatically. If you closed it, turn it on again from the View menu by choosing Toolbars, and then selecting Frames.

Frames organize the information on a Web page into easy-to-read sections. Think of a frame as a way to separate hyperlinks from content. For example, you might want the table of contents in one frame, the header in another frame, and the main text of the Web page in a third frame. You can make the table of contents frame and the header frame stay on the screen while the user jumps to other pages. Frames are a great way of "freezing" information on the page so that your readers always know where to locate certain information.

TIP

If you use the Web Page wizard and choose Vertical Frame or Horizontal Frame in the Navigation dialog box, Word inserts a frame for you.

ADD A FRAME TO A WEB PAGE

1. Open the Web page you created in the first exercise of this chapter.
2. If the Frames toolbar is not on, turn it on from the View menu by choosing Toolbars and selecting Frames.
3. Click New Frame Left, Right, Above, or Below to add a new frame to the page.
4. Click Table Of Contents In Frame to add a table of contents to the page.

NOTE

The table of contents is generated from the Heading styles in the Web page document.

VIEWING HTML SOURCE

Okay, you've seen how easy it is to create Web pages in Word. You change the appearance of the page by selecting formatting. You create hyperlinks by choosing Hyperlink from the Insert menu. Although the steps that you take to create the page *are* simple, what Word is doing behind the scenes is very complicated. You probably

didn't know that you've been programming in HTML code throughout this chapter.

Word stores HTML code for each action you take with your mouse
or keyboard. You can view this code from the <u>V</u>iew menu by choosing HTML <u>S</u>ource. Use the following exercise to take a look at what
you've done so far.

VIEW HTML SOURCE

1. From the <u>V</u>iew menu, choose HTML <u>S</u>ource (see the result in
   Figure 15.14).

NOTE

If you haven't installed the HTML Editor, you may be prompted to
install the feature.

2. Scroll through the code to see whether you recognize anything.
3. When you're ready, choose Exit HTML <u>S</u>ource from the <u>V</u>iew
   menu.
4. Close the Web page without saving.

Why tell you to look at the HTML code? Only to reinforce the idea
that all you need to create a Web page is Word 2000. Because Word
can save documents as HTML, you never need to learn how to code
in HTML or purchase any other HTML software.

FIGURE 15.14

Word created
this HTML code
as you built the
Web page.

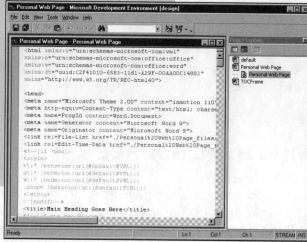

CHAPTER 16

INTEGRATING WORD WITH OTHER OFFICE APPLICATIONS

IN THIS CHAPTER

- ◆ Integrating Outlook and Word
- ◆ Using Excel and Word together
- ◆ Basic Excel functions for legal purposes
- ◆ Integrating PowerPoint and Word
- ◆ Integrating Access and Word
- ◆ Inserting Word objects
- ◆ Creating organizational charts in Word

When you go grocery shopping, you may be looking for a specific item, but once you walk up and down the aisles (or scroll through a list of products if you shop online), you often come across other items you need that you hadn't originally thought of. In a way, that's what working with Microsoft Office is like. You may have a need for Word and Outlook, but haven't yet seen how the other pieces of the suite of products fit. Prepare to be pleasantly surprised at how well Microsoft Office applications work together.

INTEGRATING OUTLOOK AND WORD

Chapter 13 discussed how to send a file as an e-mail message directly from Word. While this is a great feature, there are many other things that you can do between these two products, including a new Mail Merge feature.

NOTE

If you've used previous versions of Word and Outlook, you know that extracting contact information from Outlook and generating a mail merge did not always give you the best results. The reason for this was that you could not access all the contact fields that you needed for the merge. Most firms got into the habit of exporting the list of contacts to Excel or Access and then using this file as a data source for the mail merge. This extra step is no longer necessary if you use Outlook and Word 2000. The Mail Merge feature has vastly improved.

I can almost hear the groans now, "Mail merge a list of contacts in Outlook without exporting them to Excel?" You won't believe how well this works in Word and Outlook 2000. The feature has been totally rewritten.

Mail Merge is now available directly from within Outlook 2000 and now all the address book fields are available. The Mail Merge dialog box may be a bit more limited than from within Word but it's still very powerful.

PERFORM A MAIL MERGE FROM OUTLOOK 2000

1. Click the Contacts icon in Outlook 2000.
2. From the Tools menu, choose Mail Merge. The Mail Merge Contacts dialog box appears as shown in Figure 16.1.

FIGURE 16.1

Create a Mail
Merge from
within
Outlook 2000

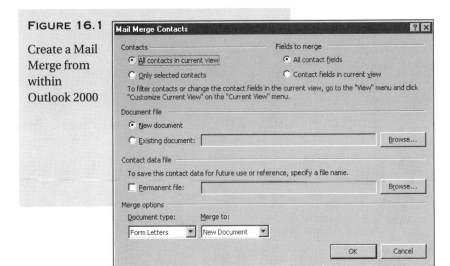

The Mail Merge Contacts dialog box allows you to specify:

+ Which contacts to use for the merge

+ What fields to merge

+ Whether to use a new or existing document

+ Whether to create a contact data file that can be used later

+ What type of document to create (form letter, mail labels, and so on)

+ Whether to merge to a new document, to a printer, or to an e-mail message

NOTE

The Mail Merge command is only available when you are in a Contact list.

3. Make your selections and click OK. The Export process begins.

4. Click Edit Mail Merge Document. Word 2000 is started and the Mail Merge toolbar is now visible in the document.

5. Click the Insert Merge Field button to view all the available address book fields. The Insert Merge field list is shown in Figure 16.2.

6. Click the Insert Word Fields button to see what options are available.

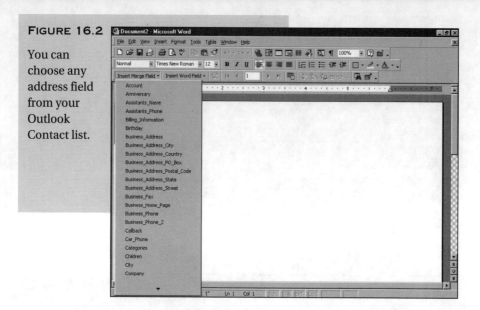

FIGURE 16.2

You can
choose any
address field
from your
Outlook
Contact list.

7. Insert Merge Fields into the document.

8. When you finish, click Merge To New Document on the Mail Merge toolbar.

EXPORTING AN OUTLOOK CONTACT LIST FOR A MAIL MERGE

If you want to create a mail merge on a machine that does not have Outlook or your Contact list, you may want to first export the information to a file.

IMPORT AND EXPORT CONTACTS

1. Open Outlook 2000.

2. From the File menu, choose Import And Export.

3. In the Import and Export wizard, choose Export A File, and then click Next.

4. Select Comma Separated Values (Windows) under Create A File Of Type. The Export to a File dialog box appears, as shown in Figure 16.3.

5. Click Next.

FIGURE 16.3

Select the desired file format for the exported records.

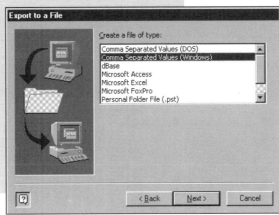

 **NOTE**

Word may need to install a filter for importing and exporting if it wasn't installed during setup.

6. Select Contacts as the folder to export and click Next.

7. Enter a file name to save the document. The file will be saved with a Comma Separated Value file extension (.csv), the file type specified in Step 4.

8. Click Next.

9. Specify where to save the exported file. For example, to save it on the C drive in the My Documents folder, type **C:\My Documents\myfile.csv**.

10. Click Next and then Finish.

11. Locate the file that you created and open it.

LETTER TO CONTACT

You can send a letter to a person on your Outlook 2000 Contact list without leaving the Outlook window. To do this, first select the contact to address the letter to. From the Actions menu, choose New Letter To Contact. Fill out the information in the four steps of the Letter wizard and click Finish. A letter is generated using the information that appears about this person in your Contact list.

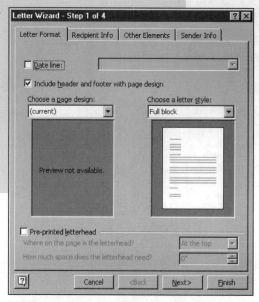

SEND A LETTER TO A CONTACT FROM OUTLOOK 2000

1. Select a contact in your Contact list.
2. From the Actions menu, choose New Letter To Contact. The Letter Wizard dialog box appears, as shown in Figure 16.4.
3. Click Finish.

INTEGRATING EXCEL AND WORD

One of the most popular software programs in the world is Microsoft Excel. Long before most firms started switching to Microsoft Word, many had discovered the power of the spreadsheet application. Excel is a number-crunching, data analysis, charting, and report-generating superstar.

Even a giant like Excel, however, has its limitations. For example, it's not optimal to do word processing or create a pleading in a spreadsheet. Luckily, when you purchase Microsoft Office, you have quick access to both products, and even better, you don't have to leave Word to get an Excel worksheet into your document.

The terms *spreadsheet* and *worksheet* are interchangeable.

Although Word is no slouch when it comes to calculations, Excel is far more powerful for this type of function. One example is how Excel works with formulas. Excel dynamically recalculates to show any changes made to a formula. If the same formula in Word changes, you have to select and then update the field containing the formula to gct thc updatcd result. Word allows you to use 18 mathematical functions, whereas Excel has hundreds available.

There are three ways to insert an Excel worksheet into a Word document: using a toolbar button, using a menu command, or copying and pasting the data from Excel into Word.

USING THE INSERT MICROSOFT EXCEL WORKSHEET BUTTON

"I'd like four rows and three columns please." These are the type of instructions that you give Word when you click the Insert Excel Worksheet button on the Standard toolbar. Starting in the upper-left corner, as you move your mouse over and down squares (or "cells" in Excel), you are telling Word how many cells tall and wide you want your spreadsheet. When you release the mouse, the spreadsheet of your design appears inside the Word document, already activated. Figure 16.5 shows the expanded Insert Excel Worksheet button.

You must have Microsoft Excel installed on your computer to complete the exercises in this section.

FIGURE 16.5

Select the number of rows and columns to insert.

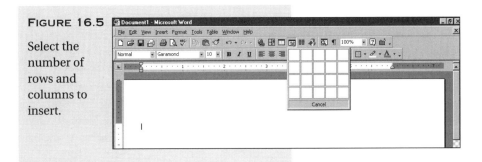

INSERT A WORKSHEET OF A SPECIFIC SIZE

1. Click the Insert Microsoft Excel Worksheet button on the Standard toolbar.

2. Highlight the number of rows and columns that you want to insert into the Word document, and click with the mouse to complete the process (this is the same process as you used to create tables, just with a different button).

3. Click in the last cell for the table and release the mouse. The worksheet is inserted in the Word document.

Keep in mind that the inserted worksheet is an object that you are placing into Word—much like a picture or graphic. If you select the worksheet and press the Delete key, you delete not just the value in a cell but the entire worksheet.

USING A MENU COMMAND TO INSERT A WORKSHEET

If you don't need to define the size of the workbook in advance, from the Insert menu, choose Object and then specify whether to insert a new Excel Worksheet, or an existing one from a file.

INSERT A WORKSHEET FROM THE INSERT MENU

1. From the Insert menu, choose Object, and select the Create New tab.

2. Select Microsoft Excel Worksheet as the Object type.

3. Click OK.

When you insert a worksheet using the Insert menu, a 7-column by 10-row worksheet is inserted into the document.

You may have noticed that you can insert the worksheet as an icon in the Object dialog box instead of as an Excel worksheet. Doing this will speed up the performance of your computer slightly but you will have to double-click the Excel icon to get to the data in the file. Unless you're working with a very large worksheet, the icon feature won't make enough difference to be worth the effort.

USING COPY AND PASTE WITH EXCEL DATA

You can transfer existing data between Excel and Word just as easily as you can insert an Excel worksheet. There are several ways to accomplish this. The method you choose depends on what you are trying to accomplish.

When you copy information in Excel and then paste it into Word, the information is transformed into a Word table and is no longer in Excel format.

COPY FROM EXCEL, PASTE INTO WORD

1. Open an existing Excel worksheet or create a new one.
2. Select and copy the Excel data.
3. Switch to Microsoft Word.
4. From the Edit menu, choose Paste. The information is pasted into a Word table and is no longer associated with Microsoft Excel.

USING COPY AND PASTE SPECIAL

If you prefer to keep the information in an Excel format, or if you wish to maintain a link between the original data and what you pasted into Word, you'll need to use Paste Special instead of the Paste command. Figure 16.6 shows the Paste Special dialog box. Two items of interest are Microsoft Excel Worksheet Object and Word Hyperlink. (The latter is out of sight in the figure; you get to it by using the vertical scrollbar in the As box.)

COPY AN EXCEL WORKSHEET OBJECT

1. Open Excel and Word.
2. From within Excel, enter information into several cells and copy it.
3. Switch to Word.
4. From the Edit menu, choose Paste Special.

FIGURE 16.6

You can paste the Excel worksheet in different formats using Paste Special.

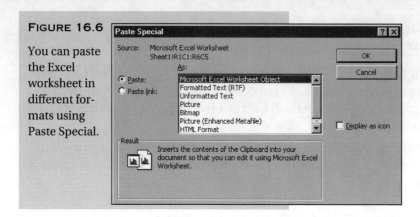

5. Select Microsoft Excel Worksheet Object and click OK. The format remains in Excel and Excel can be used to edit the information.

6. Close both documents without saving.

WORD HYPERLINK

If you create a link back to the original file, you can paste the contents of the Excel worksheet as a Word hyperlink. When you click the link from within Word, you open and can work in the worksheet in Excel.

INSERT EXCEL WORKSHEET AS A WORD HYPERLINK

1. Open both Word and Excel if they are not already open.

2. Type information into the Excel worksheet.

3. Save the Excel worksheet as **Word Hyperlink**.

4. Select and copy the information that you typed in Excel.

5. Switch to Word.

6. From the Edit menu, choose Paste Special.

7. Select Paste Link, and then select Word Hyperlink.

8. Click OK. Figure 16.7 shows data that was pasted as a Word hyperlink.

9. Click the hyperlink to work in the Excel worksheet.

10. Close the Word and Excel files without saving.

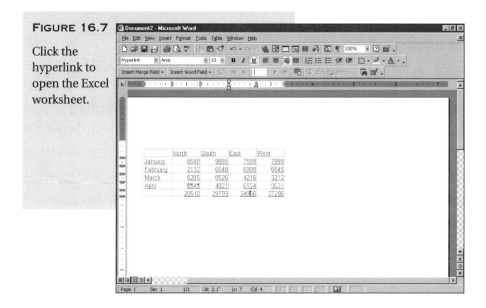

MAINTAINING A LINK BETWEEN EXCEL AND WORD

When it's important that your information be kept up to date, it's a good idea to create a link between the Excel worksheet and the Word document. To do this, you copy the information, use Paste Special to paste the information into Word, and create a link.

CREATE A LINK BETWEEN EXCEL AND WORD

1. Open an Excel worksheet.
2. Type and copy information, or copy existing data.
3. Switch to Word.
4. From the Edit menu, choose Paste Special.
5. Select Paste Link and Microsoft Excel Worksheet Object.
6. Click OK.
7. Switch to Microsoft Excel.
8. Make a change in a cell that was copied previously.
9. Switch to Word and you should see the change that was made to the Excel worksheet.
10. Close both documents without saving.

BASIC EXCEL FUNCTIONS FOR LEGAL PURPOSES

OK, so this is not supposed to be a book on how to use Excel in a law firm. But in case you're wondering why you just spent so much time learning how to insert an Excel worksheet into a Word document, here are some of the uses.

If you are a part of the subrogation workgroup within a law firm, or if you need to quickly calculate monthly payments, you can take advantage of Microsoft Excel's built-in Function wizard, which will guide you through the creation of many different types of formulas. To find the amount of a monthly payment, try the following exercise.

USE THE PMT FUNCTION TO CALCULATE MONTHLY PAYMENTS

1. Create a new Word document.

2. Use the Insert Excel Worksheet button on the Standard toolbar to insert a five-column by five-row worksheet.

3. In cell A1, type **.08** (reflects interest rate value), in cell A2 type **60** (reflects the number of months when a payment will be made), and in cell A3, type **25000** and press Enter.

4. Click in cell C3, and then, from the Insert menu, choose Function. The Paste Function dialog box appears, as shown in Figure 16.8.

FIGURE 16.8

Excel includes hundreds of functions to choose from and provides help for walking through even the most complex calculation.

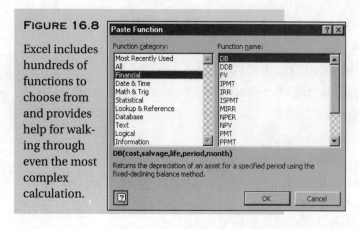

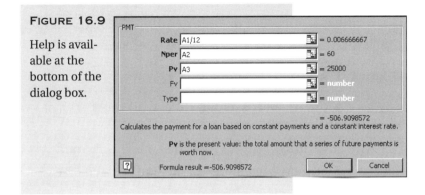

FIGURE 16.9

Help is available at the bottom of the dialog box.

5. Select **Financial** from the Function Category list. Select **PMT** from the Function Name list. Click OK.

6. In the Rate box, click in cell A1 and then type **/12**. This is the interest rate divided by twelve (twelve months in a year). Press Tab to move to the Nper field.

7. *Nper* is the total number of payments for the loan. If the loan is for 5 years and you make 12 payments per year the number here would be entered as either 60 or 5*12. Since you already entered this value in cell B1, click in cell B1 to put this reference in the Nper box. Press Tab.

8. The *PV* field is the present value of the loan. Click in cell A3 (where you put the value 25,000). All of the required fields for this function are now complete as shown in Figure 16.9.

9. Click OK. The spreadsheet will show that the calculated monthly payment is $506.91.

10. Change the value in cell A3 and the calculated value in cell C3 automatically updates.

11. Close the Excel worksheet without saving.

While the preceding exercise has legal applications, it can also be used to calculate the monthly payments on that new convertible!

EXCEL CHARTS IN WORD

Excel can create 14 different types of charts to plot your data: Column, Bar, Line, Pie, XY Scatter, Area, Doughnut, Radar, Surface, Bubble, Stock, Cylinder, Cone, and Pyramid. Within each of these chart types are different subtypes to choose from to design just the chart you need.

CHART EXCEL DATA IN WORD

1. Create a new document and insert an Excel worksheet with at least four columns and three rows.

2. In cell A1 type **Location**, in cell B1 **Attorney**, in cell C1 **Staff**.

3. Type **Boston** in Cell A2, **Chicago** in A3 and **Seattle** in cell A4.

4. Now type numbers in cells B2 through C4.

5. Select cells A1 through C4 (expressed as A1:C4).

6. From the Insert menu, choose Chart.

7. From the Chart type list, select Bar (as shown in Figure 16.10), and click Finish.

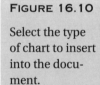

To see what your chart will look like in the selected format without finishing the process, click the Press And Hold To View Sample button on Step 1 of the Chart wizard.

8. Expand the worksheet area by clicking the lower-right corner handle and dragging it to enlarge the worksheet.

FIGURE 16.10

Select the type of chart to insert into the document.

FIGURE 16.11

Data and chart next to one another with gridlines turned off

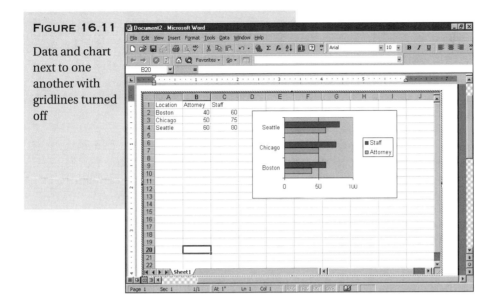

9. If you need to move the chart over to see the worksheet data, click the chart once, drag it to the new location, and release the mouse button. The finished result is shown in Figure 16.11.

TIP

To hide gridlines in the Excel worksheet, double-click in the Excel object to activate in-place editing. From the Tools menu, choose Options and select the View tab. Uncheck Gridlines under Windows options and click OK.

INTEGRATING POWERPOINT AND WORD

You've surely sat through meetings where a speaker stood in front of the room, talking endlessly, while you fought to stay awake. Unless someone is born with a story-telling personality, it can be difficult to hold the attention of an audience without some sort of visual aid.

In the past, when law firms needed a whiz-bang presentation they had to rely on an outside graphics company to provide the visuals. Microsoft PowerPoint has changed all this. Now secretaries, paralegals, attorneys, and anyone in a law firm can quickly assemble high-quality, professional presentations in a matter of minutes.

This section covers how PowerPoint and Word work together. You can import and export information from one program to the other and back again very easily.

EXPORTING POWERPOINT FILES TO WORD

Not only can you take information from a PowerPoint presentation and send it to a Word document, you can use it to create notes with the slides or create an outline. You can also add slides to Microsoft Word documents that contain a link to the original PowerPoint presentation so that if the information changes, it's changed in the Word document that contains the link as well.

When presenting a speech, it's often useful to provide handouts to the audience. When you send information from PowerPoint to Word, it makes it easy to prepare these handouts in just minutes.

EXPORT POWERPOINT PRESENTATION TO WORD AND CREATE NOTES

1. Open an existing PowerPoint presentation or create a new one.
2. From the File menu, choose Send To and select Microsoft Word. The Write-Up dialog box shown in Figure 16.12 appears.

FIGURE 16.12

Specify whether you want notes to appear with the presentation slides and if so, where on the page.

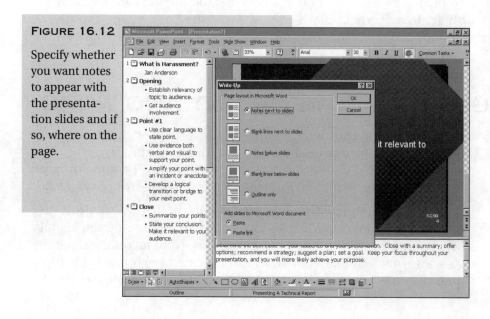

FIGURE 16.13

Make great handouts by exporting your PowerPoint presentation to Word.

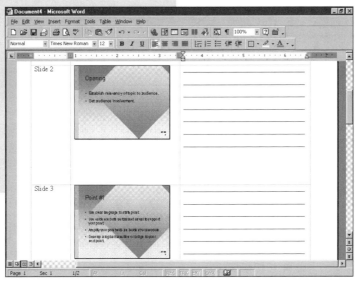

3. Select Blank Lines Next To Slide, and then click OK. The PowerPoint presentation is exported to a Word document and lines for notes are placed next to each slide. The result is shown in Figure 16.13.

NOTE

To create a link between the original PowerPoint presentation and the Word document, click Paste Link.

4. Close the document without saving.

EXPORTING MEETING MINDER NOTES TO WORD

Often in the middle of a presentation, I discover that I need to add a note about something. In PowerPoint, when you are in the process of running a slide show, it's easy to make notes and create action items, and then export them to a Microsoft Word document.

USE MEETING MINDER AND EXPORT NOTES AND ACTION ITEMS TO WORD

1. Create a PowerPoint presentation.

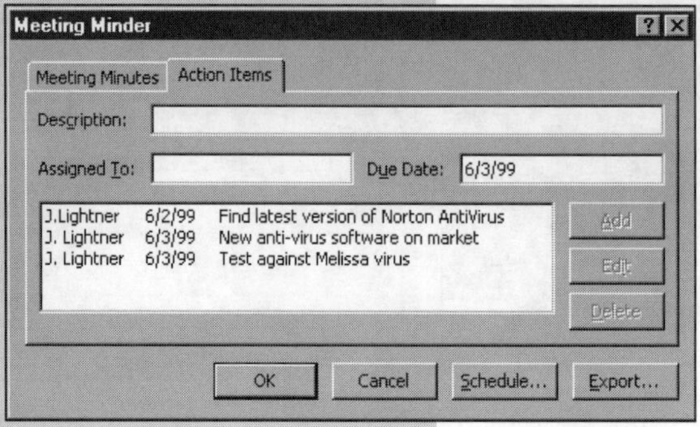

FIGURE 16.14

Use the Meeting
Minder to enter
minutes and
action items.

Figure 16.14: Use the Meeting Minder to enter minutes and action items.

2. From the View menu, choose Slide Show.

3. Alternate-click a slide and select Meeting Minder from the shortcut menu.

4. Under Meeting Minutes type **Meeting of American Bar Association on how to prevent computer viruses.**

5. Click OK.

6. Alternate-click the slide again and select the Action Items tab.

7. In the Description box type **Find latest version of Norton AntiVirus**.

8. In the Assigned to box, type your name.

9. In the Due Date box, enter a date.

10. Click the Add button and add three more action items. The filled-in dialog box is shown in Figure 16.14.

11. Click Export.

12. Select Send Meeting Minutes And Action Items To Microsoft Word.

13. Click Export Now.

EXPORTING WORD DOCUMENTS TO POWERPOINT

If you needed one more reason to use styles, here it is. If you use heading styles in your Word document, you can quickly export information from Word to a PowerPoint presentation.

EXPORT A WORD DOCUMENT TO A POWERPOINT PRESENTATION

1. Create a new Word document.

2. Apply heading styles 1, 2, and 3 to various items in the document. A document in Outline view with heading styles applied is shown in Figure 16.15.

3. From the File menu, choose Send To and select Microsoft PowerPoint.

4. Close both documents without saving.

NOTE

If you prefer, you can copy and paste information between Word and PowerPoint.

FIGURE 16.15

Use heading styles in your Word document and you can quickly create PowerPoint slides from the text.

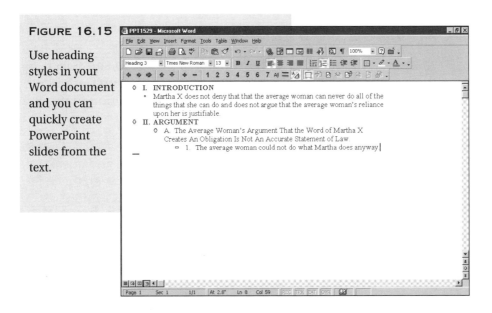

INTEGRATING ACCESS AND WORD

If your firm uses Microsoft Access as a database to store information, you can insert the contents of any of the tables or queries into a Word document. To do this, you'll need to display the Database toolbar.

INSERT A MICROSOFT ACCESS TABLE INTO WORD

1. Alternate-click any toolbar and select Database to display the Database toolbar.
2. Click Insert Database.
3. Click Get Data.
4. Change Files Of Type to MS Access Databases, and in the File Name box, enter the name of the database that you want.
5. Click Open.
6. Select the Tables or Queries tab and click the table or query that you want.
7. Click OK.
8. To insert a subset of the table, click Query Options and select the options that you want, and then click OK. To apply a Table AutoFormat, click Table AutoFormat, select the option that you want, and then click OK.
9. Click Insert Data.
10. Specify which records to include in the Word table and check the Insert Data As Field option to create a link between the original Access database and the Word table. If this option is checked, the information is inserted as a field that will update when F9 is pressed.
11. Click OK.

You can also start from within Microsoft Access to export information to Word.

EXPORT ACCESS DATA TO WORD

1. Open Microsoft Access and the database that you want to export to Word.

To export only a portion of the information, first select the rows and columns that you want.

2. From the File menu, choose Export.

3. Change Save As Type to Rich Text Format (*.rtf).

If you were exporting information to be used in a mail merge, you would select Microsoft Word Merge.

4. Click Save. The file is exported to a Rich Text File format (.rtf) that can be opened by Word.

INSERTING OBJECTS INTO WORD

You can insert all types of objects into Word documents. To see a list of all of the object types, from the Insert menu, choose Object.

SEE LIST OF OBJECTS THAT CAN BE INSERTED INTO WORD

1. From the Insert menu, choose Object.

2. Scroll through the list of object types that can be inserted into a Word document.

3. Click Cancel to close the Object dialog box.

INSERT CLIP ART INTO WORD

Word ships with all sorts of clip art that can be inserted into your documents. Also included are sounds and motion clips. To see what has been installed on your computer, from the Insert menu, choose Picture and then choose Clip Art.

INSERT A CLIP ART PICTURE

1. Create a new document.

2. Type **=RAND()** and press Enter. This inserts random text within the document.

FIGURE 16.16

Microsoft Office comes with many clip art images.

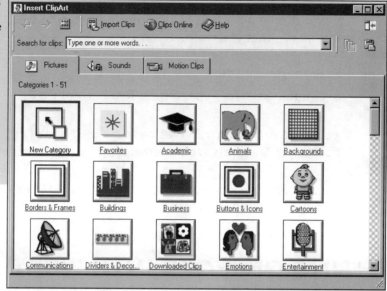

3. Click within one of the paragraphs of text.

4. From the Insert menu, choose Picture and then Clip Art.

5. Click a Category, and then click a Clip image.

6. Click Insert Clip and close the Insert ClipArt window. The Insert ClipArt window is shown in Figure 16.16.

7. Leave this file open for the next exercise.

CHANGE THE LAYOUT OF THE OBJECT

In Word 2000, the default layout of the inserted picture is now in line with the text as the wrapping style. If you are inserting text boxes, WordArt, and AutoShapes, the default is in front of text selected. To see the difference, try the following exercise.

VIEW DIFFERENT DEFAULTS FOR INSERTED OBJECTS

1. Double-click the picture that you inserted in the preceding exercise.

2. Select the Layout tab. Notice that the Wrapping style is set to In Line With Text.

3. Click Cancel.

4. Display the Drawing toolbar.

5. Click the Insert WordArt button.

6. Select a WordArt style and click OK.

7. Type your full name and click OK.

8. On the WordArt toolbar, click the Text Wrapping button. Note that the default is I<u>n</u> Front Of Text.

INSERT PICTURES INTO TABLE CELLS

In Word 2000, you can insert pictures and clip art into table cells. When you do, the cell resizes to accommodate the inserted picture. If you double-click the picture, the Format Picture dialog box opens and allows you to change the properties of the picture.

INSERT A PICTURE INTO A TABLE CELL AND CHANGE THE LAYOUT OPTIONS

1. Insert a table in a Word document.

2. Click in one of the table cells.

3. From the <u>I</u>nsert menu, choose <u>P</u>icture, and then choose <u>C</u>lip Art.

4. Select a Category, and insert the image.

5. Double-click the picture, and select the Size tab.

6. Change the Height to **150%** and click OK.

7. Double-click the picture.

8. Select the Layout tab.

9. Click Advanced and see other options that can be applied to pictures.

10. Click Cancel twice to return to the Word document.

NOTE   If you worked with objects in previous versions of Word, you may notice that the Float Over Text check box has been removed from the Insert Picture, Format Picture, Insert Object, and Convert dialog boxes in Word 2000. When a picture is inserted into a Word document, the default now is for the object to be inserted as In Line With The Text.

INSERT ORGANIZATIONAL CHARTS

Did you know that Word 2000 includes a program that inserts organizational chart objects into documents? The best part is that the process is fast and very easy to do. To insert an organizational chart into a Word document, from the Insert menu, choose Object. On the Create new tab, select Microsoft Organization Chart 2.0 and click OK. Once the organizational chart is inserted into the document, you can customize it as required.

INSERT AN ORGANIZATIONAL CHART

1. Create a new blank document.

2. From the Insert menu, choose Object.

If you don't see the Object command, double-click the menu command Insert. This expands the menu to show all available commands.

3. On the Create new tab, select Microsoft Organization Chart 2.0.

4. Click OK. The Microsoft Organization Chart Object in Document window appears, as shown in Figure 16.17. This is where you will set up the customized organizational chart.

FIGURE 16.17

The organizational chart is an object that sits on top of the Word document.

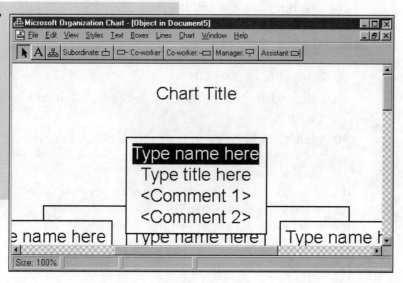

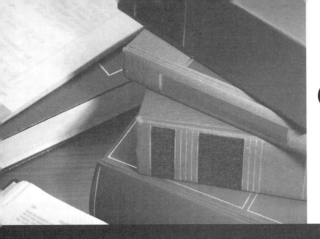

CHAPTER 17

INTRODUCTION TO VBA

IN THIS CHAPTER

- Introduction to Visual Basic for Applications

- Where macros live

- How Word 2000 works with macros

- Generating a macro with the macro recorder

- Different ways to trigger macros (buttons, menus, keyboard shortcuts)

- Editing and deleting macros

- New macro security features for Word 2000

VISUAL BASIC FOR APPLICATIONS

A *macro* is a series of instructions written using programming code that carries out an action or set of actions. Word's macro language is called Visual Basic for Applications (VBA if you want to sound cool), and it's a subset of the fastest-growing programming language in the world, Microsoft Visual Basic (VB). Even though the two are closely related, don't mix them up: VB is designed to quickly develop independent, stand-alone programs, while VBA needs to run inside an application such as Word, Excel or Outlook 2000. WordBasic was the programming language prior to Word 97. Visual Basic for Applications is now standardized for the entire Microsoft Office suite.

If your firm has a "systems person" (many firms have dozens!), you're probably already using macros. One of the main advantages of VBA is that you can use it to create procedures that appear seamless to end users. If you're responsible for making things seem seamless, you'll want to leverage your Word skills to create or fine-tune your own macros.

There are some projects that you'll be able to tackle on your own right away, and some you'll have to leave to an experienced developer. There are also products developed by third parties that may offer an immediate solution. These products, called add-ins, add functionality to Word and include VBA solutions.

The beginning of the chapter includes necessary VBA theory–information that you need to know before you get started. The rest of the chapter focuses on recording, playing back, and editing basic macros. Tips and tricks for automating legal-specific solutions are included.

NOTE

If you're concerned about the applicability of any VBA skills you acquire, just remember that VBA is the standard across the entire Microsoft Office suite. And many of the skills you learn in VBA are applicable not just to all of the components of Office, but to other applications as well. Visio, Peachtree, Great Plains accounting software, AutoCAD, and now even WordPerfect run VBA! Earlier versions of Word (prior to Word 97) used WordBasic as their macro language.

DOES MY FIRM NEED VBA?

Because Microsoft built so much whiz-bang functionality right into Word 2000, you won't need macros for many things. You should explore Word to its fullest before deciding to create a solution in VBA. One of the primary principles of programming is "Keep it in the software." That is, you shouldn't create a macro if you can perform the desired task as part of Word itself—why reinvent the wheel?

Most firms use macros to automate the creation of letters, memos, faxes, and pleadings. Some also find that a macro to assist with numbering is essential in law firms. Simplifying a task in Word will reduce the amount of training time necessary.

NOTE

For information on the Payne Consulting Group macros to simplify using Word in a law firm visit `http://www.payneconsulting.com/`.

HOW DO I KNOW IF I'M REINVENTING THE WHEEL?

After you've been using Word for a while, you'll know better when to use VBA as a solution. Your best asset in becoming a VBA programmer is to know Word inside and out. More than anything else, experience and time will help you decide whether you need to create a macro or find an experienced developer to assist you.

To get you started, however, here's a three-step checklist with questions to ask yourself when confronted with a potential automation situation. If you answer yes to any of these questions, you should consider creating a macro with VBA.

- ♦ Do you find yourself wishing you could consolidate tasks instead of performing them over and over?
- ♦ Do you *know* that a process could be simpler?
- ♦ Are you getting frustrated because you can't get Word to do what you want?

I NEED A MACRO. DO I TRY IT MYSELF OR GET A PRO?

You should be able to create and edit simple macros after reading and working through the exercises in this chapter, even if you've never programmed before. Word 2000 lets you create macros by writing the code yourself, or recording the steps of a procedure and playing them back later, much like using a video camera or cassette recorder. A caveat: while recording macros is useful for many tasks, many others are too complex to capture in a macro recorder or require more optimization for speed or size than a recorder can provide. For these types of macros, it's best to seek the advice of an experienced developer.

CAUTION Always back up important documents before creating, editing, or deleting macros. Practice on non-critical documents before you alter important files. Remember that it's easy to copy macros from one document or template to another using the Organizer (see the Chapter 10, "Creating Legal Templates," for more information on the Organizer).

A powerful feature of VBA is its *interoperability*—the way it can be used in different software products. Developers can use VBA to create powerful applications that have advanced functionality across the products included in Office 2000. A developer can create a macro that creates a pleading in Word, puts an outline of that pleading in PowerPoint, automatically integrates charts and graphs from Excel into an exhibit, adds information to an Access database, and sends the original Word document via e-mail in Outlook 2000 to a contact you've specified. All that in one macro!

Then VBA is hard, right? The answer is yes, for examples like those just mentioned; those are exciting ideas, but they're way beyond the scope of this chapter. The real power behind VBA is solving everyday problems on a smaller scale. Users and techies alike can automate routine tasks as never before. This relatively easy development environment turns an everyday word processor into a task-processing giant.

JUMPSTART TO CREATING MACROS IN VBA

In order to understand macros, you need to know quite a bit of theory–especially in regard to where macros are stored and the hierarchy of how Word handles macros when there is a conflict.

It's tempting when there is a lot of introductory information to skip over text and get right to the exercises. For this reason, we've included an introductory exercise to keep your interest as you read through this chapter.

A JUMPSTART ON CREATING A MACRO

1. Create a new blank document.

2. Press Alt+F11 to open the Visual Basic Editor. This is where macros are written and stored in VBA.

3. From the View menu, choose Code. The insertion point is in the portion of the window where VBA code is written.

4. Type the following:

```
Sub SayHello()

      MsgBox "Hello"

End Sub
```

5. Position the mouse pointer within the macro and press F5 to run the macro. The macro within the Visual Basic Editor Code window is shown in Figure 17.1.

6. Click OK.

7. From the File menu, choose Close and Return to Microsoft Word.

8. Press Alt+F11 again to return to the Visual Basic Editor.

9. Select the macro named hello that you created and delete it.

FIGURE 17.1

All macro code is written or recorded in Visual Basic Editor.

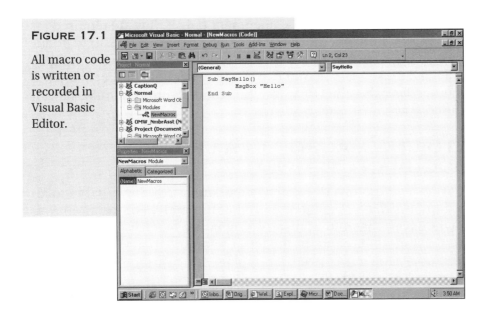

10. From the File menu, choose Close and Return to Microsoft Word.

11. Close the document without saving.

WHERE MACROS LIVE

Macros can live in a number of places:

- In the document
- In the document template
- In the Normal template
- In a global template

The intended use of the macro will determine where it should be stored and which one you should choose. An understanding of how templates and documents relate to each other will come in handy here. For more information on this issue, see Chapter 10, "Creating Legal Templates."

STORING MACROS IN A LEGAL DOCUMENT

Macros should be stored in a document only if they are required for that one specific document or user. Store macros in single documents only if you're certain that no other documents or templates will need those macros. You can always trade macros between and among files using the Organizer, but good planning should make it unnecessary to fall back on that.

STORING MACROS IN A LEGAL DOCUMENT TEMPLATE

Storing a macro in a document template makes it available to all documents that are created with that template. For example, you might have a macro that inserts a signature block into a letter. You would store that macro in the letter template to make it available each time a letter is created. If templates are distributed throughout your firm, or placed in a workgroup template folder on the network, then the macros will be available to all users creating documents with that template.

STORING MACROS IN THE NORMAL TEMPLATE

Storing a macro in the Normal template makes it available in every document that you create. Macros that live in the Normal template are available to all documents, but because that template is stored locally on user machines, it is not a desirable solution for much beyond user-specific modifications. The Normal template is used to store *user* modifications to Word. It is not where firmwide macros should be stored.

STORING MACROS IN A LEGAL GLOBAL TEMPLATE

Just like the Normal template, if you store a macro in a global template, that macro is available to all your documents. Global templates are stored in your Startup directory (check Tools, Options, File Locations if you're not sure what your Startup directory is). Global templates are ideal locations for storing firmwide macros, toolbars, AutoText, and other customizations that you want your users to take advantage of. An additional advantage of storing macros in global templates is that your users won't be able to edit, delete, or even view your macro code unless they actually unload and then open the template file itself. Another feature of macros is that they can be password protected to prevent users from accessing them.

 Like all passwords in Word, passwords used to protect macros are case sensitive. This means that you must enter the password exactly as it was originally stored to access the macro. For example, if you were to use NOACCESS (uppercase) as a password, typing noaccess (lowercase) would not register correctly.

EXPLORE MACROS STORED IN THE NORMAL TEMPLATE

1. Create a new blank document.

2. From the Tools menu, choose Macro and then select Macros from the submenu, as shown in Figure 17.2. Keyboard users can press Alt+F8.

3. Select Normal.dot (global template) from the Macros In list. The Macro Name box displays a list of macros that are available in the Normal template.

FIGURE 17.2

The Macros dialog box lists all the macros available in an open document and template.

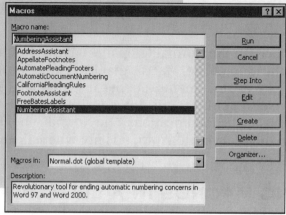

Macros	? X
Macro name:	
NumberingAssistant	
AddressAssistant	Run
AppellateFootnotes	Cancel
AutomatePleadingFooters	
AutomaticDocumentNumbering	Step Into
CaliforniaPleadingRules	
FootnoteAssistant	Edit
FreeBatesLabels	
NumberingAssistant	Create
	Delete
	Organizer...
Macros in: Normal.dot (global template)	
Description:	
Revolutionary tool for ending automatic numbering concerns in Word 97 and Word 2000.	

NOTE

If you have not customized the Normal template, there may not be any macros listed in the Macro Name box. If other templates are listed in the Macros In list, select them to see what macros, if any, they contain.

4. Click Cancel to close the Macros dialog box without running a macro.

HOW WORD 2000 WORKS WITH MACROS

Macros are accessed by Word in several ways. Word can access macros from any of the following:

- The Macros dialog box
- A menu or toolbar assignment
- A keyboard assignment
- A MacroButton field

ACCESSING LEGAL MACROS FROM THE MACROS DIALOG BOX

If you don't assign macros to a keyboard shortcut or toolbar, you can always access them from the Macros dialog box. If you intend to use macros often or wish to keep things simple, however, it's better to assign them to a toolbar button, menu command, or keyboard shortcut. Assigning macros to toolbar buttons, menu commands, and keyboard shortcuts is covered later in this chapter.

ACCESS A MACRO FROM THE MACROS DIALOG BOX

1. Create a new blank document.

2. From the Tools menu, choose Macro and then select Macros. Keyboard users can press Alt+F8.

3. Change the option in the Macros in list box to Word Commands. This will allow you to run one of Word's built-in macros.

4. Select the ListCommands macro and choose Run. This macro will create a table of all of Word's commands along with their keyboard shortcuts.

If you double-click a macro in the Macro Name box it will run automatically.

5. When the List Commands dialog box is open, select All Word Commands and then click OK. After a few seconds, Word will display a table of available commands along with the keyboard shortcuts and menu assignments for each command.

MACRO HIERARCHY

Macros in Word 2000 follow the same hierarchy as AutoText, Styles, and any other Word feature subject to the template hierarchy principles. The most common source of confusion is when two macros in different locations have the same name. Word will proceed in the order listed here to determine which macro will be activated if there is a name conflict:

1. Document

2. Document Template

3. Normal Template

4. Global Templates (in alphabetical order by file name)

This rule has one exception, which is encountered under specific conditions. If you have accessed the Macros dialog box (as you did in the previous exercise) and changed the Macros In list to default to a specific document or template rather than to all documents and templates, then that template will take precedence over the others.

It is important to keep this hierarchy in mind when you name and store macros. It's best to ensure that firmwide macros have unique names to prevent potential conflicts with macros created by users. In other words, don't name a macro that inserts a signature block "Signature." It's likely that users will create their own versions of a signature macro and use the name "Signature" for them.

You might want to spend some time developing naming conventions for your macros. One option is to use the initials of your firm as an identifier for all firmwide macros. For example, if your firm were named Johnson Myers and Smith, you might begin all macro names with "jms." The signature macro mentioned in the preceding paragraph would be named "jmsSignature." Such naming conventions not only help prevent conflicts with user-level macros but also cause all firmwide macros to appear together in the <u>M</u>acro Name box, which lists macros in alphabetical order. This is helpful when you're trying to locate specific macros.

RECORDING LEGAL MACROS

The easiest way to create a macro is to record one. The macro recorder feature in Word makes it possible to automatically store specific editing steps in a macro. Word's macro recorder is ideal for users who do not know how to write VBA macros. They can simply turn on the macro recorder and move through the steps that they want to have the macro record and repeat. The macro is created automatically. Running the recorded macro will repeat all of the commands accessed while the macro record feature was activated.

Recording is often sufficient to create macros that automate daily tasks. For example, many firms have discovered that specific editing steps must be repeated every time a document is converted from WordPerfect or another word processing application. Rather than repeat those steps each time you convert a document, you can use the macro record feature to store them to a macro. After the commands are stored, you can simply run the macro each time you need to convert a document; all the necessary clean-up work will be done automatically.

When you record a macro, Word displays the Stop Recording toolbar. This toolbar has special buttons that allow you to stop and pause recording.

Chapter 17: Introduction to VBA

RECORD A MACRO TO SEARCH AND CHANGE A CLIENT NAME

1. Create a new blank document.

2. Type **SMITH COMPANY EXPRESSLY ACKNOWLEDGES AND AGREES THAT THIS AGREEMENT IS NOT A LEASE and Smith Company shall, under no circumstances be considered a tenant under Chapter 83, Florida Statutes.**

3. From the Tools menu, choose Macro and select Record New Macro.

Another way to start recording a macro is by double-clicking on REC, located on the Status bar at the bottom of the screen.

4. Name the macro **ReplaceSmithWithJones**.

Including a description of a macro when you are creating it is a good practice. This makes finding the macro in the Macros dialog box easier when you can't remember the name.

5. Store Macro In should be the current document, and then click OK. The Stop Recording toolbar appears on the screen.

If you receive an error message saying, "Invalid Procedure Call," check the typing of the macro name. Macro names cannot contain spaces and must begin with a letter. Names can contain up to 80 letters and numbers.

Sometimes when an error occurs, the Visual Basic Editor is activated. If this happens, don't panic; you can close the Visual Basic Editor from the File menu by choosing Close And Return To Microsoft Word from the File menu.

6. Press Ctrl+Home to move to the top of the document.

7. Press Ctrl+H to display the Replace tab on the Find and Replace dialog box.

8. In the Find What box, type **Smith**.

9. In the Replace With box, type **Jones**.

10. Click Replace All and Close to close the Find and Replace dialog box.

11. On the Stop Recording toolbar, click Stop Recording (the square button).

NOTE

If you have accidentally closed the Stop Recording toolbar, from the Tools menu choose Macro, then choose Stop Recording.

12. From the Edit menu, choose Undo. You are now undoing all of the actions of the macro in one step. In the next step you will rerun the macro.

13. From the Tools menu, choose Macro and select Macros.

14. Double-click the macro ReplaceSmithWithJones to execute the macro.

15. Close the document without saving changes.

NOTE

The macro recorder in Word is useful; however, it often records more steps than necessary and may therefore take up more memory than would writing the macro yourself.

The following exercise shows a more advanced use of the macro recorder. You will record a macro that inserts your name into a memorandum each time you create a document based on the memorandum template.

For the purposes of this chapter, it is assumed that you have installed Word's default templates. If you haven't installed Word's templates, you can substitute any template available as you move through the exercises. In each exercise, you will make copies of the existing templates, so you don't have to worry about modifying the originals.

RECORD A MACRO THAT EXECUTES AUTOMATICALLY

1. From the File menu, choose New and then select the Memos tab.

2. Select Elegant Memo from the list of available templates. In the Create New section in the lower-right corner of the dialog box, select Template. This will allow you to make a copy of the existing template.

3. Click OK. A new template based on the Elegant Memo appears.

4. Insert a bookmark in the FROM line, where the author name would normally be inserted. Name the bookmark "Author." You will use this bookmark in the recorded macro.

If you need help inserting a bookmark, see "Inserting a Bookmark" in Chapter 12, "Working with Long Documents."

5. Save the template as "VBA-1 Memorandum."

6. Close the template.

7. Create a new document using the VBA-1 Memorandum template.

If you don't see the VBA-1 Memorandum template that you just created, make certain that the General tab is selected. Unless you specify the folder when saving a template, Word places it on the General tab automatically.

When recording and testing template-level macros, it's good practice to create the macro in a document based on the template rather than in the actual template. This prevents you from accidentally inserting unwanted text and formatting into the template. You can copy the macro to the working template after you finalize it.

8. From the Tools menu, choose Macro, and then choose Record New Macro to open the Record Macro dialog box, as shown in Figure 17.3.

FIGURE 17.3

The Record Macro dialog box allows you to assign a macro to toolbar buttons or keyboard shortcuts, specify the location for a macro, and provide a description of a macro.

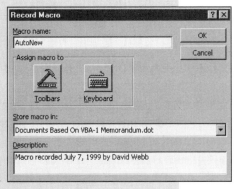

9. Type **AutoNew** in the Macro Name box. Naming a macro *AutoNew* will cause it to run automatically every time a new document is created using this template.

NOTE

Advanced users may question the use of AutoNew rather than Document_New. A Document_New procedure cannot be recorded, however. If you want to record a macro that runs automatically when you create a new document, you must use AutoNew as the macro name.

10. Because this macro will run automatically, skip the Assign Macro To section for now. (Normally, this is where you would assign a macro to a toolbar button or keyboard shortcut.)

11. Select Documents Based on VBA-1 Memorandum in the Store Macro In box.

12. Type a description for the macro in the Description box. This macro will be used to insert the author name in a memorandum when the memorandum is first created.

13. Click OK. The Stop Recording toolbar appears on the screen.

14. Record the following steps. Don't worry if you make a mistake; you can start again if necessary. You will learn how to edit macros to remove unwanted commands later in this chapter.

15. From the Insert menu, choose Bookmark.

16. Select the bookmark named Author (you inserted the Author bookmark at the beginning of this exercise), and then click Go To.

17. Click Close to close the Bookmark dialog box.

18. Type your name at the author location.

19. Press Ctrl+Home to move back to the beginning of the document.

20. On the Stop Recording toolbar, click Stop Recording (the square button).

21. Close the document. Word prompts you to save changes to the document. You don't need to save the document, so click No. Next, you will be prompted to save changes to the Memorandum template; make certain to click Yes to save the macro.

NOTE

If you accidentally stored the macro in the Normal template, you will not be prompted to save the template at this time. If you don't get the prompt, simply record the macro again. You will need to delete the macro from the Normal template to prevent it from running each time a new document other than a memorandum is created. Deleting macros is covered later in this chapter.

22. Create a new document based on the Memorandum template that you created. Your name is inserted automatically at the FROM line.

ASSIGNING LEGAL MACROS TO TOOLBAR BUTTONS, KEYBOARD SHORTCUTS, AND MACROBUTTON FIELDS

In the preceding exercise, the macro you recorded ran automatically when a new document was created based on the template. Many macros that you create will not be AutoNew macros. Instead, you'll want to create macros that you can call only when you need them. Although you can always choose to run a macro from the Macros dialog box, it makes sense to assign the macro to a toolbar button or a keyboard shortcut so that users can access it easily.

RECORD A MACRO AND ASSIGN IT TO A TOOLBAR BUTTON

1. Create a new document using the VBA-1 Memorandum template created in an earlier exercise.

2. On the Status bar, double-click REC to start recording a new macro.

3. Type **Print2Copies** in the Macro Name box.

4. In the Store Macro In box, select Documents Based On VBA-1 Memorandum.

5. In the Assign Macro To section, click Toolbars. The Customize dialog box appears, as shown in Figure 17.4.

6. In the Save In box, make certain to select the memorandum template.

FIGURE 17.4

The Customize dialog box allows you to assign macros to toolbars.

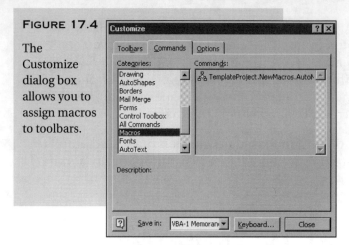

If you neglect to change the template in the Customize dialog box, the toolbar modification will be saved to the Normal template and will appear in all documents, rather than just in memorandums.

If you change to the specified template in the Record Macro dialog box, only the macro that you are recording will appear in the Commands window of the Customize dialog box. This makes it easier to locate the macro.

7. Drag the macro from the Commands window to an existing toolbar. Because the macro prints two copies of the document, a good place for it might be next to the Print icon on the Standard toolbar.

8. Close the Customize dialog box. The Stop Recording toolbar appears.

9. Record the following steps for the macro:

   ◆ From the File menu, choose Print.

   ◆ Change the Number Of Copies to 2.

   ◆ Click OK.

10. Click the square button on the Stop Recording toolbar.

11. Close the document without saving any changes. When you are prompted to save the template, click Yes.

ASSIGNING A MACRO TO A KEYBOARD SHORTCUT

You have assigned the Print2Copies macro to the toolbar in the VBA-1 Memorandum template. You can also assign the macro to a keyboard shortcut so that keyboard users can access the macro as well.

ASSIGN A MACRO TO A KEYBOARD SHORTCUT

1. Create a new document using the VBA-1 Memorandum template.
2. From the Tools menu, choose Customize.
3. Click Keyboard. The Customize Keyboard dialog box appears, as shown in Figure 17.5.
4. Select the memorandum template from the Save Changes In box.

 CAUTION If you do not select the memorandum template in the Save Changes In box, the keyboard shortcut may be assigned to the Normal template or to the document. You want the keyboard shortcut to appear in the template so that the macro is available at the template level.

5. From the Categories list, select Macros.
6. Choose Print2Copies from the list of Macros.
7. Click in the Press New Shortcut Key box and then press a new keyboard shortcut, such as Alt+2.

FIGURE 17.5

The Customize Keyboard dialog box allows you to assign macros to keyboard commands.

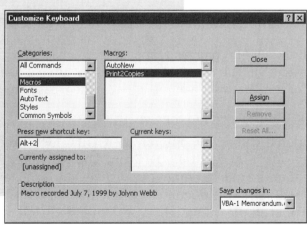

8. Click Assign to assign the keyboard shortcut to the macro in the VBA-1 Memorandum template.

9. Close the document without saving changes. Save the memorandum template when you are prompted to do so.

ASSIGNING A MACRO TO A MACROBUTTON FIELD

Sometimes it is helpful to display a macro button within a document or template. This makes the macro visible to all users and allows them to easily access it. For example, you might have a macro that sends a document via fax automatically. You might make this macro accessible to users by creating a macro button on the fax form template.

ASSIGN A MACRO TO A MACROBUTTON

1. Open the VBA-1 Memorandum template.

Because a macro button must appear within the actual text area of a template, you must open the template rather than create a new document based on the template. Creating a new document would place the macro button in the document only, not in the template.

2. Move to the end of the document by pressing Ctrl+End.

3. From the Insert menu, choose Field.

4. Select MacroButton from the list of Field Names.

5. Click Options.

6. Select Print2Copies from the list of Macro Names.

All of Word's built-in commands appear in the macro list, so the list may be extensive. This is one example of why using a naming convention for firm macros is helpful; it makes them easier to locate.

7. Click Add To Field and then click OK.

8. Position the insertion point in the Field Codes box after the text that reads "MACROBUTTON Print2Copies." Enter the display text after the macro name. The *display text* is the text that the user will see in the document where the macro button is located. For example, you might type: **Double-click here to print two copies of this document.**

9. Click OK. The macro button is inserted and the display text appears.

If Field Code view is activated, you will see the field code rather than the display text. If the field code is visible, it will appear as follows:

```
{MACROBUTTON Print2Copies Double-click here to
print two copies of this document}
```

You can turn off Field Code view by clearing the option to view field codes on the View tab of the Options dialog box. From the Tools menu, choose Options to access the Options dialog box.

Now users can double-click the MacroButton field to print two copies of the memorandum automatically. Keyboard users can select the macro button and press Alt+Shift+F9 to activate it.

If Field Code view is activated in a document, the macro button fields will not work. You must turn off Field Code view to use macro buttons. Make certain to turn off Field Code view before saving and closing a template. If users activate Field Code view, they must turn it off before attempting to use macro buttons.

EDITING MACROS

Word will store many of the commands and settings that exist in a document at the time a macro is recorded. Some of these settings may not be necessary or desired for the macro. You can edit the macro to remove the unwanted commands.

When you create a macro, the code for that macro is stored in a *VBA project*. To modify the code, you must open the project in Visual Basic Editor. The default Visual Basic Editor window is made up of three smaller windows:

 ◆ The Project Explorer Window

 ◆ The Properties Window

 ◆ The Code Window

Figure 17.6 shows all the windows in Visual Basic Editor.

FIGURE 17.6

Use Visual Basic Editor to make changes to macros that you have recorded.

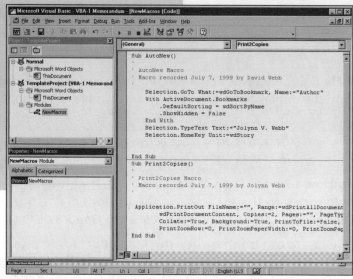

To modify the macro that you recorded in a previous exercise, you must open the macro in Visual Basic Editor.

EDIT A MACRO IN VISUAL BASIC EDITOR

1. Create a new document based on the VBA-1 Memorandum template.

2. From the Tools menu, choose Macro and then select Macros.

3. Locate the AutoNew macro stored in the VBA-1 Memorandum template.

4. Select the macro and click Edit. Visual Basic Editor appears, with the AutoNew macro selected in the Code window (see Figure 17.6).

5. In the Code window, locate the code that inserts your name into the memorandum. It should look similar to the following line of code:

```
Selection.TypeText Text:="<your name>"
```

6. Locate the following line of code and change the name to another name, or add or remove a middle initial:

```
Selection.TypeText Text:="<your name>"
```

7. From the File menu, choose Save VBA-1 Memorandum to save the macro.

8. Choose <u>C</u>lose And Return To Microsoft Word from the <u>F</u>ile menu to close Visual Basic Editor.

9. Create a new document based on the VBA-1 Memorandum template. The new name is inserted at the FROM line.

COMMENTING CODE

The lines of code that appear in green at the beginning of the macro are comments. Comments about the macro do not execute when the macro runs.

To insert a comment into a macro, precede the line with at least one apostrophe. The apostrophe tells Word that this is a comment and the text is skipped when the macro executes. Experienced developers often precede a comment with three apostrophe characters. This helps to distinguish between a comment marker and text.

Why is this useful? Let's say you want to delete all comments in your VBA code in a project. If you precede comments with a single apostrophe, when you use Find and Replace with a single apostrophe identifier, you also replace any contractions that are used in message and input boxes such as "can't, I'd, we'll, etc.". If you use three apostrophes to precede a comment, you don't have this problem.

You can insert comments on the same line as existing code, as long as the comment appears *after* the code and is preceded by an apostrophe. It's a good idea to insert comments throughout your code to explain what is happening. Doing so will help you and other developers when the code needs editing later.

NAVIGATING WITHIN VISUAL BASIC EDITOR

You may want to modify more than one macro while you're working in Visual Basic Editor.

Because a document, document template, and the Normal template can all contain macros, each is defined as a separate project within Visual Basic Editor. You can navigate from project to project using the Project Explorer window. Refer back to Figure 17.6 to see the different windows available in Visual Basic Editor.

You can navigate through the Project Explorer window in a similar manner as you navigate through the Windows Explorer. You can collapse or expand components of a project by clicking the +/- buttons.

LOCATE A TEMPLATE PROJECT

1. Create a new document using the VBA-1 Memorandum template.
2. Open Visual Basic Editor (Alt+F11).
3. Locate the VBA-1 Memorandum template project in the Project Explorer window.
4. Locate and double-click the Modules folder for the VBA-1 Memorandum template. If the Modules folder is not visible, double-click the VBA-1 Memorandum template project to open it.
5. Double-click the NewMacros module to display the module's code in the Code window. If the NewMacros module is not visible, double-click the Modules folder to open it.
6. Click anywhere in the Code window to position the insertion point within the code.
7. Use the arrow keys to move through the code of a macro.
8. Select a macro from the Procedure list to move to the beginning of the selected macro.

NOTE

In Visual Basic Editor, macros are referred to as *procedures*.

DELETING MACROS

Sometimes you will record macros that you need only briefly. For example, you might be working on a project that requires identical modifications to a large number of documents. After you finish those documents, you may no longer need the macro. Deleting unwanted macros helps keep templates organized so that necessary macros are easier to locate and manipulate within the Macros dialog box and Visual Basic Editor.

NOTE If you accidentally create a macro in the wrong template, you can move the macro to the correct template using Word's Organizer. For more information about using the Organizer, see "Using the Organizer" in Chapter 10.

DELETE A MACRO

1. Create a new document based on the VBA-1 Memorandum template.
2. From the Tools menu, choose Macro and then choose Macros.
3. Locate the AutoNew macro stored in the VBA-1 Memorandum template.
4. Select the macro and click Delete.
5. When prompted to delete the macro, choose Yes to delete it, or choose No to leave the macro in the template.
6. Click Close to close the Macros dialog box. If the macro was not deleted, the Close button will be a Cancel button instead.

TIP To delete a macro while working in Visual Basic Editor, select the entire contents of the macro (from Sub XXX to End Sub), and then press the Delete key. If you inadvertently delete a macro that you did not intend to delete, click Undo on the Standard toolbar, or press Ctrl+Z.

RUN-TIME AND MACRO ERRORS

The goal of any programmer worth his salt is to trap errors *before* a user sees them. As you become more experienced, you will want to learn to create error-handling subroutines to avoid unsightly error messages.

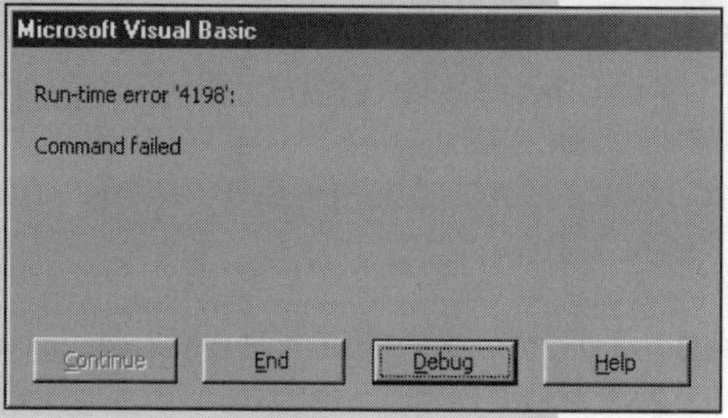

FIGURE 17.7

Test macros to avoid the user seeing error messages

```
Microsoft Visual Basic

Run-time error '4198':

Command failed

      Continue        End        Debug        Help
```

An error message occurs because either the macro was not written correctly, or something is preventing the macro from running properly. If you receive an error message you can choose to End or Debug the macro, as shown in Figure 17.7.

Clicking End stops the macro and returns you to the active document in Word. To look at the macro in Visual Basic Editor, click Debug; the offending line of code is highlighted.

MACRO SECURITY IN WORD 2000

It seems that as long as there are macros, there will be dastardly folks who write macro viruses. Broadly defined, macro viruses work like conventional computer viruses, but take advantage of Word's structure to replicate and trigger when certain events occur. Many macro viruses are harmless nuisances, but others can damage your sensitive and critical documents. Microsoft and others have responded to the need for macro virus security in Word. In Word 2000 there is a feature built in to Word that will help protect you from macro viruses.

CAUTION

While the security in Word 2000 against macro viruses is impressive, it isn't a substitute for good anti-virus software. All of the major anti-virus software products are generally reliable. If you haven't already done so, purchase and install a well-known anti-virus software package, and then keep it up to date.

To set security levels for Word 2000, from the Tools menu, choose Macro, and then select Security. You will see a dialog box with three options: High, Medium, and Low, as shown in Figure 17.8. The setting you choose depends on how much protection you desire. For more information on macro protection in Word, open the Office

FIGURE 17.8

The Security dialog box lists the built-in macro security options and allows you to choose the level of security you want.

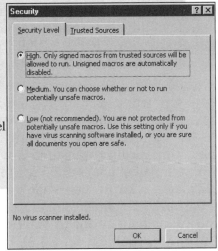

Assistant (the quickest way is to press F1) and type "Security levels in Word" or "Protection from documents that might contain viruses."

Here is a brief description of what the security levels will do for you:

◆ **High**. The only macros that will run are those that have a digital certificate (just like the ones you may have seen warnings for while Web browsing) from a trusted source. Other macros are automatically disabled. This setting is the default in Word 2000.

◆ **Medium**. Whenever Word encounters a macro that does not have a digital certificate from a trusted source, you will receive a warning and be presented with a choice to enable or disable macros.

◆ **Low**. All macros are enabled.

USING WORD 97 MACROS IN WORD 2000—AND VICE VERSA

First the good news. Because the file format is the same in both Word 97 and Word 2000, your macros should work fine at first glance. VBA in Word 2000 fully supports all the syntax, structure, objects, methods, and properties in Word 97 VBA. In other words, you won't notice any difference when you use your Word 97 macros in Word 2000.

Now the bad news: If you take advantage of any of the new features in Word 2000 VBA, like some of the new string manipulation functions, new language features, or other features that were not supported in Word 97, error messages may appear if you try to run them in Word 97.

Another potential trouble spot when attempting to run your Word 2000 macros in Word 97 is the new security features mentioned previously. Because the default security setting in Word 2000 is High, your Word 97 macros are automatically disabled in Word 2000 if you try to open documents or templates that contain the macros. If you attempt to run a Word 97 macro in Word 2000 while security is set to High, you will receive a warning: "The macros in this project are disabled. Please refer to the online help or documentation of the host application to determine how to enable macros." As with any other situation where you wish to run macros in Word 2000, make sure the macro provider (even if it's you!) has a digital certificate, otherwise you'll have to change your security setting to Medium or Low. Read the online help topic "How to obtain a digital certificate" for more information.

NOTE

If you have anti-virus software installed that works with Office 2000, it will scan all of the files you open regardless of the security setting you've chosen. Also, it's possible that your network administrator may have enforced a security level, thereby preventing you from choosing which sources are trusted sources and which are not. Consult the help files on digital certificates for more information.

ANSWERING COMMON QUESTIONS ON VBA

How do I get help on VBA?

To access VBA help, switch to the Visual Basic Editor (Alt+F11). Click in the code window and press F1. If you have a question on a specific command in VBA, first type and then select the command and press F1. For example, to obtain help on msgbox (a message box) type the command in the code window, select the text and press F1.

What is happening when I type something in the Code window and other text appears in a drop-down list?

If you type something that VBA recognizes, Word tries to help you by letting you know what other VBA commands can be used with the one that you just entered. For example, if you type **Application.** in the Code window, a drop-down list of properties and methods that can be used with an object are shown. After Application., type **ActiveDocument**. As you type the word, VBA tries to locate commands for you. Accept these commands by pressing the Tab key. Next type **Save**. The full line of code is

```
Application.ActiveDocument.Save.
```

This command, when embedded in a macro, will save the active document.

Is there a way to see all commands in VBA without having to first type them?

The Object Browser that is available in the Visual Basic Editor displays a list of all the Visual Basic methods, properties, functions, and objects. Click the Object Browser button. In the list of libraries, click the library for the program you want.

Is it possible to pause while using macro recorder?

To pause recording, click Pause Recording on the Stop Recording toolbar. When you're ready to resume recording, click the Resume Recorder button.

What is a reasonable amount of time for me to learn VBA?

Have you seen those book titles, *Learn VBA in 10 days*? Don't believe it. VBA is a complex programming language that encompasses much more than what was covered in this brief introductory chapter. If you use VBA every day as part of your job, you may become a proficient programmer in six months. To become a true expert can take years. As with everything, plan, prepare and practice.

There are classes in VBA you can take. In fact, Payne Consulting Group offers a Word VBA Workshop designed specially for law firms. For more information visit `http://www.payneconsulting.com/`. There are books on Word VBA available (make sure to get one on VBA and not VB) that teach you about objects, properties, methods, naming conventions, if statements and all of the other necessary information for learning VBA.

Microsoft also sponsors an interactive newsgroup on the Web where questions and answers are posted on Word VBA. Initially, you'll likely find yourself lurking in the newsgroup and watching what answers that are posted in response to user questions. But eventually, you may find yourself jumping in and answering questions yourself. That's how many of the developers at our company started and became recognized as experts in VBA development. The newsgroups are located at `http://support.microsoft.com/support/news/` and then click the hyperlink to Visual Basic for Applications.

INDEX

*CardText switch, 292

1.5 line spacing, 92

12 Points of Space (Ctrl+0) (zero) keyboard
shortcut, 91, 92

A

A4 size, 149

About Microsoft Word command, 35

About Microsoft Word dialog box, 35

Accept or Reject Changes command, 438

Accept or Reject Changes dialog box,
433, 438

action fields, 366

actions
redoing, 59
reversing, 58–60

Add command, 251–252

Add Row (Tab key) keyboard shortcut, 218

add-in programs, 306–307

Address Assistant, 293

agreements, special layouts, 151–156

aliases
built-in styles, 195–197
user-defined styles, 196–197

aligning decimals in tables, 232–233

Alki Software Corporation Web site, 254,
307

Alt+Ctrl+O (Online view), 61

Alt-key combinations, 5

apostrophes and converting
documents, 462

applying numbers while typing, 116–118

Arrange All command, 30

Arrange Icons view, 25

arranging documents on screen, 29–30

attached templates, 299–303

AutoCaption, 405–406

AutoCaption dialog box, 406

AutoComplete Tip
activating, 70
AutoText and, 70
AutoText feature, 72
turning off, 72

AutoCorrect
Add button, 87
adding and deleting entries, 248–250
adding misspelled words, 246–247
assigning entries, 87
AutoFormat As You Type tab, 113, 187
Automatic Bulleted Lists option, 113
Capitalize First Letter of Sentences feature,
249
commonly used phrases, 248
exceptions, 250–251
features, 246
inserting phrases, 248
legal symbols, 86
real word as code, 248
Replace box, 87
spell checking, 245–251

AutoCorrect command, 102–103, 107–108,
113, 117–118, 187, 209, 247–250

AutoCorrect dialog box
AutoCorrect tab, 247, 249–250
AutoFormat As You Type tab, 103, 108,
117–118, 209

Automatic Bulleted Lists option, 108

Automatic Numbered Lists option, 108, 117–118

Automatically Use Suggestions From The Spelling Checker option, 247

AutoText tab, 72, 327–328

With box, 248–249

Define Styles Based On Your Formatting option, 103

Delete button, 249

Exceptions button, 250

Replace box, 248–249

Replace Text As You Type option, 247

Tables check box, 209

AutoFormat, 107, 117, 187

  automatically defining styles, 103

AutoFormat dialog box, 227

automated AutoText entries, 330

automatic bullets while typing, 107–109

automatic formatting, 103

automatic paragraph numbers and converted documents, 469–470

automatically

  defining styles, 103

  formatting text, 102–103

  saving versions, 441

  selecting entire word, 74

AutoText, 69–73

  AutoComplete Tip and, 70, 72

  automated entries, 330

  deleting entries, 73

  global entries, 71

  inserting entries in documents, 69–70

  predefined entries, 69

  redefining entries, 72–73

  replicating WordPerfect for DOS macros, 69

  storing entries, 69, 71

  user-created entries, 71–72

AutoText (Alt+F3) keyboard shortcut, 136

AutoText command, 69, 71–73, 327

AutoText dialog box, 69, 71–72

  Delete button, 73

Show AutoComplete Tip For AutoText And Dates option, 70

AutoText Entry (Alt+F3) keyboard shortcut, 471

AutoText template, 303

AutoText toolbar, 72

Avery Dennison Web site, 307

B

Backspace key, 42

bar tabs, 97

Batch Conversion Wizard, 483–485

Beginning of Document (Ctrl+Home) keyboard shortcut, 174

block quote, 320

Block Quote style, 186

Body Text style, 180

bold text, 79–80

Bold Text (Ctrl+B) keyboard shortcut, 79

Bookmark command, 232, 361, 397, 399, 544

Bookmark (Ctrl+Shift+F5) keyboard shortcut, 361, 397, 399

Bookmark dialog box, 232, 361, 397, 399, 544

bookmarks, 231, 397–400

  advanced features, 399–400

  built-in locations, 398–399

  form fields, 353–354

  moving to, 398

  naming, 397–398

  pleading captions, 399

  reference fields, 360

  retrieving pleading caption with bookmark name, 399–400

borders

  automatic formatting, 103

  pages, 101–102, 154–156

  paragraphs, 100–101

  tables, 213

Borders And Shading command, 101–102, 135, 222

Borders And Shading dialog box, 100
  3-D option, 102
  Apply To setting, 156
  Art Frame option, 102
  Borders tab, 101, 155, 222
  Box option, 102, 155
  Color option, 102
  Custom option, 101
  double underline option, 101
  Horizontal Line button, 156
  Options button, 156
  Page Borders tab, 102, 155–156
  Preview box, 101
  Shadow option, 102
  Show Toolbar button, 156
  Style option, 102
  Style section, 155
  This Section - First page Only in the Apply To list box, 102
  Width option, 102

Break command, 121, 157–158, 165–166, 174

Break dialog box, 121

briefs
  special layouts, 151–156
  tables, 202

Browse Object, 18, 395
  Browse By Comment, 426
  Browse By Endnote icon, 395
  Browse By Footnote icon, 395
  Browse By Page icon, 54
  Find icon, 54
  finding and replacing text, 54

Browse Object (Alt+Ctrl+Home) keyboard shortcut, 18, 395

browsing by comments, 426

built-in styles, 178
  aliases, 195–197
  keyboard shortcuts, 199
  modifying, 189
  table of contents from, 373–375

Bullet (Ctrl+Shift+L) keyboard shortcut, 115, 199

bullets
  applying, 107–110
  automatic as you type, 107–109
  automatic formatting, 103
  Bullets And Numbering dialog box, 109
  Bullets button, 110
  changing styles, 110–111
  converting to numbers, 124 125
  customizing, 111–114
  default, 111
  disabling automatic, 108
  font attributes, 112
  hanging indents, 112
  modifying style, 114–115
  new character for, 112
  pictures as, 113–114
  position, 112
  removing, 108, 111
  resetting customized, 113
  Symbol dialog box characters as, 107

Bullets And Numbering command, 109–110, 111, 113, 118, 122–124, 126–127, 130, 132, 136–138, 504

Bullets And Numbering dialog box, 113, 119, 504
  Borders tab, 135
  Bulleted tab, 109–111, 113, 125
  bullets, 109
  Continue Previous List option, 122
  Customize button, 111, 123, 128, 132, 136–138
  gallery position, 110
  Import Clips button, 113
  Indent At Text Position option, 138
  Insert Clip button, 113
  Level box, 132
  Link Level To Style box, 132
  More option, 132, 138
  Number Position Aligned At option, 138
  Numbered Position option, 138
  Numbered tab, 118, 122–123, 125

Outline Numbered tab, 117, 126, 128, 130, 132, 136–138

Picture option, 113

Restart Numbering option, 122

buttons

adding to toolbars, 11–13

removing from toolbars, 13–14

viewing name, 7

C

calculating form fields, 353–356

calculations in tables, 229–233

Calendar wizard, 304–305

Caption command, 404

Caption dialog box, 404–405

Caption Numbering dialog box, 405

captions

AutoCaption, 405–406

table of figures, 406–407

tables, 404–405

updating, 405–406

catalog merge, 290–291

catalogs, 261

cells

aligning text, 216, 233

Fit Text feature, 217

inserting pictures, 529

merging, 214

shading, 214

splitting, 214

tab inside, 215

center tabs, 97

Centered (Ctrl+E) keyboard shortcut, 89

centered paragraphs, 88–89

centering heading information and text underneath, 137–138

Change Case command, 258

Change Case (Ctrl+F3) keyboard shortcut, 258

Change Case dialog box, 258

Change Case feature, 258

character formatting, 76, 87

commands, 79

character styles, 178

Style dialog box, 184, 188

characters

nonprinting, 86

removing manual formatting, 198

Chart command, 520

Chart wizard, 520

Check Box Form Field Options dialog box, 341

check box form fields, 340–342

Cheyenne Web site, 331

Choose Assistant command, 32

citations

formatting, 384

marking, 383–384

searching for, 384

CiteLink, 412

cleaning up converted documents

automatic paragraph numbers, 469–470

changing straight quotes to smart quotes, 467–468

copying styles, 475

locking fields, 466

Paste Special command, 473–474

quick and dirty, 465–466

reasons for, 464–465

reformatting documents, 472–473

removing field codes, 468–469

removing paragraph and character formatting, 475–476

resetting header and footer margins, 472

Sequence fields, 470–471

spic and span, 466–473

spring cleaning, 473–476

tab settings, 472

table borders, 472

templates, 473–476

updating table of contents, 471–472

widow and orphan control, 472

Clear Field (F9) keyboard shortcut, 353

clearing form fields, 352–353

clearing tabs, 97–98

Click and Type feature
>   enabling, 44
>   Flush Right feature, 43
>   formatting, 43
>   markers, 44
>   Print Layout view, 99
>   signature line, 98–99
>   tab characters and paragraph marks, 43
>   Web Layout view, 99

clip art, 527–528

Clip Art command, 527–529

Clipboard toolbar, 55–56, 74

Clippit, 32

Close All command, 36

Close (Alt+Shift+C) keyboard shortcut, 394, 424

Close button, 28, 352

Close command, 28, 36, 253

Close Full Screen (Alt+C) keyboard shortcut, 68

Close Full Screen command, 68

closing
>   documents, 28, 36
>   Word 2000, 35

Code command, 535

color and table borders, 213

color palette, 213

Column Break command, 166

Column Break (Ctrl+Shift+Enter) keyboard shortcut, 166

Column command, 220

columns
>   adding, 220
>   deleting, 220
>   pleading caption, 221–222
>   resizing, 221

Columns command, 165

Columns dialog box, 165–166

commands
>   Alt-key combinations, 5
>   character formatting, 79
>   organizing, 5

Comment command, 423

Comment pane, 425, 426–427

comments, 422–429
>   blank, 428
>   browsing by, 426
>   deleting, 426–427
>   deleting all, 427–428
>   editing, 426–427
>   embedded sound objects, 422
>   inserting, 423–424
>   macros, 551
>   PAGE field, 428–429
>   printing, 428–429
>   reviewer's ScreenTip, 424–425
>   ScreenTip, 422
>   Versions dialog box, 439
>   viewing, 425

Comments (Alt+Ctrl+M) keyboard shortcut, 423

Comments command, 425, 429

Compare Documents command, 436

CompareRite, 429

comparing documents, 435–437

concordance files, 390

continuing numbered lists, 121–122

continuous section breaks, 166

Conversions Plus, 486

Convert command, 206–207

Convert File dialog box, 456

Convert Footnote or Endnote (Alt+F10) keyboard shortcut, 396

Convert Notes dialog box, 396

Convert Text to Table dialog box, 206

Convert to Endnote command, 397

Convert to Footnote command, 397

converted table, sorting, 206–208

converting documents, 452–453
    Batch Conversion Wizard, 483–485
    clean up, 463–476
    cleanup, 452
    compatibility options, 459–460
    compatibility settings, 485–486
    export converters, 455
    field codes, 462
    file types, 453–455
    formatting options not available, 486
    header and footer margins, 462
    import converters, 454–455
    Install on First Use, 454
    MS-DOS text only, 480
    MS-DOS text with layout, 480
    multiple simultaneously, 483–485
    multiple tabs, 486
    numbered paragraphs, 462
    outgoing files, 476–482
    parallel columns, tables, and borders, 463
    to previous versions of Word, 476–478
    Private fields, 458
    process of, 455–457
    products for, 486
    quotations and apostrophes, 462
    round-tripping, 453
    RTF (Rich Text Format), 480–481
    saving document in different file format, 479–481
    section breaks, 460–461
    Sequence fields, 462
    text only, 480
    unusual tab settings, 463
    widow and orphan control, 463
    to Word 2000, 457
    Word to WordPerfect, 481–482
    from WordPerfect, 458–463
Copy command, 55, 194
Copy (Ctrl+C) keyboard shortcut, 55–56, 341
copying
    custom settings between templates, 317–319
    files to disk, 416–417
    formatting, 103–104

    paragraph styles, 194
    section formatting, 174
    styles, 193–195
    table from another application, 205
    text, 54–57
    text with drag and drop, 58
Copyright (Ctrl+Alt+C) keyboard shortcut, 86
Corel Web site, 482
court rules in pleadings and styles, 179
Create AutoText dialog box, 71
Create Data Source dialog box, 264–266
Cross-Reference command, 361, 401
Cross-Reference dialog box, 361–362, 401–402
cross-references
    hyperlinks, 401, 403
    numbered paragraph options, 401
    updating, 403
    viewing, 403
custom dictionaries, 243–244, 251–255
    editing, 251–252
custom toolbars, 14–15
custom user templates, 302
custom-AutoText entries, 71–72
customizations
    global templates, 325
    Normal template, 298–299
    templates, 298–299
Customize Bulleted List dialog box, 111–112
Customize command, 6–8, 13, 15–16, 209, 321, 323
Customize dialog box, 323
    All Commands option, 321
    button categories and command options, 14
    Categories list, 321–322
    Commands tab, 13
    listing toolbars, 9
    Options tab, 209
    Save In box, 545
    Show ScreenTips on toolbars option, 209
    Styles option, 322
    Toolbars tab, 15–16

Customize Keyboard dialog box, 16, 84–85, 547–548

Customize Numbered List dialog box, 123–124

Customize Outline Numbered List dialog box, 128–129, 136

customized styles and table of contents, 375–376

customizing
    bullets, 111–114
    main documents, 289–290
    numbered lists, 122–124
    Office Assistant, 33
    pleading templates, 314–315
    toolbars, 11–16

Cut command, 55, 119

Cut (Ctrl+X) keyboard shortcut, 55–56, 120

D

damages charts, 202

data fields, 263–264

Data Form, 266–268
    editing data source through, 272–273

Data Form (Alt+Shift+E) keyboard shortcut, 272

Data Form dialog box, 272

data records, 263–264

data source
    attaching new, 273–274
    creation of, 263–266
    data fields, 263–264
    Data Form, 266–268
    data records, 263–264
    from delimited text, 274–275
    editing, 271–273
    options, 271–275
    Pleading Index as, 278–279
    sorting, 284–285

Database toolbar, 526

Dataviz Web site, 486

Date And Time command, 327

dates, 160

decimal tabs, 97, 233

decimals, aligning in tables, 232–233

Decrease Level (Shift+Tab) keyboard shortcut, 126–127, 133

default
    bullets, 111
    fonts, 80
    margins, 144
    outline numbering, 127–129
    toolbars, 8

Define Styles Based On Your Formatting feature, 187–188

Delete Columns command, 220

Delete command, 218

Delete Comment command, 426–427

Delete key, 42

Delete Rows command, 219

Delete Table Borders (Alt+Ctrl+U) keyboard shortcut, 222

deleting
    all comments, 427–428
    AutoText entries, 73
    columns, 220
    comments, 426–427
    documents, 24
    files, 24
    folders, 24
    footnotes and endnotes, 396
    form fields, 352
    hard page break, 157
    items from Office Clipboard, 56
    large amounts of text, 43
    macros, 552–553
    multiple characters, 42
    one character at a time, 42
    rows, 218–219
    styles, 192–193
    subdocuments, 448
    table of contents, 378
    text, 41–43
    text from keyboard, 48

delimited files, 274–275

Demote Heading Style (Alt+Shift+Left Arrow) keyboard shortcut, 199

Demote Level (Shift+Tab) keyboard shortcut, 117

deselecting text, 47–48

desktop, accessing, 27

Details view, 25

Detect and Repair command, 35

diagnostic check, 35

diagonal drawing, 211

docked toolbars, 10–11

Document Map, 20–21
  not changing paragraph formatting, 65
  Outline level, 65
  Outline view, 64
  resizing, 64
  views, 64

Document Map command, 21, 64–65

documents
  AutoText entries, 69–70
  based on templates, 299–301
  bookmarks, 397–398
  closing, 28, 36
  comments, 422–429
  common search locations, 26–27
  comparing, 435–437
  converting, 452–453
  copying styles between, 194–195
  creation with wizards, 304–306
  dates, 160
  deleting, 24
  deleting all comments, 427–428
  displaying styles, 182–184
  Document Map, 20–21
  draft printed on every page, 174
  e-mailing from Word, 417–421
  entering text, 38
  Excel worksheets, 229, 513–514
  exporting to PowerPoint, 524–525
  fast saves, 27–28
  finding, 22–24

finding items, 18

finding text, 51

footnotes and endnotes, 392–394

formatted with heading styles, 130

formatting, 76

formatting page numbers, 162–163

gutters, 145

header and footer distance, 147–148

headers and footers, 152, 159–166

headings, 64

hyperlinks, 401, 408–410

index, 388–389

line numbers, 153–154

locking, 174

magnifying, 65–67

maintaining settings when printing, 175

making printed match screen, 81–82

merging, 437–439

modifying styles, 189–190

most recently used, 26

moving around in, 39–41

moving to items, 18

multiple open simultaneously, 28–31

My Documents folder, 26

name of, 4

navigating, 20, 39–41

navigating large, 64–65

new, 79

new window for, 29

Newspaper-Style Columns, 165–166

Normal view, 19

Normal.dot template, 21

only saved as templates, 331

opening, 22–24

organizing structure, 62

page breaks, 156–157

page numbers, 160

paper sizes, 149–150

partial name search, 23

previewing, 25

previewing printing, 20

previous location in, 24

Print Layout view, 20–21

Print Preview, 166–168

printer settings, 81

printing two pages on one page, 146–147

protecting, 442–444

reviewing marked changes, 433–434

saving, 7, 27–28

saving in different file format, 479–481

saving in HTML format, 503–504

scrolling, 18

searching and replacing text, 53–54

searching folders and drives for, 23

searching World Wide Web for, 24

section breaks, 158–159

sections, 143, 151–152

separated numbered lists, 136–137

sharing customizations, 112–113

splitting, 31

Style Area, 182–183

suppressing endnotes, 153

switching between, 30

tables, 135

templates, 21

titles, 64

tracking changes, 429–435

type of file, 23

versioning, 439–442

vertical alignment, 152

viewing different parts of, 29

views, 60–65

Web Layout view, 19–20

word count, 257–258

WordPerfect file, 466

wrong file type, 24

zooming, 65–67

DocXchange, 486

Dot, 32

.dot file extension, 309

double line spacing, 92

Double Space (Ctrl+2) keyboard shortcut, 154

Down Level (Alt+Shift+Left Arrow) keyboard shortcut, 127, 133

drag and drop
  disabling, 74
  moving and copying text, 57–58
  turning on, 57

dragging mouse, 45

Draw Table command, 208

drawing tables, 208–209

Drawing toolbar, 154

drives, searching for documents, 23

Drop-Down Form Field Options dialog box, 343–344

drop-down form fields, 342–344

Drop-Down List (Alt+Down Arrow) keyboard shortcut, 348

dual indents, 95–96

dynamic link libraries (.dll files), 307

E

é (Ctrl+,'e) keyboard shortcut, 83

Edit Comment command, 426–427

Edit menu, 47–48, 51, 53, 74, 182, 194, 197, 205, 219, 351, 398

editing
  comments, 426–427
  custom dictionaries, 251–252
  data source, 271–273
  macros, 549–551
  numbered lists, 119–120

Elegant Memo.dot template, 22, 542

e-mail
  addresses and hyperlinks, 410
  documents from Word, 417–421
  hyperlinks, 501
  routing slip, 419–421
  sending to mail recipient, 417–418

embedded sound objects, 422

End of Document (Ctrl+End) keyboard shortcut, 311, 447, 461

Endnote Pane (Alt+Ctrl+E) keyboard shortcut, 394

Endnote Reference, 391

endnotes, suppressing, 153

Envelope Address dialog box, 276

Envelope dialog box, 281

Envelope Options dialog box, 276, 282–283

envelopes, 261

    addressing multiple, 293

    mail merge, 275–278

    merge fields printing on, 293

    printing single, 281–284

Envelopes And Labels command, 280–282

Envelopes And Labels dialog box, 280–281

Envelopes and Labels dialog box, 282

exact line spacing, 92

exact spacing, 92

Excel

    charts in Word, 519–521

    functions for legal purposes, 518–519

    inserting worksheets in Word documents, 229

Exceptions dialog box, 250–251

exclude dictionary, 252–253

.exe file extension, 253

exhibits and headers and footers, 161

Exit (Alt+F4) keyboard shortcut, 35

Exit command, 35

Export command, 527

export converters, 455

Export dialog box, 527

exporting

    Access data to Word, 526–527

    contact list for mail merge, 510–511

    Meeting Minder notes to Word, 523–524

    Powerpoint files to Word, 522–523

    Word documents to PowerPoint, 524–525

Extend Selection, 46, 48–49

Extend Selection (F8) keyboard shortcut, 48

F

F1 the Robot, 32

fast saves, 27–28

Favorites, 27

fax template

    modifying, 309–310

    using, 311

Field Code view, 359, 361

field codes

    converting documents, 462

    interrogatories, 122

    removing from converted documents, 468–469

    requests for admissions, 122

    requests for production, 122

    table of contents, 376

    unable to hide, 412

Field Codes (Alt+F9) keyboard shortcut, 359, 376, 429, 468, 471

Field command, 316, 357, 366

Field (Ctrl+F9) keyboard shortcut, 136

Field dialog box, 316, 357–359, 366

field names, 266

field switch, 292

Field Tab (Ctrl+Tab) keyboard shortcut, 348

fields and cross-references, 403

File command, 399, 466

file folder labels from Pleading Indexes, 279–280

File menu, 6, 21–22, 26, 28, 35–36, 82, 143–144, 146, 149, 155, 166, 168, 252–253, 262, 288, 300, 304, 308, 311–312, 314–315, 327–328, 336–337, 364

files

    copying to disk, 416–417

    deleting, 24

    icons representing, 25

    information about, 25

    listing names, 25

    MS-DOS text only, 480

    MS-DOS text with layout, 480

    RTF (Rich Text Format), 480–481

    searching by type, 23

    shortcuts to, 27

    text only, 480

    types that can convert, 453–455

fill-in fields, 357–361

filtering data, 285–287

Find and Replace dialog box, 427–428, 468, 541–542

    clearing formatting options, 198

    exiting to edit text, 53

    Find tab, 51

    Find What box, 197

    going to comments, 425

    More option, 197

    Replace tab, 53–54, 468

    search options, 51–53

Find and Replace dialog box (Alt+Shift+F6) keyboard shortcut, 53

Find command, 51

Find (Ctrl+F) keyboard shortcut, 51

Find feature, 50

Find in Field dialog box, 272

Find Style dialog box, 197–198

finding and replacing text, 50–54

    Browse Object, 54

    section breaks, 174–175

finding documents, 22–24

finding items, 18

First Spelling/Grammar Error (Alt+F7) keyboard shortcut, 240

first-line indents, 93–94

Fit Text feature, 217

fixed margins, 144–145

floating toolbars, 10–12

Flush Right feature, 43, 98

folders

    creation of, 25

    deleting, 24

    searching for documents, 23

    up on level, 24

Follow Number With drop-down list, 138

Font command, 80–81, 327, 350, 479

Font dialog box, 80–81, 479

fonts

    default, 80

    Normal template, 81

    numbered lists, 123

    setting default, 81

    TrueType, 81

    WYSIWYG (What You *See* Is What You Get), 79

footers, inserting, 160–161

Footnote and Endnote dialog box, 392–393, 396

Footnote and Endnote Options dialog box, 393–394

Footnote command, 392

Footnote Pane (Alt+Ctrl+F) keyboard shortcut, 394

Footnote Reference, 178, 391

Footnote Text style, 178

footnotes and endnotes

    browsing by, 395

    converting, 396–397

    deleting, 396

    Endnote Reference, 391

    Footnote Reference, 391

    inserting in documents, 392–394

    numbering, 392–393

    options, 393

    reference mark and footnote on different pages, 412–413

    viewing and editing, 394

Footnotes command, 394

foreign languages, checking spelling and grammar, 254–255

Form Field Help Text dialog box, 363–364

Form Field Options dialog box, 350, 352, 354–355, 363–364

Form Field Options (Shift+F10) keyboard shortcut, 340

form fields, 335

    bookmark names, 350

    bookmarks, 353–354

    calculating, 353–356

    clearing, 352–353

    deleting, 352

    disabling, 351–352

    formatting, 350

    Help text, 362–364

modifying, 349–352

naming, 350–351, 353

Number type, 355

preventing update, 368

referencing named, 361–362

table calculation of, 355–356

as text placeholders, 368

viewing name only, 369

form letters, 261

form templates, 336–337

check box form fields, 340–341

drop-down form fields, 342

inserting text form fields, 337–338

naming, 337

Format menu, 65, 80–81, 91, 95, 98, 101–102, 109–111, 113, 115, 118, 122–124, 127, 130, 132, 135–138, 154, 165, 185, 188, 190–193, 196, 214, 222, 258, 327, 350, 505

Format Painter, 103–104

formatting

character, 76

citations, 384

Click and Type feature, 43

copying, 103–104

documents, 76

form fields, 350

formulas, 231

legal documents, 78

page numbers, 162–163

paragraph, 76, 87–88

removing or replacing, 50

tables, 227–229

text automatically, 102–103

Formatting toolbar, 8, 350

Bold button, 79–80

Bullets button, 109–111

Bullets or Numbering button, 135

Center button, 89, 138, 235

Decrease Indent button, 126

Increase Indent button, 126

legal documents, 78

More Buttons command, 12

Numbering button, 118–119, 120–122

paragraph alignment, 88

Size box, 66

Style box, 181–182, 185, 189

Subscript command, 12

Superscript command, 12

TrueType fonts, 81

Underline button, 80

WYSIWYG (What You *See* Is What You Get), 79

forms, 334–335

action fields, 366

additional fields, 365–368

calculating fields, 353–356

clearing form fields, 352–353

completing, 348

creation of, 335–334

disabling form fields, 351–352

fields as text placeholders, 368

fill-in fields, 357–360

Form Field Shading, 349

form fields, 335

Forms toolbar, 335

inserting fields, 366–367

limited fields, 349

macros, 334–335, 364–365

marker fields, 365

modifying form fields, 349–352

moving through, 348–349

naming fill-in fields, 360–361

naming form fields, 350–351

passwords, 346

preventing field update, 368

printing data, 368

professional-looking, 356–365

protecting and unprotecting, 345–348

reference fields, 360

referencing named fields, 361–362

result fields, 365

saving data only, 369

Status bar Help text, 349

templates, 334

using, 344–349

Forms Assistant, 307

Forms toolbar
  Check Box Form Field button, 340
  Drop-Down Form Field button, 342
  Protect Form button, 347
  Text Form Field, 338

Formula command, 230–232

Formula dialog box, 230–231

formulas, 230–231

fractions, 102–103

French, 254

Full Screen command, 68

Full Screen mode, 68

Full Screen toolbar, 68

FullAuthority, 412

Function command, 518

Function Key Display toolbar, 9

G

gallery position, 110

Genius, 32

global AutoText entries, 71

global AutoText template
  date and time field, 327–329
  fill-in field, 330

global templates, 298, 303–304
  AutoText entries, 69
  creation of, 324–329
  customizations, 325
  default directory, 304
  firmwide customizations, 304
  modifying Startup file location, 325–327
  storing macros, 537

Go To command, 351, 398

Go To (Ctrl+G) keyboard shortcut, 351

Go To dialog box, 18

Go To (F5) keyboard shortcut, 18, 397–398

GoBack command, 398

GoBack (Shift+F5) keyboard shortcut, 398–399

grammar checking
  another language, 254–255
  automatic, 238–242
  controlling on/off, 239–240
  fixing errors, 240–241
  options, 242–245
  with spell checking, 241

Grammar Settings dialog box, 245

graphics, retrieving frequently used, 69–73

gridlines, 212, 222

gutters, 145

H

hanging indents, 93
  bullets, 112

hard page breaks, 156–157

Header And Footer command, 160–162

Header and Footer toolbar, 10, 159–160
  Close button, 161, 165
  Format Page Number button, 163–165
  Insert AutoText button, 160
  Insert Date button, 160
  Number Format box, 164
  Page Number button, 160
  Page Numbering section, 164–165
  Page Setup button, 162
  Show Next button, 162, 164–165
  Switch Between Header And Footer button, 160

headers and footers, 152
  dates, 160
  different on first page, 161–162
  distance, 147–148
  exhibits, 161
  inserting information, 159–161
  margins when converting documents, 462
  page numbers, 160
  resetting margins for converted documents, 472
  same as previous, 163–165
  tab setting, 160

Heading 1 (Alt+Ctrl+1) keyboard shortcut, 130, 199

Heading 1 style, 181, 373

Heading 2 (Alt+Ctrl+2) keyboard shortcut, 130, 199

Heading 2 style, 182, 373

Heading 3 (Alt+Ctrl+3) keyboard shortcut, 130, 182, 199

Heading 3 style, 182, 373

Heading Rows Repeat command, 227–228

headings, 64
    outline numbering linked to styles, 125
    tables, 227–228

Help
    topics, 33

help
    advanced find and replace features, 50
    diagnostic check, 35
    Office On The Web command, 34
    online support, 34
    standard, 33
    WordPerfect help, 34–35

Help menu, 31, 35, 77, 79, 301

Hidden Paragraph Marks (Ctrl+Shift+H) keyboard shortcut, 135

hidden text, 242

Hide Gridlines command, 212

Highlight Changes command, 431–432, 434

Highlight Changes dialog box, 431–432, 434

highlighting text. *See* selecting text

holdings lists, 202

horizontal ruler, 141

HTML (HyperText Markup Language), 489

Hyperlink command, 408, 499–501

Hyperlink (Ctrl+K) keyboard shortcut, 408, 499

Hyperlink dialog box, 408

hyperlinks
    cross-references, 401, 403
    e-mail, 501
    e-mail addresses, 410

    following to Web addresses, 410
    integrating Excel and Word, 516
    options, 409
    other server locations, 410
    viewing, 409–410
    Web pages, 497–501

hyphenation, 256–257

hyphenation zone, 256

hyphens, 256

I

import converters, 454–455

Increase Indent (Tab) keyboard shortcut, 126–127

Increase Level (Tab) keyboard shortcut, 133

indents, 93–96

Index And Tables command, 374–375, 378–379, 383, 390, 407

Index and Tables command, 381, 385, 388

Index and Tables dialog box
    Index tab, 388–389, 390
    Table of Authorities tab, 383, 385–386
    Table of Contents tab, 374–375, 378, 379, 381
    Table of Figures tab, 407

indices
    case sensitivity of entries, 388
    concordance files, 390
    inserting in documents, 388–389
    marking entries, 387–388
    updating, 390

Insert ClipArt dialog box, 528

Insert command, 135, 217, 220, 227, 234, 278, 467

Insert Field (Ctrl+F9) keyboard shortcut, 366–367

Insert File dialog box, 399–400

Insert Hyperlink dialog box, 499, 501

Insert menu, 69, 71–73, 82–85, 87, 108, 121, 157–158, 165–166, 174, 232, 316, 327, 357, 361, 366, 374–375, 378–379, 381, 383, 385, 388, 392, 397, 399, 401, 518

Insert Merge (Alt+Shift+F) keyboard shortcut, 268, 270
Insert Merge Field dialog box, 268–269
Insert Postal Bar Code dialog box, 277
Insert Rows command, 218
Insert Subdocument dialog box, 447
Insert Table command, 229
Insert Table dialog box, 203, 234
Insert Word Field:IF dialog box, 290
inserting
    AutoText entries, 69–70
    text, 41–43
insertion point, 38
    keyboard positioning, 40
    mouse moving, 39, 40
inside margins, 146
Install on First Use, 454
integrating Access and Word, 526–527
integrating Excel and Word
    copying and pasting Excel data, 515–516
    Excel charts in Word, 519–521
    links between Excel and Word, 517
    Word hyperlinks, 516
    worksheets in Word documents, 513–514
integrating Outlook and Word
    exporting contact list for mail merge, 510–511
    letters to contacts, 511–512
    mail merge from Outlook, 508–510
integrating PowerPoint and Word
    exporting Meeting Minder notes to Word, 523–524
    exporting Powerpoint files to Word, 522–523
    exporting Word documents to PowerPoint, 524–525
international characters, 83
interrogatories, 136–137
    field codes, 122
interrupting numbered lists, 120–121
Intranets, 488
    benefits, 489
    saving documents in HTML format, 503–504
    viewing text as Web page, 19–20
    Web page creation, 489–504

J
Jenai Software Engineering Web site, 486
Justified (Ctrl+J) Justified keyboard shortcut, 89
justified paragraphs, 88–89

K
keyboard
    deleting text, 48
    deselecting text, 48
    Extend Selection, 48–49
    Full Screen mode, 68
    movement keys, 40–41
    moving through document with mouse, 41
    moving through forms, 348–349
    positioning insertion point, 40–41
    selecting text, 47–49
    switching views, 60–61
Keyboard Shortcut template, 303
keyboard shortcuts, 16–17
    adding, 16
    assigning macro to, 547–548
    built-in styles, 199
    legal symbols, 82, 84–85
    listing, 17
    Pleading toolbar, 322
    printing list of, 79
    ScreenTips, 8
    styles, 188
    unassigned, 85

L
Label Options dialog box, 279
landscape orientation, 150
Language command, 256
laptops and Web Layout view, 20, 64
Left Align (Ctrl+L) keyboard shortcut, 233
left indents, 93
left tabs, 97
Left-aligned (Ctrl+L) keyboard shortcut, 89

left-aligned paragraphs, 88–89

legal documents
  cross-references, 400–403
  formatting, 78
  Formatting toolbar, 78
  matching screen when printing, 81–82
  printing, 168–173
  standard layout, 140
  storing macros, 536
  styles, 179–180, 184–188
  tables, 202
  writing styles, 245

Legal Numbering macro, 307

Legal Pleading wizard, 305, 314
  pleading templates, 312–314

legal practice styles, 179

legal size, 149

legal symbols, 82–83
  ANSI equivalent, 85
  AutoCorrect entries, 86
  keyboard shortcuts, 82, 84–85

legal templates
  creation of, 307–315
  customizing toolbars for, 321–323
  fax template, 308–311
  pleading, 311–315
  styles, 307

legal toolbar, 14–15

letters
  Body Text style, 180
  size, 149

Letters & Faxes folder, 309

LEXIS-NEXIS Web site, 412, 430

limited fields, 349

line numbers
  patent applications, 154
  pleading, 175
  spacing, 154

Line Numbers dialog box, 153

line spacing, 90–92

links between Excel and Word, 517

Links the Cat, 32

List Bullet 1 through List Bullet 5 styles, 115

List view, 25

ListCommands macro, 17, 539

ListNum field (Alt+Ctrl+L) keyboard
    shortcut, 133

Lock Fields (Ctrl+F11) keyboard shortcut,
    368, 466

locking
  documents, 174
  fields, 466
  subdocuments, 449

M

Macro command, 364, 537, 539, 541, 550

Macro dialog box, 364

Macro Recording toolbar, 364

Macro template, 303

macro virus, 331

MacroButton field, 368
  assigning macros to, 548–549

macros, 532
  accessing, 538–540
  assigning to keyboard shortcut, 547–548
  assigning to MacroButton field, 548–549
  assigning to toolbar button, 545–546
  comments, 551
  creation of, 534–536
  deleting, 552–553
  editing, 549–551
  forms, 334–335, 364–365
  hierarchy, 539–540
  Macros dialog box, 538–539
  other versions of Word, 555–556
  recording, 540–545
  runtime errors, 553–554
  security, 554–555
  storing in global templates, 537
  storing in legal document, 536
  storing in Normal template, 537
  storing in templates, 536
  user creation, 533–534

Macros (Alt+F8) keyboard shortcut, 537, 539

Macros dialog box, 538–539

magnifying documents, 65–67

Mail Merge, 279

mail merge
  catalog merge, 290–291
  customizing main documents, 289–290
  Data Form, 266–268
  data source, 263–268
  data source options, 271–275
  defining, 260
  envelopes, 275–278
  exporting contact list for, 510–511
  filtering data, 285–287
  main documents, 260–263
  merge fields, 268–270
  merging data with document, 270–271
  from Outlook, 508–510
  previewing merged data, 269–270
  printing specific pages, 287–288
  query options, 284–287
  sorting data source, 284–285
  spelling out numeric text, 292
  WordPerfect, 288–289

Mail Merge command, 262, 273, 275, 284, 289, 291

Mail Merge Contacts dialog box, 508–509

Mail Merge Helper
  Active Window option, 275, 279, 291
  Catalog option, 291
  Create Data Source option, 264
  Create option, 275, 279, 291
  Create options, 262
  Data Source options, 264–265
  Envelopes, 275
  Get Data option, 264, 273, 275, 279
  Get data option, 291
  Mailing Labels option, 279
  Merge option, 277, 280
  Open Data Source option, 273, 276, 279, 291
  Query Options option, 284
  Set Up Main Document option, 276, 279

Mail Merge toolbar, 268
  Edit Data Source button, 272
  If...Then...Else, 290
  Insert Merge Field button, 268–269, 508
  Insert Word Field button, 290, 508
  Merge button, 286
  Merge To New Document button, 271, 509
  Query Options button, 286
  View Merged Data button, 269

Mail Recipient command, 418

mailing labels, 261

main documents, 260–263
  catalogs, 261
  customizing, 289–290
  envelopes, 261
  form letters, 261, 262
  If...Then fields, 289–290
  mailing labels, 261
  merge fields, 268–270
  restoring to normal Word document, 261

Manual Line Break (Shift+Enter) keyboard shortcut, 120–121

manual line breaks, 89

margins, 141
  default, 144
  fixed, 144–145
  gutters, 145
  inside, 146
  mirror, 145–146
  mouse, 142–143
  outside, 146
  Page Setup dialog box, 143–145
  position of document changes affect, 148
  sections, 143, 148
  setting, 142–145
  undoing, 142

Mark Citation dialog box, 383–384

Mark Index Entry (Alt+Shift+X) keyboard shortcut, 378

Mark Index Entry dialog box, 388–389

Mark Table of Contents dialog box, 380–381

Mark Table of Contents Entry (Alt+Shift+O) keyboard shortcut, 380 marker fields, 365

master documents
  adding subdocuments, 447
  creation of, 445–446
  on networks, 449–450

menu bar, 4–5

menus, 4–5

Merge dialog box, 277, 280

Merge Documents command, 438

merge fields, 268–270
  printing on envelopes, 293

Merge to New Document (Alt+Shift+N)
  keyboard shortcut, 271, 290

merging cells, 214

merging documents
  protecting documents, 437
  reviewers, 437–438

Microsoft Knowledge Base Web site, 454

Microsoft Most Valuable Professionals Web
  site, 34

Microsoft Office Language Settings dialog
  box, 255

Microsoft Web site, 301, 331, 460, 486, 558

Microsoft Word Help command, 31, 79

Microsoft Word Viewer, 486

Microsystems Web site, 486

mirror margins, 143

Mission statement, 498–499

Modify Location dialog box, 324, 326–327

Modify Style dialog box, 189–192, 196, 379

modifying
  entire tables, 223–225
  styles, 189–192

Mother Nature, 32

mouse
  deselecting text, 47
  dragging, 45
  Full Screen mode, 68
  large amount of text selection, 46
  moving through document with keyboard, 41
  moving through forms, 348–349
  positioning insertion point, 39

protecting and unprotecting forms, 347–348
  redoing actions, 59
  selecting text, 45–46
  Selection bar, 47
  setting margins, 142–143
  Shift+Click text selection, 46
  sizing pointer, 219
  Style Area, 184
  switching views, 60–61
  undoing actions, 59

moving
  around in documents, 39–41
  to items, 18
  tables, 223–224
  text, 46, 54–57
  text with drag and drop, 57
  toolbars, 10–11

MS-DOS text only files, 480

MS-DOS text with layout files, 480

Mssp3en.exc file, 253

Mssp3en.lex file, 253

multi-document interface, 4

multiple documents
  arranging on-screen, 29–30
  open simultaneously, 28–31
  tiling, 30

My Documents folder, 26

N

names and nonbreaking spaces, 85–86

navigating
  documents, 20, 39–41
  large documents, 64–65
  tables shortcuts, 215

nesting tables, 226–227

New command, 21–22, 262, 300, 304, 308,
  311–312, 314, 327, 336, 483, 490–491,
  498

New dialog box, 21
  Blank Document option, 336
  Blank Document template, 327

Calendar Wizard option, 304
Create New Template option, 337
General tab, 302, 308, 327, 336, 498–499
Legal Pleadings tab, 312, 314
Letters & Faxes tab, 262, 300, 308, 311
Memos tab, 22, 542
Other Documents tab, 304, 483
Pleading Wizard option, 312
Professional Letter template, 301
Template option, 308
templates, 299–300
Web Pages tab, 490–491
New Document (Ctrl+N) keyboard shortcut, 21–22, 79
New Style dialog box, 185–188
New Toolbar dialog box, 15
New Window command, 29
Newspaper-Style Columns, 165–166
Next Document (Ctrl+F6) keyboard shortcut, 409
Next Field
   F11 keyboard shortcut, 301
   Tab keyboard shortcut, 348
Next Footnote or Endnote (Ctrl+Page Up) keyboard shortcut, 395
Next Page section break, 158, 159
nonbreaking hyphens, 85–86
Nonbreaking Space (Ctrl+Shift+Spacebar) keyboard shortcut, 86
nonbreaking spaces, 85–86
nonprinting characters, 86
   paragraph position marks, 108
Nonprinting Characters (Ctrl+Shift+*) keyboard shortcut, 120
nonprinting symbols, 77
Normal command, 19, 157–158, 392, 396
Normal (Ctrl+Shift+N) keyboard shortcut, 199
Normal template, 296, 298–299
   AutoText entries, 69
   customizations, 298–299
   default location, 299

defaults, 140
firmwide customizations, 304
fonts, 81
global items, 298
storing AutoText entries, 71
storing macros, 537
Normal view, 19, 61, 157–158, 392, 394, 396
   columns, 166
   Style Area, 183
Normal view (Alt+Ctrl+N) keyboard shortcut, 20, 61, 392, 394, 396
Normal.dot template, 15, 21
numbered lists
   automatic formatting, 103
   Bullets And Numbering dialog box, 118
   changing or removing styles, 122
   characters before or after number, 123
   continuing, 121–122
   converting bullets to, 124–125
   customizing, 122–124
   disabling, 118
   editing, 119–120
   fonts, 123
   interrupting, 120–121
   multiple in documents, 136
   Numbering button, 118–119
   promoting and demoting levels, 117
   restarting, 121–122
   starting number, 123
   styles, 123
   undoing, 118
numbered paragraphs and converting documents, 462
Numbering Assistant, 134
Numbering button, 7
numbering lines in pleadings, 154
numbers
   applying while typing, 116–118
   centering text beneath, 137–138
   removing underline, 137

O

Object command, 514, 527

Object dialog box, 514, 527

objects
  clip art, 527–528
  defaults, 528–529
  inserting in Word, 527–529

offering statements and tables, 202

Office Assistant, 31–33, 79
  Answer Wizard tab, 33
  characters, 32
  Contents tab, 33
  customizing, 33
  F1 function key, 31
  Index tab, 33
  questioning, 33
  selecting characters, 32
  standard help, 33

Office Clipboard
  appearing automatically, 74
  copying and pasting text, 55
  deleting items from, 56–57
  Paste All button, 55
  viewing first 50 characters of text on, 55

Office Logo, 32

Office On The Web command, 34, 301

Office Services Request Form template, 334

Online Collaboration, 450

online support, 34

Open command, 416, 455

Open dialog box, 318, 416–417, 455, 457
  Back button, 24
  Create New Folder button, 25
  Delete button, 24
  Document Window, 23
  File Name box, 23
  Files Of Type box, 24
  Look In box, 23
  Places bar, 22, 26–27
  Search the Web button, 24
  sorting icons, 25

Tool button, 26
toolbar buttons, 24–26
Up One Level button, 24
View button, 25

Open Index AutoMark File dialog box, 390

opening documents, 22–24

optional hyphens, 256

Options command, 18, 26, 28, 33, 44, 51, 57,
    61, 73–74, 82, 99, 120, 127, 141, 175,
    183–184, 239–240, 242, 247, 252–254,
    324–325, 359, 361, 376, 377, 424, 428,
    430, 456, 459

Options dialog box, 141
  Allow Accented Uppercase In French
      option, 254
  Check Grammar As You Type option, 239–240
  Check Spelling As You Type option,
      239–240, 247
  Choose Options command, 89
  Compatibility tab, 82, 175, 459
  Dictionaries button, 252
  Don't Expand Character Spaces, 89
  Drag And Drop Text Editing option, 74
  Edit tab, 44, 57, 73–74, 99, 127, 254
  Enable Click And Type, 99
  Field Codes option, 359, 361
  File Locations tab, 302, 324–326
  File Types list, 324
  General tab, 26, 456
  Hide Grammar Errors In This Document
      check box, 240
  Hide Spelling Errors In This Document check
      box, 240
  Never option, 376
  Paragraph Marks option, 77
  Print tab, 377, 428
  Recheck Document button, 254
  Save tab, 28
  Spelling & Grammar tab, 239–240, 242–245,
      247, 252, 254
  Style Area Width box, 183–184
  Tabs And Backspace Set Left Indent
      option, 127

Track Changes tab, 430–431
Typing Replaces Selection, 51
Update Fields option, 377
Use Printer Metrics To Lay Out Document
    option, 175
Use Smart Cut And Paste option, 73
User Information tab, 425
View tab, 18, 77, 120, 183–184, 359, 361, 376
When Selecting, Automatically Select Entire
    Word option, 74
workgroup templates, 302
Workgroup Templates file location, 303
ordinals (1st) with superscript, 103
organizational charts, 530
Organizer, 192, 317–319
    copying styles, 475
Organizer dialog box, 193–194, 317–318
    Macro Project Items tab, 318
    Styles tab, 193
    Toolbars tab, 318
organizing
    commands, 5
    document structure, 62
outgoing files conversion
    automatic numbering and formatting,
        478–481
    to previous versions of Word, 476–478
    saving document in different file format,
        479–481
Outline command, 445
Outline level, 65
outline numbering, 117
    applying, 126–127
    built-in headings, 130–131
    complex numbers, 128–129
    customizing, 127–129
    default, 127
    fonts, 129
    increasing or decreasing level, 126
    legal style, 129
    linked to custom headings, 132
    linked to Heading Styles feature, 125
    linked to styles, 130–132

losing tab settings, 134
modifying, 127
number position, 129
Numbering Assistant, 134
numbering scheme, 128
restarting numbering, 129
Roman and Arabic numerals, 136
starting number, 128
Tab character, 129
text position, 129
Outline view, 62
    Document Map, 64
    Style Area, 183
Outline view (Alt+Ctrl+O) keyboard
    shortcut, 20, 61
Outlining toolbar
    buttons, 448–449
    Collapse Subdocuments button, 447
    Create Subdocuments button, 446–447
    Expand Subdocuments button, 449
    Insert Subdocument button, 447
    Master Document view, 445
    Remove Subdocument button, 448
outside margins, 146
overriding styles, 184
Overtype feature, 39
overwritten text, 39

P

Page Border dialog box, 156
Page Break (Ctrl+Enter) keyboard shortcut,
    157, 161–162
page breaks, 157
    preventing in rows, 220
PAGE field, 428–429
Page Number (Alt+Shift+P) keyboard
    shortcut, 160
Page Number Format dialog box, 163
page numbers, 160
    formatting, 162–163

Page Setup command, 143–144, 146, 149, 155, 225

Page Setup dialog box, 143–145
   2 Pages Per Sheet, 146
   Apply To box, 148
   Borders button, 155
   Bottom Margin option, 144
   Default button, 144
   Different First Page option, 152, 162
   First Page box, 151
   Gutter box, 145
   Height option, 150
   Landscape option, 147, 225
   Layout tab, 151, 155, 159, 162
   Line Numbers button, 153
   Margins tab, 143, 145–148
   mirror margins, 143
   Mirror Margins option, 145–146
   Orientation, 150
   Other Pages box, 151
   Paper Size box, 149
   Paper Size tab, 147, 149–150, 225
   Paper Source tab, 151
   Preview option, 147
   Suppress Endnotes option, 153
   Top Margin option, 144
   Vertical alignment option, 152
   Width option, 150

pages
   borders, 101–102, 154–156
   centering tables on, 235
   default settings, 140
   different headers and footers on first, 161–162
   keeping rows together across, 219–220
   landscape orientation, 150
   margins, 141
   orientation, 150
   portrait orientation, 150
   previewing, 147
   printing two pages on one, 146–147
   setting up, 140–156
   width on-screen, 66

pagination, turning off, 61

paper sizes, 149–150

paper source, changing, 150

Paragraph, 65

Paragraph command, 91, 95, 115

Paragraph dialog box
   After box, 91
   After setting, 115
   dual indent, 95
   Indents and Spacing tab, 90–91, 95, 115
   Left Indentation, 95
   paragraph formatting, 88
   Right Indentation, 95

paragraph marks, 108, 119, 120
   Click and Type, 43
   displaying, 77
   formatting codes, 77
   importance of, 76
   viewing, 76–77
   viewing codes in, 77

Paragraph Marks (Ctrl+Shift+*) keyboard shortcut, 135

paragraph numbers, cleaning up converted documents, 469–470

paragraph styles, 178
   copying, 194
   by example, 184–185
   Style dialog box, 185–188

Paragraph Symbol (Alt+P) keyboard shortcut, 85

paragraphs, 38
   aligning, 87–90
   automatic amount of space, 91–92
   blank line between bulleted, 114–115
   borders, 100–101
   centered, 88–89
   clearing tabs, 97–98
   copying formats, 104
   dual indent, 95
   first-line indents, 93–94
   formatting, 76, 87–88
   hanging indents, 93, 95
   indents, 93–96

justified, 88–89
left indents, 93
left-aligned, 88–89
ListNum field, 132–133
numbering items in, 132–133
removing manual formatting, 198
right indents, 93
right-aligned, 88–89
setting tabs, 97
spacing, 90–92
spacing after, 91
spacing before, 91
parallel columns in tables, 202
parentheses and pleading caption, 222
Password Confirmation dialog box, 346
passwords
case sensitivity, 347
forms, 346
levels, 444
protecting documents, 443
Paste button, 7
Paste command, 55, 119, 194, 205, 515
Paste (Ctrl+V) keyboard shortcut, 55–56,
120, 205, 341
Paste Function dialog box, 518–519
Paste Special command, 515–517
cleaning up converted documents, 473–474
Paste Special dialog box, 474
patent applications
line numbers, 154
special layouts, 151–156
Payne Consulting Group Web site, 34, 134,
307, 332, 334, 533, 557
personalized menus, 6
Picture Bullet dialog box, 504
Picture command, 527–529
pictures
as bullets, 113–114
cells, 529
Places bar, 26–27
pleading captions, 221–222
parentheses, 222

retrieving with bookmark name, 399–400
scallops, 222
pleading indexes
as data source, 278–279
file folder labels from, 278–280
pleading templates, 296
automating with fill-in fields, 315–316
copying toolbar and macros between,
317–319
creation of, 311–315
customizing, 314–315
Legal Pleading wizard, 312–314
styles, 179
Pleading toolbar, 318–319
adding heading styles, 321–322
Block Quotation button, 320
Heading 1 button, 323
Heading 1 style, 322
Heading 2 button, 323
Heading 2 style, 322
Heading 3 button, 323
Heading 3 style, 322
keyboard shortcut, 322
options, 319–320
removing buttons, 323
renaming buttons, 322
testing new buttons, 323
Pleading wizard, 175
pleadings
block quote, 320
Body Text style, 180
bookmarking caption, 399
counting words, 403
court rules, 179
formatting index, 135
If...Then fields, 289–290
line numbers, 175
line numbers don't print, 331
numbering lines, 154
special layouts, 151–156
tables, 202
wizard creation of, 305
portrait orientation, 150

Preview view, 25

previewing

documents, 25

merged data, 269–270

pages, 147

printing, 20

Previous Field (Shift+F11) keyboard shortcut, 301

Previous Field (Shift+Tab) keyboard shortcut, 348

Previous Footnote or Endnote (Ctrl+Page Down) keyboard shortcut, 395

primary mouse button moving insertion point, 39–40

Print command, 82, 168, 288, 364, 428–429

Print (Ctrl+P) keyboard shortcut, 168, 288

Print dialog box, 429

Cancel button, 169

Name box, 168

Number of Copies option, 171

Options button, 172

Page Range section, 169

Pages option, 170

Print To File option, 171

Properties button, 169

Print Layout view, 20–21, 62, 99, 141

Click and Type, 43, 99

columns, 166

margin area, 141

vertical ruler, 141

Print Layout view (Alt+Ctrl+P) keyboard shortcut, 20, 61, 141

Print Options dialog box, 172–173

Print Preview, 166–168

Print Preview command, 166

Print Preview (Ctrl+F2) keyboard shortcut, 166

Print Preview toolbar, 167168

printer metrics, 82

printers

changing paper source, 150

changing selected, 81–82

selecting, 168–169

PrintForm macro, 364

printing

comments, 428–429

to file, 171

form data, 368

legal documents, 168–173

list of keyboard shortcut, 79

maintaining document settings, 175

number of copies, 171

number of pages per sheet, 172

options, 172–173

previewing, 20

Print What feature, 171

scaling for different paper, 172

single envelope, 281–284

single label, 280–281

specific pages in mail merge, 287–288

speeding up, 175

Track Changes, 434

two pages on one page, 146–147

zooming, 171

Private fields, 458

Pro Ace, 486

Professional Fax template, 308

Professional Letter template, 301

professional-looking forms, 356–365

programs (.exe files), 307

Promote Heading Style (Alt+Style+Right Arrow) keyboard shortcut, 199

Promote Level (Tab) keyboard shortcut, 117

proofing tools, 254

properties and tables, 225–226

Properties command, 339–340

Properties view, 25

Protect Document command, 174, 346, 434, 437

Protect Document dialog box, 174, 346, 434

protecting

document for Track Changes, 433–434

documents, 442–444

documents and merging, 437

forms, 345–348

Q

Query dialog box, 285
Query Options dialog box, 285–287
quotations and converting documents, 462

R

readability statistics, 244
Record New Macro command, 541
Record New Macro dialog box, 541, 543–544
recording macros
    automatic execution, 542–545
    pausing, 557
redefining AutoText entries, 72–73
Redo command, 59
Redo (Ctrl+Y) keyboard shortcut, 59
redo stack, 59
redoing actions, 59
reference fields, 360
reformatting documents, 472–473
Registered (Ctrl+Alt+R) keyboard
    shortcut, 86
Remove Character Formatting
    (Ctrl+Spacebar) keyboard shortcut, 198
Remove Formats (Ctrl+Spacebar) keyboard
    shortcut, 80, 476
Remove Manual Formatting (Ctrl+Q)
    keyboard shortcut, 198, 475–476
Remove Split command, 31
Remove Table Border (Ctrl+Alt+U)
    keyboard shortcut, 135
removing bullets, 108, 111
renaming
    styles, 195–198
    user-defined styles, 195–196
Repeat (Ctrl+Y) keyboard shortcut, 182
Repeat (F4) keyboard shortcut, 182
Repeat Style command, 182
Replace command, 53, 197, 427, 468
Replace (Ctrl+H) keyboard shortcut, 53, 468
Replace feature, 50

replacing table of contents, 378
requests for admissions, 136–137
    field codes, 122
requests for production, 136–137
    field codes, 122
Reset Paragraph Formatting (Ctrl+O)
    keyboard shortcut, 90
resetting
    styles, 198
    toolbars, 15–16
resizing
    columns, 221
    Document Map, 64
    tables, 224
restarting numbered lists, 121–122
result fields, 365
Reveal Codes, 35, 76–77
reversing actions, 58–60
reviewers and merging documents, 437–438
reviewing marked changes, 433–434
Reviewing toolbar, 421–423, 431
right indents, 93
right tabs, 89, 97–99
Right-aligned (Ctrl+R) keyboard
    shortcut, 89
right-aligned paragraphs, 88–89
Rocky the Dog, 32
rotating text in tables, 214
round-tripping, 453
routing slip, 419–421
Routing Slip command, 419
Routing Slip dialog box, 419–420
rows
    adding at end of table, 217–218
    changing height, 219
    deleting, 218–219
    inserting between rows, 218
    keeping together across pages, 219–220
    preventing page breaks in, 220
    undoing deletion, 219
Rows Below command, 218
Rows command, 219

RTF (Rich Text Format) files, 480–481

Ruler command, 17, 94, 141, 211

rulers, 17

changing indents, 94–95

first-line indent marker, 94

Hanging Indent marker, 95

indent markers, 94

indents, 94

Left Tab, 97

margins, 141

setting tabs, 96–99

Tab Alignment, 97

Run Macro (F5) keyboard shortcut, 535

S

Same As Previous command, 163

Save As command, 252, 308, 315, 328, 337, 436, 443, 457, 467, 478–479, 481

Save As dialog box, 266, 308, 328, 457

Create New Folder button, 25

Document Template (.dot) option, 337

Document Template option, 309

Save As Type list, 337

Save As Type to Text Only, 253

Save As Web Page command, 504

Save (Ctrl+S) keyboard shortcut, 27

Save dialog box, 443

Save Version command, 440–441

Save Version dialog box, 440–441

saving

in different file format, 479–481

documents, 7, 27–28

documents in HTML format, 503–504

form data only, 369

scallops, 222

Screen Tips, 7–8

ScreenTips

about current page, 39

Clipboard, 56

comments, 422

current page number, 41

shortcut keys, 8

turning on, 7

scroll bars

Browse Object, 18

double down arrows, 18

double up arrows, 18

hiding, 68

moving through document, 39

scrolling documents, 18

Scrolling Text dialog box, 506

scrolling text in Web pages, 505–506

SDI (Single Document Interface), 4

searching for text, 50

section breaks, 156

changing type, 159

converting documents, 460–461

finding and replacing, 174–175

uses for, 158

Section Protection dialog box, 346

sections, 143

break type, 151–152

copying formatting, 174

margins, 143, 148

resetting break type, 152

same as previous, 163–165

security and macros, 554–555

Select All (Ctrl+A) keyboard shortcut, 137, 154, 446, 466

Select command, 213, 220, 235

Select File to Compare With Current Document dialog box, 436

Select File to Merge Into Current Document dialog box, 438

selecting text, 45–48

deleting text and, 47

entire word, 74

keyboard, 47–49

mouse, 45–46

Selection bar, 47

Selection bar, 47, 218

Send To command, 417, 419, 438, 525

Sequence fields, 462
  cleaning up converted documents, 470–471
shading cells, 214
sharing customizations, 112–113
sharing documents
  copying files to disk, 416–417
  e-mailing documents from Word, 417–421
  Reviewing toolbar, 421–422
Shift+Enter (Manual Line Break) keyboard
  shortcut, 89, 138
shortcuts
  creation of, 2
  to files, 27
Show Paragraph Marks (Ctrl+Shift+*)
  keyboard shortcut, 43
signature blocks, 202
signature line
  Click and Type feature, 98–99
  tabs, 96–97
single label, printing, 280–281
single line spacing, 92
sizing pointer, 219
Smart Cut And Paste, 73
soft page breaks, 156–157
Sort command, 207
Sort dialog box, 207–208
sorting
  converted table, 206–208
  data source, 284–285
spacing
  after paragraphs, 91
  before paragraphs, 91
Special Characters tab, 82–83
special layouts
  agreements, 151–156
  briefs, 151–156
  patent applications, 151–156
  pleadings, 151–156
spell checking
  another language, 254–255
  AutoCorrect, 245–251
  automatic, 238–242

controlling on/off, 239–240
custom dictionaries, 251–255
exclude dictionary, 252–253
fixing errors, 240–241
with grammar checking, 241
hidden text, 242
options, 242–245
proofing tools, 254
rechecking documents, 253–254
Spelling And Grammar command, 241
Spelling and Grammar dialog box, 240–241
Spelling and Grammar (F7) keyboard
  shortcut, 241
Spelling command, 240
spin box, 91
Split command, 31
Split Table command, 225
Split Table (Ctrl+Shift+Enter) keyboard
  shortcut, 225
splitting
  cells, 214
  documents, 31
  tables, 225
Standard toolbar, 8
  Close All button, 11, 13
  Copy button, 56
  Cut button, 56, 120
  Document Map button, 21, 64–65
  E-mail button, 417–418
  Format Painter button, 103–104
  Insert Excel Worksheet button, 513–514, 518
  Insert Table button, 204
  move handle, 11
  New button, 21–22
  New icon, 79
  Office Assistant button, 31
  Open button, 22
  Paste button, 120
  Print button, 168
  Print Preview button, 166–167, 228
  Redo button, 59
  Save button, 7
  Show/Hide button, 43, 108, 120, 242

symbol (¶), 77
Table grid, 204
Tables And Borders button, 208, 211
Undo button, 59, 74, 142
Undo list, 59
Zoom list box, 65–67
Startup file, modifying location, 325–327
Status bar, 17–18
  EXT (Extend Selection button), 46, 48–49
  hiding, 68
  icons, 18
  OVR characters, 39
  Spelling and Grammar Status icon, 240–241
  TRK (Track Changes), 431
  Web Layout view, 20
Stop Recording toolbar, 541–542
straight quotes changing to smart quotes, 467–468
Style Area, 182–184
Style command, 185, 188, 190–193, 196
Style (Ctrl+Shift+S) keyboard shortcut, 182, 185, 189, 195
Style dialog box, 188
  character styles, 184, 188
  Delete option, 192
  Modify option, 191, 196
  modifying styles, 190
  Organizer option, 192–193
  paragraph styles, 185–188
  Styles list, 190–192
style manual, 297
styles, 178–179
  adding to templates, 187
  applying, 180–182
  automatically applying, 186–187
  automatically defining, 103
  based on styles, 188
  basing styles on, 186
  built-in, 178
  bullets, 110–111
  changing or removing numbered lists, 122
  character, 178

  consistent formatting, 179
  copying, 193–195
  copying from converted documents, 475
  court rules, 179
  creation of, 185–188
  Define Styles Based On Your Formatting feature, 187–188
  deleting, 192–193
  displaying in documents, 182–184
  dual indents, 96
  hidden paragraph mark, 135
  identical names in template, 180
  indicators, 181
  legal documents, 179–180, 184–188
  legal practice, 179
  legal templates, 307
  linking outline numbering to, 130
  List Bullet 1 through List Bullet 5, 115
  listing, 181
  modifying, 189–192
  modifying bullet, 114–115
  modifying table of contents, 378–379
  name conflicts, 195
  names, 185
  numbered lists, 123
  overriding, 184
  paragraph, 178
  pleading templates, 179
  reducing editing time, 180
  reducing training time, 180
  renaming, 195–198
  replacing, 195, 197–198
  resetting, 198
  shortcut keys, 188
  tables of contents without codes, 179–180
  user-defined, 178
subdocuments
  adding to master documents, 447
  deleting, 448
  expanding and collapsing, 446–447
  locking, 449
  on networks, 449–450
Sum function, 354

superscript formatting, 102

suppressing endnotes, 153

Switch (Alt+Tab) keyboard shortcut, 205

Switch Document (Ctrl+F6) keyboard shortcut, 30

Switch Document (Ctrl+Tab) key combination, 4

switching between documents, 30

Symantec Web site, 331

Symbol command, 82–85, 87, 108

Symbol dialog box
Assign button, 85
AutoCorrect button, 87
characters as bullets, 107
Paragraph symbol, 84, 87
Shortcut Key button, 84
Special Characters tab, 82–84, 86–87
Symbols tab, 83
viewing keyboard shortcut, 84

Symbol menu, 82
Special Characters tab, 256

Synonyms command, 256

T

TA field codes, 386

Tab dialog box, 98

Tab inside Cell (Ctrl+Tab) keyboard shortcut, 215

tab leaders, 98

Table AutoFormat feature, 227

Table command, 203, 213, 220, 227, 234, 278

Table grid, 204

Table menu, 135, 203, 206–208, 212–213, 217–218, 220–221, 225–232, 234–235, 278, 298

Table Move handle, 223–224

table of authorities
easier way of generating, 412
generating, 385–386
marking citations, 383–384
page numbers incorrect, 412

passim, 385
updating, 386–387

table of contents, 135, 372
beginning of numbered paragraph in, 411
from built-in styles, 373–375
customized styles, 375–376
deleting, 378
field codes, 376
in frame, 413–414
generating from another document, 410–411
by marking entries, 380–382
modifying styles, 378–379
page numbers, 376
page numbers incorrect, 412
paragraphs other than heading paragraphs in, 411
replacing, 378
shading, 376
updating, 377
updating from converted documents, 471–472
without codes, 179–180

Table of Contents Builder macro, 135

Table of Contents Options dialog box, 375–376

table of figures, 406–407

Table of Figures dialog box, 407

Table Properties command, 217, 219, 221, 225–226

Table Properties dialog box
Allow Row To Break Across Pages option, 219
Cell tab, 217
Column tab, 221
Fit Text option, 217
Next Column option, 221
Options option, 217
Preferred Width field, 225
Preferred Width of Column option, 221
Previous Column option, 221
Row Height setting, 219
Row tab, 219
Table tab, 226
Text Wrapping option, 226

Table Resize Handle, 224

tables
adding numbers together, 229
aligning decimals, 232–233
automatically resizing columns, 215–216
bookmark calculations, 231–232
border color, 213
borders and cleaning up converted documents, 472
briefs, 202
calculating form fields, 355–356
calculations in, 229–233
captions, 404–405
cells, 216–217
centering on page, 235
changing border, 213
changing defaults, 234
changing line weight and style, 212–213
columns, 220–222
converting text to, 205–208
copying from another application, 205
creation of, 202–209
damages charts, 202
drawing, 208–209
editing with Track Changes on, 434–435
entering text, 214, 215
erasing interior lines, 212
formatting, 227–229
formulas, 230–231
gridlines, 212, 222
headings, 227–228
holdings lists, 202
inserting in document, 135
legal documents, 202
mathematical functions on noncontiguous cells, 235–236
merging cells, 214
modifying entire, 223–225
modifying structure, 216–227
moving, 223–224
navigating shortcuts, 215
nesting, 226–227
nonstandard layout, 211
offering statements, 202
parallel columns, 202

pleadings, 202
properties, 225–226
removing borders, 135, 222
repeating headings in large, 228
resizing, 224
rotating text, 214
rows, 217–220
selecting cells, 213
shading cells, 214
signature blocks, 202
sorting converted, 206–208
splitting, 225
splitting cells, 214
subtotals, 230
Table AutoFormat feature, 227
Table Move handle, 223–224
text above, 234
text form fields, 230
text wrapping, 226, 235
two-column, 135
updating calculations, 230
widening, 225
Tables And Borders toolbar
AutoSum button, 229–230, 233
Border button, 213
Border Color button, 213
buttons, 210–211
Change Text Direction button, 214
drop-down arrow, 216
Eraser button, 212
Line Style button, 212
Line Weight button, 213
Merge Cells button, 214
ScreenTip, 209
Shading Color button, 214
Split Cells button, 214
Table AutoFormat button, 227
tabs
cleaning up converted documents, 472
clearing, 97–98
Click and Type, 43
Flush Right feature, 98
paper sizes, 149

setting, 96–99

signature line, 96–97

types, 97

unusual settings and converting documents, 463

Tabs command, 98

Tabs dialog box, 97–98

templates, 21, 296–298

adding style to, 187

attached, 299–303

attaching to active document, 332

automatically loading, 329

automating, 315–316

AutoText entries, 69, 71

basing Web pages on, 490–491

cleaning up converted documents, 473–476

complexity, 332

consistency, 297

containing macros (.dot files), 307

copying custom settings between, 317–319

copying styles between, 193–194

creation from scratch, 309

custom user, 302

customizations, 298–299

documents based on, 299–301

documents only saved as, 331

.dot file extension, 309

forms, 334

global, 298, 303–304

hierarchy, 329

identical style names, 180

modifying, 309–310

New dialog box, 299–300

Normal, 298–299

provided with Word, 301

reducing employee training time, 298

saving first time, 308

saving time, 297

storing macros, 536

types, 298–307

user, 299–302

Word 97, 301

workgroup, 299, 302–303, 324

Templates And Add-Ins command, 317, 329, 475

Templates and Add-Ins dialog box, 317

text

above tables, 234

accidentally moving instead of selecting, 74

automatically formatting, 102–103

bold, 79–80

centering beneath numbers, 137–138

changing case, 258

Click and Type feature, 43–45

converting to tables, 205–208

copying, 54–57

deleting, 41–43

entering, 38–39

entering in tables, 214

finding and replacing, 50–54

hyphenation, 256–257

inserting, 41–43

losing two spaces when copying and pasting, 73

moving, 46, 54–57

nonbreaking hyphens, 85–86

nonbreaking spaces, 85–86

overwritten, 39

pagination, 61

paragraphs, 38

retrieving frequently used, 69–73

rotating in tables, 214

searching for, 50

selecting, 45–48

typing exactly where you want it, 43–45

underlined, 80

viewing as Web page, 19–20

word-wrap, 38

Text Box command, 154

Text Box dialog box, 154

Text Direction command, 214

Text Form Field Options dialog box, 339–340

text form fields, 337–340

text only files, 480

Text To Table command, 206–208

Theme command, 505

Theme dialog box, 505

Thesaurus, 255–256

Thesaurus command, 256

Thesaurus dialog box, 256

tiling multiple documents, 30

title bar, 4

titles, 64

TOA Heading style, 386

TOC styles, 178

Toggle Field Code (Shift+F9) keyboard shortcut, 230

Toggle Field Codes command, 292, 367

Tool menu, 26, 102, 141

Toolbar and Menu Customization template, 303

toolbars, 6–11
  Add Or Remove Buttons command, 11–12, 15
  adding buttons, 11–13
  Customize command, 13
  customizing, 11–16
  customizing for legal templates, 321–323
  default, 8
  displaying, 320
  docked, 10–11
  floating, 10–12
  hiding, 68
  legal, 14–15
  listing available, 9
  listing available commands, 13
  More Buttons command, 12, 14–15
  move handle, 10
  moving, 10–11
  removing buttons, 13–14
  Reset Toolbar command, 15
  resetting, 15–16
  Screen Tips, 7–8
  selecting, 319
  Spelling and Grammar button, 241
  Underline button, 137
  Undo button, 219

Toolbars command, 9, 74, 319, 335, 506

Tools menu, 6–8, 13, 15–16, 18, 28, 44, 51, 57, 61, 73–74, 77, 82, 89, 103, 107–108, 113, 117–118, 120, 127, 174–175, 183–184, 187, 209, 239–242, 248–250, 252–254, 256–257, 262, 264, 273, 275, 279–282, 284, 289, 291, 317, 321, 323–325, 329, 346–347, 359, 361, 364, 376–377, 403

Tools menu command, 99

Top of Document (Ctrl+Home) keyboard shortcut, 162

Topics Found dialog box, 79

Track Changes
  on and editing tables, 434–435
  options, 430–431
  printing, 434
  protecting document for, 433–434
  reviewing marked changes, 433–434
  turning off redline formatting, 432
  turning on, 431–432
  viewing, 432–433

Track Changes command, 431–432, 434, 436, 438

Track Changes (Ctrl+Shift+E) keyboard shortcut, 431

tracking document changes, 429–435

Trademark (Ctrl+Alt+T) keyboard shortcut, 86

TrueType fonts, 81

two-column table, 135

Typing Replaces Selection feature, 50–51

U

underlined text, 80

Underlined Text (Ctrl+U) keyboard shortcut, 80

underlining text but not number, 137

Undo command, 47–48, 58–60, 74

Undo (Ctrl+Z) keyboard shortcut, 59, 74, 108, 118, 142

Undo Delete command, 219

undo stack, 59

undoing actions, 58–60

Unlock Field (Ctrl+Shift+F11) keyboard shortcut, 368

Unprotect Document command, 347, 437

Unprotect Document dialog box, 347

unprotecting forms, 345–348

Up Level (Alt+Shift+Right Arrow) kcyboard shortcut, 127, 133

Update AutoText (F3) keyboard shortcut, 136

Update Calculation (F9) keyboard shortcut, 230

Update Citation (Alt+Shift+I) keyboard shortcut, 386

Update Field command, 377, 382, 390, 471–472

Update Field (F9) keyboard shortcut, 136–137, 367, 377, 390, 471–472

Update Table of contents dialog box, 377

updating
    captions, 405–406
    cross-references, 403
    indices, 390
    table of authorities, 386–387
    table of contents, 377

U.S. Postal Service Web site, 278

Use Printer Metrics To Lay Out Document box, 82

user templates, 299–302

user-created AutoText entries, 71–72

user-defined styles, 178
    aliases, 196–197
    modifying, 189
    renaming, 195–196, 196

V

VB-1 Memorandum template, 543

VBA (Visual Basic for Applications), 532
    help, 556

interoperability, 534
learning curve, 557–558
macro creation, 534–536
need for, 533
reasons for using, 533
viewing all commands, 557

versioning, 439–442

Versions command, 439

Versions dialog box, 439–441

vertical ruler, 141

View menu, 9, 17, 19, 21, 64–65, 68, 74, 94, 99, 141, 157–158, 160–162, 211, 335, 392, 394, 396

views, 19–21, 60–65
    changing, 67, 141
    Document Map, 64
    Normal, 19, 61
    Print Layout, 20–21
    Print Layout Outline, 62
    Web Layout, 19–20, 63–64

Visual Basic Editor, 550–551
    help typing, 557
    navigating, 551–552

Visual Basic Editor (Alt+F11) keyboard shortcut, 535

W

Web browsers viewing text as Web page, 19–20

Web Layout view, 19–20, 63–64
    Click and Type, 43, 99
    laptops, 20
    Status bar, 20

Web Page wizard
    Add Pages dialog box, 493–494
    Navigation dialog box, 492
    Organize Pages dialog box, 494–495
    Title and Location dialog box, 492
    Visual Theme dialog box, 495–496

Web pages
    adding text, 497
    backgrounds and themes, 505

basing on Web template, 490–491

changing bullet styles, 504

creation of, 489–504

enhancing, 504–506

hyperlinks, 497–501

scrolling text, 505–506

viewing text as, 19–20

Web Page wizard, 491–497

Web toolbar, 502

Web toolbar, 502

Web Tools toolbar, 506

Westlaw Web site, 412

What's This? command, 77

What's This? (Shift-F1) keyboard shortcut, 77

widening tables, 225

widow and orphan control

cleaning up converted documents, 472

converting documents, 463

wildcards and searching for text, 52

Window menu, 29–31

windows

See also Word window

elements, 3

views, 19–21

Windows 95 starting Word 2000, 2

Windows 98 starting Word 2000, 2

Windows menu, 29

Windows NT starting Word 2000, 2

Wizards, 340–306

Word 97 templates, 301

Word 2000

closing, 35

personalized menus, 5–6

Reveal codes, 35

SDI (Single Document Interface), 4

shortcut on desktop, 2

starting, 2

version information, 35

word count, 257–258

Word Count command, 257, 403

Word Count dialog box, 257, 403

Word VBA Workshop, 557

Word window, 3–6

elements, 3

menu bar, 4–5

title bar, 4

view buttons, 60

WordPerfect

converting documents from, 458–463

converting documents to, 481–482

Flush Right command, 89

inserting file in Word document, 466

mail merges, 288–289

primary file, 263

Reveal Codes, 76–77

secondary file, 263

WordPerfect Convert dialog box, 482

WordPerfect for DOS

blocking text, 45

replicating macros, 69

WordPerfect for Windows, 45

WordPerfect help, 34–35

WordPerfect Help command, 35

workgroup templates, 299, 302–303

setting location for, 324

World Wide Web

accessing folders on, 27

searching for documents, 24

Write-Up dialog box, 522–523

writing styles, 245

WYSIWYG (What You See Is What You Get), 77

Z

Zoom dialog box, 65, 67

Zoom feature, 65–67

zooming

documents, 65–67

printing, 171

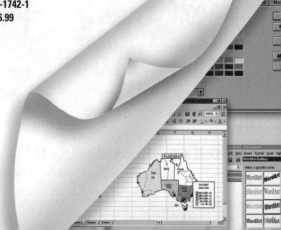